Aviation Maintenance Technician Handbook–Powerplant

Volume 2

2012

U.S. Department of Transportation
FEDERAL AVIATION ADMINISTRATION
Flight Standards Service

Published by Books Express Publishing
Copyright © Books Express, 2012
ISBN 978-1-78266-023-1

Books Express publications are available from all good retail and online booksellers. For publishing proposals and direct ordering please contact us at: info@books-express.com

Volume Contents

Volume 1

Preface v

Acknowledgments vii

Table of Contents ix

Chapter 1
Aircraft Engines 1-1

Chapter 2
Engine Fuel and Fuel Metering Systems 2-1

Chapter 3
Induction and Exhaust Systems 3-1

Chapter 4
Engine Ignition and Electrical Systems 4-1

Chapter 5
Engine Starting Systems 5-1

Volume 2

Chapter 6
Lubrication and Cooling Systems 6-1

Chapter 7
Propellers 7-1

Chapter 8
Engine Removal and Replacement 8-1

Chapter 9
Engine Fire Protection Systems 9-1

Chapter 10
Engine Maintenance and Operation 10-1

Chapter 11
Light-Sport Aircraft Engines 11-1

Preface

The Aviation Maintenance Handbook–Powerplant (FAA-H-8083-32) is one of a series of three handbooks for persons preparing for certification as a powerplant mechanic. It is intended that this handbook provide the basic information on principles, fundamentals, and technical procedures in the subject matter areas relating to the powerplant rating. It is designed to aid students enrolled in a formal course of instruction, as well as the individual who is studying on his or her own. Since the knowledge requirements for the airframe and powerplant ratings closely parallel each other in some subject areas, the chapters which discuss fire protection systems and electrical systems contain some material which is also duplicated in the Aviation Maintenance Handbook–Airframe (FAA-H-8083-31).

This handbook contains an explanation of the units that make up each of the systems that bring fuel, air, and ignition together in an aircraft engine for combustion. It also contains information on engine construction features, lubrication systems, exhaust systems, cooling systems, cylinder removal and replacement, compression checks, and valve adjustments. Because there are so many different types of aircraft in use today, it is reasonable to expect that differences exist in airframe components and systems. To avoid undue repetition, the practice of using representative systems and units is carried out throughout the handbook. Subject matter treatment is from a generalized point of view and should be supplemented by reference to manufacturer's manuals or other textbooks if more detail is desired. This handbook is not intended to replace, substitute for, or supersede official regulations or the manufacturer's instructions. Occasionally the word "must" or similar language is used where the desired action is deemed critical. The use of such language is not intended to add to, interpret, or relieve a duty imposed by Title 14 of the Code of Federal Regulations (14 CFR).

This handbook is available for download, in PDF format, from www.faa.gov.

The subject of Human Factors is contained in the Aviation Maintenance Handbook–General (FAA-H-8083-30).

This handbook is published by the United States Department of Transportation, Federal Aviation Administration, Airman Testing Standards Branch, AFS-630, P.O. Box 25082, Oklahoma City, OK 73125.

Comments regarding this publication should be sent, in email form, to the following address:

AFS630comments@faa.gov

Acknowledgments

The Aviation Maintenance Handbook–Powerplant (FAA-H-8083-32) was produced by the Federal Aviation Administration (FAA) with the assistance of Safety Research Corporation of America (SRCA). The FAA wishes to acknowledge the following contributors:

Mr. Tom Wild for images used throughout this handbook

Free Images Live (www.freeimageslive.co.uk) for image used in Chapter 1

Mr. Stephen Sweet (www.stephensweet.com) for image used in Chapter 1

Pratt & Whitney for images used in Chapters 2, 3, 6, 7, and 8

Teledyne Continental Motors (www.genuinecontinental.aero) for images used in chapter 2, 3, and 11

DeltaHawk Engines, Inc. (www.deltahawkengines.com) for image used in Chapter 6

Mr. Felix Gottwald for image used in Chapter 7

Mr. Stephen Christopher (www.schristo.com) for images used in Chapter 8

Mr. Yunjin Lee for images used in Chapter 9

Aeromax Aviation, LLC (www.aeromaxaviation.com) for images used in Chapter 11

Avid Aircraft (www.avidflyeraircraft.com) for image used in Chapter 11

Flight and Safety Design (www.eco1aircraft.com) for image used in Chapter 11

Great Plains Aircraft Supply Co., Inc. (www.greatplainsas.com) for image used in Chapter 11

Lycoming Engines (www.lycoming.textron.com) for image used in Chapter 11

Revmaster LLC Aviation (revmasteraviation.com) for images used in Chapter 11

Rotech Research Canada, Ltd. (www.rotec.com) for images used in Chapter 11

Additional appreciation is extended to Mr. Gary E. Hoyle, Dean of Students, Pittsburgh Institute of Aeronautics; Mr. Tom Wild, Purdue University; and Dr. Ronald Sterkenburg, Associate Professor of the Department of Aviation Technology, Purdue University; for their technical support and input.

Table of Contents

Volume Contents iii

Preface v

Acknowledgments vii

Table of Contents ix

Chapter 6
Lubrication and Cooling Systems 6-1
Principles of Engine Lubrication 6-1
   Types of Friction 6-2
   Functions of Engine Oil 6-2
Requirements and Characteristics of Reciprocating
Engine Lubricants 6-2
   Viscosity 6-3
   Viscosity Index 6-3
   Flash Point and Fire Point 6-3
   Cloud Point and Pour Point 6-3
   Specific Gravity 6-4
Reciprocating Engine Lubrication Systems 6-5
   Combination Splash and Pressure Lubrication ... 6-5
   Lubrication System Requirements 6-5
   Dry Sump Oil Systems 6-5
   Oil Tanks 6-5
   Oil Pump 6-7
   Oil Filters 6-8
   Oil Pressure Regulating Valve 6-8
   Oil Pressure Gauge 6-9
   Oil Temperature Indicator 6-10
   Oil Cooler 6-10
   Oil Cooler Flow Control Valve 6-10
   Surge Protection Valves 6-10
   Airflow Controls 6-11
   Dry Sump Lubrication System Operation ... 6-12
   Wet-Sump Lubrication System Operation .. 6-14
Lubrication System Maintenance Practices 6-14
   Oil Tank 6-14
   Oil Cooler 6-16
   Oil Temperature Bulbs 6-16
   Pressure and Scavenge Oil Screens 6-16
Oil Pressure Relief Valve 6-17
Recommendations for Changing Oil 6-17
   Draining Oil 6-17
   Oil and Filter Change and Screen Cleaning ... 6-18
   Oil Filter Removal Canister Type Housing .. 6-18
   Oil Filter/Screen Content Inspection 6-18
   Assembly of and Installation of Oil Filters .. 6-19
   Troubleshooting Oil Systems 6-19
Requirements for Turbine Engine Lubricants 6-19
   Turbine Oil Health and Safety Precautions ... 6-20
   Spectrometric Oil Analysis Program 6-21
   Typical Wear Metals and Additives 6-21
Turbine Engine Lubrication Systems 6-21
Turbine Lubrication System Components 6-22
   Oil Tank 6-22
   Oil Pump 6-23
   Turbine Oil Filters 6-24
   Oil Pressure Regulating Valve 6-25
   Oil Pressure Relief Valve 6-25
   Oil Jets 6-26
   Lubrication System Instrumentation 6-26
   Lubrication System Breather Systems (Vents) ... 6-26
   Lubrication System Check Valve 6-27
   Lubrication System Thermostatic Bypass Valves ... 6-27
   Air Oil Coolers 6-28
   Fuel Oil Coolers 6-28
   Deoiler 6-28
   Magnetic Chip Detectors 6-28
Typical Dry-Sump Pressure Regulated Turbine
Lubrication System 6-28
Pressure System 6-29
   Scavenge System 6-29
   Breather Pressurizing System 6-30
Typical Dry-Sump Variable Pressure Lubrication
System 6-30
   Pressure Subsystem 6-30
   Scavenger Subsystem 6-31
   Breather Subsystems 6-31
Turbine Engine Wet-Sump Lubrication System .. 6-31
Turbine Engine Oil System Maintenance 6-32
Engine Cooling Systems 6-33

Reciprocating Engine Cooling Systems 6-33
Reciprocating Engine Cooling System
Maintenance 6-35
Maintenance of Engine Cowling 6-36
Engine Cylinder Cooling Fin Inspection 6-37
Cylinder Baffle and Deflector System Inspection 6-38
Cylinder Temperature Indicating Systems 6-38
Exhaust Gas Temperature Indicating Systems 6-39
Turbine Engine Cooling 6-39
Accessory Zone Cooling 6-40
Turbine Engine Insulation Blankets 6-40

Chapter 7
Propellers 7-1
General 7-1
Basic Propeller Principles 7-2
Propeller Aerodynamic Process 7-3
Aerodynamic Factors 7-5
Propeller Controls and Instruments 7-6
Propeller Location 7-6
Tractor Propeller 7-6
Pusher Propellers 7-6
Types of Propellers 7-6
Fixed-Pitch Propeller 7-6
Test Club Propeller 7-7
Ground-Adjustable Propeller 7-7
Controllable-Pitch Propeller 7-7
Constant-Speed Propellers 7-8
Feathering Propellers 7-8
Reverse-Pitch Propellers 7-9
Propeller Governor 7-9
Governor Mechanism 7-10
Underspeed Condition 7-10
Overspeed Condition 7-10
On-Speed Condition 7-10
Governor System Operation 7-12
Propellers Used on General Aviation Aircraft 7-12
Fixed-Pitch Wooden Propellers 7-12
Metal Fixed-Pitch Propellers 7-14
Constant-Speed Propellers 7-14
Hartzell Constant-Speed, Nonfeathering 7-14
Constant-Speed Feathering Propeller 7-15
Unfeathering 7-17
Propeller Auxiliary Systems 7-17
Ice Control Systems 7-17
Anti-Icing Systems 7-17
Deicing Systems 7-18
Propeller Synchronization and Synchrophasing 7-20
Autofeathering System 7-20
Propeller Inspection and Maintenance 7-20
Wood Propeller Inspection 7-21

Metal Propeller Inspection 7-21
Aluminum Propeller Inspection 7-21
Composite Propeller Inspection 7-21
Propeller Vibration 7-22
Blade Tracking 7-22
Checking and Adjusting Propeller Blade Angles 7-23
Universal Propeller Protractor 7-23
Propeller Balancing 7-24
Static Balancing 7-24
Dynamic Balancing 7-26
Balancing Procedure 7-26
Propeller Removal and Installation 7-27
Removal 7-27
Installation 7-27
Servicing Propellers 7-27
Cleaning Propeller Blades 7-27
Charging the Propeller Air Dome 7-28
Propeller Lubrication 7-28
Propeller Overhaul 7-28
The Hub 7-29
Prop Reassembly 7-30
Troubleshooting Propellers 7-30
Hunting and Surging 7-30
Engine Speed Varies With Flight Attitude
(Airspeed) 7-30
Failure to Feather or Feathers Slowly 7-30
Turboprop Engines and Propeller Control Systems 7-30
Reduction Gear Assembly 7-31
Turbo-Propeller Assembly 7-31
Pratt and Whitney PT6 Hartzell Propeller System 7-32
Hamilton Standard Hydromatic Propellers 7-35
Principles of Operation 7-37
Feathering Operation 7-38
Unfeathering Operation 7-39
Setting the Propeller Governor 7-41

Chapter 8
Engine Removal and Replacement 8-1
Introduction 8-1
Reasons for Removal of Reciprocating Engines 8-2
Engine or Component Lifespan Exceeded 8-2
Sudden Stoppage 8-2
Sudden Reduction in Speed 8-2
Metal Particles in the Oil 8-3
Spectrometric Oil Analysis Engine Inspection
Program 8-3
Turbine Engine Condition Monitoring Programs 8-3
Engine Operational Problems 8-3
General Procedures for Engine Removal and
Installation 8-3
Preparation of Engines for Installation 8-3

QECA Buildup Method for Changing of Engines 8-4
Depreservation of an Engine 8-5
Inspection and Depreservation of Accessories 8-5
Inspection and Replacement of Powerplant External
Units and Systems 8-6
Preparing the Engine for Removal 8-7
Draining the Engine 8-7
Electrical Disconnects 8-7
Disconnection of Engine Controls 8-8
Disconnection of Lines 8-9
Other Disconnections 8-9
Removing the Engine 8-9
Hoisting the Engine 8-10
Hoisting and Mounting the Engine for Installation 8-10
Connections and Adjustments 8-11
Preparation of Engine for Ground and Flight
Testing 8-13
Pre-Oiling 8-13
Fuel System Bleeding 8-13
Propeller Check 8-14
Checks and Adjustments After Engine Runup and
Operation 8-14
Removal and Installation of an Opposed-Type
Engine 8-14
Engine Removal 8-14
Engine Installation 8-15
Turbine Engine Powerplant Removal and
Installation 8-16
Removal and Replacement of an Auxiliary
Power Unit (APU) 8-16
Install APU Powerplant 8-16
Turbofan Powerplant QECA Removal 8-18
Removal of QECA Accessories 8-19
Installation of Turbofan Engines 8-19
Installation With Dolly 8-19
Installation with Cable Hoist 8-19
Completing the Installation 8-19
Rigging, Inspections, and Adjustments 8-20
Rigging Power Controls 8-20
Adjusting the Fuel Control 8-21
Turboprop Powerplant Removal and Installation 8-22
Reciprocating Helicopter Engine and QECA 8-23
Removal of Helicopter QECA 8-23
Installation, Rigging, and Adjustment of
Helicopter QECA 8-23
Testing the Engine Installation 8-23
Engine Mounts 8-23
Mounts for Reciprocating Engines 8-23
Mounts for Turbofan Engines 8-24
Turbine Vibration Isolation Engine Mounts 8-24
Preservation and Storage of Engines 8-24

Corrosion-Preventive Materials 8-24
Corrosion-Preventive Compounds 8-25
Dehydrating Agents 8-25
Engine Preservation and Return to Service 8-26
Engine Shipping Containers 8-27
Inspection of Stored Engines 8-28
Preservation and Depreservation of Gas Turbine
Engines 8-28

Chapter 9
Engine Fire Protection Systems 9-1
Introduction 9-1
Components 9-2
Engine Fire Detection Systems 9-2
Thermal Switch System 9-2
Thermocouple Systems 9-3
Optical Fire Detection Systems 9-4
Pneumatic Thermal Fire Detection 9-5
Continuous-Loop Detector Systems 9-5
Fire Zones 9-7
Engine Fire Extinguishing System 9-8
Fire Extinguishing Agents 9-8
Turbine Engine Ground Fire Protection 9-9
Containers 9-9
Discharge Valves 9-9
Pressure Indication 9-9
Two-Way Check Valve 9-9
Discharge Indicators 9-9
Thermal Discharge Indicator (Red Disk) 9-10
Yellow Disk Discharge Indicator 9-10
Fire Switch 9-10
Warning Systems 9-11
Fire Detection System Maintenance 9-11
Fire Detection System Troubleshooting 9-12
Fire Extinguisher System Maintenance Practices 9-13
Boeing 777 Aircraft Fire Detection and
Extinguishing System 9-14
Overheat Detection 9-14
Fire Detection 9-14
Nacelle Temperature Recording 9-14
Continuous Fault Monitoring 9-14
Single/Dual Loop Operation 9-14
System Test 9-14
Boeing 777 Fire Extinguisher System 9-14
Fire Extinguisher Containers 9-14
Squib 9-16
Engine Fire Switches 9-16
Engine Fire Operation 9-17
APU Fire Detection and Extinguishing System 9-19
APU Fire Warning 9-19
Fire Bottle Discharge 9-19

Chapter 10
Engine Maintenance and Operation 10-1
Reciprocating Engine Overhaul 10-1
   Top Overhaul... 10-2
   Major Overhaul and Major Repairs.......................... 10-2
General Overhaul Procedures 10-2
Receiving Inspection 10-2
Disassembly 10-2
Inspection Process 10-3
   Visual Inspection... 10-3
   Cylinder Head.. 10-5
   Piston, Valve Train, and Piston Pin 10-5
   Crankshaft and Connecting Rods 10-5
Cleaning 10-6
   Degreasing... 10-6
   Removing Hard Carbon... 10-6
Structural Inspection 10-7
   Dye Penetrant Inspection.. 10-7
   Eddy Current Inspection... 10-7
   Ultrasonic Inspection.. 10-8
      Pulse-Echo 10-8
      Through Transmission 10-8
      Resonance 10-8
   Magnetic Particle Inspection 10-8
   X-ray... 10-8
Dimensional Inspection 10-8
   Cylinder Barrel.. 10-8
   Valves and Valve Springs 10-10
   Crankshaft 10-11
   Checking Alignment... 10-11
   Repair and Replacement.. 10-12
   Cylinder Assembly Reconditioning 10-12
   Piston and Piston Pins 10-13
   Valves and Valve Springs 10-13
   Refacing Valve Seats... 10-13
   Valve Reconditioning.. 10-16
   Valve Lapping and Leak Testing 10-18
   Piston Repairs... 10-18
   Cylinder Grinding and Honing............................... 10-18
Reassembly 10-20
Installation and Testing 10-20
   Engine Testing of Reciprocating Engines.............. 10-20
   Test Cell Requirements 10-21
   Engine Instruments... 10-21
   Carburetor Air Temperature (CAT) Indicator........ 10-22
   Fuel Pressure Indicator 10-22
   Oil Pressure Indicator 10-23
   Oil Temperature Indicator 10-23
   Fuel Flow Meter 10-23
   Manifold Pressure Indicator 10-23
   Tachometer Indicator 10-24

   Cylinder Head Temperature Indicator..................... 10-24
   Torquemeter 10-25
   Warning Systems... 10-25
Reciprocating Engine Operation................................... 10-25
   Engine Instruments... 10-25
   Engine Starting 10-26
   Pre-Oiling 10-26
   Hydraulic Lock.. 10-26
   Engine Warm-Up 10-26
   Ground Check... 10-27
   Fuel Pressure and Oil Pressure Check................... 10-28
   Propeller Pitch Check 10-28
   Power Check 10-28
   Idle Speed and Idle Mixture Checks 10-29
   Engine Stopping 10-29
Basic Engine Operating Principles 10-30
   Combustion Process 10-30
   Detonation 10-30
   Pre-Ignition 10-31
   Backfiring 10-31
   Afterfiring 10-31
Factors Affecting Engine Operation 10-32
   Compression.. 10-32
   Fuel Metering 10-32
   Idle Mixture 10-34
   Induction Manifold.. 10-34
   Operational Effect of Valve Clearance 10-34
Engine Troubleshooting.. 10-36
   Valve Blow-By... 10-40
Cylinder Compression Tests 10-40
   Differential Pressure Tester................................... 10-40
   Cylinder Replacement 10-42
Cylinder Removal 10-42
Cylinder Installation.. 10-43
Cold Cylinder Check... 10-44
Turbine Engine Maintenance 10-46
   Compressor Section.. 10-46
   Inspection and Cleaning 10-46
   Causes of Blade Damage.. 10-46
   Blending and Replacement.................................... 10-48
Combustion Section Inspection 10-49
   Marking Materials for Combustion Section
   Parts.. 10-50
   Inspection and Repair of Combustion
   Chambers 10-50
   Fuel Nozzle and Support Assemblies..................... 10-51
   Turbine Disk Inspection 10-51
   Turbine Blade Inspection 10-51
   Turbine Blade Replacement Procedure................. 10-52
   Turbine Nozzle Inlet Guide Vane Inspection......... 10-52
   Clearances 10-55

Exhaust Section 10-55
Engine Ratings 10-55
Turbine Engine Instruments 10-56
    Engine Pressure Ratio Indicator 10-56
    Torquemeter (Turboprop Engines) 10-56
    Tachometer 10-56
    Exhaust Gas Temperature Indicator (EGT) 10-56
    Fuel-Flow Indicator 10-58
    Engine Oil Pressure Indicator 10-58
    Engine Oil Temperature Indicator 10-58
Turbine Engine Operation 10-58
    Ground Operation Engine Fire 10-58
    Engine Checks 10-58
    Checking Takeoff Thrust 10-59
    Ambient Conditions 10-59
Engine Shutdown 10-60
Troubleshooting Turbine Engines 10-60
Turboprop Operation 10-60
    Troubleshooting Procedures for Turboprop
    Engines 10-60
Turbine Engine Calibration and Testing 10-62
    Turbine Engine Analyzer Uses 10-62
    Analyzer Safety Precautions 10-64
    Continuity Check of Aircraft EGT Circuit 10-64
    Functional Check of Aircraft EGT Circuit 10-65
    EGT Indicator Check 10-65
    Resistance and Insulation Check 10-65
    Tachometer Check 10-65
Troubleshooting EGT System 10-65
    One or More Inoperative Thermocouples in
    Engine Parallel Harness 10-66
    Engine Thermocouples Out of Calibration 10-66
    EGT Circuit Error 10-66
    Resistance of Circuit Out of Tolerance 10-66
    Shorts to Ground/Shorts Between Leads 10-66
Troubleshooting Aircraft Tachometer System 10-66

Chapter 11
Light-Sport Aircraft Engines 11-1
Engine General Requirements 11-1
Personnel Authorized to Perform Inspection and
Maintenance on Light-Sport Engines 11-2
    Authorized Personnel That Meet FAA
    Regulations 11-4
Types of Light-Sport and Experimental Engines 11-4
    Light-Sport Aircraft Engines 11-4
    Two-Cycle, Two Cylinder Rotax Engine 11-4
    Single Capacitor Discharge Ignition (SCDI) 11-4
    Dual Capacitor Discharge Ignition (DCDI) 11-4
    Rotax 447 UL (SCDI) and Rotax 503 UL
    (DCDI) 11-4

Rotax 582 UL DCDI 11-5
Description of Systems for Two-Stroke Engines 11-5
    Cooling System of Rotax 447 UL SCDI and
    Rotax 503 UL DCDI 11-5
    Cooling System of the Rotax 582 UL DCDI 11-5
    Lubrication Systems 11-6
    Oil Injection Lubrication of Rotax 503 UL
    DCDE, 582 UL DCDI, and 582 UL DCDI 11-6
    Electric System 11-6
    Fuel System 11-6
    Fuel/Oil Mixing Procedure 11-6
Opposed Light-Sport, Experimental, and Certified
Engines 11-7
    Rotax 912/914 11-7
    Description of Systems 11-7
        Cooling System 11-7
        Fuel System 11-7
        Lubrication System 11-7
        Electric System 11-8
        Turbocharger and Control System 11-10
    HKS 700T Engine 11-10
    Jabiru Light-Sport Engines 11-10
        Jabiru 2200 Aircraft Engine 11-12
        Aeromax Aviation 100 (IFB) Aircraft Engine 11-12
Direct Drive VW Engines 11-13
    Revmaster R-2300 Engine 11-13
    Great Plains Aircraft Volkswagen (VW)
    Conversions 11-15
    Teledyne Continental 0-200 Engine 11-16
    Lycoming 0-233 Series Light-Sport Aircraft
    Engine 11-16
General Maintenance Practices on Light-Sport
Rotax Engines 11-16
Maintenance Schedule Procedures and Maintenance
Checklist 11-17
    Carburetor Synchronization 11-17
    Pneumatic Synchronization 11-18
    Idle Speed Adjustment 11-20
    Optimizing Engine Running 11-20
    Checking the Carburetor Actuation 11-20
Lubrication System 11-20
Oil Level Check 11-20
Oil Change 11-21
Cleaning the Oil Tank 11-21
Inspecting the Magnetic Plug 11-21
Checking the Propeller Gearbox 11-22
Checking the Friction Torque in Free Rotation 11-22
Daily Maintenance Checks 11-22
Pre-flight Checks 11-23
Troubleshooting and Abnormal Operation 11-23

Troubleshooting 11-23
    Engine Keeps Running With Ignition OFF 11-24
    Knocking Under Load 11-24
  Abnormal Operating 11-24
    Exceeding the Maximum Admissible Engine Speed 11-24
    Exceeding of Maximum Admissible Cylinder Head Temperature 11-24
    Exceeding of Maximum Admissible Exhaust Gas Temperature 11-24
Engine Preservation 11-24
General Maintenance Practices for the Light-Sport Jabiru Engines 11-24
  Engine and Engine Compartment Inspection 11-24
  Lubrication System 11-25
  Carburetor Adjustment and Checks 11-25
  Spark Plugs 11-25
  Exhaust System 11-25
  Head Bolts 11-25
  Tachometer and Sender 11-25
Engine Inspection Charts 11-26

Glossary G-1

Index I-1

Chapter 6
Lubrication and Cooling Systems

Principles of Engine Lubrication

The primary purpose of a lubricant is to reduce friction between moving parts. Because liquid lubricants or oils can be circulated readily, they are used universally in aircraft engines. In theory, fluid lubrication is based on the actual separation of the surfaces so that no metal-to-metal contact occurs. As long as the oil film remains unbroken, metallic friction is replaced by the internal fluid friction of the lubricant. Under ideal conditions, friction and wear are held to a minimum. Oil is generally pumped throughout the engine to all areas that require lubrication. Overcoming the friction of the moving parts of the engine consumes energy and creates unwanted heat. The reduction of friction during engine operation increases the overall potential power output. Engines are subjected to several types of friction.

Types of Friction

Friction may be defined as the rubbing of one object or surface against another. One surface sliding over another surface causes sliding friction, as found in the use of plain bearings. The surfaces are not completely flat or smooth and have microscopic defects that cause friction between the two moving surfaces. *[Figure 6-1]* Rolling friction is created when a roller or sphere rolls over another surface, such as with ball or roller bearings, also referred to as antifriction bearings. The amount of friction created by rolling friction is less than that created by sliding friction and this bearing uses an outer race and an inner race with balls, or steel spheres, rolling between the moving parts or races. Another type of friction is wiping friction, which occurs between gear teeth. With this type of friction, pressure can vary widely and loads applied to the gears can be extreme, so the lubricant must be able to withstand the loads.

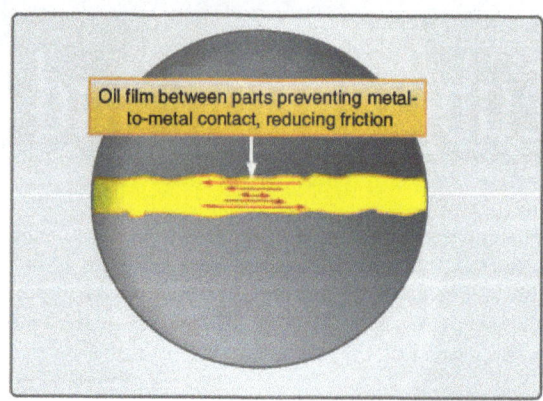

Figure 6-2. *Oil film acts as a cushion between two moving surfaces.*

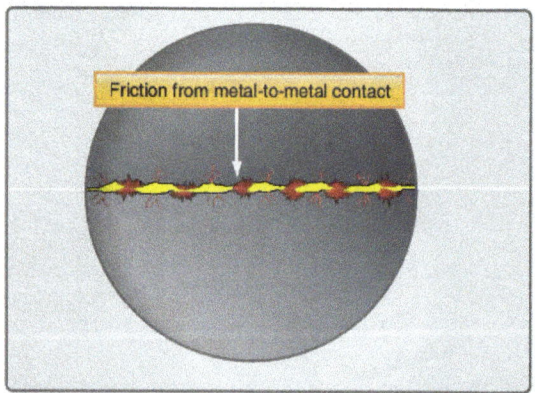

Figure 6-1. *Two moving surfaces in direct contact create excessive friction.*

Functions of Engine Oil

In addition to reducing friction, the oil film acts as a cushion between metal parts. *[Figure 6-2]* This cushioning effect is particularly important for such parts as reciprocating engine crankshafts and connecting rods, which are subject to shock-loading. As the piston is pushed down on the power stroke, it applies loads between the connecting rod bearing and the crankshaft journal. The load-bearing qualities of the oil must prevent the oil film from being squeezed out, causing metal-to-metal contact in the bearing. Also, as oil circulates through the engine, it absorbs heat from the pistons and cylinder walls. In reciprocating engines, these components are especially dependent on the oil for cooling.

Oil cooling can account for up to 50 percent of the total engine cooling and is an excellent medium to transfer the heat from the engine to the oil cooler. The oil also aids in forming a seal between the piston and the cylinder wall to prevent leakage of the gases from the combustion chamber.

Oils clean the engine by reducing abrasive wear by picking up foreign particles and carrying them to a filter where they are removed. The dispersant, an additive, in the oil holds the particles in suspension and allows the filter to trap them as the oil passes through the filter. The oil also prevents corrosion on the interior of the engine by leaving a coating of oil on parts when the engine is shut down. This is one of the reasons why the engine should not be shut down for long periods of time. The coating of oil preventing corrosion will not last on the parts, allowing them to rust or corrode.

The engine's oil is the life blood of the engine and it is very important for the engine to perform its function and to extend the length between overhauls.

Requirements and Characteristics of Reciprocating Engine Lubricants

While there are several important properties that satisfactory reciprocating engine oil must possess, its viscosity is most important in engine operation. The resistance of an oil to flow is known as its viscosity. Oil that flows slowly is viscous or has a high viscosity; if it flows freely, it has a low viscosity. Unfortunately, the viscosity of oil is affected by temperature. It was not uncommon for earlier grades of oil to become practically solid in cold weather, increasing drag and making circulation almost impossible. Other oils may become so thin at high temperatures that the oil film is broken, causing a low load carrying ability, resulting in rapid wear of the moving parts.

The oil selected for aircraft engine lubrication must be light enough to circulate freely at cold temperatures, yet heavy enough to provide the proper oil film at engine operating temperatures. Since lubricants vary in properties and since no one oil is satisfactory for all engines and all operating conditions, it is extremely important that only the approved grade or Society of Automotive Engineers (SAE) rating be used.

Several factors must be considered in determining the proper grade of oil to use in a particular engine, the most important of which are the operating load, rotational speeds, and operating temperatures. The grade of the lubricating oil to be used is determined by the operating conditions to be met in the various types of engines. The oil used in aircraft reciprocating engines has a relatively high viscosity required by:

1. Large engine operating clearances due to the relatively large size of the moving parts, the different materials used, and the different rates of expansion of the various materials;
2. High operating temperatures; and
3. High bearing pressures.

Viscosity

Generally, commercial aviation oils are classified by a number, (such as 80, 100, 140, etc.) that is an approximation of the viscosity as measured by a testing instrument called the Saybolt Universal Viscosimeter. In this instrument, a tube holds a specific quantity of the oil to be tested. The oil is brought to an exact temperature by a liquid bath surrounding the tube. The time in seconds required for exactly 60 cubic centimeters of oil to flow through an accurately calibrated orifice is recorded as a measure of the oil's viscosity. If actual Saybolt values were used to designate the viscosity of oil, there would probably be several hundred grades of oil.

To simplify the selection of oils, they are often classified under an SAE system that divides all oils into seven groups (SAE 10 to 70) according to viscosity at either 130 °F or 210 °F. SAE ratings are purely arbitrary and bear no direct relationship to the Saybolt or other ratings.

The letter W occasionally is included in the SAE number giving a designation, such as SAE 20W. This W indicates that the oil, in addition to meeting the viscosity requirements at the testing temperature specifications, is satisfactory oil for winter use in cold climates. This should not be confused with the W used in front of the grade or weight number that indicates the oil is of the ashless dispersant type.

Although the SAE scale has eliminated some confusion in the designation of lubricating oils, it must not be assumed that this specification covers all the important viscosity requirements. An SAE number indicates only the viscosity grade or relative viscosity; it does not indicate quality or other essential characteristics. It is well known that there are good oils and inferior oils that have the same viscosities at a given temperature and, therefore, are subject to classification in the same grade.

The SAE letters on an oil container are not an endorsement or recommendation of the oil by the SAE. Although each grade of oil is rated by an SAE number, depending on its specific use, it may be rated with a commercial aviation grade number or an Army and Navy specification number. The correlation between these grade numbering systems is shown in *Figure 6-3*.

Commercial Aviation No.	Commercial SAE No.	Army and Navy Specification No.
65	30	1065
80	40	1080
100	50	1100
120	60	1120
140	70	

Figure 6-3. *Grade designations for aviation oils.*

Viscosity Index

The viscosity index is a number that indicates the effect of temperature changes on the viscosity of the oil. When oil has a low viscosity index, it signifies a relatively large change of viscosity of increased temperature. The oil becomes thin at high temperatures and thick at low temperatures. Oils with a high viscosity index have small changes in viscosity over a wide temperature range.

The best oil for most purposes is one that maintains a constant viscosity throughout temperature changes. Oil having a high viscosity index resists excessive thickening when the engine is subjected to cold temperatures. This allows for rapid cranking speeds during starting and prompt oil circulation during initial start up. This oil resists excessive thinning when the engine is at operating temperature and provides full lubrication and bearing load protection.

Flash Point and Fire Point

Flash point and fire point are determined by laboratory tests that show the temperature at which a liquid begins to give off ignitable vapors, flash, and the temperature at which there are sufficient vapors to support a flame, fire. These points are established for engine oils to determine that they can withstand the high temperatures encountered in an engine.

Cloud Point and Pour Point

Cloud point and pour point also help to indicate suitability. The cloud point of oil is the temperature at which its wax content, normally held in solution, begins to solidify and separate into tiny crystals, causing the oil to appear cloudy or hazy. The pour point of oil is the lowest temperature at which it flows or can be poured.

Specific Gravity

Specific gravity is a comparison of the weight of the substance to the weight of an equal volume of distilled water at a specified temperature. As an example, water weighs approximately 8 pounds to the gallon; oil with a specific gravity of 0.9 would weigh 7.2 pounds to the gallon.

In the early years, the performance of aircraft piston engines was such that they could be lubricated satisfactorily by means of straight mineral oils, blended from specially selected petroleum base stocks. Oil grades 65, 80, 100, and 120 are straight mineral oils blended from selected high-viscosity index base oils. These oils do not contain any additives except for very small amounts of pour point depressant, which helps improve fluidity at very low temperatures, and an antioxidant. This type of oil is used during the break-in period of a new aviation piston engine or those recently overhauled.

Demand for oils with higher degrees of thermal and oxidation stability necessitated fortifying them with the addition of small quantities of nonpetroleum materials. The first additives incorporated in straight mineral piston engine oils were based on the metallic salts of barium and calcium. In most engines, the performance of these oils with respect to oxidation and thermal stability was excellent, but the combustion chambers of the majority of engines could not tolerate the presence of the ash deposits derived from these metal-containing additives. To overcome the disadvantages of harmful combustion chamber deposits, a nonmetallic (i.e., non-ash forming, polymeric) additive was developed that was incorporated in blends of selected mineral oil base stocks. W oils are of the ashless type and are still in use. The ashless dispersant grades contain additives, one of which has a viscosity stabilizing effect that removes the tendency of the oil to thin out at high oil temperatures and thicken at low oil temperatures.

The additives in these oils extend operating temperature range and improve cold engine starting and lubrication of the engine during the critical warm-up period permitting flight through wider ranges of climatic changes without the necessity of changing oil.

Semi-synthetic multigrade SAE W15 W50 oil for piston engines has been in use for some time. Oils W80, W100, and W120 are ashless dispersant oils specifically developed for aviation piston engines. They combine nonmetallic additives with selected high viscosity index base oils to give exceptional stability, dispersancy, and antifoaming performance. Dispersancy is the ability of the oil to hold particles in suspension until they can either be trapped by the filter or drained at the next oil change. The dispersancy additive is not a detergent and does not clean previously formed deposits from the interior of the engine.

Some multigrade oil is a blend of synthetic and mineral-based oil semisynthetic, plus a highly effective additive package, that is added due to concern that fully synthetic oil may not have the solvency to handle the lead deposits that result from the use of leaded fuel. As multigrade oil, it offers the flexibility to lubricate effectively over a wider range of temperatures than monograde oils. Compared to monograde oil, multigrade oil provides better cold-start protection and a stronger lubricant film (higher viscosity) at typical operating temperatures. The combination of nonmetallic, antiwear additives and selected high viscosity index mineral and synthetic base oils give exceptional stability, dispersancy, and antifoaming performance. Start up can contribute up to 80 percent of normal engine wear due to lack of lubrication during the start-up cycle. The more easily the oil flows to the engine's components at start up, the less wear occurs.

The ashless dispersant grades are recommended for aircraft engines subjected to wide variations of ambient temperature, particularly the turbocharged series engines that require oil to activate the various turbo controllers. At temperatures below 20 °F, preheating of the engine and oil supply tank is normally required regardless of the type of oil used.

Premium, semisynthetic multigrade ashless dispersant oil is a special blend of a high-quality mineral oil and synthetic hydrocarbons with an advanced additive package that has been specifically formulated for multigrade applications. The ashless antiwear additive provides exceptional wear protection for wearing surfaces.

Many aircraft manufacturers add approved preservative lubricating oil to protect new engines from rust and corrosion at the time the aircraft leaves the factory. This preservative oil should be removed at end of the first 25 hours of operation. When adding oil during the period when preservative oil is in the engine, use only aviation grade straight mineral oil or ashless dispersant oil, as required, of the viscosity desired.

If ashless dispersant oil is used in a new engine, or a newly overhauled engine, high oil consumption might possibly be experienced. The additives in some of these ashless dispersant oils may retard the break in of the piston rings and cylinder walls. This condition can be avoided by the use of mineral oil until normal oil consumption is obtained, then change to the ashless dispersant oil. Mineral oil should also be used following the replacement of one or more cylinders or until the oil consumption has stabilized.

In all cases, refer to the manufacturers' information when oil type or time in service is being considered.

Reciprocating Engine Lubrication Systems

Aircraft reciprocating engine pressure lubrication systems can be divided into two basic classifications: wet sump and dry sump. The main difference is that the wet sump system stores oil in a reservoir inside the engine. After the oil is circulated through the engine, it is returned to this crankcase-based reservoir. A dry sump engine pumps the oil from the engine's crankcase to an external tank that stores the oil. The dry sump system uses a scavenge pump, some external tubing, and an external tank to store the oil.

Other than this difference, the systems use similar types of components. Because the dry sump system contains all the components of the wet sump system, the dry sump system is explained as an example system.

Combination Splash and Pressure Lubrication

The lubricating oil is distributed to the various moving parts of a typical internal combustion engine by one of the three following methods: pressure, splash, or a combination of pressure and splash.

The pressure lubrication system is the principal method of lubricating aircraft engines. Splash lubrication may be used in addition to pressure lubrication on aircraft engines, but it is never used by itself; aircraft-engine lubrication systems are always either the pressure type or the combination pressure and splash type, usually the latter.

The advantages of pressure lubrication are:

1. Positive introduction of oil to the bearings.
2. Cooling effect caused by the large quantities of oil that can be pumped, or circulated, through a bearing.
3. Satisfactory lubrication in various attitudes of flight.

Lubrication System Requirements

The lubrication system of the engine must be designed and constructed so that it functions properly within all flight attitudes and atmospheric conditions that the aircraft is expected to operate. In wet sump engines, this requirement must be met when only half of the maximum lubricant supply is in the engine. The lubrication system of the engine must be designed and constructed to allow installing a means of cooling the lubricant. The crankcase must also be vented to the atmosphere to preclude leakage of oil from excessive pressure.

Dry Sump Oil Systems

Many reciprocating and turbine aircraft engines have pressure dry sump lubrication systems. The oil supply in this type of system is carried in a tank. A pressure pump circulates the oil through the engine. Scavenger pumps then return it to the tank as quickly as it accumulates in the engine sumps. The need for a separate supply tank is apparent when considering the complications that would result if large quantities of oil were carried in the engine crankcase. On multiengine aircraft, each engine is supplied with oil from its own complete and independent system.

Although the arrangement of the oil systems in different aircraft varies widely and the units of which they are composed differ in construction details, the functions of all such systems are the same. A study of one system clarifies the general operation and maintenance requirements of other systems.

The principal units in a typical reciprocating engine dry sump oil system include an oil supply tank, an engine-driven pressure oil pump, a scavenge pump, an oil cooler with an oil cooler control valve, oil tank vent, necessary tubing, and pressure and temperature indicators. *[Figure 6-4]*

Oil Tanks

Oil tanks are generally associated with a dry sump lubrication system, while a wet sump system uses the crankcase of the engine to store the oil. Oil tanks are usually constructed of aluminum alloy and must withstand any vibration, inertia, and fluid loads expected in operation.

Each oil tank used with a reciprocating engine must have expansion space of not less than the greater of 10 percent of the tank capacity or 0.5 gallons. Each filler cap of an oil tank that is used with an engine must provide an oil-tight seal. The oil tank usually is placed close to the engine and high enough above the oil pump inlet to ensure gravity feed.

Oil tank capacity varies with the different types of aircraft, but it is usually sufficient to ensure an adequate supply of oil for the total fuel supply. The tank filler neck is positioned to provide sufficient room for oil expansion and for foam to collect.

The filler cap or cover is marked with the word OIL. A drain in the filler cap well disposes of any overflow caused by the filling operation. Oil tank vent lines are provided to ensure proper tank ventilation in all attitudes of flight. These lines are usually connected to the engine crankcase to prevent the loss of oil through the vents. This indirectly vents the tanks to the atmosphere through the crankcase breather.

Early large radial engines had many gallons of oil in their tank. To help with engine warm up, some oil tanks had a built-in hopper or temperature accelerating well. *[Figure 6-5]* This well extended from the oil return fitting on top of the oil tank

Figure 6-4. *Oil system schematic.*

Figure 6-5. *Oil tank with hopper.*

to the outlet fitting in the sump in the bottom of the tank. In some systems, the hopper tank is open to the main oil supply at the lower end. Other systems have flapper-type valves that separate the main oil supply from the oil in the hopper.

The opening at the bottom of the hopper in one type and the flapper valve-controlled openings in the other allow oil from the main tank to enter the hopper and replace the oil consumed by the engine. Whenever the hopper tank includes the flapper controlled openings, the valves are operated by differential oil pressure. By separating the circulating oil from the surrounding oil in the tank, less oil is circulated. This hastens the warming of the oil when the engine was started. Very few of these types of tanks are still in use and most are associated with radial engine installations.

Generally, the return line in the top of the tank is positioned to discharge the returned oil against the wall of the tank in a swirling motion. This method considerably reduces foaming that occurs when oil mixes with air. Baffles in the bottom of the oil tank break up this swirling action to prevent air from being drawn into the inlet line of the oil pressure pump. Foaming oil increases in volume and reduces its ability to provide proper lubrication. In the case of oil-controlled propellers, the main outlet from the tank may be in the form of a standpipe so that there is always a reserve supply of oil for propeller feathering in case of engine failure. An oil tank sump, attached to the undersurface of the tank, acts as a trap for moisture and sediment. *[Figure 6-4]* The water and sludge can be drained by manually opening the drain valve in the bottom of the sump.

Most aircraft oil systems are equipped with the dipstick-type quantity gauge, often called a bayonet gauge. Some larger aircraft systems also have an oil quantity indicating system that shows the quantity of oil during flight. One type system consists essentially of an arm and float mechanism that rides the level of the oil and actuates an electric transmitter on top of the tank. The transmitter is connected to a cockpit gauge that indicates the quantity of oil.

Oil Pump

Oil entering the engine is pressurized, filtered, and regulated by units within the engine. They are discussed along with the external oil system to provide a concept of the complete oil system.

As oil enters the engine, it is pressurized by a gear-type pump. *[Figure 6-6]* This pump is a positive displacement pump that consists of two meshed gears that revolve inside the housing. The clearance between the teeth and housing is small. The pump inlet is located on the left and the discharge port is connected to the engine's system pressure line. One gear is attached to a splined drive shaft that extends from the pump housing to an accessory drive shaft on the engine. Seals are used to prevent leakage around the drive shaft. As the lower gear is rotated counterclockwise, the driven idler gear turns clockwise.

As oil enters the gear chamber, it is picked up by the gear teeth, trapped between them and the sides of the gear chamber, is carried around the outside of the gears, and discharged from the pressure port into the oil screen passage. The pressurized oil flows to the oil filter, where any solid particles suspended in the oil are separated from it, preventing possible damage to moving parts of the engine.

Oil under pressure then opens the oil filter check valve mounted in the top of the filter. This valve is used mostly with dry sump radial engines and is closed by a light spring loading of 1 to 3 pounds per square inch (psi) when the engine is not operating to prevent gravity-fed oil from entering the engine and settling in the lower cylinders or sump area of the engine. If oil were allowed to gradually seep by the rings of the piston and fill the combustion chamber, it could cause a liquid lock. This could happen if the valves on the cylinder were both closed and the engine was cranked for start. Damage could occur to the engine.

The oil filter bypass valve, located between the pressure side of the oil pump and the oil filter, permits unfiltered oil to bypass the filter and enter the engine if the oil filter is clogged or during cold weather if congealed oil is blocking the filter during engine start. The spring loading on the bypass valve allows the valve to open before the oil pressure collapses the filter; in the case of cold, congealed oil, it provides a low-resistance path around the filter. Dirty oil in an engine is better than no lubrication.

Figure 6-6. *Engine oil pump and associated units.*

Oil Filters

The oil filter used on an aircraft engine is usually one of four types: screen, Cuno, canister, or spin-on. A screen-type filter with its double-walled construction provides a large filtering area in a compact unit. *[Figure 6-6]* As oil passes through the fine-mesh screen, dirt, sediment, and other foreign matter are removed and settle to the bottom of the housing. At regular intervals, the cover is removed and the screen and housing cleaned with a solvent. Oil screen filters are used mostly as suction filters on the inlet of the oil pump.

The Cuno oil filter has a cartridge made of disks and spacers. A cleaner blade fits between each pair of disks. The cleaner blades are stationary, but the disks rotate when the shaft is turned. Oil from the pump enters the cartridge well that surrounds the cartridge and passes through the spaces between the closely spaced disks of the cartridge, then through the hollow center, and on to the engine. Any foreign particles in the oil are deposited on the outer surface of the cartridge. When the cartridge is rotated, the cleaner blades comb the foreign matter from the disks. The cartridge of the manually operated Cuno filter is turned by an external handle. Automatic Cuno filters have a hydraulic motor built into the filter head. This motor, operated by engine oil pressure, rotates the cartridge whenever the engine is running. There is a manual turning nut on the automatic Cuno filter for rotating the cartridge manually during inspections. This filter is not often used on modern aircraft.

A canister housing filter has a replaceable filter element that is replaced with rest of the components other than seals and gaskets being reused. *[Figure 6-7]* The filter element is designed with a corrugated, strong steel center tube supporting each convoluted pleat of the filter media, resulting in a higher collapse pressure rating. The filter provides excellent filtration, because the oil flows through many layers of locked-in-fibers.

Full flow spin-on filters are the most widely used oil filters for reciprocating engines. *[Figure 6-8]* Full flow means that all the oil is normally passed through the filter. In a full flow system, the filter is positioned between the oil pump and the engine bearings, which filters the oil of any contaminants before they pass through the engine bearing surfaces. The filter also contains an antidrain back valve and a pressure relief valve, all sealed in a disposable housing. The relief valve is used in case the filter becomes clogged. It would open to allow the oil to bypass, preventing the engine components from oil starvation. A cutaway of the micronic filter element shows the resin-impregnated cellulosic full-pleat media that is used to trap harmful particles, keeping them from entering the engine. *[Figure 6-9]*

Figure 6-7. *Housing filter element type oil filter.*

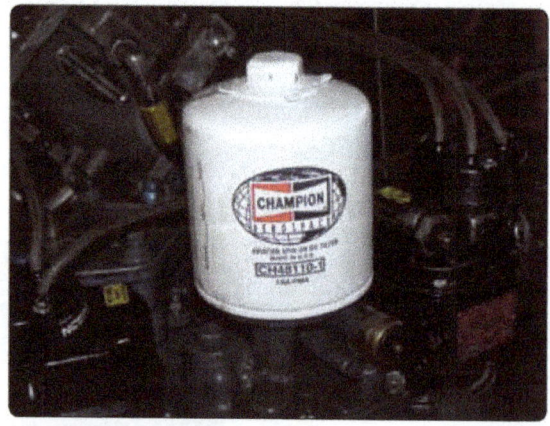

Figure 6-8. *Full flow spin-on filter.*

Oil Pressure Regulating Valve

An oil pressure regulating valve limits oil pressure to a predetermined value, depending on the installation. *[Figure 6-6]* This valve is sometimes referred to as a relief valve but its real function is to regulate the oil pressure at a present pressure level. The oil pressure must be sufficiently high to ensure adequate lubrication of the engine and its accessories at high speeds and powers. This pressure helps ensure that the oil film between the crankshaft journal and bearing is maintained. However, the pressure must not be too

Figure 6-9. *Cutaway view of a filter.*

high, as leakage and damage to the oil system may result. The oil pressure is generally adjusted by loosening the locknut and turning the adjusting screw. *[Figure 6-10]* On most aircraft engines, turning the screw clockwise increases the tension of the spring that holds the relief valve on its seat and increases the oil pressure; turning the adjusting screw counterclockwise decreases the spring tension and lowers the pressure. Some engines use washers under the spring that are either removed or added to adjust the regulating valve and pressure. The oil pressure should be adjusted only after the engine's oil is at operating temperature and the correct viscosity is verified. The exact procedure for adjusting the oil pressure and the factors that vary an oil pressure setting are included in applicable manufacturer's instructions.

Oil Pressure Gauge

Usually, the oil pressure gauge indicates the pressure that oil enters the engine from the pump. This gauge warns of possible engine failure caused by an exhausted oil supply, failure of the oil pump, burned-out bearings, ruptured oil lines, or other causes that may be indicated by a loss of oil pressure.

One type of oil pressure gauge uses a Bourdon-tube mechanism that measures the difference between oil pressure and cabin, or atmospheric, pressure. This gauge is constructed similarly to other Bourdon-type gauges, except that it has a small restriction built into the instrument case, or into the nipple connection leading to the Bourdon tube. This restriction prevents the surging action of the oil pump from damaging the gauge or causing the pointer to oscillate

Figure 6-10. *Oil pressure adjustment screw.*

too violently with each pressure pulsation. The oil pressure gauge has a scale ranging from 0–200 psi, or from 0–300 psi. Operation range markings are placed on the cover glass, or the face of the gauge, to indicate the safe range of oil pressure for a given installation.

A dual-type oil pressure gauge is available for use on multiengine aircraft. The dual indicator contains two Bourdon tubes, housed in a standard instrument case; one tube being used for each engine. The connections extend from the back of the case to each engine. There is one common movement assembly, but the moving parts function independently. In some installations, the line leading from the engine to the pressure gauge is filled with light oil. Since the viscosity of this oil does not vary much with changes in temperature, the gauge responds better to changes in oil pressure. In time, engine oil mixes with some of the light oil in the line to the transmitter; during cold weather, the thicker mixture causes sluggish instrument readings. To correct this condition, the gauge line must be disconnected, drained, and refilled with light oil.

The current trend is toward electrical transmitters and indicators for oil and fuel pressure-indicating systems in all aircraft. In this type of indicating system, the oil pressure being measured is applied to the inlet port of the electrical transmitter where it is conducted to a diaphragm assembly by a capillary tube. The motion produced by the diaphragm's expansion and contraction is amplified through a lever and gear arrangement. The gear varies the electrical value of the indicating circuit, which in turn, is reflected on the indicator in the cockpit. This type of indicating system replaces long fluid-filled tubing lines with an almost weightless piece of wire.

Oil Temperature Indicator

In dry-sump lubricating systems, the oil temperature bulb may be anywhere in the oil inlet line between the supply tank and the engine. Oil systems for wet-sump engines have the temperature bulb located where it senses oil temperature after the oil passes through the oil cooler. In either system, the bulb is located so that it measures the temperature of the oil before it enters the engine's hot sections. An oil temperature gauge in the cockpit is connected to the oil temperature bulb by electrical leads. The oil temperature is indicated on the gauge. Any malfunction of the oil cooling system appears as an abnormal reading.

Oil Cooler

The cooler, either cylindrical or elliptical shaped, consists of a core enclosed in a double-walled shell. The core is built of copper or aluminum tubes with the tube ends formed to a hexagonal shape and joined together in the honeycomb effect. *[Figure 6-11]* The ends of the copper tubes of the core are soldered, whereas aluminum tubes are brazed or mechanically joined. The tubes touch only at the ends so that a space exists between them along most of their lengths. This allows oil to flow through the spaces between the tubes while the cooling air passes through the tubes.

The space between the inner and outer shells is known as the annular or bypass jacket. Two paths are open to the flow of oil through a cooler. From the inlet, it can flow halfway around the bypass jacket, enter the core from the bottom, and then pass through the spaces between the tubes and out to the oil tank. This is the path the oil follows when it is hot enough to require cooling. As the oil flows through the core, it is guided by baffles that force the oil to travel back and forth several times before it reaches the core outlet. The oil can also pass from the inlet completely around the bypass jacket to the outlet without passing through the core. Oil follows this bypass route when the oil is cold or when the core is blocked with thick, congealed oil.

Oil Cooler Flow Control Valve

As discussed previously, the viscosity of the oil varies with its temperature. Since the viscosity affects its lubricating properties, the temperature at which the oil enters an engine must be held within close limits. Generally, the oil leaving an engine must be cooled before it is recirculated. Obviously, the amount of cooling must be controlled if the oil is to return to the engine at the correct temperature. The oil cooler flow control valve determines which of the two possible paths the oil takes through the oil cooler. *[Figure 6-12]*

There are two openings in a flow control valve that fit over the corresponding outlets at the top of the cooler. When the oil is cold, a bellows within the flow control contracts and lifts a valve from its seat. Under this condition, oil entering the cooler has a choice of two outlets and two paths. Following the path of least resistance, the oil flows around the jacket and out past the thermostatic valve to the tank. This allows the oil to warm up quickly and, at the same time, heats the oil in the core. As the oil warms up and reaches its operating temperature, the bellows of the thermostat expand and closes the outlet from the bypass jacket. The oil cooler flow control valve, located on the oil cooler, must now flow oil through the core of the oil cooler. No matter which path it takes through the cooler, the oil always flows over the bellows of the thermostatic valve. As the name implies, this unit regulates the temperature by either cooling the oil or passing it on to the tank without cooling, depending on the temperature at which it leaves the engine.

Surge Protection Valves

When oil in the system is congealed, the scavenger pump may build up a very high pressure in the oil return line. To prevent this high pressure from bursting the oil cooler or blowing off the hose connections, some aircraft have surge protection valves in the engine lubrication systems. One type of surge valve is incorporated in the oil cooler flow control valve; another type is a separate unit in the oil return line. *[Figure 6-12]*

Figure 6-11. *Oil cooler.*

Figure 6-12. *Control valve with surge protection.*

The surge protection valve incorporated in a flow control valve is the more common type. Although this flow control valve differs from the one just described, it is essentially the same except for the surge protection feature. The high-pressure operation condition is shown in *Figure 6-12*, in which the high oil pressure at the control valve inlet has forced the surge valve (C) upward. Note how this movement has opened the surge valve and, at the same time, seated the poppet valve (E). The closed poppet valve prevents oil from entering the cooler proper; therefore, the scavenge oil passes directly to the tank through outlet (A) without passing through either the cooler bypass jacket or the core. When the pressure drops to a safe value, the spring forces the surge and poppet valves downward, closing the surge valve (C) and opening the poppet valve (E). Oil then passes from the control valve inlet (D), through the open poppet valve, and into the bypass jacket (F). The thermostatic valve, according to oil temperature, determines oil flow either through the bypass jacket to port (H) or through the core to port (G). The check valve (B) opens to allow the oil to reach the tank return line.

Airflow Controls

By regulating the airflow through the cooler, the temperature of the oil can be controlled to fit various operating conditions. For example, the oil reaches operating temperature more quickly if the airflow is cut off during engine warm-up. There are two methods in general use: shutters installed on the rear of the oil cooler, and a flap on the air-exit duct. In some cases, the oil cooler air-exit flap is opened manually and closed by a linkage attached to a cockpit lever. More often, the flap is opened and closed by an electric motor.

One of the most widely used automatic oil temperature control devices is the floating control thermostat that provides manual and automatic control of the oil inlet temperatures. With this type of control, the oil cooler air-exit door is opened and closed automatically by an electrically operated actuator. Automatic operation of the actuator is determined by electrical impulses received from a controlling thermostat inserted in the oil pipe leading from the oil cooler to the oil supply tank. The actuator may be operated manually by an oil cooler air-exit door control switch. Placing this switch in the "open" or "closed" position produces a corresponding movement of the cooler door. Placing the switch in the "auto" position puts the actuator under the automatic control of the floating control thermostat. *[Figure 6-13]* The thermostat shown in *Figure 6-13* is adjusted to maintain a normal oil temperature so that it does not vary more than approximately 5° to 8 °C, depending on the installation.

During operation, the temperature of the engine oil flowing over the bimetal element causes it to wind or unwind slightly. *[Figure 6-13B]* This movement rotates the shaft (A) and the grounded center contact arm (C). As the grounded contact arm is rotated, it is moved toward either the open or closed floating contact arm (G). The two floating contact arms are oscillated by the cam (F), which is continuously rotated by an electric motor (D) through a gear train (E). When the grounded center contact arm is positioned by the bimetal element so that it touches one of the floating contact arms, an electric circuit to the oil cooler exit-flap actuator motor is completed, causing the actuator to operate and position the

A	Shaft
B	Bimetal element
C	Grounded center contact arm
D	Electric motor
E	Gear train
F	Cam
G	Floating contact arm

Figure 6-13. *Floating control thermostat.*

oil cooler air-exit flap. Newer systems use electronic control systems, but the function or the overall operation is basically the same regarding control of the oil temperature through control of the air flow through the cooler.

In some lubrication systems, dual oil coolers are used. If the typical oil system previously described is adapted to two oil coolers, the system is modified to include a flow divider, two identical coolers and flow regulators, dual air-exit doors, a two-door actuating mechanism, and a Y-fitting. *[Figure 6-14]* Oil is returned from the engine through a single tube to the flow divider (E), where the return oil flow is divided equally into two tubes (C), one for each cooler. The coolers and regulators have the same construction and operations as the cooler and flow regulator just described. Oil from the coolers is routed through two tubes (D) to a Y-fitting, where the floating control thermostat (A) samples oil temperature and positions the two oil cooler air-exit doors through the use of a two-door actuating mechanism. From the Y-fitting, the lubricating oil is returned to the tank where it completes its circuit.

Dry Sump Lubrication System Operation

The following lubrication system is typical of those on small, single-engine aircraft. The oil system and components are those used to lubricate a 225 horsepower (hp) six-cylinder, horizontally opposed, air-cooled engine. In a typical dry sump pressure-lubrication system, a mechanical pump supplies oil under pressure to the bearings throughout the engine. *[Figure 6-4]* The oil flows into the inlet or suction side of the oil pump through a suction screen and a line connected to the external tank at a point higher than the bottom of the oil sump. This prevents sediment that falls into the sump from being drawn into the pump. The tank outlet is higher than the pump inlet, so gravity can assist the flow into the pump. The engine-driven, positive-displacement, gear-type pump forces the oil into the full flow filter. *[Figure 6-6]* The oil either passes through the filter under normal conditions or, if the filter were to become clogged, the filter bypass valve would open as mentioned earlier. In the bypass position, the oil would not be filtered. As seen in *Figure 6-6*, the regulating (relief) valve senses when system pressure is reached and opens enough to bypass oil to the inlet side of the oil pump. Then, the oil flows into a manifold that distributes the oil through drilled passages to the crankshaft bearings and other bearings throughout the engine. Oil flows from the main bearings through holes drilled in the crankshaft to the lower connecting rod bearings. *[Figure 6-15]*

A	Floating control thermostat	D	Outlet from cooler tubes
B	Y-fitting	E	Flow divider
C	Inlet to cooler tubes		

Figure 6-14. *Dual oil cooler system.*

Figure 6-15. *Oil circulation through the engine.*

Oil reaches a hollow camshaft (in an inline or opposed engine), or a cam plate or cam drum (in a radial engine), through a connection with the end bearing or the main oil manifold; it then flows out to the various camshaft, cam drum, or cam plate bearings and the cams.

The engine cylinder surfaces receive oil sprayed from the crankshaft and also from the crankpin bearings. Since oil seeps slowly through the small crankpin clearances before it is sprayed on the cylinder walls, considerable time is required for enough oil to reach the cylinder walls, especially on a cold day when the oil flow is more sluggish. This is one of the chief reasons for using modern multiviscosity oils that flow well at low temperatures.

When the circulating oil has performed its function of lubricating and cooling the moving parts of the engine, it drains into the sumps in the lowest parts of the engine. Oil collected in these sumps is picked up by gear or gerotor-type scavenger pumps as quickly as it accumulates. These pumps have a greater capacity than the pressure pump. This is needed because the volume of the oil has generally increased due to foaming (mixing with air). On dry sump engines, this oil leaves the engine, passes through the oil cooler, and returns to the supply tank.

A thermostat attached to the oil cooler controls oil temperature by allowing part of the oil to flow through the cooler and part to flow directly into the oil supply tank. This arrangement allows hot engine oil with a temperature still below 65 °C (150 °F) to mix with the cold uncirculated oil in the tank. This raises the complete engine oil supply to operating temperature in a shorter period of time.

Wet-Sump Lubrication System Operation

A simple form of a wet-sump system is shown in *Figure 6-16*. The system consists of a sump or pan in which the oil supply is contained. The oil supply is limited by the sump (oil pan) capacity. The level (quantity) of oil is indicated or measured by a vertical rod that protrudes into the oil from an elevated hole on top of the crankcase. In the bottom of the sump (oil pan) is a screen strainer having a suitable mesh, or series of openings, to strain undesirable particles from the oil and yet pass sufficient quantity to the inlet or (suction) side of the oil pressure pump. *Figure 6-17* shows a typical oil sump that has the intake tube running through it. This preheats the fuel-air mixture before it enters the cylinders.

Figure 6-16. *Basic wet-sump oil system.*

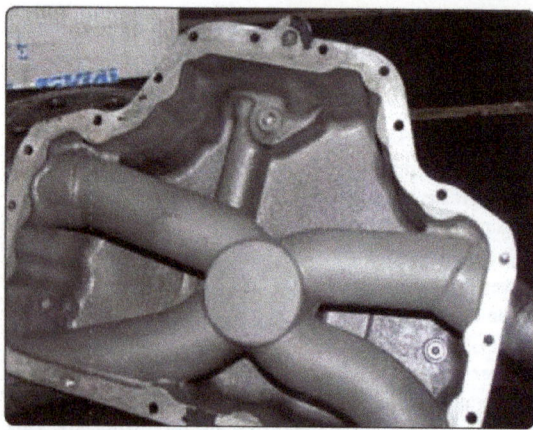

Figure 6-17. *Wet-sump system's sump with intake tube running through it.*

The rotation of the pump, which is driven by the engine, causes the oil to pass around the outside of the gears. *[Figure 6-6]* This develops a pressure in the crankshaft oiling system (drilled passage holes). The variation in the speed of the pump from idling to full-throttle operating range of the engine and the fluctuation of oil viscosity because of temperature changes are compensated by the tension on the relief valve spring. The pump is designed to create a greater pressure than required to compensate for wear of the bearings or thinning out of oil. The parts oiled by pressure throw a lubricating spray into the cylinder and piston assemblies. After lubricating the various units it sprays, the oil drains back into the sump and the cycle is repeated. The system is not readily adaptable to inverted flying since the entire oil supply floods the engine.

Lubrication System Maintenance Practices

Oil Tank

The oil tank, constructed of welded aluminum, is serviced (filled) through a filler neck located on the tank and equipped with a spring-loaded locking cap. Inside the tank, a weighted, flexible rubber oil hose is mounted so that it is repositioned automatically to ensure oil pickup during all maneuvers. A dipstick guard is welded inside the tank for the protection of the flexible oil hose assembly. During normal flight, the oil tank is vented to the engine crankcase by a flexible line at the top of the tank. The location of the oil system components in relation to each other and to the engine is shown in *Figure 6-18*.

Repair of an oil tank usually requires that the tank be removed. The removal and installation procedures normally remain the same regardless of whether the engine is removed or not. First, the oil must be drained. Most light aircraft provide an oil drain similar to that shown in *Figure 6-19*. On some aircraft, the normal ground attitude of the aircraft may prevent the oil tank from draining completely. If the amount of undrained oil is excessive, the aft portion of the tank can be raised slightly after the tank straps have been loosened to complete the drainage.

After disconnecting the oil inlet and vent lines, the scupper drain hose and bonding wire can be removed. *[Figure 6-20]* The securing straps fitted around the tank can now be removed. *[Figure 6-21]* Any safety wire securing the clamp must be removed before the clamp can be loosened and the strap disconnected. The tank can now be lifted out of the aircraft. The tank is reinstalled by reversing the sequence used in the tank removal. After installation, the oil tank should be filled to capacity. *[Figure 6-22]*

After the oil tank has been filled, the engine should be run for at least two minutes. Then, the oil level should be checked and, if necessary, sufficient oil should be added to bring the oil up to the proper level on the dipstick. *[Figure 6-23]*

Figure 6-18. *Oil system perspective.*

Figure 6-19. *Oil tank drain.*

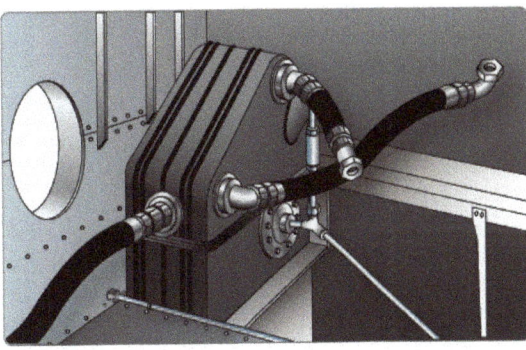

Figure 6-20. *Disconnect oil lines.*

6-15

Figure 6-21. *Removal of securing straps.*

Figure 6-22. *Filling an oil tank.*

Figure 6-23. *Checking oil level with dipstick.*

Oil Cooler
The oil cooler used with this aircraft's opposed-type engine is the honeycomb type. *[Figure 6-24]* With the engine operating and an oil temperature below 65 °C (150 °F), oil cooler bypass valve opens allowing oil to bypass the core.

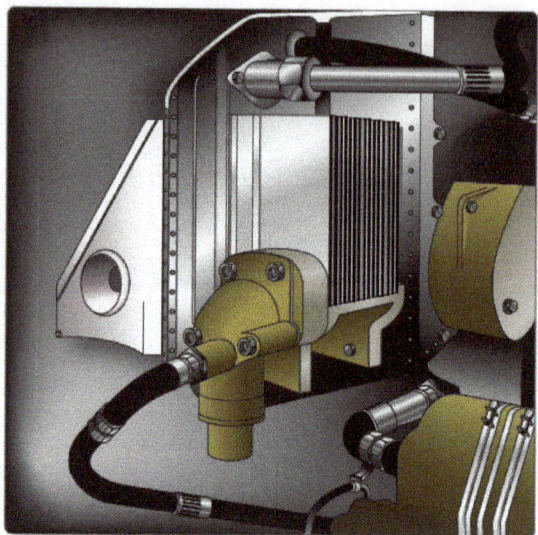

Figure 6-24. *Oil cooler.*

This valve begins to close when the oil temperature reaches approximately 65 °C (150 °F). When the oil temperature reaches 85 °C (185 °F), ±2 °C, the valve is closed completely, diverting all oil flow through the cooler core.

Oil Temperature Bulbs
Most oil temperature bulbs are mounted in the pressure oil screen housing. They relay an indication of engine oil inlet temperature to the oil temperature indicators mounted on the instrument panel. Temperature bulbs can be replaced by removing the safety wire and disconnecting the wire leads from the temperature bulbs, then removing the temperature bulbs using the proper wrench. *[Figure 6-25]*

Pressure and Scavenge Oil Screens
Sludge accumulates on the pressure and scavenges oil screens during engine operation. *[Figure 6-26]* These screens must be removed, inspected, and cleaned at the intervals specified by the manufacturer.

Typical removal procedures include removing the safety devices and loosening the oil screen housing or cover plate. A suitable container should be provided to collect the oil that drains from the filter housing or cavity. The container must be clean so that the oil collected in it can be examined for foreign particles. Any contamination already present in the container gives a false indication of the engine condition. This could result in a premature engine removal.

After the screens are removed, they should be inspected for contamination and for the presence of metal particles that may indicate possible engine internal wear, damage, or in extreme cases, engine failure. The screen must be

Figure 6-25. *Removing oil temperature bulb.*

cleaned prior to reinstalling in the engine. In some cases, it is necessary to disassemble the filter for inspection and cleaning. The manufacturer's procedures should be followed when disassembling and reassembling an oil screen assembly. When reinstalling a filter or screen, use new O-rings and gaskets and tighten the filter housing or cover retaining nuts to the torque value specified in the applicable maintenance manual. Filters should be safetied as required.

Oil Pressure Relief Valve

An oil pressure regulating (relief) valve limits oil pressure to the value specified by the engine manufacturer. Oil pressure settings can vary from around 35 psi minimum to around 90 psi maximum, depending on the installation. The oil pressure must be high enough to ensure adequate lubrication of the engine and accessories at high speeds and power settings. On the other hand, the pressure must not be too high, since leakage and damage to the oil system may result. Before any attempt is made to adjust the oil pressure, the engine must be at the correct operating temperature and a check should be made to assure that the correct viscosity oil is being used in the engine. One example of adjusting the oil pressure is done by removing a cover nut, loosening a locknut, and turning the adjusting screw. *[Figure 6-27]* Turn the adjusting screw clockwise to increase the pressure, or counterclockwise to decrease the pressure. Make the pressure adjustments while the engine is idling and tighten the adjustment screw lock-nut after each adjustment. Check the oil pressure reading while the engine is running at the rpm specified in the manufacturer's maintenance manual. This may be from around 1,900 rpm to 2,300 rpm. The oil pressure reading should be between the limits prescribed by the manufacturer at all throttle settings.

Recommendations for Changing Oil

Draining Oil

Oil, in service, is constantly exposed to many harmful substances that reduce its ability to protect moving parts.

Figure 6-26. *Oil pressure screen (A) and scavenge oil screen assembly (B).*

Figure 6-27. *Oil pressure relief valve adjustment.*

The main contaminants are:

- Gasoline
- Moisture
- Acids
- Dirt
- Carbon
- Metallic particles

Because of the accumulation of these harmful substances, common practice is to drain the entire lubrication system at regular intervals and refill with new oil. The time between oil changes varies with each make and model aircraft and engine combination.

In engines that have been operating on straight mineral oil for several hundred hours, a change to ashless dispersant oil should be made with a degree of caution as the cleaning action of some ashless dispersant oils tends to loosen sludge deposits and cause plugged oil passages. When an engine has been operating on straight mineral oil, and is known to be in excessively dirty condition, the switch to ashless dispersant oil should be deferred until after the engine is overhauled.

When changing from straight mineral oil to ashless dispersant oil, the following precautionary steps should be taken:

1. Do not add ashless dispersant oil to straight mineral oil. Drain the straight mineral oil from the engine and fill with ashless dispersant oil.
2. Do not operate the engine longer than 5 hours before the first oil change.
3. Check all oil filters and screens for evidence of sludge or plugging. Change oil every 10 hours if sludge conditions are evident. Repeat 10-hour checks until clean screen is noted, then change oil at recommended time intervals.
4. All turbocharged engines must be broken in and operated with ashless dispersant oil.

Oil and Filter Change and Screen Cleaning

One manufacturer recommends that for new, remanufactured; or newly overhauled engines and for engines with any newly installed cylinders, the oil should be changed after the first replacement/screen cleaning at 25 hours. The oil should be changed, filter replaced or pressure screen cleaned, and oil sump suction screen cleaned and inspected. A typical interval for oil change is 25 hours, along with a pressure screen cleaning and oil sump suction screen check for all engines employing a pressure screen system. Typical 50-hour interval oil changes generally include the oil filter replacement and suction screen check for all engines using full-flow filtration systems. A time maximum of 4 months between servicing is also recommended for oil system service.

Oil Filter Removal Canister Type Housing

Remove the filter housing from the engine by removing the safety wire and loosening the hex head screw and housing by turning counterclockwise and removing the filter from the engine. *[Figure 6-7]* Remove the nylon nut that holds the cover plate on the engine side of the filter. Remove the cover plate, hex head screw from the housing. To remove the spin-on type of filter, cut the safety wire and use the wrench pad on the rear of the filter to turn the filter counterclockwise, and remove filter. Inspect the filter element as described in the following paragraph. Discard old gaskets and replace with new replacement kit gaskets.

Oil Filter/Screen Content Inspection

Check for premature or excessive engine component wear that is indicated by the presence of metal particles, shavings, or flakes in the oil filter element or screens. The oil filter can be inspected by opening the filter paper element. Check the condition of the oil from the filter for signs of metal contamination. Then, remove the paper element from the filter and carefully unfold the paper element; examine the material trapped in the filter. If the engine employs a pressure screen system, check the screen for metal particles. After draining the oil, remove the suction screen from the oil sump and check for metal particles. *[Figure 6-28]* If examination of the used oil filter or pressure screen and the oil sump suction screen indicates abnormal metal content, additional service may be required to determine the source and possible need for corrective maintenance. To inspect the spin on filter the can must be cut open to remove the filter element for inspection. Using the special filter cutting tool, slightly tighten the cutter blade against filter and rotate 360° until the mounting plate separates from the can. *[Figure 6-29]* Using a clean plastic bucket containing varsol, move the filter to remove contaminants. Use a clean magnet and check for any ferrous

Figure 6-28. *Oil sump screen.*

metal particles in the filter or varsol solution. Then, take the remaining varsol and pour it through a clean filter or shop towel. Using a bright light, inspect for any nonferrous metals.

Assembly of and Installation of Oil Filters

After cleaning the parts, installation of the canister or filter element type filter is accomplished by lightly oiling the new rubber gaskets and installing a new copper gasket on the hex head screw. Assemble the hex head screw into the filter case using the new copper gasket. Install the filter element and place the cover over the case, then manually thread on the nylon nut by hand. Install the housing on the engine by turning it clockwise, then torque and safety it. Spin-on filters generally have installation instructions on the filter. Place a coating of engine oil on the rubber gasket, install the filter, torque and safety it. Always follow the manufacturer's current instructions to perform any maintenance.

Troubleshooting Oil Systems

The outline of malfunctions and their remedies listed in *Figure 6-30* can expedite troubleshooting of the lubrication system. The purpose of this section is to present typical troubles. It is not intended to imply that any of the troubles are exactly as they may be in a particular airplane.

Requirements for Turbine Engine Lubricants

There are many requirements for turbine engine lubricating oils. Due to the absence of reciprocating motion and the presence of ball and roller bearings (antifriction bearings), the turbine engine uses a less viscous lubricant. Gas turbine engine oil must have a high viscosity for good load-carrying ability but must also be of sufficiently low viscosity to provide good flowability. It must also be of low volatility to prevent loss by evaporation at the high altitudes at which the engines operate. In addition, the oil should not foam and should be essentially nondestructive to natural or synthetic rubber seals in the lubricating system. Also, with high-speed antifriction bearings, the formation of carbons or varnishes must be held to a minimum. Synthetic oil for turbine engines are usually supplied in sealed one-quart cans.

The many requirements for lubricating oils are met in the synthetic oils developed specifically for turbine engines. Synthetic oil has two principal advantages over petroleum oil. It has a lower tendency to deposit lacquer and coke (solids left after solvents have been evaporated) because it does not evaporate the solvents from the oil at high temperature. Oil grades used in some turbine engines normally contain thermal and oxidation preventives, load-carrying additives, and substances that lower the pour point in addition to synthetic chemical-base materials. MIL-L-7808, which is a military specification for turbine oil, was type I turbine oil. Turbine synthetic oil has a viscosity of around 5 to 5.5 centistokes at 210° F that is approved against the military specification MIL-PRF-23699F. This oil is referred to as type II turbine oil. Most turbine oils meet this type II specification and are made with the following characteristics:

1. Vapor phase deposits—carbon deposits formed from oil mist and vapor contact with hot engine surfaces.
2. Load-carrying ability—provides for heavy loads on the bearing systems of turbine engines.
3. Cleanliness—minimum formation of sludge deposits during severe operation.

Figure 6-29. *Cutting open a spin-on type oil filter using a special filter cutter.*

Trouble	Isolation Procedure	Remedy
1 Excessive oil consumption		
Oil line leakage	Check external lines for evidence of oil leakage.	Replace or repair defective lines.
Accessory seal leakage	Check for leak at accessories immediately after engine operation.	Replace accessory and/or defective accessory oil seal.
Low grade of oil		Fill tank with proper grade oil.
Failing or failed bearing	Check sump and oil pressure pump screen for material particles.	Replace engine if metal particles are found.
2 High or low indicated oil pressure		
Defective pressure gauge	Check indicator.	Replace indicator if defective.
Improper operation of oil pressure	Erratic pressure indications either excessively high or low.	Remove, clean, and inspect relief valve accessory oil seal.
Inadequate oil supply	Check oil quantity.	Fill oil tank.
Diluted or contaminated oil		Drain engine and tank; refill tank.
Clogged oil screen		Remove and clean oil screen.
Oil viscosity incorrect	Make sure correct oil is being used.	Drain engine and tank; refill tank.
Oil pump pressure relief valve adjustment incorrect	Check pressure relief valve adjustment.	Make correct adjustment on oil pump pressure relief valve.
3 High or low indicated oil temperature		
Defective temperature gauge	Check indicator.	Replace indicator if defective.
Inadequate oil supply	Check oil quantity.	Fill oil tank.
Diluted or contaminated oil		Drain engine and tank; refill tank.
Obstruction in oil tank	Check tank.	Drain oil and remove obstruction.
Clogged oil screen		Remove and clean oil screens.
Obstruction in oil cooler passages	Check cooler for blocked or deformed passages.	Replace oil cooler if defective.
4 Oil foaming		
Diluted or contaminated oil		Drain engine and tank; refill tank.
Oil level in tank too high	Check oil quantity.	Drain excess oil from tank.

Figure 6-30. *Oil system troubleshooting procedures.*

4. Bulk stability—resistance to physical or chemical change resulting from oxidation. Permits long periods of serve operation without significant increase in viscosity or total acidity, the main indicators of oxidation.

5. Compatibility—most turbine oil is compatible with other oils that meet the same military specification. But, most engine manufacturers do not recommend the indiscriminate mixing of approved oil brands and this is not a generally accepted practice.

6. Seal Wear—essential for the life of engines with carbon seals that lubricant properties prevent wear of the carbon at the carbon seal face.

Turbine Oil Health and Safety Precautions

Under normal conditions, the use of turbine oil presents a low health risk for humans. Although each person reacts somewhat differently to exposure, contact with liquids, vapors, and mist of turbine oil should be minimized. Information on established limits on exposure to turbine oil can generally be found in the material safety data sheets (MSDS). Prolonged breathing of hydrocarbon vapor concentrations in excess of the prescribed limits may result in lightheadedness, dizziness, and nausea. If turbine oil is ingested, call a doctor immediately; identify the product and how much was ingested. Because of the risk of ingestion, petroleum products should never be siphoned by mouth.

Prolonged or repeated contact of turbine oil with the skin can cause irritation and dermatitis. In case of skin contact, wash the skin thoroughly with soap and warm water. Promptly remove oil-soaked clothing and wash. If turbine oil contacts the eyes, flush the eyes with fresh water until the irritation subsides. Protective clothing, gloves, and eye protection should be used when handling turbine oil.

During operation, it is possible for the oil to be subjected to very high temperatures that can break down the oil and produce a product of unknown toxicity. If this happens, all precautions to avoid explosive should be taken. It can also have a tendency to blister, discolor, or remove paint whenever it is spilled. Painted surfaces should be wiped clean with a petroleum solvent after spillage.

Spectrometric Oil Analysis Program

The Spectrometric Oil Analysis Program allows an oil sample to be analyzed and searched for the presence of minute metallic elements. Due to oil circulation throughout an aircraft engine, every lubricant that is in service contains microscopic particles of metallic elements called wear metals. As the engine operates over time, the oil picks up very small particles that stay suspended in the oil. Oil analysis programs identify and measure these particles in parts per million (PPM) by weight. The analyzed elements are grouped into categories, such as wear metals and additives, and their measurement in PPM provides data that expert analysts can use as one of many tools to determine the engine's condition. An increase in PPM of certain materials can be a sign of component wear or impending failure of the engine. When you take a sample, note and record the amount of wear metals. If the amount of wear metals increases beyond a normal rate, then the operator can be notified quickly so repair or a recommend specific maintenance procedure or inspection can be ordered.

Oil analysis increases safety by identifying an engine problem before engine failure. It also saves money by finding engine problems before they become large problems or complete engine failure. This procedure can be used for both turbine and reciprocating engines.

Typical Wear Metals and Additives

The following examples of wear metals are associated with areas of the engine that could be lead to their source. Identifying the metal can help identify the engine components that are wearing or failing.

- Iron—wear from rings, shafts, gears, valve train, cylinder walls, and pistons in some engines.
- Chromium—primary sources are chromed parts (such as rings, liners, etc.) and some coolant additives.
- Nickel—secondary indicator of wear from certain types of bearings, shafts, valves, and valve guides.
- Aluminum—indicates wear of pistons, rod bearings, and certain types of bushings.
- Lead—mostly from tetraethyl lead contamination.
- Copper—wear from bearings, rocker arm bushings, wrist pin bushings, thrust washers, and other bronze or brass parts, and oil additive or antiseize compound.
- Tin—wear from bearings.
- Silver—wear of bearings that contain silver and, in some instances, a secondary indicator of oil cooler problems.
- Titanium—alloy in high-quality steel for gears and bearings.
- Molybdenum—gear or ring wear and used as an additive in some oils.
- Phosphorous—antirust agents, spark plugs, and combustion chamber deposits.

Turbine Engine Lubrication Systems

Both wet- and dry-sump lubrication systems are used in gas turbine engines. Wet-sump engines store the lubricating oil in the engine proper, while dry-sump engines utilize an external tank mounted on the engine or somewhere in the aircraft structure near the engine, similar to reciprocating piston engines mentioned earlier.

Turbine engine's oil systems can also be classified as a pressure relief system that maintains a somewhat constant pressure: the full flow type of system, in which the pressure varies with engine speed, and the total loss system, used in engines that are for short duration operation (target drones, missiles, etc.). The most widely used system is the pressure relief system with the full flow used mostly on large fan-type engines. One of the main functions of the oil system in turbine engines is cooling the bearings by carrying the heat away from the bearing by circulating oil around the bearing.

The exhaust turbine bearing is the most critical lubricating point in a gas turbine engine because of the high temperature normally present. In some engines, air cooling is used in addition to oil cooling the bearing, which supports the turbine. Air cooling, referred to as secondary air flow, is cooling air provide by bleed air from the early stages of the compressor. This internal air flow has many uses on the inside of the engine. It is used to cool turbine disk, vanes, and blades. Also, some turbine wheels may have bleed air flowing over the turbine disk, which reduces heat radiation to the bearing surface. Bearing cavities sometimes use compressor air to aid in cooling the turbine bearing. This bleed air, as it is called, is usually bled off a compressor stage at a point where air has enough pressure but has not yet become too warm (as the air is compressed, it becomes heated).

The use of cooling air substantially reduces the quantity of oil necessary to provide adequate cooling of the bearings. Since cooling is a major function of the oil in turbine engines, the lubricating oil for bearing cooling normally requires an oil cooler. When an oil cooler is required, usually a greater quantity of oil is necessary to provide for circulation between the cooler and engine. To ensure proper temperature, oil is routed through either air-cooled and/or fuel-cooled oil coolers. This system is used to also heat (regulate) the fuel to prevent ice in the fuel.

Turbine Lubrication System Components

The following component descriptions include most found in the various turbine lubrication systems. However, since engine oil systems vary somewhat according to engine model and manufacturer, not all of these components are necessarily found in any one system.

Oil Tank

Although the dry-sump systems use an oil tank that contains most of the oil supply, a small sump is usually included on the engine to hold a small supply of oil. It usually contains the oil pump, the scavenge and pressure inlet strainers, scavenge return connection, pressure outlet ports, an oil filter, and mounting bosses for the oil pressure gauge and temperature bulb connections.

A view of a typical oil tank is shown in *Figure 6-31*. It is designed to furnish a constant supply of oil to the engine during any aircraft attitude. This is done by a swivel outlet assembly mounted inside the tank, a horizontal baffle mounted in the center of the tank, two flapper check valves mounted on the baffle, and a positive vent system.

The swivel outlet fitting is controlled by a weighted end that is free to swing below the baffle. The flapper valves in the baffle are normally open; they close only when the oil in the bottom of the tank tends to rush to the top of the tank during decelerations. This traps the oil in the bottom of the tank where it is picked up by the swivel fitting. A sump drain is located in the bottom of the tank. The vent system inside the tank is so arranged that the airspace is vented at all times even though oil may be forced to the top of the tank by deceleration of the aircraft.

All oil tanks are provided with expansion space. This allows expansion of the oil after heat is absorbed from the bearings and gears and after the oil foams as a result of circulating through the system. Some tanks also incorporate a deaerator tray for separating air from the oil returned to the top of the tank by the scavenger system. Usually these deaerators are the can type in which oil enters at a tangent. The air released

Figure 6-31. *Oil tank.*

is carried out through the vent system in the top of the tank. In most oil tanks, a pressure buildup is desired within the tank to ensure a positive flow of oil to the oil pump inlet. This pressure buildup is made possible by running the vent line through an adjustable check relief valve. The check relief valve is usually set to relieve at about 4 psi, keeping positive pressure on the oil pump inlet. If the air temperature is abnormally low, the oil may be changed to a lighter grade. Some engines may provide for the installation of an immersion-type oil heater.

Oil Pump

The oil pump is designed to supply oil under pressure to the parts of the engine that require lubrication, then circulate the oil through coolers as needed, and return the oil to the oil tank. Many oil pumps consist of not only a pressure supply element, but also scavenge elements, such as in a dry-sump system. However, there are some oil pumps that serve a single function; that is, they either supply or scavenge the oil. These pump elements can be located separate from each other and driven by different shafts from the engine. The numbers of pumping elements (two gears that pump oil), pressure and scavenge, depend largely on the type and model of the engine. Several scavenge oil pump elements can be used to accommodate the larger capacity of oil and air mix. The scavenge elements have a greater pumping capacity than the pressure element to prevent oil from collecting in the bearing sumps of the engine.

The pumps may be one of several types, each type having certain advantages and limitations. The two most common oil pumps are the gear and gerotor, with the gear-type being the most commonly used. Each of these pumps has several possible configurations.

The gear-type oil pump has only two elements: one for pressure oil and one for scavenging. *[Figure 6-32]* However, some types of pumps may have several elements: one or more elements for pressure and two or more for scavenging. The clearances between the gear teeth and the sides of the pump wall and plate are critical to maintain the correct output of the pump.

Figure 6-32. *Cutaway view of gear oil pump.*

6-23

A regulating (relief) valve in the discharge side of the pump limits the output pressure of the pump by bypassing oil to the pump inlet when the outlet pressure exceeds a predetermined limit. *[Figure 6-32]* The regulating valve can be adjusted, if needed, to bring the oil pressure within limits. Also shown is the shaft shear section that causes the shaft to shear if the pump gears should seize up and not turn.

The gerotor pump, like the gear pump, usually contains a single element for oil pressure and several elements for scavenging oil. Each of the elements, pressure and scavenge, is almost identical in shape; however, the capacity of the elements can be controlled by varying the size of the gerotor elements. For example, the pressure element may have a pumping capacity of 3.1 gallon per minute (gpm) as compared to 4.25 gpm capacity for the scavenge elements. Consequently, the pressure element is smaller since the elements are all driven by a common shaft. The pressure is determined by engine rpm with a minimum pressure at idling speed and maximum pressure at intermediate and maximum engine speeds.

A typical set of gerotor pumping elements is shown in *Figure 6-33*. Each set of gerotors is separated by a steel plate, making each set an individual pumping unit consisting of an inner and an outer element. The small star-shaped inner element has external lobes that fit within and are matched with the outer element that has internal lobes. The small element fits on and is keyed to the pump shaft and acts as a drive for the outer free-turning element. The outer element fits within a steel plate having an eccentric bore. In one engine model, the oil pump has four elements: one for oil feed and three for scavenge. In some other models, pumps have six elements: one for feed and five for scavenge. In each case, the oil flows as long as the engine shaft is turning.

Figure 6-33. *Typical gerotor pumping elements.*

Turbine Oil Filters

Filters are an important part of the lubrication system because they remove foreign particles that may be in the oil. This is particularly important in gas turbines as very high engine speeds are attained; the antifriction types of ball and roller bearings would become damaged quite rapidly if lubricated with contaminated oil. Also, there are usually numerous drilled or core passages leading to various points of lubrication. Since these passages are usually rather small, they are easily clogged.

There are several types and locations of filters used for filtering the turbine lubricating oil. The filtering elements come in a variety of configurations and mesh sizes. Mesh sizes are measured in microns, which is a linear measurement equal to one millionth of a meter (a very small opening).

A main oil strainer filter element is shown in *Figure 6-34*. The filtering element interior is made of varying materials including paper and metal mesh. *[Figure 6-35]* Oil normally flows through the filter element from the outside into the filter body. One type of oil filter uses a replaceable laminated paper element, while others use a very fine stainless steel metal mesh of about 25–35 microns.

Figure 6-34. *Turbine oil filter element.*

Most filters are located close to the pressure pump and consist of a filter body or housing, filter element, a bypass valve, and a check valve. The filter bypass valve prevents the oil flow from being stopped if the filter element becomes clogged. The bypass valve opens whenever a certain pressure is reached. If this occurs, the filtering action is lost, allowing unfiltered oil to be pumped to the bearings. However, this prevents the bearings from receiving no oil at all. In the bypass mode, many engines have a mechanical indicator that pops out to indicate the filter is in the bypass mode. This indication is visual and can only be seen by inspecting the engine directly. An antidrain check valve is incorporated into the assembly to prevent the oil in the tank from draining down into the engine sumps when the engine is not operating. This check valve is normally spring loaded closed with 4 to 6 psi needed to open it.

The filters generally discussed are used as main oil filters; that is, they strain the oil as it leaves the pump before being

Figure 6-35. *Turbine oil filter paper element.*

piped to the various points of lubrication. In addition to the main oil filters, there are also secondary filters located throughout the system for various purposes. For instance, there may be a finger screen filter that is sometimes used for straining scavenged oil. These screens tend to be large mesh screens that trap larger contaminants. Also, there are fine-mesh screens called last chance filters for straining the oil just before it passes from the spray nozzles onto the bearing surfaces. *[Figure 6-36]* These filters are located at each bearing and help screen out contaminants that could plug the oil spray nozzle.

Oil Pressure Regulating Valve

Most turbine engine oil systems are the pressure regulating type system that keeps the pressure fairly constant. An oil pressure regulating valve is included in the oil system on the pressure side of the pressure pump. A regulating valve system controls the systems pressure to a limited pressure within the system. It is more of a regulating valve than a relief valve because it keeps the pressure in the system within certain limits other than only opening when the absolute maximum pressure of the system is exceeded.

The regulating valve *Figure 6-37* has a valve held against a seat by a spring. By adjusting the tension (increase) on the spring, you change the pressure at which the valve opens and you also increase the system pressure. A screw pressing on the spring adjusts the tension on the valve and the system pressure.

Figure 6-37. *Pressure regulating valve.*

Oil Pressure Relief Valve

Some large turbofan oil systems do not have a regulating valve. The system pressure varies with engine rpm and pump speed. There is a wide range of pressure in this system. A relief valve is used to relieve pressure only if it exceeds the maximum limit for the system. *[Figure 6-38]* This true relief valve system is preset to relieve pressure and bypass the oil back to the inlet side of the oil pump whenever the pressure exceeds the maximum preset system limit. This relief valve is especially important when oil coolers are incorporated

Figure 6-36. *Last-chance filter before spray nozzle.*

6-25

Figure 6-38. *Pressure relief valve.*

in the system since the coolers are easily ruptured because of their thin-wall construction. Under normal operation, it should never open.

Oil Jets

Oil jets (or nozzles) are located in the pressure lines adjacent to, or within, the bearing compartments and rotor shaft couplings. *[Figure 6-39]* The oil from these nozzles is delivered in the form of an atomized spray. Some engines use an air-oil mist spray that is produced by tapping high-pressure bleed air from the compressor to the oil nozzle outlet. This method is considered adequate for ball and roller bearings; however, the solid oil spray method is considered the better of the two methods.

The oil jets are easily clogged because of the small orifice in their tips; consequently, the oil must be free of any foreign particles. If the last-chance filters in the oil jets should become clogged, bearing failure usually results since nozzles are not accessible for cleaning except during engine maintenance. To prevent damage from clogged oil jets, main oil filters are checked frequently for contamination.

Lubrication System Instrumentation

Gauge connection provisions are incorporated in the oil system for oil pressure, oil quantity, low oil pressure, oil filter differential pressure switch, and oil temperature. The oil pressure gauge measures the pressure of the lubricant as it leaves the pump and enters the pressure system. The oil pressure transmitter connection is located in the pressure line between the pump and the various points of lubrication. An electronic sensor is placed to send a signal to the Full Authority Digital Engine Control (FADEC) control unit and through the Engine Indicating and Crew Alerting System (EICAS) computers, and on to the displays in the flight deck. *[Figure 6-40]* The tank quantity transmitter information is sent to the EICAS computers. The low oil pressure switch alerts the crew if the oil pressure falls below a certain pressure during engine operation. The differential oil pressure switch alerts the flight crew of an impending oil filter bypass because of a clogged filter. A message is sent to the display in the upper EICAS display in the flight deck as can be seen in *Figure 6-40*. Oil temperature can be sensed at one or more points in the engine's oil flow path. The signal is sent to the FADEC/EICAS computer and is displayed on the lower EICAS display.

Lubrication System Breather Systems (Vents)

Breather subsystems are used to remove excess air from the bearing cavities and return the air to the oil tank where it is separated from any oil mixed in the vapor of air and oil by the deaerator. Then, the air is vented overboard and back to the atmosphere. All engine bearing compartments, oil tanks, and accessory cases are vented together so the pressure in the system remains the same.

The vent in an oil tank keeps the pressure within the tank from rising above or falling below that of the outside atmosphere. However, the vent may be routed through a check relief valve that is preset to maintain a slight (approximately 4 psi) pressure on the oil to assure a positive flow to the oil pump inlet.

Figure 6-39. *Oil nozzles spray lubricate on bearings.*

Figure 6-40. *Oil indicating system.*

In the accessory case, the vent (or breather) is a screen-protected opening that allows accumulated air pressure within the accessory case to escape to the atmosphere. The scavenged oil carries air into the accessory case and this air must be vented. Otherwise, the pressure buildup within the accessory case would stop the flow of oil draining from the bearing, forcing this oil past the bearing oil seals and into the compressor housing. If in enough quantity, oil leakage could cause burning and seal and bearing malfunction. The screened breathers are usually located in the front center of the accessory case to prevent oil leakage through the breather when the aircraft is in unusual flight attitudes. Some breathers may have a baffle to prevent oil leakage during flight maneuvers. A vent that leads directly to the bearing compartment may be used in some engines. This vent equalizes pressure around the bearing surface so that the lower pressure at the first compressor stage does not cause oil to be forced past the bearing rear oil seal into the compressor.

Lubrication System Check Valve
Check valves are sometimes installed in the oil supply lines of dry-sump oil systems to prevent reservoir oil from seeping (by gravity) through the oil pump elements and high-pressure lines into the engine after shutdown. Check valves, by stopping flow in an opposite direction, prevent accumulations of undue amounts of oil in the accessory gearbox, compressor rear housing, and combustion chamber. Such accumulations could cause excessive loading of the accessory drive gears during starts, contamination of the cabin pressurization air, or internal oil fires. The check valves are usually the spring-loaded ball-and-socket type constructed for free flow of pressure oil. The pressure required to open these valves varies, but the valves generally require from 2 to 5 psi to permit oil to flow to the bearings.

Lubrication System Thermostatic Bypass Valves
Thermostatic bypass valves are included in oil systems using an oil cooler. Although these valves may be called different names, their purpose is always to maintain proper oil temperature by varying the proportion of the total oil flow passing through the oil cooler. A cutaway view of a typical thermostatic bypass valve is shown in *Figure 6-41*. This valve consists of a valve body, having two inlet ports and one outlet port, and a spring-loaded thermostatic element valve. The valve is spring loaded because the pressure drop through the oil cooler could become too great due to denting

Figure 6-41. *Typical thermostatic bypass valve.*

or clogging of the cooler tubing. In such a case, the valve opens, bypassing the oil around the cooler.

Air Oil Coolers

Two basic types of oil coolers in general use are the air-cooled and the fuel-cooled. Air oil coolers are used in the lubricating systems of some turbine engines to reduce the temperature of the oil to a degree suitable for recirculation through the system. The air-cooled oil cooler is normally installed at the forward end of the engine. It is similar in construction and operation to the air-cooled cooler used on reciprocating engines. An air oil cooler is usually included in a dry-sump oil system. *[Figure 6-42]* This cooler may be air-cooled or fuel-cooled and many engines use both. Dry-sump lubrication systems require coolers for several reasons. First, air cooling of bearings by using compressor bleed-air is not sufficient to cool the turbine bearing cavities because of the heat present in area of the turbine bearings. Second, the large turbofan engines normally require a greater number of bearings, which means that more heat is transferred to the oil. Consequently, the oil coolers are the only means of dissipating the oil heat.

Figure 6-42. *Air oil cooler.*

Fuel Oil Coolers

The fuel-cooled oil cooler acts as a fuel oil heat exchanger in that the fuel cools the hot oil and the oil heats the fuel for combustion. *[Figure 6-43]* Fuel flowing to the engine must pass through the heat exchanger; however, there is a thermostatic valve that controls the oil flow, and the oil may bypass the cooler if no cooling is needed. The fuel/oil heat exchanger consists of a series of joined tubes with an inlet and outlet port. The oil enters the inlet port, moves around the fuel tubes, and goes out the oil outlet port.

Deoiler

The deoiler removes the oil from the breather air. The breather air goes into an impeller that turns in the deoiler housing. Centrifugal force drives the oil towards the outer wall of the impeller. Then, the oil drains from the deoiler into a sump or oil tank. Because the air is much lighter than the oil, it goes through the center of the impeller and is vented overboard.

Magnetic Chip Detectors

Magnetic chip detectors are used in the oil system to detect and catch ferrous (magnetic) particles present in the oil. *[Figure 6-44]* Scavenge oil generally flows past chip detectors so any magnetic particles are attracted and stick to the chip detector. Chip detectors are placed in several locations but generally are in the scavenge lines for each scavenge pump, oil tank, and in the oil sumps. Some engines have several detectors to one detector. During maintenance, the chip detectors are removed from the engine and inspected for metal; if none is found, the detector is cleaned, replaced, and safety wired. If metal is found on a chip detector, an investigation should be made to find the source of the metal on the chip.

Typical Dry-Sump Pressure Regulated Turbine Lubrication System

The turbine lubrication system is representative of turbine engines using a dry-sump system. *[Figure 6-45]* The lubrication system is a pressure regulated, high-pressure design. It consists of the pressure, scavenge, and breather subsystems.

The pressure system supplies oil to the main engine bearings and to the accessory drives. The scavenger system returns the oil to the engine oil tank that is usually mounted on the compressor case. It is connected to the inlet side of the pressure oil pump and completes the oil flow cycle. A breather system connecting the individual bearing compartments and the oil tank with the breather pressurizing valve completes the engine lubrication system. In a turbine pressure relief dry-sump lubrication system, the oil supply is carried in a tank mounted on the engine. With this type of system, a larger

Figure 6-43. *Fuel oil heat exchanger cooler.*

Figure 6-44. *Chip detector.*

oil supply can be carried and the temperature of the oil can be readily controlled.

Pressure System

The oil pressure branch of the engine lubrication system is pressurized by a gear-type pressure pump located in the oil pump and accessory drive housing. *[Figure 6-45]* The pressure pump receives engine oil at its lower (inlet) side and discharges pressurized oil to an oil filter located on the housing. From the oil filter, which is equipped with a bypass valve for operation in case the filter clogs, the pressurized oil is transmitted to a cored passage running through to the pressure regulating (relief) valve that maintains system pressure. The pressure regulating (relief) valve is located downstream of the pump. It is adjusted to maintain a proper pressure to the oil metering jets in the engine. The pressure regulating (relief) valve is usually easily accessible for adjustment. Then, the oil flows through the fuel oil cooler and on to the bearing cavities through last-chance filters and out spray nozzles to the bearings. Pressurized oil distributed to the engine main bearings is sprayed on the bearings through fixed orifice nozzles providing a relatively constant oil flow at all engine operating speeds.

Scavenge System

The scavenge system scavenges the main bearing compartments and circulates the scavenged oil back to the tank. The scavenge oil system includes five gear-type pumps. *[Figure 6-45]* The No.1 bearing oil scavenge pump scavenges accumulated oil from the front bearing case. It directs the oil through an external line to a central collecting point in the main accessory gearbox. The oil return from No. 2 and 3 bearings is through internal passages to a central collecting point in the main accessory case. The accessory gearbox oil suction pump, located in the main accessory gearbox, scavenges oil from the gearbox housing to the oil tank. Oil from the No. 4, No.

6-29

Figure 6-45. *Typical turbine dry-sump pressure regulated lubrication system.*

4½ and No. 5 bearing accumulates in the bearing cavity and is scavenged to the accessory gearbox.

The turbine rear bearing oil suction pump scavenges oil from the No. 6 bearing compartment and directs the scavenged oil through a passage in the turbine case strut. From there, it is directed to the bearing cavity for the 4, 4½, and 5 bearing cavity where it joins this oil and is returned to the oil tank. The scavenge oil passes through the deaerator as it enters the oil tank, which separates the air mixed in the return oil. The oil stays in the tank while the air flow into the accessory gearbox and enters the deoiler.

Breather Pressurizing System

The breather pressurizing system ensures a proper oil spray pattern from the main bearing oil jets and furnishes a pressure head to the scavenge system. Breather tubes in the compressor inlet case, the oil tank, the diffuser case, and the turbine exhaust case are connected to external tubing at the top of the engine. By means of this tubing, the vapor-laden atmospheres of the various bearing compartments and the oil tank are brought together in the deoiler in the accessory gearbox. The deoiler separates out the oil from the air/oil mist and vents the air back to the atmosphere.

Typical Dry-Sump Variable Pressure Lubrication System

The dry-sump variable-pressure lubrication system uses the same basic subsystems that the regulated systems used (pressure Scavenge breather). *[Figure 6-46]* The main difference is that the pressure in this system is not regulated by a regulating bypass valve. Most large turbofan engine pressure systems are variable-pressure systems in which the pump outlet pressure (oil pressure) depends on the engine rpm. In other words, the pump output pressure is proportional to the engine speed. Since the resistance to flow in the system does not vary much during operation and the pump has only the variable of turning faster or slower, the pressure is a function of engine speed. As an example, oil pressure can vary widely in this type of system, from 100 psi to over 260 psi, with the relief valve opening at about 540 psi.

Pressure Subsystem

The oil flows from the oil tank down to the pressure stage of the oil pump. A slight pressure in the tank assures that the flow of oil into the pressure pump is continuous. After being pressurized, it moves on to the oil filter where it is filtered.

Figure 6-46. *Typical turbine dry-sump variable pressure lubrication system.*

If the filter is clogged, the bypass valve sends the oil around the filter. There is no regulating valve but there is a relief valve to prevent the system pressure from exceeding the maximum limits. This valve is usually set to open well above the systems operating pressure. The oil flows from the filter housing to the engine air/oil cooler. The oil either bypasses the cooler (cold) or passes through the cooler (hot) and then on to the fuel oil cooler. Through the use of the coolers, the fuel temperature is adjusted to meet the requirements needed for the engine. Some of the oil passes through the classified oil pressure trim orifice that helps adjust oil pressure at low speeds. The oil now flows through the last-chance oil filters (strainers) that remove particles from the oil if the oil filter has been bypassed. The engine oil passes through the nozzles to lubricate the bearings, gearboxes, seals, and accessory drive splines. After performing its functions of lubricating, cleaning, and cooling the bearings, the oil needs to be returned to the old tank by the scavenge system.

Scavenger Subsystem

The scavenger oil pump has several stages that pull oil from the bearing compartments and gear boxes and sends the oil to the tank. At the tank, the oil enters the deaerator, which separates the air from the scavenge oil. The oil returns to the tank and the air is vented through a check valve overboard. Each stage of the scavenge pump has a magnetic chip detector that can be removed for inspection.

Breather Subsystems

The purpose of the breather system is to remove air from the bearing compartments, separate breather air from oil, and vent the air overboard. The breather air from the bearing compartments is drawn to the gearbox by the deoiler. The deoiler is turned at high speed and causes the oil to separate from the air. The air is then vented with air from the deaerator overboard. By referring to *Figure 6-46*, notice that the deaerator is in the oil tank and the deoiler is in the main gear box.

Turbine Engine Wet-Sump Lubrication System

In some engines, the lubrication system is the wet-sump type. There are relatively few engines using a wet-sump type of oil system. A schematic diagram of a wet-sump oil system is shown in *Figure 6-47*. The components of a wet-sump system are similar to those of a dry-sump system. The major difference between the two systems is the location of the oil reservoir. The reservoir for the wet-sump oil system may be the accessory gear case or it may be a sump mounted on the bottom of the accessory case. Regardless of configuration, reservoirs for wet-sump systems are an integral part of the engine and contain the bulk of the engine oil supply. *[Figure 6-47]*

Figure 6-47. *Typical turbine wet sump system.*

Included in the wet-sump reservoir are the following components:

1. A sight gauge indicates the oil level in the sump.
2. A vent or breather equalizes pressure within the accessory casing.
3. A magnetic drain plug may be provided to drain the oil and also to trap any ferrous metal particles in the oil. This plug should always be examined closely during inspections. The presence of metal particles may indicate gear or bearing failure.
4. Provision may also be made for a temperature bulb and an oil pressure fitting.

This system is typical of all engines using a wet-sump lubrication system. The bearing and drive gears in the accessory drive casing are lubricated by a splash system. The oil for the remaining points of lubrication leaves the pump under pressure and passes through a filter to jet nozzles that direct the oil into the rotor bearings and couplings. The oil is returned to the reservoir (sump) by gravity. Oil from the compressor bearing and the accessories drive coupling shaft drains directly into the reservoir. Turbine oil drains into a sump where the oil was originally pumped.

Turbine Engine Oil System Maintenance

Maintenance of gas turbine lubrication systems consists mainly of adjusting, removing, cleaning, and replacing various components. Oil filter maintenance and oil change intervals for turbine engines vary widely from model to model, depending on the severity of the oil temperature conditions imposed by the specific airframe installation and engine configuration. The applicable manufacturer's instructions should be followed. The oil filter should be removed at every regular inspection. It should be disassembled, cleaned, and any worn or damaged filter elements replaced. The following steps illustrate typical oil filter removal cleaning and replacement procedures:

1. Provide a suitable container for collecting the drained oil, if needed.
2. Remove the filter housing and withdraw the filter assembly. *[Figure 6-48]* Discard the old seals.

Figure 6-48. *Oil filter housing.*

3. Immerse the screen or filter in an approved carbon remover at room temperature for a few minutes. Rinse them in a degreaser fluid or cleaning solvent. Then, blow them dry with an air jet.
4. Then, install the filter in the filter housing assembly. Place a new seal and tightened to the torque prescribed in the manufacturer's instructions.
5. Secure with lock wire.

To adjust the oil pressure, first remove the adjusting screw acorn cap on the oil pressure relief valve. Then, loosen the locknut and turn the adjusting screw clockwise to increase, or counterclockwise to decrease, the oil pressure. In a typical turbojet lubrication system, the adjusting screw is adjusted to provide an oil pressure of 45, ±5 psi, at approximately 75 percent of normal rated thrust. The adjustment should be made while the engine is idling; it may be necessary to perform several adjustments before the desired pressure is obtained. When the proper pressure setting is achieved, tighten the adjusting screw locknut, and install the acorn cap with a new gasket, then tighten and secure with lock wire.

Maintenance of scavenge and breather systems at regular inspections includes checks for oil leaks and security of mounting of system components. Also, check chip detectors for particles of ferrous material and clean last-chance filters; install and safety.

Engine Cooling Systems

Excessive heat is always undesirable in both reciprocating and turbine aircraft engines. If means were not available for its control or elimination, major damage or complete engine failure would occur. Although the vast majority of reciprocating engines are air cooled, some diesel liquid-cooled engines are being made available for light aircraft. *[Figure 6-49]* In a liquid-cooled engine, around the cylinder are water jackets, in which liquid coolant is circulated and the coolant takes away the excess heat. The excess heat is then dissipated by a heat exchanger or radiator using air flow. Turbine engines use secondary airflow to cool the inside components and many of the exterior components.

Figure 6-49. *Diesel liquid-cooled aircraft engine.*

Reciprocating Engine Cooling Systems

An internal-combustion engine is a heat machine that converts chemical energy in the fuel into mechanical energy at the crankshaft. It does not do this without some loss of energy, however, and even the most efficient aircraft engines may waste 60 to 70 percent of the original energy in the fuel. Unless most of this waste heat is rapidly removed, the cylinders may become hot enough to cause complete engine failure. Excessive heat is undesirable in any internal-combustion engine for three principal reasons:

1. It affects the behavior of the combustion of the fuel/air charge.
2. It weakens and shortens the life of engine parts.
3. It impairs lubrication.

If the temperature inside the engine cylinder is too great, the fuel-air mixture is preheated, and combustion occurs before the desired time. Since premature combustion causes detonation, knocking, and other undesirable conditions, there must be a way to eliminate heat before it causes damage.

One gallon of aviation gasoline has enough heat value to boil 75 gallons of water; thus, it is easy to see that an engine that burns 4 gallons of fuel per minute releases a tremendous amount of heat. About one-fourth of the heat released is changed into useful power. The remainder of the heat must be dissipated so that it is not destructive to the engine. In a typical aircraft powerplant, half of the heat goes out with the exhaust and the other is absorbed by the engine. Circulating oil picks up part of this soaked-in heat and transfers it to the airstream through the oil cooler. The engine cooling system takes care of the rest. Cooling is a matter of transferring the excess heat from the cylinders to the air, but there is more to such a job than just placing the cylinders in the airstream. A cylinder on a large engine is roughly the size of a gallon jug. Its outer surface, however, is increased by the use of cooling fins so that it presents a barrel-sized exterior to the cooling air. Such an arrangement increases the heat transfer by radiation. If too much of the cooling fin area is broken off, the cylinder cannot cool properly, and a hotspot develops. Therefore, cylinders are normally replaced if a specified number of square inches of fins are missing.

Cowling and baffles are designed to force air over the cylinder cooling fins. *[Figure 6-50]* The baffles direct the air close around the cylinders and prevent it from forming hot pools of stagnant air while the main streams rush by unused. Blast tubes are built into the baffles to direct jets of cooling air onto the rear spark plug elbows of each cylinder to prevent overheating of ignition leads.

An engine can have an operating temperature that is too low. For the same reasons that an engine is warmed up before takeoff, it is kept warm during flight. Fuel evaporation and distribution and oil circulation depend on an engine being kept at its optimum operating temperature. The aircraft engine

Figure 6-50. *Cylinder baffle and deflector system.*

Figure 6-51. *Regulating the cooling airflow.*

has temperature controls that regulate air circulation over the engine. Unless some controls are provided, the engine could overheat on takeoff and get too cold in high altitude, high-speed and low-power letdowns.

The most common means of controlling cooling is the use of cowl flaps. *[Figure 6-51]* These flaps are opened and closed by electric motor-driven jackscrews, by hydraulic actuators, or manually in some light aircraft. When extended for increased cooling, the cowl flaps produce drag and sacrifice streamlining for the added cooling. On takeoff, the cowl flaps are opened only enough to keep the engine below the red-line temperature. Heating above the normal range is allowed so that drag is as low as possible. During ground operations, the cowl flaps should be opened wide since drag does not matter and cooling needs to be set at maximum. Cowl flaps are used mostly with older aircraft and radial engine installations.

Some aircraft use augmentors to provide additional cooling airflow. *[Figure 6-52]* Each nacelle has two pairs of tubes running from the engine compartment to the rear of the nacelle. The exhaust collectors feed exhaust gas into the inner augmentor tubes. The exhaust gas mixes with air that has passed over the engine and heats it to form a high-temperature, low-pressure, jet-like exhaust. This low-pressure area in the augmentors draws additional cooling air over the engine. Air entering the outer shells of the augmentors is heated through contact with the augmentor tubes but is not contaminated with exhaust gases. The heated air from the shell goes to the cabin heating, defrosting, and anti-icing system.

Augmentors use exhaust gas velocity to cause airflow over the engine so that cooling is not entirely dependent on the prop wash. Vanes installed in the augmentors control the volume of air. These vanes are usually left in the trail position to permit maximum flow. They can be closed to increase the heat for cabin or anti-icing use or to prevent the engine from cooling too much during descent from altitude. In addition to augmentors, some aircraft have residual heat doors or nacelle flaps that are used mainly to let the retained heat escape after engine shutdown. The nacelle flaps can be opened for more

Figure 6-52. *Augmentor.*

6-34

cooling than that provided by the augmentors. A modified form of the previously described augmentor cooling system is used on some light aircraft. *[Figure 6-53]* Augmentor systems are not used much on modern aircraft.

As shown in *Figure 6-53*, the engine is pressure cooled by air taken in through two openings in the nose cowling, one on each side of the propeller spinner. A pressure chamber is sealed off on the top side of the engine with baffles properly directing the flow of cooling air to all parts of the engine compartment. Warm air is drawn from the lower part of the engine compartment by the pumping action of the exhaust gases through the exhaust ejectors. This type of cooling system eliminates the use of controllable cowl flaps and assures adequate engine cooling at all operating speeds.

Reciprocating Engine Cooling System Maintenance

The engine cooling system of most reciprocating engines usually consists of the engine cowling, cylinder baffles, cylinder fins, and some use a type of cowl flaps. In addition to these major units, there are also some temperature-indicating systems, such as cylinder head temperature, oil temperature, and exhaust gas temperature.

The cowling performs two functions:

1. It streamlines the bulky engine to reduce drag.
2. It forms an envelope around the engine that forces air to pass around and between the cylinders, absorbing the heat dissipated by the cylinder fins.

The cylinder bases are metal shields, designed and arranged to direct the flow of air evenly around all cylinders. This even distribution of air aids in preventing one or more cylinders from being excessively hotter than the others. The cylinder fins radiate heat from the cylinder walls and heads. As the air passes over the fins, it absorbs this heat, carries it away from the cylinder, and is exhausted overboard through the bottom rear of the cowl.

The controllable cowl flaps provide a means of decreasing or increasing the exit area at the rear of the engine cowling. *[Figure 6-54]* Closing the cowl flaps decreases the exit area, which effectively decreases the amount of air that can circulate over the cylinder fins. The decreased airflow cannot carry away as much heat; therefore, there is a tendency engine temperature tends to increase. Opening the cowl flaps makes the exit area larger. The flow of cooling air over the cylinders

Figure 6-53. *Engine cooling and exhaust system.*

Figure 6-54. *Small aircraft cowl flaps.*

increases, absorbing more heat and the engine temperature tends to decrease. Good inspection and maintenance in the care of the engine cooling system aids in overall efficient and economical engine operation.

Maintenance of Engine Cowling

Of the total ram airflow approaching the airborne engine nacelle, only about 15 to 30 percent enters the cowling to provide engine cooling. The remaining air flows over the outside of the cowling. Therefore, the external shape of the cowl must be faired in a manner that permits the air to flow smoothly over the cowl with a minimum loss of energy.

The engine cowling discussed in this section is typical of that used on many radial or horizontally opposed engines. All cooling systems function in the same manner, with minor engineering changes designed for specific installations.

The cowl is manufactured in removable sections, the number varies with the aircraft make and model. The installation shown in *Figure 6-55* contains two sections that are locked together when installed.

The cowl panels, made from sheet aluminum or composite material, have a smooth external surface to permit undisturbed airflow over the cowl. The internal construction is designed to give strength to the panel and, in addition, to provide receptacles for the toggle latches, cowl support, and engine air seal.

An air seal is constructed of rubber material, bolted to a metal rib riveted to the cowl panel. *[Figure 6-55]* This seal, as the name implies, seals the air in the engine section, preventing the air from escaping along the inner surface of the panel without circulating around the cylinders. The engine air seal must be used on engines that have a complete cylinder baffling system that covers the cylinder heads. Its purpose is to force the air to circulate around and through the baffle system. Inspect the cowl panels during each regular engine and aircraft inspection. Removing the cowling for maintenance provides an opportunity for more frequent inspection of the cowling.

Inspect the cowling panels for scratches, dents, and tears in the panels. This type of damage causes weakness of the panel structure, increases drag by disrupting airflow, and contributes to the starting of corrosion. The cowling panel latches should be inspected for pulled rivets and loose or damaged handles. The internal construction of the panel should be examined to see that the reinforcing ribs are not cracked and that the air seal is not damaged. The cowl flap hinges, if equipped, and cowl flap hinge bondings should be checked for security of mounting and for breaks or cracks. These inspections are visual checks and should be performed frequently to ensure that the cowling is serviceable and is contributing to efficient engine cooling.

Figure 6-55. *Differential air cooling.*

Engine Cylinder Cooling Fin Inspection

The cooling fins are of the utmost importance to the cooling system, since they provide a means of transferring the cylinder heat to the air. Their condition can mean the difference between adequate or inadequate cylinder cooling. The fins are inspected at each regular inspection. Fin area is the total area (both sides of the fin) exposed to the air. During the inspection, the fins should be examined for cracks and breaks. *[Figure 6-56]* Small cracks are not a reason for cylinder removal. These cracks can be filled or even sometimes stop-drilled to prevent any further cracking. Rough or sharp corners on fins can be smoothed out by filing, and this action eliminates a possible source of new cracks. However, before reprofiling cylinder cooling fins, consult the manufacturer's service or overhaul manual for the allowable limits.

The definition of fin area becomes important in the examination of fins for broken areas. It is a determining factor for cylinder acceptance or removal. For example, on

Figure 6-56. *Regulating the cooling airflow.*

6-37

a certain engine, if more than 12 inches in length of any one fin, as measured at its base, is completely broken off, or if the total fins broken on any one cylinder head exceed 83 square inches of area, the cylinder is removed and replaced. The reason for removal in this case is that an area of that size would cause a hot spot on the cylinder; since very little heat transfer could occur.

Where adjacent fins are broken in the same area, the total length of breakage permissible is six inches on any two adjacent fins, four inches on any three adjacent fins, two inches on any four adjacent fins, and one inch on any five adjacent fins. If the breakage length in adjacent fins exceeds this prescribed amount, the cylinder should be removed and replaced. These breakage specifications are applicable only to the engine used in this discussion as a typical example. In each specific case, applicable manufacturer's instructions should be consulted.

Cylinder Baffle and Deflector System Inspection
Reciprocating engines use some type of intercylinder and cylinder head baffles to force the cooling air into close contact with all parts of the cylinders. *Figure 6-50* shows a baffle and deflector system around a cylinder. The air baffle blocks the flow of air and forces it to circulate between the cylinder and the deflectors. *Figure 6-57* illustrates a baffle and deflector arrangement designed to cool the cylinder head. The air baffle prevents the air from passing away from the cylinder head and forces it to go between the head and deflector. Although the resistance offered by baffles to the passage of the cooling air demands that an appreciable pressure differential be maintained across the engine to obtain the necessary airflow, the volume of cooling air required is greatly reduced by employing properly designed and located cylinder deflectors.

Figure 6-57. *Cylinder head baffle and deflector system.*

As shown in *Figure 6-55*, the airflow approaches the nacelle and piles up at the top of the engine, creating a high pressure in the top of the cylinders. This piling up of the air reduces the air velocity. The outlet at the bottom rear of the cowling produces a low-pressure area. As the air nears the cowl exit, it is speeded up again and merges smoothly with the airstream. The pressure differential between the top and the bottom of the engine forces the air past the cylinders through the passages formed by the deflectors. The baffles and deflectors normally are inspected during the regular engine inspection, but they should be checked whenever the cowling is removed for any purpose. Checks should be made for cracks, dents, or loose hold down studs. Cracks or dents, if severe enough, would necessitate repair or removal and replacement of these units. However, a crack that has just started can be stop-drilled, and dents can be straightened, permitting further service from these baffles and deflectors.

Cylinder Temperature Indicating Systems
This system usually consists of an indicator, electrical wiring, and a thermocouple. The wiring is between the instrument and the nacelle firewall. At the firewall, one end of the thermocouple leads connects to the electrical wiring, and the other end of the thermocouple leads connects to the cylinder. The thermocouple consists of two dissimilar metals, generally constantan and iron, connected by wiring to an indicating system. If the temperature of the junction is different from the temperature where the dissimilar metals are connected to wires, a voltage is produced. This voltage sends a current through wires to the indicator, a current-measuring instrument graduated in degrees.

The thermocouple end that connects to the cylinder is either the bayonet or gasket type. To install the bayonet type, the knurled nut is pushed down and turned clockwise until it is snug. *[Figure 6-58]* In removing this type, the nut is pushed down and turned counterclockwise until released. The gasket type fits under the spark plug and replaces the normal spark plug gasket. *[Figure 6-59]* When installing a thermocouple lead, remember not to cut off the lead because it is too long, but coil and tie up the excess length. The thermocouple is designed to produce a given amount of resistance. If

Figure 6-58. *Bayonet type CHT probe.*

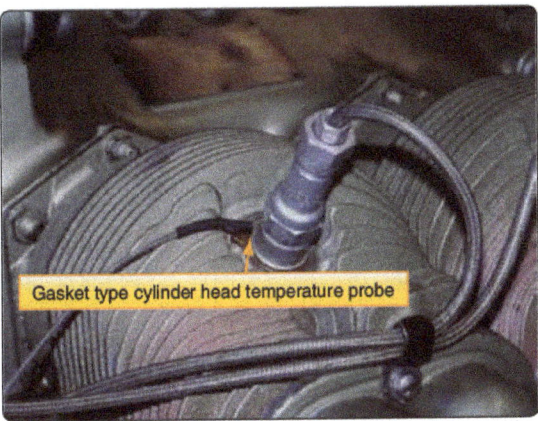

Figure 6-59. *Gasket type CHT probe.*

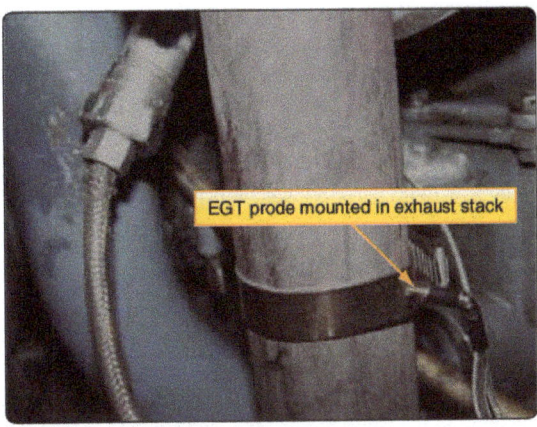

Figure 6-60. *EGT probe in exhaust stack.*

the length of the lead is reduced, an incorrect temperature reading results. The bayonet or gasket of the thermocouple is inserted or installed on the hottest cylinder of the engine, as determined in the block test. When the thermocouple is installed and the wiring connected to the instrument, the indicated reading is the cylinder temperature. Prior to operating the engine, provided it is at ambient temperature, the cylinder head temperature indicator indicates the free outside air temperature; that is one test for determining that the instrument is working correctly. The cover glass of the cylinder head temperature indicator should be checked regularly to see that it has not slipped or cracked. The cover glass should be checked for indications of missing or damaged decals that indicate temperature limitations. If the thermocouple leads were excessive in length and had to be coiled and tied down, the tie should be inspected for security or chafing of the wire. The bayonet or gasket should be inspected for cleanness and security of mounting. When operating the engine, all of the electrical connections should be checked if the cylinder head temperature pointer fluctuates.

Exhaust Gas Temperature Indicating Systems

The exhaust gas temperature indicator consists of a thermocouple placed in the exhaust stream just after the cylinder port. *[Figure 6-60]* It is then connected to the instrument in the instrument panel. This allows for the adjustment of the mixture, which has a large effect on engine temperature. By using this instrument to set the mixture, the engine temperature can be controlled and monitored.

Turbine Engine Cooling

The intense heat generated when fuel and air are burned necessitates that some means of cooling be provided for all internal combustion engines. Reciprocating engines are cooled either by passing air over fins attached to the cylinders or by passing a liquid coolant through jackets that surround the cylinders. The cooling problem is made easier because combustion occurs only during every fourth stroke of a four-stroke-cycle engine.

The burning process in a gas turbine engine is continuous, and nearly all of the cooling air must be passed through the inside of the engine. If only enough air were admitted to the engine to provide an ideal air/fuel ratio of 15:1, internal temperatures would increase to more than 4,000 °F. In practice, a large amount of air in excess of the ideal ratio is admitted to the engine. The large surplus of air cools the hot sections of the engine to acceptable temperatures ranging from 1,500° to 2,100 °F. Because of the effect of cooling, the temperatures of the outside of the case are considerably less than those encountered within the engine. The hottest area occurs in and around the turbines. Although the gases have begun to cool a little at this point, the conductivity of the metal in the case carries the heat directly to the outside skin.

The secondary air passing through the engine cools the combustion-chamber liners. The liners are constructed to induce a thin, fast-moving film of air over both the inner and outer surfaces of the liner. Can-annular-type burners frequently are provided with a center tube to lead cooling air into the center of the burner to promote high combustion-efficiency and rapid dilution of the hot combustion gases while minimizing pressure losses. In all types of gas turbines, large amounts of relatively cool air join and mix with the burned gases aft of the burners to cool the hot gases just before they enter the turbines.

Cooling-air inlets are frequently provided around the exterior of the engine to permit the entrance of air to cool the turbine case, the bearings, and the turbine nozzle. Internal air is bled from the engine compressor section and is vented to the bearings and other parts of the engine. Air vented into or from the engine is ejected into the exhaust stream. When located on the side of the engine, the case is cooled by outside air flowing around it. The engine exterior and the engine nacelle are cooled by passing fan air around the engine and the nacelle. The engine compartment frequently is divided into two sections. The forward section is referred to as the cold section and the aft section (turbine) is referred to as the hot section. Case drains drain almost potential leaks overboard to prevent fluids from building up in the nacelle.

Accessory Zone Cooling

Turbine powerplants can be divided into primary zones that are isolated from each other by fireproof bulkheads and seals. The zones are the fan case compartment, intermediate compressor case compartment, and the core engine compartment. *[Figure 6-61]* Calibrated airflows are supplied to the zones to keep the temperatures around the engine at levels that are acceptable. The airflow provides for proper ventilation to prevent a buildup of any harmful vapors. Zone 1, for example, is around the fan case that contains the accessory case and the electronic engine control (EEC). This area is vented by using ram air through an inlet in the nose cowl and is exhausted through a louvered vent in the right fan cowling.

If the pressure exceeds a certain limit, a pressure relief door opens and relieves the pressure. Zone 2 is cooled by fan air from the upper part of the fan duct and is exhausted at the lower end back into the fan air stream. This area has both fuel and oil lines, so removing any unwanted vapors would be important.

Zone 3 is the area around the high-pressure compressor to the turbine cases. This zone also contains fuel and oil lines and other accessories. Air enters from the exhaust of the precooler and other areas and is exhausted from the zone through the aft edge of the thrust reverser inner wall and the turbine exhaust sleeve.

Turbine Engine Insulation Blankets

To reduce the temperature of the structure in the vicinity of the exhaust duct or thrust augmentor (afterburner) and to eliminate the possibility of fuel or oil coming in contact with the hot parts of the engine, it is sometimes necessary to provide insulation on the exhaust duct of gas turbine engines. The exhaust duct surface temperature runs quite high. A typical insulation blanket and the temperatures

Figure 6-61. *Accessory zone cooling.*

obtained at various locations are shown in *Figure 6-62*. This blanket contains fiberglass as the low conductance material and aluminum foil as the radiation shield. The blanket is suitably covered so that it does not become oil soaked. Insulation blankets have been used rather extensively on many installations in which long exhaust is needed. Some auxiliary power units (APU) mounted in the tail cone of transport aircraft have air that surrounds the exhaust tail pipe that provides cooling and protects the surrounding structure.

Figure 6-62. *Typical engine insulation blanket.*

Chapter 7
Propellers

General

The propeller, the unit that must absorb the power output of the engine, has passed through many stages of development. Although most propellers are two-bladed, great increases in power output have resulted in the development of four- and six-bladed propellers of large diameters. However, all propeller-driven aircraft are limited by the revolutions per minute (rpm) at which propellers can be turned.

There are several forces acting on the propeller as it turns; a major one is centrifugal force. This force at high rpm tends to pull the blades out of the hub, so blade weight is very important to the design of a propeller. Excessive blade tip speed (rotating the propeller too fast) may result not only in poor blade efficiency, but also in fluttering and vibration. Since the propeller speed is limited, the aircraft speed of a propeller driven aircraft is also limited—to approximately 400 miles per hour (mph). As aircraft speeds increased, turbofan engines were used for higher speed aircraft. Propeller-driven aircraft have several advantages and are widely used for applications in turboprops and reciprocating engine installations. Takeoff and landing can be shorter and less expensive. New blade materials and manufacturing techniques have increased the efficiency of propellers. Many smaller aircraft will continue to use propellers well into the future.

Speeder spring
Flyweight
Toe
Flyweight head
By-pass plug "B"
Passage "C"
Propeller control line

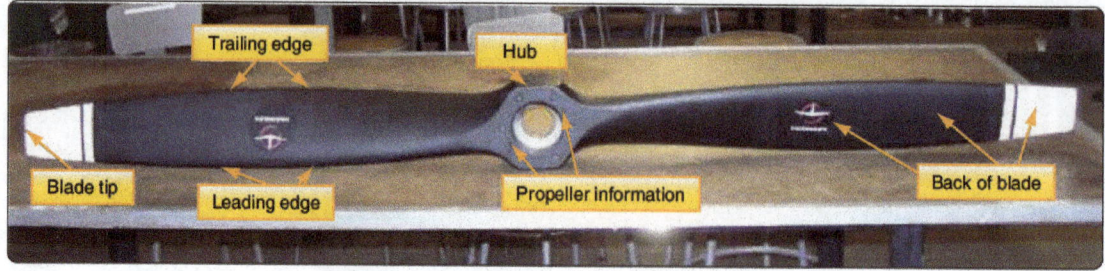

Figure 7-1. *Basic nomenclature of propellers.*

The basic nomenclature of the parts of a propeller is shown in *Figure 7-1* for a simple fixed-pitch, two-bladed wood propeller. The aerodynamic cross-section of a blade in *Figure 7-2* includes terminology to describe certain areas shown.

Figure 7-2. *Cross-sectional area of a propeller blade airfoil.*

The many different types of propeller systems have been developed for specific aircraft installation, speed, and mission. Propeller development has encouraged many changes as propulsion systems have evolved. The first propellers were fabric-covered sticks made to force air in a rearward direction. Propellers started as simple two-bladed wood propellers and have advanced to the complex propulsion systems of turboprop aircraft that involve more than just the propeller. As an outgrowth of operating large, more complex propellers, a variable-pitch, constant-speed feathering and reversing propeller system was developed. This system allows the engine rpm to be varied only slightly during different flight conditions and, therefore, increases flying efficiency. A basic constant-speed system consists of a flyweight-equipped governor unit that controls the pitch angle of the blades so that the engine speed remains constant. The governor can be regulated by controls in the cockpit so that any desired blade angle setting and engine operating speed can be obtained. A low-pitch, high-rpm setting, for example, can be utilized for takeoff. Then, after the aircraft is airborne, a higher pitch and lower rpm setting can be used. *Figure 7-3* shows normal propeller movement with the positions of low pitch, high pitch, feather (used if the engine quits to reduce drag), and zero pitch into negative pitch, or reverse pitch.

Basic Propeller Principles

The aircraft propeller consists of two or more blades and a central hub to which the blades are attached. Each blade of an aircraft propeller is essentially a rotating wing. As a result of their construction, the propeller blades produce forces that create thrust to pull or push the airplane through the air. The power needed to rotate the propeller blades is furnished by the engine. The propeller is mounted on a shaft, which may be an extension of the crankshaft on low-horsepower engines; on high-horsepower engines, it is mounted on a propeller

Figure 7-3. *Propeller range positions.*

shaft that is geared to the engine crankshaft. In either case, the engine rotates the airfoils of the blades through the air at high speeds, and the propeller transforms the rotary power of the engine into thrust.

Propeller Aerodynamic Process

An airplane moving through the air creates a drag force opposing its forward motion. If an airplane is to fly on a level path, there must be a force applied to it that is equal to the drag but acting forward. This force is called thrust. The work done by thrust is equal to the thrust times the distance it moves the airplane.

$$\text{Work} = \text{Thrust} \times \text{Distance}$$

The power expended by thrust is equal to the thrust times the velocity at which it moves the airplane.

$$\text{Power} = \text{Thrust} \times \text{Velocity}$$

If the power is measured in horsepower units, the power expended by the thrust is termed thrust horsepower.

The engine supplies brake horsepower through a rotating shaft, and the propeller converts it into thrust horsepower. In this conversion, some power is wasted. For maximum efficiency, the propeller must be designed to keep this waste as small as possible. Since the efficiency of any machine is the ratio of the useful power output to the power input, propeller efficiency is the ratio of thrust horsepower to brake horsepower. The usual symbol for propeller efficiency is the Greek letter η (eta). Propeller efficiency varies from 50 percent to 87 percent, depending on how much the propeller slips.

Pitch is not the same as blade angle, but because pitch is largely determined by blade angle, the two terms are often used interchangeably. An increase or decrease in one is usually associated with an increase or decrease in the other. Propeller slip is the difference between the geometric pitch of the propeller and its effective pitch. *[Figure 7-4]* Geometric pitch is the distance a propeller should advance in one revolution with no slippage; effective pitch is the distance it actually advances. Thus, geometric or theoretical pitch is based on no slippage. Actual, or effective, pitch recognizes propeller slippage in the air. The relationship can be shown as:

$$\text{Geometric pitch} - \text{Effective pitch} = \text{slip}$$

Geometric pitch is usually expressed in pitch inches and calculated by using the following formula:

$$GP = 2 \times \pi \text{ R} \times \text{tangent of blade angle at 75 percent station}$$

R = Radius at the 75 percent blade station

$$\pi = 3.14$$

Although blade angle and propeller pitch are closely related, blade angle is the angle between the face or chord of a blade section and the plane in which the propeller rotates. *[Figure 7-5]* Blade angle, usually measured in degrees, is the angle between the chordline of the blade and the plane of rotation. The chordline of the propeller blade is determined in about the same manner as the chordline of an airfoil. In fact, a propeller blade can be considered as being composed of an infinite number of thin blade elements, each of which is a miniature airfoil section whose chord is the width of the propeller blade at that section. Because most propellers have a flat blade face, the chord line is often drawn along the face of the propeller blade.

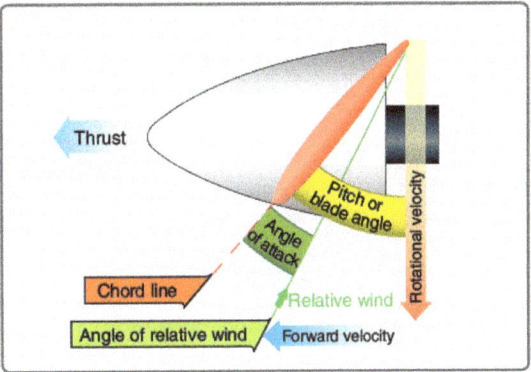

Figure 7-5. *Propeller aerodynamic factors.*

The typical propeller blade can be described as a twisted airfoil of irregular planform. Two views of a propeller blade are shown in *Figure 7-6*. For purposes of analysis, a blade can be divided into segments that are located by station numbers in inches from the center of the blade hub. The cross-sections of each 6-inch blade segment are shown as airfoils in the right side of *Figure 7-6*. Also identified in *Figure 7-6* are the blade shank and the blade butt. The blade shank is the thick, rounded portion of the propeller blade near the hub and is designed to give strength to the blade. The blade butt, also called the blade base or root, is the end of the blade that fits

Figure 7-4. *Effective pitch and geometric pitch.*

7-3

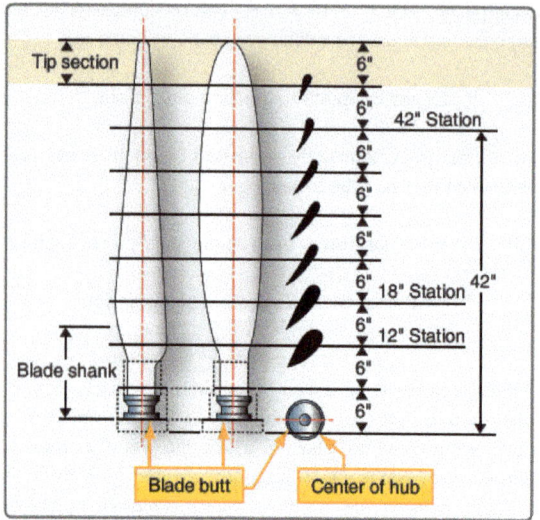

Figure 7-6. *Typical propeller blade elements.*

in the propeller hub. The blade tip is that part of the propeller blade farthest from the hub, generally defined as the last 6 inches of the blade.

A cross-section of a typical propeller blade is shown in *Figure 7-7*. This section or blade element is an airfoil comparable to a cross-section of an aircraft wing. The blade back is the cambered or curved side of the blade, similar to the upper surface of an aircraft wing. The blade face is the flat side of the propeller blade. The chord line is an imaginary line drawn through the blade from the leading edge to the trailing edge. The leading edge is the thick edge of the blade that meets the air as the propeller rotates.

A rotating propeller is acted upon by centrifugal twisting, aerodynamic twisting, torque bending, and thrust bending forces. The principal forces acting on a rotating propeller are illustrated in *Figure 7-8*.

Centrifugal force is a physical force that tends to throw the rotating propeller blades away from the hub. *[Figure 7-8A]* This is the most dominant force on the propeller. Torque bending force, in the form of air resistance, tends to bend the propeller blades in the direction opposite that of rotation. *[Figure 7-8B]* Thrust bending force is the thrust load that tends to bend propeller blades forward as the aircraft is pulled through the air. *[Figure 7-8C]* Aerodynamic twisting force tends to turn the blades to a high blade angle. *[Figure 7-8D]* Centrifugal twisting force, being greater than the aerodynamic twisting force, tends to force the blades toward a low blade angle.

At least two of these forces acting on the propellers blades are used to move the blades on a controllable pitch propeller. Centrifugal twisting force is sometimes used to move the blades to the low pitch position, while aerodynamic twisting force is used to move the blades into high pitch. These forces can be the primary or secondary forces that move the blades to the new pitch position.

A propeller must be capable of withstanding severe stresses, which are greater near the hub, caused by centrifugal force and thrust. The stresses increase in proportion to the rpm. The blade face is also subjected to tension from the centrifugal force and additional tension from the bending. For these reasons, nicks or scratches on the blade may cause very serious consequences. These could lead to cracks and failure of the blade and are addressed in the repair section later in this chapter.

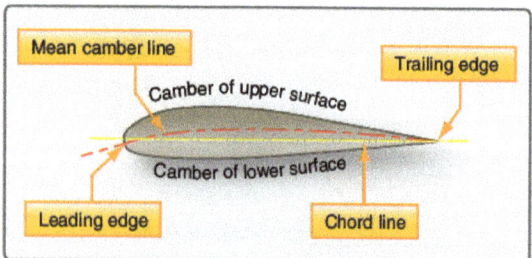

Figure 7-7. *Cross-section of a propeller blade.*

Figure 7-8. *Forces acting on a rotating propeller.*

A propeller must also be rigid enough to prevent fluttering, a type of vibration in which the ends of the blade twist back and forth at high frequency around an axis perpendicular to the engine crankshaft. Fluttering is accompanied by a distinctive noise, often mistaken for exhaust noise. The constant vibration tends to weaken the blade and eventually causes failure.

Aerodynamic Factors

To understand the action of a propeller, consider first its motion, which is both rotational and forward. Thus, as shown by the vectors of propeller forces in *Figure 7-9*, a section of a propeller blade moves downward and forward. As far as the forces are concerned, the result is the same as if the blade were stationary and the air coming at it from a direction opposite its path. The angle at which this air (relative wind) strikes the propeller blade is called angle of attack (AOA). The air deflection produced by this angle causes the dynamic pressure at the engine side of the propeller blade to be greater than atmospheric pressure, creating thrust.

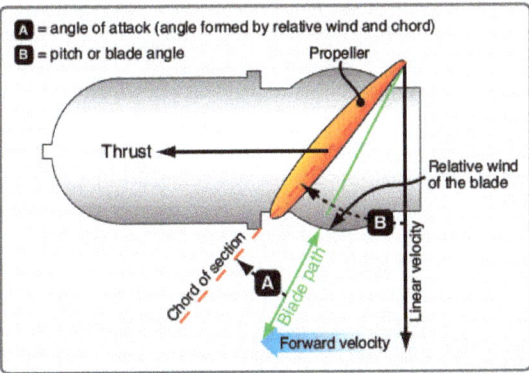

Figure 7-9. *Propeller forces.*

The shape of the blade also creates thrust because it is shaped like a wing. As the air flows past the propeller, the pressure on one side is less than that on the other. As in a wing, this difference in pressure produces a reaction force in the direction of the lesser pressure. The area above a wing has less pressure, and the force (lift) is upward. The area of decreased pressure is in front of a propeller which is mounted in a vertical instead of a horizontal position, and the force (thrust) is in a forward direction. Aerodynamically, thrust is the result of the propeller shape and the AOA of the blade.

Another way to consider thrust is in terms of the mass of air handled. In these terms, thrust is equal to the mass of air handled multiplied by the slipstream velocity minus the velocity of the airplane. Thus, the power expended in producing thrust depends on the mass of air moved per second. On the average, thrust constitutes approximately 80 percent of the torque (total horsepower absorbed by the propeller). The other 20 percent is lost in friction and slippage. For any speed of rotation, the horsepower absorbed by the propeller balances the horsepower delivered by the engine. For any single revolution of the propeller, the amount of air displaced (moved) depends on the blade angle, which determines the quantity or amount of mass of air the propeller moves. Thus, the blade angle is an excellent means of adjusting the load on the propeller to control the engine rpm. If the blade angle is increased, more load is placed on the engine, tending to slow it down unless more power is applied. As an airfoil is moved through the air, it produces two forces: lift and drag. Increasing propeller blade angle increases the AOA and produces more lift and drag; this action increases the horsepower required to turn the propeller at a given rpm. Since the engine is still producing the same horsepower, the propeller slows down. If the blade angle is decreased, the propeller speeds up. Thus, the engine rpm can be controlled by increasing or decreasing the blade angle.

The blade angle is also an excellent method of adjusting the AOA of the propeller. On constant-speed propellers, the blade angle must be adjusted to provide the most efficient AOA at all engine and airplane speeds. Lift versus drag curves, which are drawn for propellers as well as wings, indicate that the most efficient AOA is a small one varying from 2° to 4° positive. The actual blade angle necessary to maintain this small AOA varies with the forward speed of the airplane. This is due to a change in the relative wind direction, which varies with aircraft speed.

Fixed-pitch and ground-adjustable propellers are designed for best efficiency at one rotation and forward speed. In other words, they are designed to fit a given airplane and engine combination. A propeller may be used that provides the maximum propeller efficiency for takeoff, climb, cruising, or high speeds. Any change in these conditions results in lowering the efficiency of both the propeller and the engine. A constant-speed propeller, however, keeps the blade angle adjusted for maximum efficiency for most conditions encountered in flight. During takeoff, when maximum power and thrust are required, the constant-speed propeller is at a low propeller blade angle or pitch. The low blade angle keeps the AOA small and efficient with respect to the relative wind. At the same time, it allows the propeller to handle a smaller mass of air per revolution. This light load allows the engine to turn at high rpm and to convert the maximum amount of fuel into heat energy in a given time. The high rpm also creates maximum thrust. Although the mass of air handled per revolution is small, the engine rpm is high, the slipstream velocity (air coming off the propeller) is high, and, with the low airplane speed, the thrust is maximum.

After liftoff, as the speed of the airplane increases, the constant-speed propeller changes to a higher angle (or pitch). Again, the higher blade angle keeps the AOA small and efficient with respect to the relative wind. The higher blade angle increases the mass of air handled per revolution. This decreases the engine rpm, reducing fuel consumption and engine wear, and keeps thrust at a maximum.

For climb after takeoff, the power output of the engine is reduced to climb power by decreasing the manifold pressure and increasing the blade angle to lower the rpm. Thus, the torque (horsepower absorbed by the propeller) is reduced to match the reduced power of the engine. The AOA is again kept small by the increase in blade angle. The greater mass of air handled per second, in this case, is more than offset by the lower slipstream velocity and the increase in airspeed.

At cruising altitude, when the airplane is in level flight and less power is required than is used in takeoff or climb, engine power is again reduced by lowering the manifold pressure and increasing the blade angle to decrease the rpm. Again, this reduces torque to match the reduced engine power; for, although the mass of air handled per revolution is greater, it is more than offset by a decrease in slipstream velocity and an increase in airspeed. The AOA is still small because the blade angle has been increased with an increase in airspeed. Pitch distribution is the twist in the blade from the shank to the blade tip, due to the variation in speeds that each section of the blade is traveling. The tip of the blade is traveling much faster than the inner portion of the blade.

Propeller Controls and Instruments

Fixed pitch propellers have no controls and require no adjustments in flight. The constant-speed propeller has a propeller control in the center pedestal between the throttle and the mixture control. *[Figure 7-10]* The two positions for the control are increase rpm (full forward) and decrease rpm (pulled aft). This control is directly connected to the propeller governor and, by moving the control, adjusts the tension on the governor speeder spring. This control can also be used to feather the propeller in some aircraft by moving the control to the full decrease rpm position. The two main instruments used with the constant-speed propeller are the engine tachometer and the manifold pressure gauge. Rotations per minute (rpm) is controlled by the propeller control and the manifold pressure is adjusted by the throttle.

Propeller Location
Tractor Propeller

Tractor propellers are those mounted on the upstream end of a drive shaft in front of the supporting structure. Most aircraft are equipped with this type of propeller. The tractor type of propeller comes in all types of propellers. A major advantage of the tractor propeller is that lower stresses are induced in the propeller as it rotates in relatively undisturbed air.

Pusher Propellers

Pusher propellers are those mounted on the downstream end of a drive shaft behind the supporting structure. Pusher propellers are constructed as fixed- or variable-pitch propellers. Seaplanes and amphibious aircraft have used a greater percentage of pusher propellers than other kinds of aircraft. On land planes, where propeller-to-ground clearance usually is less than propeller-to-water clearance of watercraft, pusher propellers are subject to more damage than tractor propellers. Rocks, gravel, and small objects dislodged by the wheels are quite often thrown or drawn into a pusher propeller. Similarly, planes with pusher propellers are apt to encounter propeller damage from water spray thrown up by the hull during landing or takeoff airspeed. Consequently, the pusher propeller is mounted above and behind the wings to prevent such damage.

Types of Propellers

There are various types or classes of propellers, the simplest of which are the fixed-pitch and ground-adjustable propellers. The complexity of propeller systems increases from these simpler forms to controllable-pitch and complex constant-speed systems (automatic systems). Various characteristics of several propeller types are discussed in the following paragraphs, but no attempt is made to cover all types of propellers.

Fixed-Pitch Propeller

As the name implies, a fixed-pitch propeller has the blade pitch, or blade angle, built into the propeller. *[Figure 7-11]* The blade angle cannot be changed after the propeller is built. Generally, this type of propeller is one piece and is constructed of wood or aluminum alloy.

Figure 7-10. *Turboprop propeller controls.*

Test Club Propeller

A test club is used to test and break in reciprocating engines. *[Figure 7-12]* They are made to provide the correct amount of load on the engine during the test break-in period. The multi-blade design also provides extra cooling air flow during testing.

Figure 7-12. *Test club.*

Ground-Adjustable Propeller

The ground-adjustable propeller operates as a fixed-pitch propeller. The pitch, or blade angle, can be changed only when the propeller is not turning. This is done by loosening the clamping mechanism that holds the blades in place. After the clamping mechanism has been tightened, the pitch of the blades cannot be changed in flight to meet variable flight requirements. The ground-adjustable propeller is not often used on present-day airplanes.

Controllable-Pitch Propeller

The controllable-pitch propeller permits a change of blade pitch, or angle, while the propeller is rotating. This allows the propeller to assume a blade angle that gives the best performance for particular flight conditions. The number of pitch positions may be limited, as with a two-position controllable propeller, or the pitch may be adjusted to any angle between the minimum and maximum pitch settings of a given propeller. The use of controllable-pitch propellers also makes it possible to attain the desired engine rpm for a particular flight condition.

This type of propeller is not to be confused with a constant-speed propeller. With the controllable-pitch type, the blade angle can be changed in flight, but the pilot must change the propeller blade angle directly. The blade angle will not change again until the pilot changes it. The use of a governor is the next step in the evolution of propeller development, making way for constant-speed propellers with governor

Figure 7-11. *Fixed-pitch propeller.*

Fixed-pitch propellers are designed for best efficiency at one rotational and forward speed. They are designed to fit a set of conditions of both airplane and engine speeds and any change in these conditions reduces the efficiency of both the propeller and the engine. The fixed-pitch propeller is used on airplanes of low power, speed, range, or altitude. Many single-engine aircraft use fixed-pitch propellers and the advantages to these are less expense and their simple operation. This type of propeller does not require any control inputs from the pilot in flight.

systems. An example of a two-position propeller is a Hamilton Standard counterweight two-position propeller. These types of propeller are not in wide use today.

Constant-Speed Propellers

The propeller has a natural tendency to slow down as the aircraft climbs and to speed up as the aircraft dives because the load on the engine varies. To provide an efficient propeller, the speed is kept as constant as possible. By using propeller governors to increase or decrease propeller pitch, the engine speed is held constant. When the airplane goes into a climb, the blade angle of the propeller decreases just enough to prevent the engine speed from decreasing. The engine can maintain its power output if the throttle setting is not changed. When the airplane goes into a dive, the blade angle increases sufficiently to prevent overspeeding and, with the same throttle setting, the power output remains unchanged. If the throttle setting is changed instead of changing the speed of the airplane by climbing or diving, the blade angle increases or decreases as required to maintain a constant engine rpm. The power output (not the rpm) changes in accordance with changes in the throttle setting. The governor-controlled, constant-speed propeller changes the blade angle automatically, keeping engine rpm constant.

One type of pitch-changing mechanism is operated by oil pressure (hydraulically) and uses a piston-and-cylinder arrangement. The piston may move in the cylinder, or the cylinder may move over a stationary piston. The linear motion of the piston is converted by several different types of mechanical linkage into the rotary motion necessary to change the blade angle. The mechanical connection may be through gears, the pitch-changing mechanism that turns the butt of each blade. Each blade is mounted with a bearing that allows the blade to rotate to change pitch. *[Figure 7-13]*

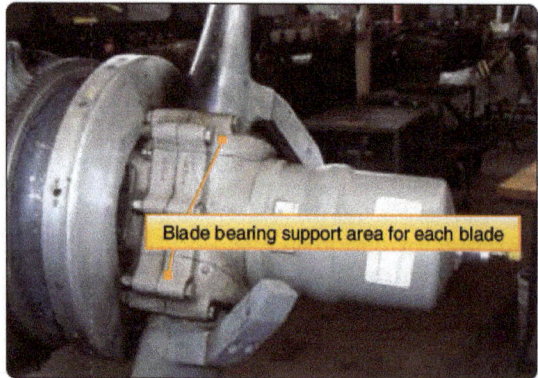

Figure 7-13. *Blade bearing areas in hub.*

In most cases, the oil pressure for operating the different types of hydraulic pitch-changing mechanisms comes directly from the engine lubricating system. When the engine lubricating system is used, the engine oil pressure is usually boosted by a pump that is integral with the governor to operate the propeller. The higher oil pressure (approximately 300 pounds per square inch (psi)) provides a quicker blade-angle change. The governors direct the pressurized oil for operation of the hydraulic pitch-changing mechanisms.

The governors used to control hydraulic pitch-changing mechanisms are geared to the engine crankshaft and are sensitive to changes in rpm. When rpm increases above the value for which a governor is set, the governor causes the propeller pitch-changing mechanism to turn the blades to a higher angle. This angle increases the load on the engine, and rpm decreases. When rpm decreases below the value for which a governor is set, the governor causes the pitch-changing mechanism to turn the blades to a lower angle; the load on the engine is decreased, and rpm increases. Thus, a propeller governor tends to keep engine rpm constant.

In constant-speed propeller systems, the control system adjusts pitch through the use of a governor, without attention by the pilot, to maintain a specific preset engine rpm within the set range of the propeller. For example, if engine speed increases, an overspeed condition occurs and the propeller needs to slow down. The controls automatically increase the blade angle until desired rpm has been reestablished. A good constant-speed control system responds to such small variations of rpm that for all practical purposes, a constant rpm is maintained.

Each constant-speed propeller has an opposing force that operates against the oil pressure from the governor. Flyweights mounted to the blades move the blades in the high pitch direction as the propeller turns. *[Figure 7-13]* Other forces used to move the blades toward the high pitch direction include air pressure (contained in the front dome), springs, and aerodynamic twisting moment.

Feathering Propellers

Feathering propellers must be used on multi-engine aircraft to reduce propeller drag to a minimum under one or more engine failure conditions. A feathering propeller is a constant-speed propeller used on multi-engine aircraft that has a mechanism to change the pitch to an angle of approximately 90°. A propeller is usually feathered when the engine fails to develop power to turn the propeller. By rotating the propeller blade angle parallel to the line of flight, the drag on the aircraft is greatly reduced. With the blades parallel to the airstream, the propeller stops turning and minimum windmilling, if any, occurs. The blades are held in feather by aerodynamic forces.

Almost all small feathering propellers use oil pressure to take the propeller to low pitch and blade flyweights, springs, and compressed air to take the blades to high pitch. Since the blades would go to the feather position during shutdown, latches lock the propeller in the low pitch position as the propeller slows down at shutdown. *[Figure 7-14]* These can be internal or external and are contained within the propeller hub. In flight, the latches are prevented from stopping the blades from feathering because they are held off their seat by centrifugal force. Latches are needed to prevent excess load on the engine at start up. If the blade were in the feathered position during engine start, the engine would be placed under an undue load during a time when the engine is already subject to wear.

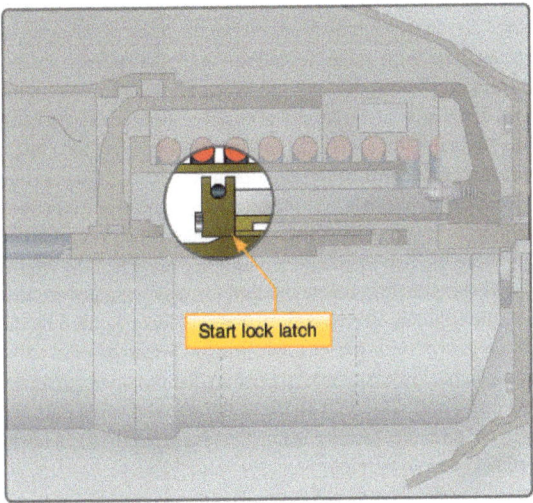

Figure 7-14. *Feathering latches.*

Reverse-Pitch Propellers

Additional refinements, such as reverse-pitch propellers (mainly used on turbo props), are included in some propellers to improve their operational characteristics. Almost all reverse-pitch propellers are of the feathering type. A reverse-pitch propeller is a controllable propeller in which the blade angles can be changed to a negative value during operation.

The purpose of the reversible pitch feature is to produce a negative blade angle that produces thrust opposite the normal forward direction. Normally, when the landing gear is in contact with the runway after landing, the propellers blades can be moved to negative pitch (reversed), which creates thrust opposite of the aircraft direction and slows the aircraft. As the propeller blades move into negative pitch, engine power is applied to increase the negative thrust. This aerodynamically brakes the aircraft and reduces ground roll after landing. Reversing the propellers also reduces aircraft speed quickly on the runway just after touchdown and minimizes aircraft brake wear.

Propeller Governor

A governor is an engine rpm-sensing device and high-pressure oil pump. In a constant-speed propeller system, the governor responds to a change in engine rpm by directing oil under pressure to the propeller hydraulic cylinder or by releasing oil from the hydraulic cylinder. The change in oil volume in the hydraulic cylinder changes the blade angle and maintains the propeller system rpm. The governor is set for a specific rpm via the cockpit propeller control, which compresses or releases the governor speeder spring.

A propeller governor is used to sense propeller and engine speed and normally provides oil to the propeller for low pitch position. *[Figure 7-15]* There are a couple of nonfeathering propellers that operate opposite to this; they are discussed later in this chapter. Fundamental forces, some already discussed, are used to control blade angle variations required for constant-speed propeller operation. These forces are:

1. Centrifugal twisting moment—a component of the centrifugal force acting on a rotating blade that tends at all times to move the blade into low pitch.

2. Propeller-governor oil on the propeller piston side—balances the propeller blade flyweights, which moves the blades toward high pitch.

3. Propeller blade flyweights—always move the blades toward high pitch.

4. Air pressure against the propeller piston—pushes toward high pitch.

5. Large springs—push in the direction of high pitch and feather.

Figure 7-15. *Parts of a governor.*

6. Centrifugal twisting force—moves the blades toward low pitch.
7. Aerodynamic twisting force—moves the blades toward high pitch.

All of the forces listed are not equal in strength. The most powerful force is the governor oil pressure acting on the propeller piston. This piston is connected mechanically to the blades; as the piston moves, the blades are rotated in proportion. By removing the oil pressure from the governor, the other forces can force the oil from the piston chamber and move the propeller blades in the other direction.

Governor Mechanism

The engine-driven single-acting propeller governor (constant-speed control) receives oil from the lubricating system and boosts its pressure to that required to operate the pitch-changing mechanism. *[Figure 7-16]* It consists of a gear pump to increase the pressure of the engine oil, a pilot valve controlled by flyweights in the governor to control the flow of oil through the governor to and away from the propeller, and a relief valve system that regulates the operating oil pressures in the governor. A spring called the speeder spring opposes the governor flyweight's ability to fly outward when turning. The tension on this spring can be adjusted by the propeller control on the control quadrant. The tension of the speeder spring sets the maximum rpm of the engine in the governor mode. As the engine and propeller rpm is increased at the maximum set point (maximum speed) of the governor, the governor flyweights overcome the tension of the speeder spring and move outward. This action moves the pilot valve in the governor to release oil from the propeller piston and allows the blade flyweights to increase blade pitch, which increases the load on the engine, slowing it down or maintaining the set speed.

In addition to boosting the engine oil pressure to produce one of the fundamental control forces, the governor maintains the required balance between control forces by metering to, or draining from, the propeller piston the exact quantity of oil necessary to maintain the proper blade angle for constant-speed operation. The position of the pilot valve, with respect to the propeller-governor metering port, regulates the quantity of oil that flows through this port to or from the propeller.

A speeder spring above the rack opposes the action of the governor flyweights, which sense propeller speed. If the flyweights turn faster than the tension on the speeder spring, they fly out; this is an overspeed condition. To slow the engine propeller combination down, the blade angle (pitch) must be increased. Oil is allowed to flow away from the propeller piston and the flyweights increase the pitch or blade angle

slowing the propeller until it reaches an on-speed condition where the force on the governor flyweights and the tension on the speeder spring are balanced. This balance of forces can be disturbed by the aircraft changing attitude (climb or dive) or the pilot changing the tension on the speeder spring with the propeller control on the instrument panel (i.e., if the pilot selects a different rpm).

Underspeed Condition

When the engine is operating below the rpm set by the pilot using the cockpit control, the governor is operating in an underspeed condition. *[Figure 7-17]* In this condition, the flyweights tilt inward because there is not enough centrifugal force on the flyweights to overcome the force of the speeder spring. The pilot valve, forced down by the speeder spring, meters oil flow to decrease propeller pitch and raise engine rpm. If the nose of the aircraft is raised or the blades are moved to a higher blade angle, this increases the load on the engine and the propeller tries to slow down. To maintain a constant speed, the governor senses the decrease in speed and increases oil flow to the propeller, moving the blades to a lower pitch and allowing them to maintain the same speed. When the engine speed starts to drop below the rpm for which the governor is set, the resulting decrease in centrifugal force exerted by the flyweights permits the speeder spring to lower the pilot valve (flyweights inward), thereby opening the propeller-governor metering port. The oil then flows through the valve port and into the propeller piston causing the blades to move to a lower pitch (a decrease in load).

Overspeed Condition

When the engine is operating above the rpm set by the pilot using the cockpit control, the governor is operating in an overspeed condition. *[Figure 7-18]* In an overspeed condition, the centrifugal force acting on the flyweights is greater than the speeder spring force. The flyweights tilt outward and raise the pilot valve. The pilot valve then meters oil flow to increase propeller pitch and lower engine rpm. When the engine speed increases above the rpm for which the governor is set, note that the flyweights move outward against the force of the speeder spring, raising the pilot valve. This opens the propeller-governor metering port, allowing governor oil flow from the propeller piston allowing counterweights on the blades to increase pitch and slow the engine.

On-Speed Condition

When the engine is operating at the rpm set by the pilot using the cockpit control, the governor is operating on speed. *[Figure 7-19]* In an on-speed condition, the centrifugal force acting on the flyweights is balanced by the speeder spring, and the pilot valve is neither directing oil to nor from the propeller hydraulic cylinder. In the on-speed condition, the forces of

Figure 7-16. *Typical governor.*

the governor flyweights and the tension on the speeder spring are equal; the propeller blades are not moving or changing pitch. If something happens to unbalance these forces, such as if the aircraft dives or climbs, or the pilot selects a new rpm range through the propeller control (changes tension on the speeder spring), then these forces are unequal and an underspeed or overspeed condition would result. A change in rpm comes about in the governing mode by pilot selection of a new position of the propeller control, which changes the tension of the governor speeder spring or by the aircraft changing attitude. The governor, as a speed-sensing device, causes the propeller to maintain a set rpm regardless of the

7-11

Figure 7-17. *Underspeed condition.*

Figure 7-18. *Overspeed condition.*

Figure 7-19. *On-speed condition.*

aircraft attitude. The speeder spring propeller governing range is limited to about 200 rpm. Beyond this rpm, the governor cannot maintain the correct rpm.

Governor System Operation

If the engine speed drops below the rpm for which the governor is set, the rotational force on the engine-driven governor flyweights becomes less. *[Figure 7-17]* This allows the speeder spring to move the pilot valve downward. With the pilot valve in the downward position, oil from the gear type pump flows through a passage to the propeller and moves the cylinder outward. This in turn decreases the blade angle and permits the engine to return to the on-speed setting. If the engine speed increases above the rpm for which the governor is set, the flyweights move against the force of the speeder spring and raise the pilot valve. This permits the oil in the propeller to drain out through the governor drive shaft. As the oil leaves the propeller, the centrifugal force acting on the counterweights turns the blades to a higher angle, which decreases the engine rpm. When the engine is exactly at the rpm set by the governor, the centrifugal reaction of the flyweights balances the force of the speeder spring, positioning the pilot valve so that oil is neither supplied to nor drained from the propeller. With this condition, propeller blade angle does not change. Note that the rpm setting is made by varying the amount of compression in the speeder spring. Positioning of the speeder rack is the only action controlled manually. All others are controlled automatically within the governor.

Propellers Used on General Aviation Aircraft

An increasing number of light aircraft are designed for operation with governor-regulated, constant-speed propellers. Significant segments of general aviation aircraft are still operated with fixed-pitch propellers. Light sport aircraft (LSA) use multiblade fixed-pitch composite propellers on up to medium size turbo prop aircraft with reversing propeller systems. Larger transport and cargo turbo prop aircraft use propeller systems with dual or double-acting governors and differential oil pressure to change pitch. Some types of propeller system are beyond the scope of this text, but several propellers and their systems are described.

Fixed-Pitch Wooden Propellers

Although many of the wood propellers were used on older airplanes, some are still in use. The construction of a fixed-pitch, wooden propeller is such that its blade pitch cannot be changed after manufacture. *[Figure 7-20]* The choice of the blade angle is decided by the normal use of the propeller on an aircraft during level flight when the engine performs at maximum efficiency. The impossibility of changing the blade pitch on the fixed-pitch propeller restricts its use to small aircraft with low horsepower engines in which maximum engine efficiency during all flight conditions is of lesser importance than in larger aircraft. The wooden, fixed-pitch propeller is well suited for such small aircraft because of its light weight, rigidity, economy of production, simplicity of construction, and ease of replacement.

Figure 7-20. *Fix-pitch wooden propeller assembly.*

A wooden propeller is not constructed from a solid block, but is built up of a number of separate layers of carefully selected and well-seasoned hardwoods. Many woods, such as mahogany, cherry, black walnut, and oak, are used to some extent, but birch is the most widely used. Five to nine separate layers are used, each about ¾ inch thick. The several layers are glued together with a waterproof, resinous glue and allowed to set. The blank is then roughed to the approximate shape and size of the finished product. The roughed-out propeller is then allowed to dry for approximately one week to permit the moisture content of the layers to become equalized. This additional period of seasoning prevents warping and cracking that might occur if the blank were immediately carved. Following this period, the propeller is carefully constructed. Templates and bench protractors are used to assure the proper contour and blade angle at all stations.

After the propeller blades are finished, a fabric covering is cemented to the outer 12 or 15 inches of each finished blade. A metal tipping is fastened to most of the leading edge and tip of each blade to protect the propeller from damage caused by flying particles in the air during landing, taxiing, or takeoff. [Figure 7-21] Metal tipping may be of terneplate, Monel metal, or brass. Stainless steel has been used to some extent. It is secured to the leading edge of the blade by countersunk wood screws and rivets. The heads of the screws are soldered to the tipping to prevent loosening, and the solder is filed to make a smooth surface. Since moisture condenses on the tipping between the metal and the wood, the tipping is provided with small holes near the blade tip to allow this moisture to drain away or be thrown out by centrifugal force. It is important that these drain holes be kept open at all times. Since wood is subject to swelling, shrinking, and warping because of changes of moisture content, a protective coating is applied to the finished propeller to prevent a rapid change of moisture content. The finish most commonly used is a number of coats of water-repellent, clear varnish. After these processes are completed, the propeller is mounted on a spindle and very carefully balanced.

Figure 7-21. *Installation of metal sheath and tipping.*

Several types of hubs are used to mount wooden propellers on the engine crankshaft. The propeller may have a forged steel hub that fits a splined crankshaft; it may be connected to a tapered crankshaft by a tapered, forged steel hub; or it may be bolted to a steel flange forged on the crankshaft. In any case, several attaching parts are required to mount the propeller on the shaft properly.

Hubs fitting a tapered shaft are usually held in place by a retaining nut that screws onto the end of the shaft. On one model, a locknut is used to safety the retaining nut and to provide a puller for removing the propeller from the shaft. This nut screws into the hub and against the retaining nut. The locknut and the retaining nut are safetied together with lock-wire or a cotter pin.

Front and rear cones may be used to seat the propeller properly on a splined shaft. The rear cone is a one-piece bronze cone that fits around the shaft and against the thrust nut (or spacer) and seats in the rear-cone seat of the hub.

The front cone is a two-piece, split-type steel cone that has a groove around its inner circumference so that it can be fitted over a flange of the propeller retaining nut. Then, the retaining nut is threaded into place and the front cone seats in the front cone hub. A snap ring is fitted into a groove in the hub in front of the front cone so that when the retaining nut is unscrewed from the propeller shaft, the front cone acts against the snap ring and pulls the propeller from the shaft.

One type of hub incorporates a bronze bushing instead of a front cone. When this type of hub is used, it may be necessary to use a puller to start the propeller from the shaft. A rear-cone spacer is sometimes provided with the splined-shaft propeller assembly to prevent the propeller from interfering with the engine cowling. The wide flange on the rear face of some types of hubs eliminates the use of a rear-cone spacer.

One type of hub assembly for the fixed-pitch, wooden propeller is a steel fitting inserted in the propeller to mount it on the propeller shaft. It has two main parts: the faceplate and the flange plate. *[Figure 7-22]* The faceplate is a steel disk that forms the forward face of the hub. The flange plate is a steel flange with an internal bore splined to receive the propeller shaft. The end of the flange plate opposite the flange disk is externally splined to receive the faceplate; the faceplate bore has splines to match these external splines. Both faceplate and flange plates have a corresponding series of holes drilled on the disk surface concentric with the hub center. The bore of the flange plate has a 15° cone seat on the rear end and a 30° cone seat on the forward end to center the hub accurately on the propeller shaft.

Duralumin. Compared to wooden propellers, they were lighter in weight because of elimination of blade-clamping devices, offered a lower maintenance cost because they were made in one piece, provided more efficient cooling because of the effective pitch nearer the hub, and, because there was no joint between the blades and the hub, the propeller pitch could be changed, within limits, by twisting the blade slightly by a propeller repair station.

Propellers of this type are now manufactured as one-piece anodized aluminum alloy. They are identified by stamping the propeller hub with the serial number, model number, Federal Aviation Administration (FAA) type certificate number, production certificate number, and the number of times the propeller has been reconditioned. The complete model number of the propeller is a combination of the basic model number and suffix numbers to indicate the propeller diameter and pitch. An explanation of a complete model number, using the McCauley 1B90/CM propeller, is provided in *Figure 7-23*.

Figure 7-23. *Complete propeller model numbers.*

Constant-Speed Propellers

Hartzell Constant-Speed, Nonfeathering

Hartzell propellers can be divided by Aluminum hub (compact) and steel hub. Hartzell compact aluminum propellers represent new concepts in basic design. They combine low weight and simplicity in design and rugged construction. In order to achieve these ends, the hub is made as compact as possible, utilizing aluminum alloy forgings for most of the parts. The hub shell is made in two halves, bolted together along the plane of rotation. This hub shell carries the pitch change mechanism and blade roots internally. The hydraulic cylinder, which provides power for changing the pitch, is mounted at the front of the hub. The propeller can be installed only on engines with flanged mounting provisions.

Figure 7-22. *Hub assembly.*

Metal Fixed-Pitch Propellers

Metal fixed-pitch propellers are similar in general appearance to a wooden propeller, except that the sections are usually thinner. The metal fixed-pitch propeller is widely used on many models of light aircraft and LSA. Many of the earliest metal propellers were manufactured in one piece of forged

One model of nonfeathering aluminum hub constant-speed propeller utilizes oil pressure from a governor to move the blades into high pitch (reduced rpm). The centrifugal twisting moment of the blades tends to move them into low pitch (high rpm) in the absence of governor oil pressure. This is an exception to most of the aluminum hub models and feathering models. Most of the Hartzell propeller aluminum and steel hub models use centrifugal force acting on blade counterweights to increase blade pitch and governor oil pressure for low pitch. Many types of light aircraft use governor-regulated, constant-speed propellers in two-bladed and up to six-bladed versions. These propellers may be the nonfeathering type, or they may be capable of feathering and reversing. The steel hub contains a central "spider," that supports aluminum blades with a tube extending inside the blade roots. Blade clamps connect the blade shanks with blade retention bearings. A hydraulic cylinder is mounted on the rotational axis connected to the blade clamps for pitch actuation. *[Figure 7-24]*

The basic hub and blade retention is common to all models described. The blades are mounted on the hub spider for angular adjustment. The centrifugal force of the blades, amounting to as much as 25 tons, is transmitted to the hub spider through blade clamps and then through ball bearings. The propeller thrust and engine torque is transmitted from the blades to the hub spider through a bushing inside the blade shank. In order to control the pitch of the blades, a hydraulic piston-cylinder element is mounted on the front of the hub spider. The piston is attached to the blade clamps by means of a sliding rod and fork system for nonfeathering models and a link system for the feathering models. The piston is actuated in the forward direction by means of oil pressure supplied by a governor, which overcomes the opposing force created by the counterweights. Hartzell and McCauley propellers for light aircraft are similar in operation. The manufacturer's specifications and instructions must be consulted for information on specific models.

Constant-Speed Feathering Propeller

The feathering propeller utilizes a single oil supply from a governing device to hydraulically actuate a change in blade angle. *[Figure 7-25]* This propeller has five blades and is used primarily on Pratt & Whitney turbine engines. A two piece aluminum hub retains each propeller blade on a thrust bearing. A cylinder is attached to the hub and contains a feathering spring and piston. The hydraulically actuated piston transmits linear motion through a pitch change rod and fork to each blade to result in blade angle change.

While the propeller is operating, the following forces are constantly present: 1) spring force, 2) counterweight force, 3) centrifugal twisting moment of each blade, and 4) blade aerodynamic twisting forces. The spring and counterweight forces attempt to rotate the blades to higher blade angle, while the centrifugal twisting moment of each blade is generally

Figure 7-24. *Constant speed non-feathering propeller.*

Figure 7-25. *Constant-speed feathering propeller.*

toward lower blade angle. Blade aerodynamic twisting force is usually very small in relation to the other forces and can attempt to increase or decrease blade angle. The summation of the propeller forces is toward higher pitch (low rpm) and is opposed by a variable force toward lower pitch (high rpm).

The variable force is oil under pressure from a governor with an internal pump that is mounted on and driven by the engine. The oil from the governor is supplied to the propeller and hydraulic piston through a hollow engine shaft. Increasing the volume of oil within the piston and cylinder decreases the blade angle and increases propeller rpm. If governor-supplied oil is lost during operation, the propeller increases pitch and feather. Feathering occurs because the summation of internal propeller forces causes the oil to drain out of the propeller until the feather stop position is reached. Normal in-flight feathering is accomplished when the pilot retards the propeller condition lever past the feather detent. This permits control oil to drain from the propeller and return to the engine sump. Engine shutdown is normally accomplished during the feathering process. Normal in-flight unfeathering is accomplished when the pilot positions the propeller condition lever into the normal flight (governing) range and restarts the engine. As engine speed increases, the governor supplies oil to the propeller and the blade angle decreases. Decreasing the volume of oil increases blade angle and decrease propeller rpm. By changing blade angle, the governor can vary the load on the engine and maintain constant engine rpm (within limits), independent of where the power lever is set. The governor uses engine speed sensing mechanisms that permit it to supply or drain oil as necessary to maintain constant engine speed (rpm). Most of the steel hub Hartzell propellers and many of the aluminum hub are full feathering. These feathering propellers operate similarly to the nonfeathering ones except the feathering spring assists the counterweights to increase the pitch.

Feathering is accomplished by releasing the governor oil pressure, allowing the counterweights and feathering spring to feather the blades. This is done by pulling the condition lever (pitch control) back to the limit of its travel, which opens up a port in the governor allowing the oil from the propeller to drain back into the engine. Feathering occurs because the summation of internal propeller forces causes the oil to drain out of the propeller until the feather stop position is reached. The time necessary to feather depends upon the size of the oil passage from the propeller to the engine, and the force exerted by the spring and counterweights. The larger the passage is through the governor and the heavier the spring, the quicker the feathering action is. An elapsed time for feathering of between 3 and 10 seconds is usual with this system. Engine shutdown is normally accomplished during the feathering process.

In order to prevent the feathering spring and counterweights from feathering the propeller when the engine is shut down and the engine stopped, automatically removable high-pitch stops were incorporated in the design. These consist of spring-loaded latches fastened to the stationary hub that engage high-pitch stop plates bolted to the movable blade clamps. When the propeller is in rotation at speeds over 600–800 rpm, centrifugal force acts to disengage the latches from the high-pitch stop plates so that the propeller pitch may be increased to the feathering position. At lower rpm, or when the engine is stopped, the latch springs engage the latches with the high-pitch stops, preventing the pitch from increasing further due to the action of the feathering spring. As mentioned earlier, the engine load would be excessive, especially on fixed-turbine turboprop engines. One safety feature inherent in this method of feathering is that the propeller feathers if the governor oil pressure drops to zero for any reason. As the governor obtains its supply of oil from the engine lubricating system, it follows that if the engine runs out of oil or if oil pressure fails due to breakage of a part of the engine, the propeller feathers automatically. This action may save the engine from further damage in case the pilot is not aware of trouble.

Unfeathering

Unfeathering can be accomplished by any of several methods, as follows:

1. Start the engine, so the governor can pump oil back into the propeller to reduce pitch. In most light twins, this procedure is considered adequate since the feathering of the propeller would happen infrequently. Vibration can occur when the engine starts and the propeller starts to come out of feather.

2. Provide an accumulator connected to the governor with a valve to trap an air-oil charge when the propeller is feathered, but released to the propeller when the rpm control is returned to normal position. This system is used with training aircraft because it unfeathers the propeller in a very short time and starts the engine wind milling.

3. Provide an unfeathering pump that provides pressure to force the propeller back to low pitch quickly using engine oil.

Normal in-flight unfeathering is accomplished when the pilot positions the propeller condition lever into the normal flight (governing) range. *[Figure 7-26]* This causes the governor to disconnect the propeller oil supply from drain and reconnects it to the governed oil supply line from the governor. At that point, there is no oil available from the engine oil pump to the governor; therefore, no governed oil is available from the governor for controlling the propeller blade angle and rpm. As the engine is started, its speed increases, the governor supplies oil to the propeller, and the blade angle decreases. As soon as the engine is operating, the governor starts to unfeather the blades. Soon, windmilling takes place, which speeds up the process of unfeathering.

In general, restarting and unfeathering of propellers can be classified as reciprocating engine restart unfeathering, turboprop engine restart unfeathering, and accumulator unfeathering. When reciprocating unfeathering is used, the engine takes a little longer to start turning enough to provide oil pressure to the governor and then to the propeller. This delay can cause vibration as the propeller is unfeathered. Many aircraft can use an accumulator to provide stored pressure to unfeather the propeller much quicker.

Special unfeathering systems are available for certain aircraft where restarting the engine is difficult or for training purposes. The system consists of an oil accumulator connected to the governor through a valve. *[Figure 7-26]* The air or nitrogen pressure in one side of the accumulator pushes a piston to force oil from the other side of the accumulator through the governor to the propeller piston to move the propeller blades from feather to a lower blade angle. The propeller then begins to windmill and permits the engine to start. When the unfeathering pump is used, it is an additional pump that, once the propeller control is in the correct position, the (full increase rpm) pump is actuated and the oil pressure from the pump unfeathers the propeller.

Propeller Auxiliary Systems

Ice Control Systems

Ice formation on a propeller blade, in effect, produces a distorted blade airfoil section that causes a loss in propeller efficiency. Generally, ice collects asymmetrically on a propeller blade and produces propeller unbalance and destructive vibration and increases the weight of the blades.

Anti-Icing Systems

A typical fluid system includes a tank to hold a supply of anti-icing fluid. *[Figure 7-27]* This fluid is forced to each propeller by a pump. The control system permits variation in the pumping rate so that the quantity of fluid delivered to a propeller can be varied, depending on the severity of icing. Fluid is transferred from a stationary nozzle on the engine nose case into a circular U-shaped channel (slinger ring) mounted on the rear of the propeller assembly. The fluid under pressure of centrifugal force is transferred through nozzles to each blade shank.

Because airflow around a blade shank tends to disperse anti-icing fluids to areas where ice does not collect in large quantities, feed shoes, or boots, are installed on the blade

Figure 7-26. *Unfeathering system.*

Figure 7-27. *Typical propeller fluid anti-icing system.*

leading edge. These feed shoes are a narrow strip of rubber extending from the blade shank to a blade station that is approximately 75 percent of the propeller radius. The feed shoes are molded with several parallel open channels in which fluid flows from the blade shank toward the blade tip by centrifugal force. The fluid flows laterally from the channels over the leading edge of the blade.

Isopropyl alcohol is used in some anti-icing systems because of its availability and low cost. Phosphate compounds are comparable to isopropyl alcohol in anti-icing performance and have the advantage of reduced flammability. However, phosphate compounds are comparatively expensive and, consequently, are not widely used. This system has disadvantages in that it requires several components that add weight to the aircraft, and the time of anti-ice available is limited to the amount of fluid on board. This system is not used on modern aircraft, giving way to the electric deicing systems.

Deicing Systems

An electric propeller-icing control system consists of an electrical energy source, a resistance heating element, system controls, and necessary wiring. *[Figure 7-28]* The heating elements are mounted internally or externally on the propeller spinner and blades. Electrical power from the aircraft system is transferred to the propeller hub through electrical leads,

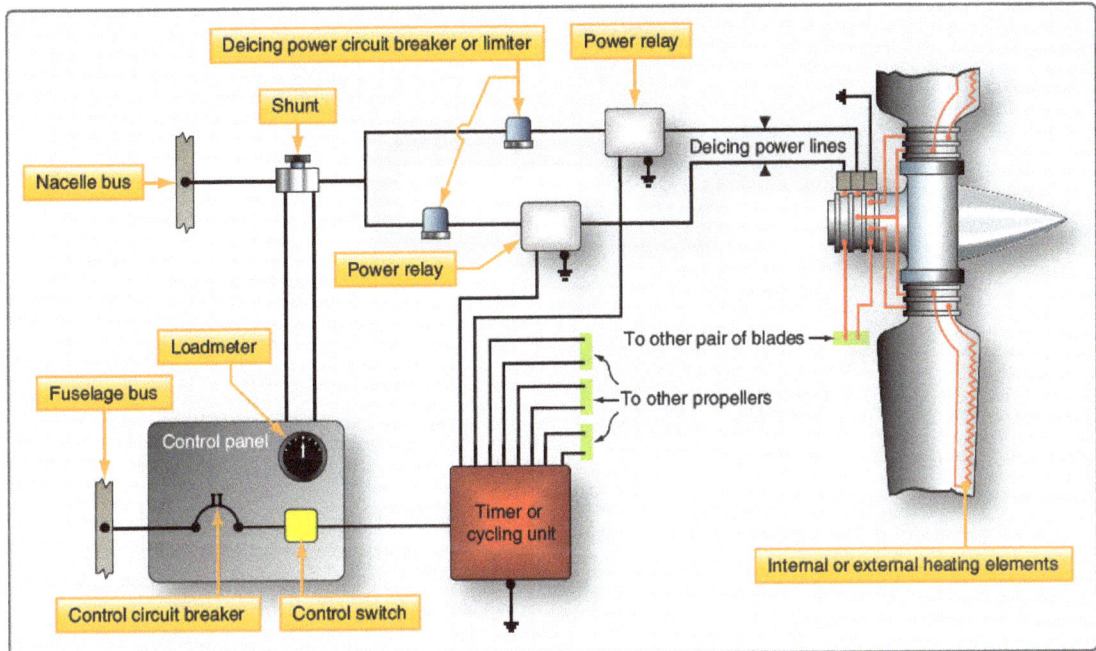

Figure 7-28. *Typical electrical deicing system.*

which terminate in slip rings and brushes. Flexible connectors are used to transfer power from the hub to the blade elements.

A deice system consists of one or more on-off switches. The pilot controls the operation of the deice system by turning on one or more switches. All deice systems have a master switch, and may have another toggle switch for each propeller. Some systems may also have a selector switch to adjust for light or heavy icing conditions or automatic switching for icing conditions.

The timer or cycling unit determines the sequence of which blades (or portion thereof) are currently being deiced, and for what length of time. The cycling unit applies power to each deice boot, or boot segment, in a sequence or all on order.

A brush block, which is normally mounted on the engine just behind the propeller, is used to transfer electricity to the slip ring. A slip ring and brush block assembly is shown in *Figure 7-29*. The slip ring rotates with the propeller and provides a current path to the blade deice boots. A slip ring wire harness is used on some hub installations to electrically connect the slip ring to the terminal strip connection screw. A deice wire harness is used to electrically connect the deice boot to the slip ring assembly.

A deice boot contains internal heating elements or dual elements. *[Figure 7-30]* The boot is securely attached to the leading edge of each blade with adhesive.

Figure 7-29. *Deicing brush block and slip ring assembly.*

Icing control is accomplished by converting electrical energy to heat energy in the heating element. Balanced ice removal from all blades must be obtained as nearly as possible if excessive vibration is to be avoided. To obtain balanced ice removal, variation of heating current in the blade elements is controlled so that similar heating effects are obtained in opposite blades.

Electric deicing systems are usually designed for intermittent application of power to the heating elements to remove ice after formation but before excessive accumulation. Proper control of heating intervals aids in preventing runback,

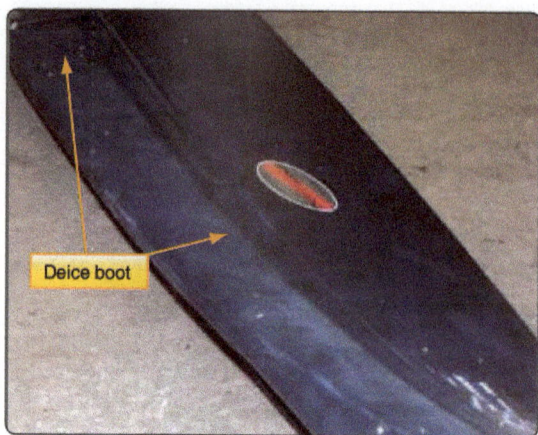

Figure 7-30. *Electric deice boot.*

Figure 7-31. *Synchrophasing system.*

since heat is applied just long enough to melt the ice face in contact with the blade. If heat supplied to an icing surface is more than that required for melting just the inner ice face, but insufficient to evaporate all the water formed, water will run back over the unheated surface and freeze. Runback of this nature causes ice formation on uncontrolled icing areas of the blade or surface.

Cycling timers are used to energize the heating element circuits for periods of 15 to 30 seconds, with a complete cycle time of 2 minutes. A cycling timer is an electric motor driven contactor that controls power contactors in separate sections of the circuit. Controls for propeller electrical deicing systems include on-off switches, ammeters or loadmeters to indicate current in the circuits, and protective devices, such as current limiters or circuit breakers. The ammeters or loadmeters permit monitoring of individual circuit currents and reflect operation of the timer. To prevent element overheating, the propeller deicing system is used only when the propellers are rotating and for short test periods of time during the takeoff check list or system inspection.

Propeller Synchronization and Synchrophasing

Most multi-engine aircraft are equipped with propeller synchronization systems. Synchronization systems provide a means of controlling and synchronizing engine rpm. Synchronization reduces vibration and eliminates the unpleasant beat produced by unsynchronized propeller operation.

A typical synchrophasing system is an electronic system. *[Figure 7-31]* It functions to match the rpm of both engines and establish a blade phase relationship between the left and right propellers to reduce cabin noise. The system is controlled by a two-position switch located forward of the throttle quadrant. Turning the control switch on supplies direct current (DC) power to the electronic control box. Input signals representing propeller rpm are received from magnetic pickup on each propeller. The computed input signals are corrected to a command signal and sent to an rpm trimming coil located on the propeller governor of the slow engine. Its rpm is adjusted to that of the other propeller.

Autofeathering System

An autofeather system is used normally only during takeoff, approach, and landing. It is used to feather the propeller automatically if power is lost from either engine. The system uses a solenoid valve to dump oil pressure from the propeller cylinder (this allows the prop to feather) if two torque switches sense low torque from the engine. This system has a test-off-arm switch that is used to arm the system.

Propeller Inspection and Maintenance

Propellers must be inspected regularly. The exact time interval for particular propeller inspections is usually specified by the propeller manufacturer. The regular daily inspection of propellers varies little from one type to another.

Typically, it is a visual inspection of propeller blades, hubs, controls, and accessories for security, safety, and general condition. Visual inspection of the blades does not mean a careless or casual observation. The inspection should be meticulous enough to detect any flaw or defect that may exist. Inspections performed at greater intervals of time (e.g., 25, 50, or 100 hours) usually include a visual check of:

1. Blades, spinners, and other external surfaces for excessive oil or grease deposits.

2. Weld and braze sections of blades and hubs for evidence of failure.

3. Blade, spinner, and hubs for nicks, scratches, or other flaws. Use a magnifying glass if necessary.

4. Spinner or dome shell attaching screws for tightness.
5. The lubricating requirements and oil levels, when applicable.

If a propeller is involved in an accident, and a possibility exists that internal damage may have occurred, or if a propeller has had a ground strike or sudden stoppage, the recommendations of the engine and propeller need to be adhered to. The propeller should be disassembled and inspected. Whenever a propeller is removed from a shaft, the hub cone seats, cones, and other contact parts should be examined to detect undue wear, galling, or corrosion.

It is also vitally important to keep up-to-date airworthiness directives (ADs) or service bulletins (SBs) for a propeller. Compliance with ADs is required to make the airplane legally airworthy, but it is also important to follow the SBs. All work performed on the propeller, including AD and SB compliance, should be noted in the propeller logbook.

The propeller inspection requirements and maintenance procedures discussed in this section are representative of those in widespread use on most of the propellers described in this chapter. No attempt has been made to include detailed maintenance procedures for a particular propeller, and all pressures, figures, and sizes are solely for the purpose of illustration and do not have specific application. For maintenance information on a specific propeller, always refer to applicable manufacturer instructions.

Wood Propeller Inspection

Wood propellers should be inspected frequently to ensure airworthiness. Inspect for defects, such as cracks, dents, warpage, glue failure, delamination defects in the finish, and charring of the wood between the propeller and the flange due to loose propeller mounting bolts. Examine the wood close to the metal sleeve of wood blades for cracks extending outward on the blade. These cracks sometimes occur at the threaded ends of the lag screws and may be an indication of internal cracking of the wood. Check the tightness of the lag screws, which attach the metal sleeve to the wood blade, in accordance with the manufacturer's instructions. In-flight tip failures may be avoided by frequent inspections of the metal cap, leading edge strip, and surrounding areas. Inspect for such defects as looseness or slipping, separation of soldered joints, loose screws, loose rivets, breaks, cracks, eroded sections, and corrosion. Inspect for separation between the metal leading edge and the cap, which would indicate the cap is moving outward in the direction of centrifugal force. This condition is often accompanied by discoloration and loose rivets. Inspect the tip for cracks by grasping it with the hand and slightly twisting about the longitudinal blade centerline and by slightly bending the tip backward and forward. If the leading edge and the cap have separated, carefully inspect for cracks at this point. Cracks usually start at the leading edge of the blade. Inspect moisture holes are open. A fine line appearing in the fabric or plastic may indicate a crack in the wood. Check the trailing edge of the propeller blades for bonding, separation, or damage.

Metal Propeller Inspection

Metal propellers and blades are generally susceptible to fatigue failure resulting from the concentration of stresses at the bottoms of sharp nicks, cuts, and scratches. It is necessary, therefore, to frequently and carefully inspect them for such defects. The inspection of steel blades may be accomplished by either visual, fluorescent penetrant (see chapter 5), or magnetic particle inspection. The visual inspection is easier if the steel blades are covered with engine oil or rust-preventive compound. The full length of the leading edge (especially near the tip), the full length of the trailing edge, the grooves and shoulders on the shank, and all dents and scars should be examined with a magnifying glass to decide whether defects are scratches or cracks.

Tachometer inspection is a very important part of the overall propeller inspection. Operation with an inaccurate tachometer may result in restricted rpm operation and damaging high stresses. This could shorten blade life and could result in catastrophic failure. If the tachometer is inaccurate, then the propeller could be turning much faster than it is rated to turn, providing extra stress. Accuracy of the engine tachometer should be verified at 100-hour intervals or at annual inspection, whichever occurs first. Hartzell Propeller recommends using a tachometer that is accurate within ± 10 rpm, and has an appropriate calibration schedule.

Aluminum Propeller Inspection

Carefully inspect aluminum propellers and blades for cracks and other flaws. A transverse crack or flaw of any size is cause for rejection. Multiple deep nicks and gouges on the leading edge and face of the blade is cause for rejection. Use dye penetrant or fluorescent dye penetrant to confirm suspected cracks found in the propeller. Refer any unusual condition or appearance revealed by these inspections to the manufacturer.

Composite Propeller Inspection

Composite blades need to be visually inspected for nicks, gouges, loose material, erosion, cracks and debonds, and lightning strike. *[Figure 7-32]* Composite blades are inspected for delaminations and debonds by tapping the blade or cuff (if applicable) with a metal coin. If an audible change is apparent, sounding hollow or dead, a debond or delamination is likely. *[Figure 7-33]* Blades that incorporate a "cuff" have a different tone when coin tapped in the cuff

Figure 7-32. *Composite blade construction*

Figure 7-33. *Coin-tap test to check for debonds and delaminations.*

area. To avoid confusing the sounds, coin tap the cuff area and the transition area between the cuff and the blade separately from the blade area. Additional nondestructive testing (NDT) techniques for composite materials, such as phased array inspections, and ultrasound inspections, are available for more detailed inspections.

Repairs to propellers are often limited to minor type repairs. Certificated mechanics are not allowed to perform major repairs on propellers. Major repairs need to be accomplished by a certificated propeller repair station.

Propeller Vibration

Although vibration can be caused by the propeller, there are numerous other possible sources of vibration that can make troubleshooting difficult. If a propeller vibrates, whether due to balance, angle, or track problems, it typically vibrates throughout the entire rpm range, although the intensity of the vibration may vary with the rpm. If a vibration occurs only at one particular rpm or within a limited rpm range (e.g., 2200–2350 rpm), the vibration is not normally a propeller problem but a problem of a poor engine-propeller match. If a propeller vibration is suspected but cannot be positively determined, the ideal troubleshooting method is to temporarily replace the propeller with one known to be airworthy and then test fly the

aircraft if possible. Blade shake is not the source of vibration problems. Once the engine is running, centrifugal force holds the blades firmly (approximately 30,000–40,000 pounds) against blade bearings. Cabin vibration can sometimes be improved by reindexing the propeller to the crankshaft. The propeller can be removed, rotated 180°, and reinstalled. The propeller spinner can be a contributing factor to an out-of-balance condition. An indication of this would be a noticeable spinner wobble while the engine is running. This condition is usually caused by inadequate shimming of the spinner front support or a cracked or deformed spinner.

When powerplant vibration is encountered, it is sometimes difficult to determine whether it is the result of engine vibration or propeller vibration. In most cases, the cause of the vibration can be determined by observing the propeller hub, dome, or spinner while the engine is running within a 1,200- to 1,500-rpm range, and determining whether or not the propeller hub rotates on an absolutely horizontal plane. If the propeller hub appears to swing in a slight orbit, the vibration is usually caused by the propeller. If the propeller hub does not appear to rotate in an orbit, the difficulty is probably caused by engine vibration.

When propeller vibration is the reason for excessive vibration, the difficulty is usually caused by propeller blade imbalance, propeller blades not tracking, or variation in propeller blade angle settings. Check the propeller blade tracking and then the low-pitch blade angle setting to determine if either is the cause of the vibration. If both propeller tracking and low blade angle setting are correct, the propeller is statically or dynamically unbalanced and should be replaced, or rebalanced if permitted by the manufacturer.

Blade Tracking

Blade tracking is the process of determining the positions of the tips of the propeller blades relative to each other (blades rotating in the same plane of rotation). Tracking shows only the relative position of the blades, not their actual path. The blades should all track one another as closely as possible. The difference in track at like points must not exceed the tolerance specified by the propeller manufacturer. The design and manufacture of propellers is such that the tips of the blades give a good indication of tracking. The following method for checking tracking is normally used:

1. Chock the aircraft so it cannot be moved.
2. Remove one spark plug from each cylinder. This makes the propeller easier and safer to turn.
3. Rotate one of the blades so it is pointing down.
4. Place a solid object (e.g., a heavy wooden block that is at least a couple of inches higher off the ground than the

distance between the propeller tip and the ground) next to the propeller tip so that it just touches or attaches a pointer/indicator to the cowling itself. *[Figure 7-34]*

Figure 7-34. *Propeller blade tracking.*

Figure 7-35. *Blade angle measurement.*

5. Rotate the propeller slowly to determine if the next blade tracks through the same point (touches the block/pointer). Each blade track should be within 1/16 inch (plus or minus) from the opposite blade's track.

6. An out-of-track propeller, may be due to one or more propeller blades being bent, a bent propeller flange, or propeller mounting bolts that are either over- or undertorqued. An out-of-track propeller causes vibration and stress to the airframe and engine and may cause premature propeller failure.

Checking and Adjusting Propeller Blade Angles

When you find an improper blade angle setting during installation or is indicated by engine performance, follow basic maintenance guidelines. From the applicable manufacturer's instructions, obtain the blade angle setting and the station at which the blade angle is checked. Do not use metal scribes or other sharply pointed instruments to mark the location of blade stations or to make reference lines on propeller blades, since such surface scratches can eventually result in blade failure. Use a bench-top protractor if the propeller is removed from the aircraft. *[Figure 7-35]* Use a handheld protractor (a digital protractor provides an easy measurement) to check blade angle if the propeller is installed on the aircraft or is placed on the knife-edge balancing stand. *[Figure 7-36]*

Universal Propeller Protractor

The universal propeller protractor can be used to check propeller blade angles when the propeller is on a balancing

Figure 7-36. *Bench top protractor.*

stand or installed on the aircraft engine. *Figure 7-37* shows the parts and adjustments of a universal propeller protractor. The following instructions for using the protractor apply to a propeller installed on the engine:

Turn the propeller until the first blade to be checked is horizontal with the leading edge up. Place the corner spirit level at right angles to the face of the protractor. Align degree and vernier scales by turning the disk adjuster before the disk is locked to the ring. The locking device is a pin that is held in the engaged position by a spring. The pin can be released by pulling it outward and turning it 90°.

Release the ring-to-frame lock (a right-hand screw with thumb nut) and turn the ring until both ring and disk zeros are at the top of the protractor.

Check the blade angle by determining how much the flat side of the block slants from the plane of rotation. First, locate a point to represent the plane of rotation by placing the protractor vertically against the end of the hub nut or any convenient surface known to lie in the plane of propeller

7-23

Figure 7-37. *Universal proptractor.*

rotation. Keep the protractor vertical by the corner spirit level, and turn the ring adjuster until the center spirit level is horizontal. This sets the zero of the vernier scale at a point representing the plane of propeller rotation. Then, lock the ring to the frame.

While holding the protractor by the handle with the curved edge up, release the disk-to-ring lock. Place the forward vertical edge (the edge opposite the one first used) against the blade at the station specified in the manufacturer's instructions. Keep the protractor vertical by the corner spirit level, and turn the disk adjuster until the center spirit level is horizontal. The number of degrees and tenths of a degree between the two zeros indicates the blade angle.

In determining the blade angle, remember that ten points on the vernier scale are equal to nine points on the degree scale. The graduations on the vernier scale represent tenths of a degree, but those of the degree scale represent whole degrees. The number of tenths of a degree in the blade angle is given by the number of vernier scale spaces between the zero of the vernier scale and the vernier scale graduation line nearest to perfect alignment with a degree scale graduation line. This reading should always be made on the vernier scale. The vernier scale increases in the same direction that the protractor scale increases. This is opposite to the direction of rotation of the moving element of the protractor. After making any necessary adjustment of the blade, lock it in position and repeat the same operations for the remaining blades of the propeller.

Propeller Balancing

Propeller unbalance, which is a source of vibration in an aircraft, may be either static or dynamic. Propeller static imbalance occurs when the center of gravity (CG) of the propeller does not coincide with the axis of rotation. Dynamic unbalance results when the CG of similar propeller elements, such as blades or counterweights, does not follow in the same plane of rotation. Since the length of the propeller assembly along the engine crankshaft is short in comparison to its diameter, and since the blades are secured to the hub so they lie in the same plane perpendicular to the running axis, the dynamic unbalance resulting from improper mass distribution is negligible, provided the track tolerance requirements are met. Another type of propeller unbalance, aerodynamic unbalance, results when the thrust (or pull) of the blades is unequal. This type of unbalance can be largely eliminated by checking blade contour and blade angle setting.

Static Balancing

The knife-edge test stand has two hardened steel edges mounted to allow the free rotation of an assembled propeller between them. *[Figure 7-38]* The knife-edge test stand must be located in a room or area that is free from any air motion, and preferably removed from any source of heavy vibration.

The standard method of checking propeller assembly balance involves the following sequence of operations:

1. Insert a bushing in the engine shaft hole of the propeller.
2. Insert a mandrel or arbor through the bushing.
3. Place the propeller assembly so that the ends of the arbor are supported upon the balance stand knife-edges. The propeller must be free to rotate.

If the propeller is properly balanced statically, it remains at any position in which it is placed. Check two-bladed propeller assemblies for balance: first with the blades in a vertical position and then with the blades in a horizontal position. Repeat the vertical position check with the blade positions reversed; that is, with the blade that was checked in the downward position placed in the upward position.

Check a three-bladed propeller assembly with each blade placed in a downward vertical position. *[Figure 7-39]*

During a propeller static balance check, all blades must be at the same blade angle. Before conducting the balance check, inspect to see that each blade has been set at the same blade angle.

Figure 7-38. *Positions of two-bladed propeller during a balance check.*

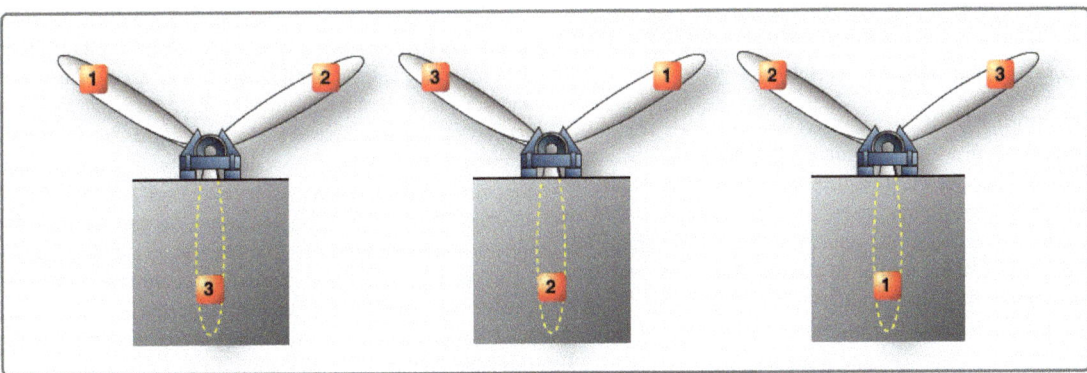

Figure 7-39. *Positions of three-bladed propeller during balance check.*

Unless otherwise specified by the manufacturer, an acceptable balance check requires that the propeller assembly have no tendency to rotate in any of the positions previously described. If the propeller balances perfectly in all described positions, it should also balance perfectly in all intermediate positions. When necessary, check for balance in intermediate positions to verify the check in the originally described positions. *[Figure 7-40]*

When a propeller assembly is checked for static balance and there is a definite tendency of the assembly to rotate, certain corrections to remove the unbalance are allowed.

1. The addition of permanent fixed weights at acceptable locations when the total weight of the propeller assembly or parts is under the allowable limit.

2. The removal of weight at acceptable locations when the total weight of the propeller assembly or parts is equal to the allowable limit.

The location for removal or addition of weight for propeller unbalance correction has been determined by the propeller manufacturer. The method and point of application of unbalance corrections must be checked to see that they are according to applicable drawings.

Figure 7-40. *Static propeller balancing.*

Dynamic Balancing

Propellers can also be dynamically balanced (spin balanced) with an analyzer kit to reduce the vibration levels of the propeller and spinner assembly. Some aircraft have the system hardwired in the aircraft and on other aircraft the sensors and cables need to be installed before the balancing run. Balancing the propulsion assembly can provide substantial reductions in transmitted vibration and noise to the cabin and also reduces excessive damage to other aircraft and engine components. The dynamic imbalance could be caused by mass imbalance or any aerodynamic imbalance. Dynamic balancing only improves the vibration caused by mass unbalance of the externally rotating components of the propulsion system. Balancing does not reduce the vibration level if the engine or aircraft is in poor mechanical condition. Defective, worn, or loose parts will make balancing impossible. Several manufacturers make dynamic propeller balancing equipment, and their equipment operation could differ. The typical dynamic balancing system consists of a vibration sensor that is attached to the engine close to the propeller, and an analyzer unit that calculates the weight and location of balancing weights.

Balancing Procedure

Face the aircraft directly into the wind (maximum 20 knots) and place chocks at the wheels. When you have installed the analyzing equipment, run the engine up at low cruise rpm; the dynamic analyzer calculates the balancing weight required at each blade position. After installing the balancing weights, run the engine up again to check if the vibration levels have diminished. This process may have to be repeated several times before satisfactory results are achieved.

A dynamic balancing example procedure is listed here, but always refer to the aircraft and propeller manuals when performing any balancing procedure. Dynamic balance is accomplished by using an accurate means of measuring the amount and location of the dynamic imbalance. The number of balance weights installed must not exceed the limits specified by the propeller manufacturer. Follow the dynamic balance equipment manufacturer's instructions for dynamic balance in addition to the specifications of the propeller.

Most equipment use an optical pickup that senses reflective tape for rpm reading. Also, there is an accelerometer mounted to the engine that senses vibration in inches per second (ips).

Visually inspect the propeller assembly before dynamic balancing. The first runup of a new or overhauled propeller assembly may leave a small amount of grease on the blades and inner surface of the spinner dome. Use Stoddard solvent (or equivalent) to completely remove any grease on the blades or inner surface of the spinner dome. Visually examine each propeller blade assembly for evidence of grease leakage. Visually examine the inner surface of the spinner dome for evidence of grease leakage. If there is no evidence of grease leakage, lubricate the propeller in accordance with the maintenance manual. If grease leakage is evident, determine the location of the leak and correct before relubricating the propeller and dynamic balancing. Before dynamic balance, record the number and location of all balance weights. Static balance is accomplished at a propeller overhaul facility when an overhaul or major repair is performed. Twelve equally spaced locations are recommended for weight attachment. Install the balancing weights using aircraft quality 10-32 or AN-3 type screws or bolts. Balance weight screws attached to the spinner bulkhead must protrude through the self-locking nuts or nut plates a minimum of one thread and a maximum of four threads. Unless otherwise specified by the engine or airframe manufacturer, Hartzell recommends that the propeller be dynamically balanced to a reading of 0.2 ips, or less. If reflective tape is used for dynamic balancing, remove the tape immediately after balancing is completed. Make a record in the propeller logbook of the number and location of dynamic balance weights, and static balance weights if they have been reconfigured.

Propeller Removal and Installation

Removal

The following procedure is for demonstration purposes only. Always use the current manufacturer's information when removing and installing any propeller.

1. Remove the spinner dome in accordance with the spinner removal procedures. Cut and remove the safety wire (if installed) on the propeller mounting studs.
2. Support the propeller assembly with a sling. If the propeller IS reinstalled and has been dynamically balanced, make an identifying mark (with a felt-tipped pen only) on the propeller hub and a matching mark on the engine flange to make sure of proper orientation during reinstallation to prevent dynamic imbalance.
3. Unscrew the four mounting bolts from the engine bushings. Unscrew the two mounting nuts and the attached studs from the engine bushings. If the propeller is removed between overhaul intervals, mounting studs, nuts, and washers may be reused if they are not damaged or corroded.

    CAUTION: remove the propeller from the mounting flange with care to prevent damaging the propeller mounting studs. Using the support sling, remove the propeller from the mounting flange.

4. Place the propeller on a cart for transport.

Installation

A flange propeller has six studs configured in a four-inch circle. Two special studs that also function as dowel pins are provided to transfer torque and index the propeller with respect to the engine crankshaft. The dowel pin locations used on a particular propeller installation are indicated in the propeller model stamped on the hub. Perform the applicable steps under Spinner Pre-Installation and clean the engine flange and propeller flange with quick dry stoddard solvent or methyl ethyl ketone (MEK). Install the O-ring in the O-ring groove in the hub bore. NOTE: When the propeller is received from the factory, the O-ring has usually been installed. With a suitable support, such as a crane hoist or similar equipment, carefully move the propeller assembly to the aircraft engine mounting flange in preparation for installation.

Install the propeller on the engine flange. Make certain to align the dowel studs in the propeller flange with the corresponding holes in the engine mounting flange. The propeller may be installed on the engine flange in a given position, or 180° from that position. Check the engine and airframe manuals to determine if either manual specifies a propeller mounting position.

CAUTION: Mounting hardware must be clean and dry to prevent excessive preload of the mounting flange.

CAUTION: Tighten nuts evenly to avoid hub damage.

Install the propeller mounting nuts (dry) with spacers. Torque the propeller mounting nuts (dry) in accordance with the proper specifications and safety wire the studs in pairs (if required by the aircraft maintenance manual) at the rear of the propeller mounting flange.

Servicing Propellers

Propeller servicing includes cleaning, lubricating, and replenishing operating lubrication supplies.

Cleaning Propeller Blades

Aluminum and steel propeller blades and hubs are usually cleaned by washing the blades with a suitable cleaning solvent, using a brush or cloth. Do not use acid or caustic materials. Power buffers, steel wool, steel brushes, or any other tool or substance that may scratch or mar the blade should be avoided. If a high polish is desired, a number of good grades of commercial metal polish are available. After completing the polishing operation, immediately remove all traces of polish. When the blades are clean, coat them with a clean film of engine oil or suitable equivalent.

To clean wooden propellers, use warm water and a mild soap, together with brushes or cloth. If a propeller has been subjected to salt water, flush it with fresh water until all traces of salt have been removed. This should be accomplished as soon as possible after the salt water has splashed on the propeller, regardless of whether the propeller parts are aluminum alloy, steel, or wood. After flushing, thoroughly dry all parts, and coat metal parts with clean engine oil or a suitable equivalent.

To remove grease or oil from propeller surfaces, apply Stoddard Solvent or equivalent to a clean cloth and wipe the part clean. Using a noncorrosive soap solution, wash the propeller. Thoroughly rinse with water. Permit to dry. Aluminum and steel propeller blades and hubs usually are cleaned by washing the blades with a suitable cleaning solvent, using a brush or cloth. Do not use acid or caustic materials. Avoid power buffers, steel wool, steel brushes, or any other tool or substance that may scratch or mar the blade. If a high polish is desired, a number of good grades of commercial metal polish are available. After completing the polishing operation, immediately remove all traces of polish. When the blades are clean, coat them with a clean film of engine oil or suitable equivalent.

Charging the Propeller Air Dome

These instructions are general in nature and do not represent any aircraft procedure. Always check the correct manual before servicing any propeller system. Examine the propeller to make sure that it is positioned on the start locks and using the proper control, then charge the cylinder with dry air or nitrogen. The air charge valve is located on the cylinder as indicated in *Figure 7-41*. Nitrogen is the preferred charging medium. The correct charge pressure is identified by checking the correct table shown. The temperature is used to find the correct pressure to charge the hub air pressure.

Propeller Lubrication

Hydromatic propellers operated with engine oil and some sealed propellers do not require lubrication. Electric propellers require oils and greases for hub lubricants and pitch change drive mechanisms. Proper propeller lubrication procedures, with oil and grease specifications, are usually published in the manufacturer's instructions. Experience indicates that water sometimes gets into the propeller blade bearing assembly on some models of propellers. For this reason, the propeller manufacturer's greasing schedule must be followed to ensure proper lubrication of moving parts and protection from corrosion. Observe overhaul periods because most defects in propellers are not external, but unseen internal corrosion. Dissimilar metals in the prop and hub create an environment ripe for corrosion, and the only way to properly inspect many of these areas is through a teardown. Extensive corrosion can dramatically reduce the strength of the blades or hub. Even seemingly minor corrosion may cause a blade or hub to fail an inspection. Because of the safety implications (blade loss), this is clearly an area in which close monitoring is needed.

One example of the lubrication requirements and procedures is detailed here for illustration purposes only. Lubrication intervals are important to adhere to because of corrosion implications. The propeller must be lubricated at intervals not to exceed 100 hours or at 12 calendar months, whichever occurs first. If annual operation is significantly less than 100 hours, calendar lubrication intervals should be reduced to 6 months. If the aircraft is operated or stored under adverse atmospheric conditions, such as high humidity, salt air, calendar lubrication intervals should be reduced to 6 months. Hartzell recommends that new or newly overhauled propellers be lubricated after the first 1 or 2 hours of operation because centrifugal loads pack and redistribute grease, which may result in a propeller imbalance. Redistribution of grease may also result in voids in the blade bearing area where moisture can collect. Remove the lubrication fitting from the cylinder-side hub half installed in the engine-side hub half. *[Figure 7-42]* Pump 1 fluid ounce (30 milliliters (ml)) grease into the fitting located nearest the leading edge of the blade on a tractor installation, or nearest the trailing edge on a pusher installation, until grease emerges from the hole where the fitting was removed, whichever occurs first.

NOTE: 1 fluid ounce (30 ml) is approximately six pumps with a hand-operated grease gun. Reinstall the removed lubrication fittings. Tighten the fittings until snug. Make sure that the ball of each lubrication fitting is properly seated. Reinstall a lubrication fitting cap on each lubrication fitting. Perform grease replacement through attached pressure fittings (zerks) in accordance with the manufacturer's instructions.

Propeller Overhaul

Propeller overhaul should be accomplished at the maximum hours or calendar time limit, whichever occurs first. Upon

Figure 7-41. *Servicing air charge in propeller.*

Figure 7-42. *Lubricating propeller bearings.*

receipt for overhaul, prepare a document that tracks the propeller components throughout the overhaul process. Research all applicable ADs, current specifications, and manufacturers' SBs for incorporation during the overhaul process. Double check the serial number and make notes on the work order regarding the general condition in which the propeller was received. As you disassemble and clean the unit, perform a preliminary inspection on all related parts. Record those revealing discrepancies requiring rework or replacement in the overhaul record by part number, along with the reason for the required action. Discard all threaded fasteners during disassembly and, with a few exceptions permitted by the manufacturer, replace with new components. Many specialized tools and fixtures are required in the disassembly and proper reassembly of propellers. These tools are generally model specific and range from massive 15-foot torque adapter bars and 100-ton presses down to tiny dowel pin alignment devices. Dimensionally inspect components that are subject to wear to the manufacturer's specifications. After passing inspection, anodize aluminum parts and cadmium plate steel parts for maximum protection against corrosion.

The Hub

Strip nonferrous hubs and components of paint and anodize and inspect for cracks using a liquid penetrant inspection (LPI) procedure. Etch, rinse, dry, and then immerse the parts in a fluorescent penetrant solution. After soaking in the penetrant, rinse them again and blow dry. Then, apply developer, which draws any penetrant caught in cracks or defects to the surface. Under an ultraviolet inspection lamp, the penetrant clearly identifies the flaw. Certain models of hubs are also eddy-current inspected around critical, high-stress areas. Eddy-current testing passes an electrical current through a conductive material that, when disturbed by a crack or other flaw, causes a fluctuation on a meter or CRT display. This method of inspection can detect flaws that are below the surface of the material and not exposed to the eye. Magnetic particle inspection (MPI) is used to locate flaws in steel parts. The steel parts of the propeller are magnetized by passing a strong electrical current through them. A suspension of fluorescent iron oxide powder and solvent is spread over the parts. While magnetized, the particles within the fluid on the parts surface immediately align themselves with the discontinuity. When examined under black light, the crack or fault shows as a bright fluorescent line.

The first step in blade overhaul is the precise measurement of blade width, thickness, face alignment, blade angles, and length. Then, record the measurements on each blade's inspection record and check against the minimum acceptable overhaul specifications established by the manufacturer. Blade overhaul involves surface grinding and repitching, if necessary. Occasionally, blade straightening is also required. The manufacturer's specification dictates certain allowable limits within which a damaged blade may be cold straightened and returned to airworthy condition. Specialized tooling and precision measuring equipment permit pitch changes or corrections of less than one-tenth of one degree. To ensure accuracy, take frequent face alignment and angle measurements during the repair process. Precision hand grind the blade airfoil to remove all corrosion, scratches, and surface flaws. After completely removing all stress risers and faults, take final blade measurements and record on each blade's inspection record. Balance and match the propeller blades, and anodize and paint them for long-term corrosion protection.

Prop Reassembly

When both the hubs and the blades have completed the overhaul process, the propeller is ready for final assembly. Recheck part numbers with the manufacturer's specifications. Lubricate and install the parts per each unit's particular overhaul manual. After final assembly, check both high- and low-pitch blade angles on constant-speed propellers for proper operation and leaks by cycling the propeller with air pressure through its blade angle range. Then, check the assembled propeller for static balance. If necessary, place weights on the hub areas of each "light" blade socket to bring about its proper balance. These weights should be considered part of the basic hub assembly and should not be moved during subsequent dynamic balancing to the engine. As with most aircraft components, all of the hardware on the propeller assembly must be safety wired, unless secured by self-locking devices. Then, the final inspector fills out and signs maintenance release tags reflecting the work accomplished, applicable ADs, and all incorporated service documents. These documents certify that the major repairs and/or alterations that have been made meet established standards and that the propeller is approved for return to service. All minor repairs and minor alterations on propellers must be accomplished by a certified repair station, an airframe and powerplant technician (A&P), or a person working under the direct supervision of such a technician or an appropriately rated air carrier. Major repairs or alterations, including the overhaul of controllable pitch propellers, must be done by an appropriately rated repair station, manufacturer, or air carrier.

Troubleshooting Propellers

Some brief examples of troubleshooting problems and possible causes are provided in the following subsections. Always refer to the correct manual for actual information on troubleshooting.

Hunting and Surging

Hunting is characterized by a cyclic variation in engine speed above and below desired speed. Surging is characterized by a large increase/decrease in engine speed, followed by a return to set speed after one or two occurrences. If propeller is hunting, an appropriately licensed repair facility should check:

1. Governor,
2. Fuel control, and
3. Synchrophaser or synchronizer.

Engine Speed Varies With Flight Attitude (Airspeed)

Small variances in engine speed are normal and are no cause for concern. An increase in engine speed while descending or increasing airspeed with a nonfeathering propeller could be.

A. The governor not increasing oil volume in the propeller.

B. Engine transfer bearing leaking excessively.

C. Excessive friction in blade bearings or pitch changing mechanism.

Failure to Feather or Feathers Slowly

Failure to feather or slow feathering of the propeller requires the FAA-certificated A&P technician to:

1. Refer to the air charge section in the maintenance manual if the air charge is lost or low.
2. Check for proper function and rigging of propeller/ governor control linkage.
3. Check the governor drain function.
4. Check the propeller for misadjustment or internal corrosion (usually in blade bearings or pitch change mechanism) that results in excessive friction. This must be performed at an appropriately licensed propeller repair facility.

Turboprop Engines and Propeller Control Systems

Turboprop engines are used for many single, twin, and commuter aircraft. *[Figure 7-43]* Smaller turboprop engines, such as the PT-6, are used on single and twin engine designs; the power ranges from 500 to 2,000 shaft horsepower. *[Figure 7-44]* Large commuter aircraft use turboprop engines, such as the P&W 150 and AE2100 that can deliver up to 5,000 shaft horsepower to power mid-sized to large turboprop aircraft. *[Figure 7-45]* The turboprop propeller is operated by a gas turbine engine through a reduction-gear assembly. It has proved to be an extremely efficient power source. The combination of propeller, reduction-gear assembly, and turbine engine is referred to as a turboprop powerplant.

Figure 7-43. *Turboprop commuter.*

The turbofan engine produces thrust directly; the turboprop engine produces thrust indirectly because the compressor and turbine assembly furnishes torque to a propeller, producing the major portion of the propulsive force that drives the aircraft. The turboprop fuel control and the propeller governor are connected and operate in coordination with each other.

Figure 7-44. *Pratt & Whitney PT6 engine.*

Figure 7-45. *Pratt & Whitney 150 turboprop engine.*

The power lever directs a signal from the cockpit to the fuel control for a specific amount of power from the engine. The fuel control and the propeller governor together establish the correct combination of rpm, fuel flow, and propeller blade angle to create sufficient propeller thrust to provide the desired power.

The propeller control system is divided into two types of control: one for flight and one for ground operation. For flight, the propeller blade angle and fuel flow for any given power lever setting are governed automatically according to a predetermined schedule. Below the "flight idle" power lever position, the coordinated rpm blade angle schedule becomes incapable of handling the engine efficiently. Here, the ground handling range, referred to as the beta range, is encountered. In the beta range of the throttle quadrant, the propeller blade angle is not governed by the propeller governor, but is controlled by the power lever position. When the power lever is moved below the start position, the propeller pitch is reversed to provide reverse thrust for rapid deceleration of the aircraft after landing.

A characteristic of the turboprop is that changes in power are not related to engine speed, but to turbine inlet temperature. During flight, the propeller maintains a constant engine speed. This speed is known as the 100 percent rated speed of the engine, and it is the design speed at which most power and best overall efficiency can be obtained. Power changes are effected by changing the fuel flow. An increase in fuel flow causes an increase in turbine inlet temperature and a corresponding increase in energy available at the turbine. The turbine absorbs more energy and transmits it to the propeller in the form of torque. The propeller, in order to absorb the increased torque, increases blade angle, thus maintaining constant engine rpm with added thrust.

Reduction Gear Assembly

The function of the reduction gear assembly is to reduce the high rpm from the engine to a propeller rpm that can be maintained without exceeding the maximum propeller tip speed (speed of sound). Most reduction gear assemblies use a planetary gear reduction. *[Figure 7-46]* Additional power takeoffs are available for propeller governor, oil pump, and other accessories. A propeller brake is often incorporated into the gearbox. The propeller brake is designed to prevent the propeller from windmilling when it is feathered in flight, and to decrease the time for the propeller to come to a complete stop after engine shutdown.

Figure 7-46. *Reduction gearbox.*

Turbo-Propeller Assembly

The turbo-propeller provides an efficient and flexible means of using the power of the engine at any condition in flight (alpha range). *[Figure 7-47]* For ground handling and reversing (beta range), the propeller can be operated to provide either zero or negative thrust. The major subassemblies of the propeller assembly are the barrel, dome, low-pitch stop assembly, overspeed governor, pitch control unit, auxiliary pump, feather and unfeather valves, torque motor, spinner, deice timer, beta feedback assembly, and propeller electronic control. Modern turboprop engines use dual Full Authority Digital Engine Control (FADEC) to control both engine and propeller. The spinner assembly is a cone-shaped configuration that mounts on the propeller and encloses the dome and barrel to reduce drag.

Figure 7-47. *Turboprop propeller.*

The synchrophasing system is designed to maintain a preset angular relationship between the designated master propeller and the slave propellers. Propeller operation is controlled by a mechanical linkage from the cockpit-mounted power lever and the emergency engine shutdown handle (if the aircraft is provided with one) to the coordinator, which, in turn, is linked to the propeller control input lever. Newer designs use electronic throttle control that is linked to the FADEC controller.

Turbo-propeller control assemblies have a feathering system that feather the propeller when the engine is shut down in flight. The propeller can also be unfeathered during flight, if the engine needs to be started again. Propeller control systems for large turboprop engines differ from smaller engines because they are dual acting, which means that hydraulic pressure is used to increase and decrease propeller blade angle. *[Figure 7-48]*

Pratt and Whitney PT6 Hartzell Propeller System

The PT6 Hartzell propeller system incorporates three-, four-, or six-bladed propellers made of aluminum or composite materials. It is a constant-speed, feathering, reversing propeller system using a single-acting governor. Oil from the propeller governor feeds into the propeller shaft and to the servo piston via the oil transfer sleeve mounted on the propeller shaft. *[Figure 7-49]* As oil pressure increases, the servo piston is pushed forward and the feather spring is compressed. Servo piston movement is transmitted to the propeller blade collars via a system of levers. When oil pressure is decreased, the return spring and counterweights force the oil out of the servo piston and change the blade pitch to a high pitch position. An increase in oil pressure drives the blades towards low pitch.

Engine oil is supplied to the governor from the engine oil supply. A gear pump, mounted at the base of the governor, increases the flow of oil going to the constant speed unit (CSU) relief valve. When the oil pressure reaches the desired

Figure 7-48. *Propeller control system schematic.*

level, the relief valve opens to maintain the governor oil pressure. When the speed selected by the pilot is reached, the flyweight force equals the spring tension of the speeder spring. The governor flyweights are then on speed. When the engine output power is increased, the power turbines tend to increase speed. The flyweights in the CSU sense this acceleration and the flyweights go into an overspeed condition because of the increase centrifugal force. This force causes the control valve to move up and restrict oil flow to the propeller dome. *[Figure 7-50]* The feathering spring increases the propeller pitch to maintain the selected speed. Reducing power causes an under-speed of the flyweights, downward movement of the control valve, more oil in propeller dome, resulting in a lower pitch to control propeller speed. The propeller governor houses an electro-magnetic coil, which is used to match the rpm of both propellers during cruise. An aircraft supplied synchrophaser unit controls this function.

At low power, the propeller and governor flyweights do not turn fast enough to compress the speeder spring. *[Figure 7-51]* In this condition, the control valve moves down and high pressure oil pushes the dome forward moving the blades towards low pitch. Any further movement pulls the beta rod and slip ring forward. The forward motion of the slip ring is transmitted to the beta valve via the beta lever and the carbon block. Forward movement of the beta valve stops the oil supply to the propeller. This prevents the blade angles from going any lower. This is the primary blade angle (PBA) and is the minimum blade angle allowed for flight operation. From this point, the propeller is in the beta mode. If the engine power is reduced when the propeller is at the primary blade angle, the propeller speed decreases since the blade angle does not change.

The lock-pitch solenoid valve prevents the propeller from going into reverse or below the primary blade angle in the event of a beta system malfunction in flight. The solenoid is energized by a switch (airframe supplied) mechanically connected to the propeller slip-ring linkage via a second carbon block. As oil pressure leaks off around the propeller shaft oil transfer sleeve, the blade angle slowly drifts back toward high pitch. This deactivates the low pitch solenoid valve and restores the oil supply to the propeller servo. The low pitch solenoid valve cycles (close/open) as backup to the beta valve function. Moving the power lever backwards causes the reversing cam and cable to move the beta valve backward, allowing more oil to flow into the propeller dome, and causing the blades to go towards reverse pitch. *[Figure 7-52]*

As the blades move to reverse, the dome pulls the slip ring forward and moves the beta valve outward, restricting the oil flow. This stops the blade movement toward reverse. To

Figure 7-49. *Pitch change mechanism.*

obtain more reverse thrust, move the power lever back more to reset the beta valve inward, and repeat the process. Move the reset arm on the CSU rearward by the interconnecting rod at the same time the blade angle moves toward reverse. This causes the reset lever and reset post to move down in the CSU, bringing the reset lever closer to the speeder spring cup. As propeller speed increases due to the increase in engine power, the governor flyweights begin to move outwards. Since the reset lever is closer to the speeder spring cup, the cup contacts the reset lever before the flyweights would normally reach the on-speed position (95 percent propeller speed instead of 100 percent). As the reset lever is pushed up by the flyweights/speeder spring cup, the Py air bleeds from the fuel control unit (FCU) which lowers the fuel flow, engine power, and thus propeller speed. In reverse, propeller speed remains 5 percent below the selected propeller speed so that the control valve remains fully open, and only the beta valve controls the oil flow to the propeller dome.

In this mode, the propeller speed is no longer controlled by changing the blade angle. It is now controlled by limiting engine power. Bringing the propeller lever to the feather position causes the speed selection lever on the CSU to push the feathering valve plunger and allows propeller servo oil to dump into the reduction gearbox sump. The pressure loss in the propeller hub causes the feathering spring and the propeller counterweights to feather the propeller. In the event of a propeller overspeed not controlled by the propeller overspeed governor (oil governor), the flyweights in the propeller governor move outward until the speeder spring cup contacts the reset lever. *[Figure 7-53]* The movement of the reset lever around its pivot point opens the Py air passage. Py bleeds into the reduction gearbox limiting the fuel supply to the engine. This prevents the propeller/power turbines from accelerating beyond 106 percent rpm.

The oil overspeed governor houses a set of flyweights connected to a control valve that is driven by a beveled gear mounted on the propeller shaft. *[Figure 7-54]* The flyweight's centrifugal force is acting against two springs: a speeder spring and a reset spring. When the propeller speed reaches a specified limit (4 percent over maximum propeller speed), the governor flyweights lift the control valve and bleed off propeller servo oil into the reduction gearbox sump, causing the blade angle to increase. An increase in blade pitch puts more load on the engine and slows down the propeller. To

Figure 7-50. *Governing mode.*

test the unit, the speed reset solenoid is activated and servo oil pressure pushes against the reset piston to cancel the effect of the reset spring. With less spring tension acting on the flyweights, the overspeed governor can be tested at speeds lower than maximum.

On twin installation, a second solenoid valve is mounted on the overspeed governor and is used in conjunction with the aircraft autofeather system. The system is switched on for takeoff and, in the event of an engine malfunction, energizes the solenoid valve to dump propeller servo oil into the reduction gearbox sump. The feathering spring and propeller counterweights move the blade quickly to feather.

Hamilton Standard Hydromatic Propellers

Many of the hydromatic propellers are used with older type aircraft involved in cargo operations. A hydromatic propeller has a double-acting governor that uses oil pressure on both sides of the propeller piston. Many larger turboprop systems also use this type of system. The governors are similar in construction and principle of operation in normal constant-speed systems. The major difference is in the pitch-changing mechanism. In the hydromatic propeller, no counterweights are used, and the moving parts of the mechanism are completely enclosed. Oil pressure and the centrifugal twisting moment of the blades are used together to turn the blades to a lower angle. The main advantages of the hydromatic propeller are the large blade angle range and the feathering and reversing features.

This propeller system is a double-acting hydraulic propeller system in which the hydraulic pressure (engine oil pressure) on one piston dome is used against governor oil pressure on the other side of the piston. These two opposing hydraulic forces are used to control and change blade angle or pitch. Although hydromatic propeller systems are very old, some are still used on radial engines. Larger new turboprop systems also use this opposing hydraulic force and double-acting governor systems.

Figure 7-51. *Beta mode forward operation.*

The distributor valve or engine-shaft-extension assembly provides oil passages for governor or auxiliary oil to the inboard side of the piston and for engine oil to the outboard side. During unfeathering operation, the distributor shifts under auxiliary pressure and reverses these passages so that oil from the auxiliary pump flows to the outboard side of the piston and oil on the inboard side flows back to the engine. The engine-shaft-extension assembly is used with propellers that do not have feathering capabilities.

The hydromatic propeller *[Figure 7-55]* is composed of four major components:

1. The hub assembly,
2. The dome assembly,
3. The distributor valve assembly (for feathering on single-acting propellers) or engine-shaft-extension assembly (for nonfeathering or double-acting propellers), and
4. The anti-icing assembly.

The hub assembly is the basic propeller mechanism. It contains both the blades and the mechanical means for holding them in position. The blades are supported by the spider and retained by the barrel. Each blade is free to turn about its axis under the control of the dome assembly.

The dome assembly contains the pitch-changing mechanism for the blades. Its major components are the:

1. Rotating cam,
2. Fixed cam,
3. Piston, and
4. Dome shell.

When the dome assembly is installed in the propeller hub, the fixed cam remains stationary with respect to the hub. The rotating cam, which can turn inside the fixed cam, meshes with gear segments on the blades. The piston operates inside the dome shell and is the mechanism that converts engine and

Figure 7-52. *Beta mode reverse operation.*

governor oil pressure into forces that act through the cams to turn propeller blades.

Principles of Operation

The pitch-changing mechanism of hydromatic propellers is a mechanical-hydraulic system in which hydraulic forces acting on a piston are transformed into mechanical twisting forces acting on the blades. Linear movement of the piston is converted to rotary motion by a cylindrical cam. A bevel gear on the base of the cam mates with bevel gear segments attached to the butt ends of the blades, thereby turning the blades. This blade pitch-changing action can be understood by studying the schematic in *Figure 7-56*.

The centrifugal force acting on a rotating blade includes a component force that tends to move the blade toward low pitch. As shown in *Figure 7-56*, a second force, engine oil pressure, is supplied to the outboard side of the propeller piston to assist in moving the blade toward low pitch.

Propeller governor oil, taken from the engine oil supply and boosted in pressure by the engine-driven propeller governor, is directed against the inboard side of the propeller piston. It acts as the counterforce, which can move the blades toward higher pitch. By metering this high-pressure oil to, or draining it from, the inboard side of the propeller piston by means of the constant-speed control unit, the force toward high pitch can balance and control the two forces toward low pitch. In this way, the propeller blade angle is regulated to maintain a selected rpm.

The basic propeller control forces acting on the Hamilton Standard propeller are centrifugal twisting force and high pressure oil from the governor. The centrifugal force acting on each blade of a rotating propeller includes a component force that results in a twisting moment about the blade center line that tends, at all times, to move the blade toward low pitch. Governor pump output oil is directed by the governor to either side of the propeller piston. The oil on the side of the piston opposite this high-pressure oil returns to the intake

Figure 7-53. *Nf overspeed governor.*

side of the governor pump and is used over again. Engine oil at engine supply pressure does not enter the propeller directly but is supplied only to the governor. During constant-speed operations, the double-acting governor mechanism sends oil to one side or the other of the piston as needed to keep the speed at a specified setting.

Feathering Operation

A typical hydromatic propeller feathering installation is shown in *Figure 7-57*. When the feathering push-button switch is depressed, the low current circuit is established from the battery through the push-button holding coil and from the battery through the solenoid relay. As long as the circuit remains closed, the holding coil keeps the push button in the depressed position. Closing the solenoid establishes the high current circuit from the battery to the feathering motor pump unit. The feathering pump picks up engine oil from the oil supply tank, boosts its pressure, if necessary, to the relief valve setting of the pump, and supplies it to the governor high-pressure transfer valve connection. Auxiliary oil entering the high-pressure transfer valve connection shifts the governor transfer valve, which hydraulically disconnects the governor from the propeller and at the same time opens the propeller governor oil line to auxiliary oil. The oil flows through the engine transfer rings, through the propeller shaft governor oil passage, through the distributor valve port, between lands, and finally to the inboard piston end by way of the valve inboard outlet.

The distributor valve does not shift during the feathering operation. It merely provides an oil passageway to the inboard piston end for auxiliary oil and the outboard piston end for engine oil. The same conditions described for underspeed operation exist in the distributor valve, except that oil at auxiliary pressure replaces drain oil at the inboard end of the land and between lands. The distributor-valve spring is backed up by engine oil pressure, which means that at all times the pressure differential required to move the piston is identical with that applied to the distributor valve.

The propeller piston moves outboard under the auxiliary oil pressure at a speed proportional to the rate the oil is supplied. This piston motion is transmitted through the piston rollers operating in the oppositely inclined cam tracks of the fixed cam and the rotating cam, and is converted by the bevel gears into the blade-twisting moment. Only during feathering or unfeathering is the low mechanical advantage portion of the cam tracks used. (The low mechanical advantage portion lies

Figure 7-54. *Propeller overspeed governor.*

between the break and the outboard end of the track profile.) Oil at engine pressure, displaced from the outboard piston end, flows through the distributor valve outboard inlet, past the outboard end of the valve land, through the valve port, into the propeller shaft engine oil passage, and is finally delivered into the engine lubricating system. Thus, the blades move toward the full high-pitch (or feathered) angle.

Having reached the full-feathered position, further movement of the mechanism is prevented by contact between the high-angle stop ring in the base of the fixed cam and the stop lugs set in the teeth of the rotating cam. The pressure in the inboard piston end now increases rapidly, and upon reaching a set pressure, the electric cutout switch automatically opens. This cutout pressure is less than that required to shift the distributor valve.

Opening the switch deenergizes the holding coil and releases the feathering push-button control switch. Release of this switch breaks the solenoid relay circuit, which shuts off the feathering pump motor. The pressures in both the inboard and outboard ends of the piston drop to zero, and, since all the forces are balanced, the propeller blades remain in the feathered position. Meanwhile, the governor high-pressure transfer valve has shifted to its normal position as soon as the pressure in the propeller governor line drops below that required to hold the valve open.

Unfeathering Operation

To unfeather a hydromatic propeller, depress and hold in the feathering switch push-button control switch. As in the case of feathering a propeller, the low-current control circuits from the battery through the holding coil and from the battery through the solenoid are completed when the solenoid closes. The high-current circuit from the battery starts the motor-pump unit, and oil is supplied at a high pressure to the governor transfer valve.

Auxiliary oil entering through the high-pressure transfer valve connection shifts the governor transfer valve and

Figure 7-55. *Typical hydromatic propeller installation.*

disconnects the governor from the propeller line; in the same operation, auxiliary oil is admitted. The oil flows through the engine oil transfer rings, through the propeller shaft governor oil passage, and into the distributor valve assembly.

When the unfeathering operation begins, the piston is in the extreme outboard position. The oil enters the inboard piston end of the cylinder by way of the distributor valve inboard outlet. As the pressure on the inboard end of the piston increases, the pressure against the distributor valve land builds up. When the pressure becomes greater than the combined opposing force of the distributor valve spring and the oil pressure behind this spring, the valve shifts. Once the valve shifts, the passages through the distributor valve assembly to the propeller are reversed. A passage is opened between lands and through a port to the outboard piston end by way of the distributor valve outlet. As the piston moves inboard under the auxiliary pump oil pressure, oil is displaced from the inboard piston end through the inlet ports between the valve lands, into the propeller shaft engine oil lands, and into the propeller shaft engine oil passage where it is discharged into the engine lubricating system. At the same time, the pressure at the cutout switch increases and the switch opens. However, the circuit to the feathering pump and motor unit remains complete as long as the feathering switch is held in.

7-40

Figure 7-56. *Diagram of hydromatic propeller operational forces.*

With the inboard end of the propeller piston connected to drain and auxiliary pressure flowing to the outboard end of the piston, the piston moves inboard, unfeathering the blades. As the blades are unfeathered, they begin to windmill and assist the unfeathering operation by the added force toward low pitch brought about by the centrifugal twisting moment. When the engine speed has increased to approximately 1,000 rpm, the operator shuts off the feathering pump motor. The pressure in the distributor valve and at the governor transfer valve decreases, allowing the distributor valve to shift under the action of the governor high-pressure transfer valve spring. This action reconnects the governor with the propeller and establishes the same oil passages through the distributor valve that are used during constant-speed and feathering operations.

Setting the Propeller Governor

The propeller governor incorporates an adjustable stop that limits the maximum speed at which the engine can run. As soon as the takeoff rpm is reached, the propeller moves off the low-pitch stop. The larger propeller blade angle increases the load on the engine, thus maintaining the prescribed maximum engine speed. At the time of propeller, propeller governor, or engine installation, the following steps are normally taken to ensure that the powerplant obtains takeoff rpm. During ground runup, move the throttle to takeoff position and note the resultant rpm and manifold pressure. If the rpm obtained is higher or lower than the takeoff rpm prescribed in the manufacturer's instructions, reset the adjustable stop on the governor until the prescribed rpm is obtained.

Figure 7-57. *Typical feathering installation.*

Chapter 8
Engine Removal and Replacement

Introduction

Procedures for removing or installing an aircraft engine usually vary widely with the type of aircraft and the type of engine. Thus, no single list of instructions can be provided as a guideline for all engines. Because of the many types of engine and aircraft installations and the large number of design variations within each type or category, representative examples have been selected to illustrate the most typical installation procedures for reciprocating, turboprop, and turbofan engines. There are some common tasks that must be accomplished when replacing an aircraft engine. Most engines require disconnecting and reconnecting electrical, hydraulic, fuel supply, intake and exhaust air path components, engine controls, and engine mounting connections to the airframe.

Reciprocating engines and gas turbine engines are used in this chapter to describe and represent general and typical procedures for engine buildup, removal, preservation, storage, and installation. Although these two types of engines have some common areas, each procedure has been included to ensure adequate coverage of the engines used in both heavy and light aircraft. It should be emphasized that while procedures for specific engines and aircraft are included in this chapter, many pertinent or mandatory references have been omitted because of their irrelevance to a general discussion. For this reason, always reference the applicable manufacturer's instructions before performing any phase of engine removal or installation.

Reasons for Removal of Reciprocating Engines

The following paragraphs outline the most common reasons for removing and replacing an engine. Information to aid in determining engine conditions that require removal is included; however, in every case, consult applicable manufacturer's instructions as the final authority in establishing the basis for engine replacement.

Engine or Component Lifespan Exceeded

Engine life is dependent upon such factors as operational use, the quality of manufacture or overhaul, the type of aircraft in which the engine is installed, the kind of operation being carried out, and the degree to which maintenance is accomplished. Thus, the manufacturer sets engine removal times. Based on service experience, it is possible to establish a maximum expected time before overhaul (TBO) or span of time within which an engine needs to be overhauled. Regardless of condition, an engine should be removed when it has accumulated the recommended maximum allowable time since the last overhaul.

Sudden Stoppage

Sudden stoppage is a very rapid and complete stoppage of the engine. It can be caused by engine seizure or by one or more of the propeller blades striking an object in such a way that revolutions per minute (rpm) goes to zero in less than one complete revolution of the propeller. Sudden stoppage may occur under such conditions as complete and rapid collapse of the landing gear, nosing over of the aircraft, or crash landing. Sudden stoppage can cause internal damage, such as cracked propeller gear teeth, gear train damage, crankshaft counterweights becoming detuned or misalignment, or damaged propeller bearings. When sudden stoppage occurs, the engine usually requires replacement or disassembly and inspection as per manufacturer's instructions.

Sudden Reduction in Speed

Sudden reduction in engine speed can occur when one or more of the propeller blades strike an object at a low engine rpm. After impact, the foreign object is cleared and the engine recovers rpm and continues to run unless stopped to prevent further damage. While taxiing an aircraft, sudden reduction in speed can occur when the propeller strikes a foreign object, such as a raised section in the runway, a tool box, or a portion of another airplane. When the accident occurs at high engine rpm, shocks are much more severe. When sudden reduction in rpm occurs, the following procedure can be used as a general rule, but you must comply with the manufacturer's information.

Make a thorough external inspection of the engine mount, crankcase, and nose section to determine whether any parts have been damaged. If damage is found that cannot be corrected by line maintenance, remove the engine. Internal components can be damaged, especially counter weights on the crankshaft.

Remove the engine oil screens or filters. Inspect them for the presence of metal particles. Remove the engine sump plugs, drain the oil into a clean container, strain it through a clean cloth, and check the cloth and the strained oil for metal particles. Heavy metal particles in the oil indicate a definite engine failure, and the engine must be removed. However, if the metal particles present are similar to fine filings, continue the inspection of the engine to determine its serviceability. If there are no heavy metal particles in the engine oil, check again for metal in the oil system after operating the engine. Metal in the screens is a sign that the bearings have been compromised and are in the process of failing.

Remove the propeller and check the crankshaft, or the propeller drive shaft on reduction-gear engines, for misalignment. Clamp a test indicator to the nose section of the engine. Use the dial-indicator that has $1/1,000$-inch graduations. Remove the spark plugs from all the cylinders. Then, turn the crankshaft, and observe if the crankshaft, propeller shaft, or flange turns straight without any bending taking place. If there is an excessive runout (bend in the crankshaft or propeller flange) reading at the crankshaft or propeller-drive shaft at the front seat location, the engine should be removed. Consult the applicable manufacturer's instructions for permissible limits. If the crankshaft or propeller drive shaft runout does not exceed these limits, install a serviceable propeller. Make an additional check by tracking the propeller at the tip in the same plane, perpendicular to the axis of rotation, to assure that blade track tolerance is within the prescribed limits.

Start the engine to see if operation is smooth, without vibration, and the power output adequate. If the engine operates properly during this ground check, shut the engine down and repeat the inspection for metal particles in the oil system.

Metal Particles in the Oil

Metal particles in the engine oil screens or the magnetic chip detectors are generally an indication of partial internal failure of the engine. Carbon tends to break loose from the interior of the engine in rock-like pieces that have the appearance of metal. It is necessary to consider these possibilities when foreign particles are found on the engine oil screens or magnetic chip detectors.

Before removing an engine for suspected internal failure, as indicated by foreign material on the oil screens or oil sump plugs, determine if the foreign particles are ferrous metal by placing them close to a magnet to see if they are magnetic. If the material is not magnetic, it is not attracted by the magnet. Any ferrous metal in the oil screens is cause for concern. Very small amounts of nonferrous metal, especially after major engine maintenance, can sometimes be normal. If the particles are metal, determine the probable extent of internal damage. For example, if only small particles are found that are similar in nature to filings, drain the oil system, and refill it. Then, ground-run the engine and reinspect the oil screens and magnetic chip detectors. If no further evidence of foreign material is found, continue the engine in service or per the manufacturer's instructions. However, engine performance should be closely observed for any indication of difficulty or internal failure.

Spectrometric Oil Analysis Engine Inspection Program

Spectrometric oil analysis program allows an oil sample to be analyzed and searched for the presence of minute metallic elements. Due to oil circulation throughout an aircraft engine, every lubricant that is in service contains microscopic particles of metallic elements called wear metals. As the engine operates over a certain amount of time, the oil picks up very small particles that stay suspended in the oil. Oil analysis programs identify and measure these particles in parts per million (PPM) by weight. The analyzed elements are grouped into categories, such as wear metals and additives, and their measurement in PPM provides the data that expert analysts can use as one of many tools to determine the engine's condition. If certain metals have an increase in PPM, it can be a signal of component wear or pending failure of the engine. The amount of wear metals is recorded and noted each time a sample is taken. If the amount of wear metals increases beyond a normal rate, then the operator can be notified quickly so repair, a recommended specific maintenance procedure, or inspection can be ordered.

The advantage of oil analysis is an increase in safety by noticing an engine problem before engine failure. It also saves money by finding engine problems before they become large problems or complete engine failure. This procedure can be used for both turbine and reciprocating engines. Oil analysis can be used to diagnose impending engine failure, and would be a reason for removing the engine from the aircraft and sending it to overhaul.

Turbine Engine Condition Monitoring Programs

Many turbine engines are monitored by an engine condition program that helps determine the health of the engine in service. This can also be called trend analysis performance monitoring, but it consists mainly of monitoring certain engine parameters daily and watching for trend shifts or changes in the engine parameters. A shift in key parameters (change over time) could be a warning that the engine has serious internal deterioration and should be overhauled.

Engine Operational Problems

Engines are usually removed when there are consistent engine operational problems. Engine operational problems generally include, but are not limited to, one or more of the following conditions:

1. Excessive engine vibration; this is especially true with turbine engines.

2. Backfiring, or misfiring, either consistent or intermittent due to valve train or other mechanical defect in reciprocating engines.

3. Turbine engines that exceed normal operating parameters or life limited components exceeding maximum time in service or cycles.

4. Low power output, generally caused by low compression, with reciprocating engines and internal engine deterioration or damage with turbines.

General Procedures for Engine Removal and Installation

Preparation of Engines for Installation

After the decision has been made to remove an engine, the preparation of the replacement engine must be considered. The maintenance procedures and methods used vary widely. Commercial operators, whose maintenance operations require the most efficient and expeditious replacement of aircraft engines, usually rely on a system that utilizes the quick-engine-change assembly (QECA), also sometimes referred to as the engine power package. The QECA is essentially a powerplant and the necessary accessories installed in the engine.

Other operators of aircraft equipped with reciprocating engines sometimes use a different replacement method in these repair facilities because engine changes often occur at random intervals. Such replacement engines may be partially or wholly built up with the necessary accessories and subassemblies, or they may be stored as received from the manufacturer in packing boxes, cases, or cans and are uncrated and built up for installation only when needed to replace an engine.

QECA Buildup Method for Changing of Engines

Because the QECA system is most commonly used with large turbine engines used in the airlines, such engines are used to describe QECA buildup and installation procedures. Many of these procedures are applicable to all other methods of engine buildup and installation.

The following study of QECA buildup is not designed to outline procedures to follow in a practical application; always use those recommended by the manufacturer. The procedures included in this chapter provide a logical sequence in following a QECA and its components through the stages of a typical buildup to gain a better understanding of units and systems interconnection. The components of a QECA are illustrated in *Figure 8-1*. As shown, the QECA consists of several units. On many aircraft, the engines are mounted in streamlined housings called nacelles that extend from the wings. These nacelles are divided into two main sections: wing nacelle and engine nacelle. The wing nacelle is that portion of the nacelle that is attached to the wing structure. The engine nacelle is that portion of the nacelle that is constructed separately from the wing. Also, the wing nacelles normally contain lines and units of the oil, fuel, and hydraulic systems, as well as linkages and other controls for the operation of the engine.

Figure 8-1. *Open cowling view of a typical power package.*

The firewall is usually the foremost bulkhead of the engine nacelle and differs from most other aircraft bulkheads in that it is constructed of stainless steel or some other fire-resistant material. *[Figure 8-2]* The primary purpose of the firewall is to confine any engine fire to the engine nacelle. It also provides a mounting surface for units within the engine nacelle and a point of disconnect for lines, linkages, and electrical wiring that are routed between the engine and the aircraft. Without this firewall, an engine fire would have ready access to the interior of the aircraft. Since the consequences of an engine fire are obvious, the necessity of sealing all unused openings in the firewall cannot be overstressed.

Figure 8-2. *Typical firewall with components mounted on it.*

An aircraft engine and its accessories that have been in storage must undergo careful depreservation and inspection before they may be installed in an aircraft. This involves more than removing an engine from its container and bolting it to the aircraft. If the engine is stored in a pressurized metal container, the air valve should be opened to bleed off the air pressure. Depending upon the size of the valve, the air pressure should bleed off in somewhat less than 30 minutes.

Prepare the container for opening by removing the bolts that hold the two sections together. Then, attach a hoist to the "hoisting points" and lift the top section clear of the container and place it away from the work area. If the engine is installed in a wooden shipping case, it is necessary to carefully break the seal of the protective envelope and fold it down around the engine. Remove the dehydrating agent or desiccant bags and the humidity indicator from the outside of the engine. Also, remove and set safely aside any accessories that are not installed on the engine but are mounted on a special stand or otherwise installed inside the protective envelope with the engine.

Depreservation of an Engine

After the engine has been secured to an engine stand, all covers must be removed from the points where the engine was sealed or closed with ventilatory covers, such as the engine breathers, exhaust outlets, and accessory mounting-pad cover plates. As each cover is removed, inspect the uncovered part of the engine for signs of corrosion. Also, as the dehydrator plugs are removed from each cylinder, make a very careful check of the walls of any cylinder for which the dehydrator plug color indicates an unsafe condition. Care is emphasized in the inspection of the cylinders, even if it is necessary to remove a cylinder.

On radial engines, the inside of the lower cylinders and intake pipes should be carefully checked for the presence of excessive corrosion-preventive compound that has drained from throughout the interior of the engine and settled at these low points. This excessive compound could cause the engine to become damaged from a hydraulic lock (also referred to as liquid-lock) when a starting attempt is made.

The check for excessive corrosion-preventive compound in the cylinders of reciprocating engines can be made as the dehydrator plugs are removed from each cylinder. Much of the compound drains from the spark plug holes of the lower cylinders of a radial engine when the dehydrator plugs are removed. But some of the mixture remains in the cylinder head below the level of the spark plug hole and can be removed with a hand pump. *[Figure 8-3]* A more positive method is to remove the lower intake pipes and open the intake valve of the cylinder by rotating the crankshaft. This latter method allows the compound to drain from the cylinder through the open intake valve. If excessive compound is present in an upper cylinder, it can be removed with a hand pump.

The oil screens should be removed from the engine and thoroughly washed in an approved solvent to remove all accumulations that could restrict the oil circulation and cause engine failure. After the screens are cleaned, immerse them in clean oil and then reinstall them in the engine.

When the cover has been removed from the intake area, the silica gel desiccant bags (used to remove moisture from the engine in storage) must be removed from the engine area. If the engine uses a propeller, remove the protective covering from the propeller shaft and wash all corrosion-preventive compounds from both the inside and outside surfaces of the shaft. Then, coat the propeller shaft lightly with engine oil. Turbine engines require the removal of several covers on many external areas on the engine.

As a final check, see that the exterior of the engine is clean. Usually a quantity of compound runs out of the engine when the dehydrator plugs and oil screens are removed. To clean the engine, spray it with an approved commercial solvent.

Inspection and Depreservation of Accessories

An engine's performance is no better than that of its accessories. Though the engine has been completely overhauled and is in top condition, any oversight or error in installing the accessories can result in improper engine operation or even irreparable damage to it.

Before depreserving any of the accessories enclosed with the engine, consult the storage data usually stenciled on the outside of the engine container or the records enclosed with the engine to determine how long the engine and accessories were in storage. Certain accessories that normally accompany an engine from overhaul are considered unsafe for use if their time in storage has exceeded a specified period. This time varies according to the limits prescribed by the manufacturer.

Any accessory that has been removed from an old engine that can be installed on the new one must be given a thorough inspection to determine its condition. This inspection includes a check for general condition, cleanliness, absence of corrosion, and absence of wear as evidenced by excessive play in the moving parts.

Some accessories must be replaced, regardless of their operating time, if the engine is being changed because of internal failure. Such accessories may have been contaminated by metal particles carried into their operating mechanisms by the engine oil that lubricates them.

Figure 8-3. *Draining corrosion preventive compound.*

Before installing any replacement accessory, check it visually for signs of corrosion and for freedom of operation. Always wipe the mounting pad, flange, and coupling clean before mounting the accessory, and install the proper gasket between the mounting pad and the accessory mounting flange. Lubricate the accessory drive shaft if so indicated in the manufacturer's instructions.

Inspection and Replacement of Powerplant External Units and Systems

The engine nacelle must be cleaned thoroughly before it is inspected. The design of an engine nacelle varies with different aircraft. Basically, it is a framework covered with removable cowling, in which the engine is mounted. This assembly is attached to the aircraft and incorporates an insulating firewall between the engine and the airframe. The interconnecting wiring, tubing, and linkages between the engine and its various systems and controls pass through the firewall.

Inspect the complete engine nacelle for condition of the framework and the sheet-metal cowling and riveted plates that cover the nacelle. The engine mounting frame assembly should be checked for any distortion of the steel tubing, such as bends, dents, flat spots, corrosion, or cracks. Use the dye penetrant inspection method to reveal a crack, porous area, or other defects.

The engine mounting bolts are usually checked for condition by magnetic particle inspection or other approved process. While the bolts are removed, the bolt holes should be checked for elongation caused by the movement of an improperly tightened bolt.

Check the outer surface of all exposed electrical wiring for breaks, chafing, or other damage. Also, check the security of crimped or soldered cable ends. In addition, carefully inspect connector plugs for overall condition. Any item that is damaged must be repaired or replaced, depending on the extent of the damage.

Before installing an engine, inspect all tubing in the nacelle for dents, nicks, scratches, chafing, or corrosion. Check all tubing carefully for indications of fatigue or excessive flatness caused by improper or accidental bending. Thoroughly inspect all hoses used in various engine systems. Weather checking (a cracking of the outside covering of the hose) sometimes penetrates to the hose reinforcement. Replace any length of hose that shows indications of the cover peeling or flaking, or has exposed fabric reinforcement. Replace a hose that shows indications of excessive cold flow. Cold flow is a term used to describe the deep and permanent impressions or cracks caused by hose clamp pressure.

Always replace a control rod if it is nicked or corroded deeply enough to affect its strength. If the corrosion cannot be removed by rubbing with steel wool, the pitting is too deep for safety.

On older aircraft, check the pulleys in the control system for freedom of movement. It is easy to spot a pulley that is not turning freely, for both it and the cable are worn from the cable sliding over the pulley instead of rolling free. The bearings of a pulley may be checked by inspecting the pulley for excessive play or wobble with the tension removed from the cable. The cable must also be inspected for corrosion and broken strands. Locate any broken strands by wiping the cable with a cloth.

Check bonding for fraying, loose attachment, and cleanness of terminal ends. The electrical resistance of the complete bond must not exceed the resistance values specified in the applicable manufacturer's instructions.

Inspect the exhaust stacks, collector ring, and tailpipe assembly for security, cracks, or excessive corrosion. Depending on the installation, these units, or parts of them, may be mounted on the engine before it is installed in the aircraft.

Check all air ducts for dents and for the condition of the fabric or rubber anti-chafing strips at the points where sections of duct are joined. The dents may be pounded out; the anti-chafing strips should be replaced if they are pulled loose from the duct or are worn to the point at which they no longer form a tight seal at the joint.

Thoroughly inspect the engine oil system, and perform any required special maintenance upon it before installing a replacement engine. If an engine is being changed at the end of its normal time in service, it is usually necessary only to flush the oil system; however, if an engine has been removed for internal failure, usually some units of the oil system must be replaced and others thoroughly cleaned and inspected.

If the engine has been removed because of internal failure, the oil tank is generally removed to permit thorough cleaning. Also, the oil cooler and temperature regulator must be removed and sent to a repair facility for overhaul. The vacuum pump pressure line and the oil separator in the vacuum system must also be removed, cleaned, and inspected. Internal failure also requires that the propeller governor and feathering pump mechanism be replaced if these units are operated by engine oil pressure.

Preparing the Engine for Removal

Before starting to work on the aircraft or reciprocating engine, always be sure that the magneto switch is in the off position. Aircraft engines can be started accidentally by turning the propeller if the magneto switch is on.

Check to see that all fuel selectors or solenoid-operated fuel shutoff valves are closed. The fuel selector valves are either manually or solenoid operated. If solenoid-operated fuel shutoff valves are installed, it may be necessary to turn the battery switch on before the valves can be closed, since the solenoid depends on electricity for operation. These valves close the fuel line at the firewall between the engine and the aircraft. After ensuring that all fuel to the engine is shut off, disconnect the battery to eliminate the possibility of a hot wire starting a fire. If it is anticipated that the aircraft will be out of service for more than 6 days, the battery is usually removed and taken to the battery shop and placed on charge.

Also, a few other preparations should be made before starting to work on the engine removal. First, make sure that there are enough fire extinguishers near at hand to meet any possible emergency. Check the seals on these extinguishers to be sure the extinguishers have not been discharged. Then, check the wheel chocks. If these are not in place, the aircraft can, and probably will, inch forward or back during some crucial operation. Also, if the aircraft has a tricycle landing gear, be sure that the tail is supported so that the aircraft cannot tip back when the weight of the engine is removed from the forward end. It is not necessary to support the tail on some multiengine aircraft if only one engine is to be removed. In addition, the landing gear shock struts can be deflated to prevent them from extending as the engine weight is removed from the aircraft.

After taking these necessary precautions, begin removing the cowling from around the engine. As it is removed, clean it and check for cracks so that the necessary repairs can be made while the engine change is in progress. Place all cowling that does not need repair on a rack where it can be readily found when the time comes to reinstall it on the new engine. After removing the cowling, the propeller should be removed for inspection or repair.

Draining the Engine

Place a large metal pan (drip pan) on the floor under the engine to catch any spilled mixture or oil. Next, secure a clean container in which to drain the oil or corrosion-preventive mixture. Place the container beneath the engine, open the drain valve, and allow the oil to drain. *Figure 8-4* shows the points at which a typical aircraft engine oil system is drained. Other points at which the oil system is drained can typically include the oil cooler, oil return line, and engine sumps. All valves, drains, and lines must remain open until the oil system has been completely drained. After draining the oil, reinstall all drain plugs and close all drain valves. Then, wipe all excess oil from around the drain points.

Figure 8-4. *Oil system drain points.*

Electrical Disconnects

Electrical disconnections are usually made at the engine firewall. When the basic engine is being removed, the electrical leads to such accessories as the starter and generators are disconnected at the units themselves. When disconnecting electrical leads, it is a good safety habit to disconnect the magnetos first and immediately ground them at some point on the engine or the assembly being removed. Most firewall disconnections of electrical conduit and cable are simplified by use of (Army/Navy) AN or (Military Standard) MS connectors. Each connector consists of two parts: a plug assembly and a receptacle assembly. To prevent accidental disconnection during airplane operation, the outlet is threaded to permit a knurled sleeve nut to be screwed to the outlet and then fastened with safety wire, if necessary.

A typical plug fitting assembly is shown in *Figure 8-5*. It also shows a typical junction box assembly, which is used as a disconnect on some aircraft engine installations. After the safety wire is broken, remove all of it from the sleeve nuts that hold the conduit to the junction boxes, as well as from the nuts on the connectors. Wrap moisture proof tape over the exposed ends of connectors to protect them from dirt and moisture. Also, do not leave long electrical cables or conduits hanging loose, since they may become entangled with some part of the aircraft while the engine is being hoisted. It is a good practice to coil all lengths of cable or flexible conduit neatly, and tie or tape them to some portion of the assembly being removed.

Figure 8-5. *Electrical connections.*

Disconnection of Engine Controls

The engine control rods and cables connect such units as the carburetor or fuel control throttle valve and the mixture control valve with their manually actuated control in the cockpit. The controls are sometimes disconnected by removing the turnbuckle that joins the cable ends. *[Figure 8-6]* A typical reciprocating engine control linkage consisting of a control rod attached to a bell crank is illustrated in *Figure 8-7*.

The control rod in the linkage shown has two rod-end assemblies, a clevis, and an eye screwed onto opposite ends. These rod-end assemblies determine the length of the control rod by the distance they are screwed onto it, and they are locked into position by cheek nuts. An antifriction bearing is usually mounted in the eye end of a rod. This eye is slipped over a bolt in the bell crank arm and is held in position by a castle nut safety with a cotter pin. The clevis rod end is slipped over the end of a bell crank arm, which also usually contains an antifriction bearing. A bolt is passed through the clevis and the bell crank eye, fastened with a castle nut, and safetied with a cotter pin.

Sometimes linkage assemblies do not include the antifriction bearings and are held in position only by a washer and cotter pin in the end of a clevis pin that passes through the bell crank and rod end. After the engine control linkages have been disconnected, the nuts and bolts should be replaced in the rod ends or bell crank arms to prevent their being lost. All control rods should be removed completely or tied back

Figure 8-6. *Engine control cable and turnbuckle assembly.*

Figure 8-7. *Engine control linkage assembly.*

8-8

to prevent them from being bent or broken if they are struck by the replacement engine or QECA as it is being hoisted.

Disconnection of Lines

The lines between units within the aircraft and the engine are either flexible hose or aluminum-alloy tubes joined by lengths of hose clamped to them. Lines that must withstand high pressure, such as hydraulic lines, are often made of stainless steel tubing.

Figure 8-8 shows the basic types of line disconnects. Most lines leading from a QECA are secured to a threaded fitting at the firewall by a sleeve nut around the tubing. Hoses are sometimes secured in this manner but may also be secured by a threaded fitting on the unit to which they lead, or by a hose clamp. The firewall fittings for some lines have a quick-disconnect fitting that contains a check valve to prevent the system from losing fluid when the line is disconnected. Metal tubing on some installations may also be disconnected at a point at which two lengths of it are joined together by a length of rubber hose. Such a disconnection is made by loosening the hose clamps and sliding the length of rubber hose over the length of tubing that remains on the aircraft. There may be some further variations in these types of disconnections, but they follow the same basic pattern.

Some type of a container should be used to collect any fuel, oil, or other fluid that may drain from the disconnected lines.

After the lines have drained, they should be immediately plugged or covered with moisture-proof tape to prevent foreign matter from entering them, as well as to prevent any accumulated fluid from dripping out.

Other Disconnections

The points at which the various air ducts are disconnected depend upon the engine and the aircraft in which it is installed. Usually, the air intake ducts and the exhaust system must be disconnected so the basic engine or the QECA can be removed. After the engine connections are free (except the engine mounts) and all the disconnections are entirely clear so they do not bind or become entangled, the engine can be prepared for hoisting.

Removing the Engine

If a QECA is being removed, the engine mount accompanies the engine. The mount remains on the aircraft if only the engine is being removed. Before the engine can be freed from its attachment points, a sling must be installed so the engine's weight can be supported with a hoist when the mounting bolts are removed.

Aircraft engines, or QECAs, have marked points for attaching a hoisting sling. The location of these attaching points varies according to the size and weight distribution of the engine. *Figure 8-9* shows a sling supporting an engine that has two attaching points. As a matter of safety, carefully inspect the sling for condition before installing it on the engine.

Figure 8-8. *Types of line disconnects.*

Figure 8-9. *Hoisting sling attached to engine.*

Before attaching the sling to the hoist, be sure that the hoist has sufficient capacity to lift the engine safely. The engine's center of gravity (CG) should also be taken into account as the engine is hoisted. A manually operated hoist mounted in a portable frame is shown in *Figure 8-10*. This hoist assembly aircraft. If the engine binds at any point, maneuver it with the hoist until it slips free.

The procedure just discussed applies to removal of most reciprocating and turbine aircraft engines. Any variation in details is outlined in the manufacturer's instructions. Before attempting any engine removal, always consult these instructions for the aircraft concerned. When the engine has been removed, it can be carefully lowered onto a stand. The engine should be fastened to the stand and prepared for the removal of accessories.

Hoisting and Mounting the Engine for Installation

When the new or overhauled engine is ready to be hoisted for installation, move the engine stand as close as possible to the nacelle in which the replacement is to be installed. Then, attach the sling to the engine and hook the hoist to the sling. Take up the slack until the hoist is supporting most of the engine weight. Next, remove the engine attaching bolts from the stand and hoist the engine clear.

The engine stand may be moved and the hoist frame positioned so the engine can be hoisted easily into the nacelle. To prevent injury to the crew or damage to the aircraft or engine, be sure that the engine is steadied when moving the hoist frame.

Engine nacelles are rarely designed for the engine to be fitted and bolted into place as though it were being mounted on a bare wall. The engine must be guided into position and mated with its various connections, such as the mounting bolt holes and the exhaust tailpipe. This must be done despite such obstacles as the nacelle framework, ducts, or firewall connections and without leaving a trail of broken and bent parts, scratched paint, or crushed fingers.

When the engine has been aligned correctly in the nacelle, insert the mounting bolts into their holes and start all of the nuts on them. Always use the type of bolt and nut recommended by the manufacturer. Never use an unauthorized substitution of a different type or specification of nut and bolt than that prescribed.

The nuts on the engine mount bolts must be tightened to the torque recommended by the aircraft manufacturer. While the nuts are being tightened, the hoist should support the engine weight sufficiently to allow alignment of the mounting bolts. If the engine is permitted to exert upward or downward pressure on the bolts, it is necessary for the nuts to pull the engine into proper alignment. This results in nuts being tightened to the proper torque value without actually holding the engine securely to the aircraft.

Figure 8-10. *Hoist and frame assembly used for engine removal.*

is specifically manufactured for the purpose of removing engines and other large assemblies from aircraft. Some frames are fitted with power-operated hoists. These should be used with care, since considerable damage can be done if an inexperienced operator allows a power-operated hoist to overrun. The hoist and frame should also be checked for condition before being used to lift the engine.

Hoisting the Engine

Before the hoist is hooked onto the engine sling, recheck the aircraft tail supports and the wheel chocks. Fasten lines to the engine, at points on the sides or rear, so that the engine can be controlled as it is being hoisted. Hook the hoist onto the sling and hoist the engine just enough to relieve the engine weight from the mount attachments. Remove the nuts from the mount attachments in the order recommended in the manufacturer's instructions for the aircraft. As the last nuts are being removed, pull back on the lines fastened to the engine (or force it back by other means if lines are not being used), thus steadying the engine. If bolts must be removed from the mount attachments, be sure the engine is under control before doing so. If the bolts are to remain in the mount attachments, the hoist can be gently maneuvered upward or downward as necessary after all the nuts have been removed. Meanwhile, gently relax the backward force on the engine just enough to allow the engine gradual forward movement when it is free from the mount attachments. When the hoist has removed all engine weight from the mount attachments, the engine should be eased gently forward, away from the

The applicable manufacturer's instructions outline the sequence for tightening the mounting bolts to ensure security of fastening. After the nuts are safetied and the engine sling and hoist are removed, bonding strips should be connected across each engine mount to provide an electrical path from the mount to the airframe.

Mounting the engine in the nacelle is, of course, only the beginning. All the ducts, electrical leads, controls, tubes, and conduits must be connected before the engine can be operated.

Connections and Adjustments

There are no hard-and-fast rules that direct the order in which units or systems should be connected to the engine. Each maintenance organization normally supplies a worksheet or checklist to be followed during this procedure. This list is based upon past engine installations on each particular aircraft. If this is followed carefully, it serves as a guide for an efficient installation. The following instructions are not a sequence of procedures but a discussion of correct methods for completing an engine installation.

The system of ducts for routing air to the engine varies with all types of aircraft. In connecting them, the goal is to fit the ducts closely at all points of disconnect so that the air they route does not escape its intended path. The duct systems of some aircraft must be pressure checked for leaks. This is done by blocking the system at one end, supplying compressed air at a specified pressure at the other end, and then checking the rate of leakage.

The filters in the air induction system must be cleaned to ensure an unrestricted flow of clean air to the engine and its units. Because methods for cleaning air filters vary with the materials used in the filtering element, clean them in accordance with the technical instructions for the aircraft being serviced.

The exhaust system should also be carefully connected to prevent the escape of hot gases into the nacelle. When assembling the exhaust system, check all clamps, nuts, and bolts, and replace any in doubtful condition. During assembly, the nuts should be gradually and progressively tightened to the correct torque. The clamps should be tapped with a rawhide mallet as they are being tightened to prevent binding at any point. On some systems, a ball joint connects the stationary portion of the exhaust system to the portion that is attached to the engine. This ball joint absorbs the normal engine movement caused by the unbalanced forces of the engine operation. Ball joints must be installed with the specified clearance to prevent binding when expanded by hot exhaust gases.

Hoses used inside low-pressure systems are generally fastened into place with clamps. Before using a hose clamp, inspect it for security of welding or riveting and for smooth operation of the adjusting screw. A clamp that is badly distorted or materially defective should be rejected. Material defects include extremely brittle or soft areas that may easily break or stretch when the clamp is tightened. After a hose is installed in a system, it should be supported with rubber-lined supporting clamps at regular intervals.

Before installing metal tubing with threaded fittings, ensure the threads are clean and in good condition. Apply sealing compound, of the correct specification for the system, to the threads of the fittings before installing them. While connecting metal tubing, follow the same careful procedure for connecting hose fittings to prevent cross-threading and to ensure correct torque.

When connecting the starter, generator, or various other electrical units within the nacelle, make sure that all lead connections are clean and properly secured. On leads that are fastened to a threaded terminal with a nut, a lock washer is usually inserted under the nut to prevent the lead from working loose. When required, connector plugs can be safetied with steel wire to hold the knurled nut in the full-tight position.

Electrical leads within the engine nacelle are usually passed through either flexible or rigid conduit. The conduit must be anchored, as necessary, to provide a secure installation and bonded when required.

All engine controls must be accurately adjusted to ensure instantaneous response to the control setting. For flexibility, the engine controls are usually a combination of rods and cables. Since these controls are tailored to the model of aircraft in which they are installed, their adjustment must follow exactly the step-by-step procedure outlined in the manufacturer's instructions for each particular model of aircraft.

Figure 8-11 illustrates a simplified schematic drawing of a throttle control system for a reciprocating aircraft engine. Follow a general procedure for adjusting throttle controls. First, loosen the serrated throttle control arm at the carburetor and back off the throttle stop until the throttle valve is in the fully closed position. After locking the cable drum into position with the locking pin, adjust the control rod to a specified length. Then, attach one end of the control rod to the locked cable drum, and reinstall the throttle control arm on the carburetor in the serrations that allow the other end of the control rod to be attached to it. This correctly connects the control arm to the cable drum.

Figure 8-11. *Schematic drawing of throttle control system.*

Now, loosen the cable turnbuckles until the throttle control can be locked at the quadrant with the locking pin. Then, with both locking pins in place, adjust the cables to the correct tension as measured with a tensiometer. Remove the locking pins from the cable drum and quadrant.

Next, adjust the throttle control so that it has a slight cushion action at two positions on the throttle quadrant: one when the carburetor throttle valve is in the full-open position and the other when it is closed to the idle position (stop to stop).

Adjust the cushion by turning the cable turnbuckles equally in opposite directions until the throttle control cushion is correct at the full-open position of the throttle valve. Then, when the throttle arm stop is adjusted to the correct idle speed setting, the amount of cushion should be within tolerance at the idle speed position of the throttle valve. The presence of this cushion ensures that the travel of the throttle valve is not limited by the stops on the throttle control quadrant, but that they are opening fully and closing to the correct idle speed as determined by the throttle arm stop.

Adjustment of the engine controls is basically the same on all aircraft regarding the linkage adjustment to a predetermined length for a specific setting of the unit to be controlled. Then adjust cables, if used in the control system, to a specific tension with the control system locked. Finally, the full travel of the unit to be controlled is ensured by establishing the correct cushion in the controls. In general, the same basic procedure is used to connect the linkage of the remaining engine controls. After rigging the engine controls, safety the turnbuckles and castle nuts, and make certain the jam nuts on all control rods are tightened.

On multiengine aircraft, the amount of cushion of all engine controls on each quadrant must be equal so that all are aligned at any specific setting chosen. This eliminates the necessity of setting each control individually to synchronize engine operations.

After the engine has been installed, it is necessary to adjust the cowl flaps, if installed, so that the passage of the cooling air over the engine can be regulated accurately. Operate the system and recheck for opening and closing to the specified limits. Also, check the cowl flap position indicators, if installed, to ensure that they indicate the true position of the cowl flaps. Cowl flaps are doors at the bottom of the rear cowling that are used to control air flow through the cowling.

The oil cooler doors are adjusted in a manner similar to that used to adjust the cowl flaps. In some cases, the procedure is reversed in so far as the door is first adjusted to retract to a specified point, and the limit switch on the motor is set to cut out at this point. Then, the jackscrew is adjusted to permit the door to open only a specified distance, and the open limit switch is set to stop the motor when this point is reached.

After the engine has been completely installed and connected, install the propeller on the aircraft. Before doing so, the thrust bearing retaining nut should be checked for correct torque. If required, the propeller shaft must be coated with light engine oil before the propeller is installed; the propeller governor and anti-icing system must be connected according to applicable manufacturer's instructions.

Preparation of Engine for Ground and Flight Testing

Pre-Oiling

Before the new engine is flight tested, it must undergo a thorough ground check. Before this ground check can be made, several operations are usually performed on the engine.

To prevent failure of the engine bearings during the initial start, the engine should be pre-oiled. When an engine has been idle for an extended period of time, its internal bearing surfaces are likely to become dry at points where the corrosion-preventive mixture has dried out or drained away from the bearings. Hence, it is necessary to force oil throughout the entire engine oil system. If the bearings are dry when the engine is started, the friction at high rpm destroys the bearings before lubricating oil from the engine-driven oil pump can reach them.

There are several methods of pre-oiling an engine. The method selected should provide an expeditious and adequate pre-oiling service. Before using any pre-oiling method, remove one spark plug from each cylinder to allow the engine to be turned over more easily with the starter. Also, connect an external source of electrical power (auxiliary power unit) to the aircraft electrical system to prevent an excessive drain on the aircraft battery.

In using some types of pre-oilers, such as that shown in *Figure 8-12*, the oil line from the inlet side of the engine-driven oil pump must be disconnected to permit the pre-oiler tank to be connected at this point. Then, a line must be disconnected, or an opening made in the oil system at the nose of the engine, to allow oil to flow out of the engine.

Figure 8-12. *Pre-oiler tank.*

Oil flowing out of the engine indicates the completion of the pre-oiling operation, since the oil has now passed through the entire system.

In order to force oil from the pre-oiler tank through the engine, apply air pressure to the oil in the tank while the engine is being turned through with the starter. When this action has forced oil through the disconnection at the nose of the engine, stop cranking the engine and disconnect the pre-oiler tank. A motor-driven oil pump can also be used to pump oil through the engine during the pre-oiling operation.

When no external means of pre-oiling an engine are available, the engine oil pump may be used. Fill the engine oil tank, or crankcase, to the proper level. Then, with the mixture in the idle cutoff position (reciprocating engine), the fuel shutoff valve and ignition switches in the off position, and the throttles fully open, crank the engine with the starter until the oil pressure gauge mounted on the instrument panel indicates oil pressure.

After the engine has been pre-oiled, replace the spark plugs and connect the oil system. Generally, the engine should be operated within 4 hours of being pre-oiled; otherwise, the pre-oiling procedure normally must be repeated.

Fuel System Bleeding

To purge the fuel system of air locks, and to aid in flushing any traces of preservative oil from a pressure carburetor, fuel injector unit, or fuel control (turbine), remove the drain plug in the fuel unit chamber that is farthest from the fuel inlet to the fuel unit. In its place, screw a threaded fitting to a length of hose leading to a suitable container. Then, set the fuel control unit to flow fuel so that fuel is permitted to flow through the system. After ensuring the fuel shutoff and main fuel tank valves are open, turn on the fuel boost pump until there are no traces of preservative oil in the fuel being pumped through the system. The passage of air is indicated by the absence of air mixed in the fuel emerging from the end of the hose submerged in the container of fuel. Air trapped in the system should not be confused with the numerous small air bubbles that may appear as a result of the velocity of the fuel being ejected from the engine's fuel unit. Usually, after approximately a gallon of fuel has been bled off, the system can be considered safe for operation. After completing the bleeding operation, return all switches and controls to their normal, or off, position, and replace and safety all fuel unit connections disturbed.

Propeller Check

The propeller, if equipped, must be checked before, during, and after the engine has been ground operated. The propeller should be checked for proper torque on the mounting bolts, leaks, vibration, and for correct safety.

A propeller whose pitch-changing mechanism is electrically actuated may be checked before the engine is operated. Propellers whose pitch-changing mechanisms are oil actuated must be checked during engine operation after the normal operating oil temperature has been reached. In addition to checking the increase or decrease in rpm, the feathering cycle of the propeller should also be checked.

Checks and Adjustments After Engine Runup and Operation

After the engine has been ground operated, and again after flight test, operational factors must be adjusted, as necessary, and the entire installation given a thorough visual inspection. These adjustments often include fuel pressure and oil pressure, as well as rechecks of such factors as ignition timing, valve clearances, and idle speed and mixture. If these rechecks are indicated by the manner in which the engine performs.

After both the initial ground runup and the test flight, remove the oil sump plugs and screens and inspect for metal particles. Clean the screens before reinstalling them.

Check all lines for leakage and security of attachment. Especially, check the oil system hose clamps for security as evidenced by oil leakage at the hose connections. Also, inspect the cylinder holddown nuts or cap screws for security and safety. This check should also be performed after the flight immediately succeeding the test flight.

Removal and Installation of an Opposed-Type Engine

The previous general information related to the removal, buildup, inspection, preservation, storage, and installation of engines is in most instances applicable to horizontally opposed aircraft engines. Finally, the number of accessories, together with fewer engine controls, electrical and hydraulic lines and connections, and the increased ease of accessibility to all parts of the engine generally preclude extensive use of QECA on opposed engines.

Engine Removal

The manufacturer's instructions should always be used as a guide in engine removal or installation. The following is a typical engine removal and installation procedure for a horizontally opposed engine:

1. Remove the propeller.
2. Release the cowl fasteners holding the top cowling, and remove the top cowlings.
3. Remove the screws at the rear of the top and bottom cowling assembly; remove the cowling and store out of the way. *[Figure 8-13]*

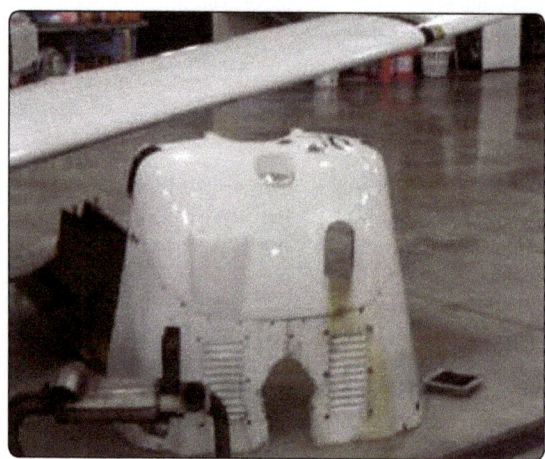

Figure 8-13. *Cowling removed and stored out of the way.*

4. Disconnect the mechanical fuel pump inlet line.
5. Disconnect the battery leads, then the generator and starter leads.
6. If installed, remove the cylinder head temperature thermocouple.
7. Disconnect the oil pressure and manifold pressure lines.
8. Disconnect the oil return line.
9. Remove the bonding strap from the rear of the engine.
10. Disconnect the governor control cable from the governor.
11. Disconnect the tachometer cable from the rear of the engine.
12. Disconnect engine oil cooler hoses.

13. Disconnect the engine oil temperature lead.
14. Disconnect the engine breather line.
15. Remove the four carburetor mounting nuts and allow the carburetor and carburetor air box to hang by means of the attached engine controls.
16. Attach a hoist to the engine-lifting eye and relieve the tension on the mounts. *[Figure 8-14]*

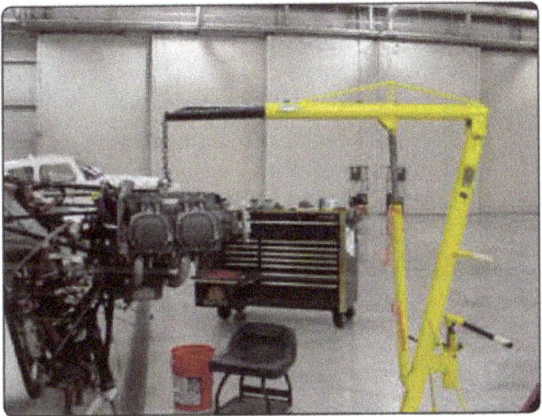

Figure 8-14. *Relieve tension on engine mounts.*

17. Disconnect magneto P-leads.
18. Remove the cotter pin, nuts, washer, and front rubber mount from each bolt and remove the sleeve. Slide bolts out of attaching points. Swing engine free, being careful not to damage any attached parts, and remove rear rubber mounts, as shown in *Figure 8-15*.

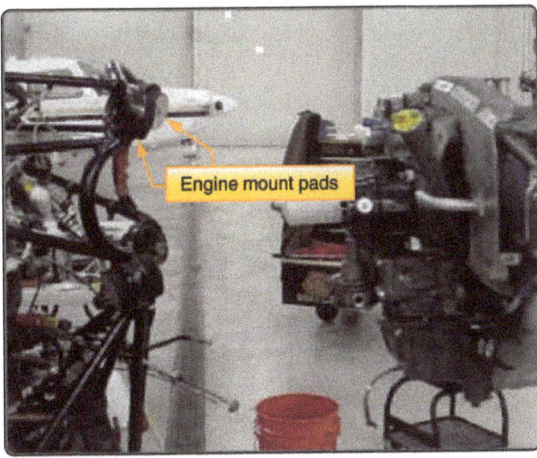

Figure 8-15. *Engine clear of mount.*

Engine Installation

The following procedure is typical of those used for installing a horizontally opposed engine after the accessories are mounted on the engine. Insert engine mounting bolts into the engine mount and slide the shock mounts onto the bolts so that the flat surface of the shock mount is flush with the engine mounting pad. *[Figure 8-16]*

Figure 8-16. *Rubber shock mount in steel engine mount.*

1. Slide the shock mount spacers onto the engine mounting bolts.
2. Attach a hoist to the lifting eye and lift the engine. Tilt the rear of the engine downward until the magnetos clear the engine mount. Position the mounting lugs of the engine so they align with the engine mount attaching points.
3. Insert an upper mounting bolt into the engine until its threaded end extends one or two threads from the mount itself.
4. Slide a shock mount between the engine mount and the engine.
5. Repeat the procedure described in steps 5 and 6 above for the remaining attachment points.
6. Install the front engine rubber mounts on the bolts and over the forward end of the sleeve; check to see that shock mounts are not binding.
7. Insert the magneto P-leads, tighten and safety.
8. Install a washer and castellated nut on each mounting bolt. Tighten the nuts progressively, following a circular sequence, to the torque value specified by the manufacturer. Install cotter pins.
9. Install gasket and carburetor air box.
10. Connect the engine breather line.

11. Connect the engine oil cooler air duct boot.
12. Connect the engine oil temperature lead.
13. Connect the oil cooler hoses.
14. Connect the tachometer cable.
15. Attach the propeller governor control cable.
16. Connect the bonding strap to the engine mount ring.
17. Connect the oil pressure line.
18. Reconnect the starter generator and battery leads.
19. Install the cylinder head temperature thermocouple.
20. Connect the primer line.
21. Reconnect the lines to the vacuum pump.
22. Reconnect the hydraulic pump lines.
23. Attach the exhaust system and generator blast tube.
24. Slide the complete cowl assembly in position and attach the bottom sections.
25. Install the top cowling with the cowl fasteners.
26. Install the propeller.

Turbine Engine Powerplant Removal and Installation

The aircraft engine used in this discussion provides a typical example of a turbofan powerplant removal and installation procedures. The engine and all engine-mounted accessories form a QECA.

Access to the engine is provided by doors that can be raised and locked open. Directional references, such as right and left and clockwise and counterclockwise, apply to the engine as viewed from the aft or exhaust end of the engine.

Removal and Replacement of an Auxiliary Power Unit (APU)

1. Open APU compartment access door latches and open door. Install door support rods. Open circuit breakers and switches as needed. *[Figure 8-17]*
2. Remove lower support shroud.
3. Disconnect APU harness, APU starter motor, and APU generator plugs from receptacles in upper shroud.
4. Disconnect APU generator control plug from receptacle in upper shroud.
5. Disconnect exhaust gas temperature (EGT) indicating system plug from receptacle in upper shroud.
6. Disconnect bleed load control air line from fitting in upper shroud.
7. Disconnect fuel hose from elbow on low pressure fuel filter. Collect dripping fuel in a suitable container.
8. Disconnect fire detection sensor element plug from receptacle in upper shroud.
9. Disconnect APU to upper shroud bonding jumper.
10. Remove clamp attaching bleed air duct coupling to turbine plenum bleed air flange.
11. Push bleed air duct coupling outboard as far as it will go.
12. Move compressor air inlet duct lock handle outboard until heel of cam is free from spring arm.
13. Rotate compressor plenum downward so that compressor air inlet opening in plenum no longer matches air inlet duct in upper shroud.
14. Install hoist assemblies to brackets in APU compartment with pins.
15. When using F80002 cradle, insert tubes in cradle base and secure in place with pins.
16. Attach hoist cables to cradle assembly tubes with pins.
17. Install cradle base on APU powerplant and secure in place with pins.
18. Pull hoist cables taut to remove load from APU engine mounts.
19. Remove nuts, washers, and bolt fastening mount caps to engine mount brackets. Do not remove cap and mount bracket hinge bolts. Open mount caps.
20. Lower powerplant slowly. Guide unit to clear bleed air duct coupling, fuel line, and airplane structure.
21. After the unit is set on transportation dolly, slacken hoist cables.
22. Disconnect hoist cables from tubes by removing pins.

Install APU Powerplant

1. Position APU powerplant, installed on a cradle base, directly under APU compartment.
2. Connect hoist cables to tubes with pins.
3. Rotate compressor plenum air inlet opening down. Slowly raise APU powerplant. Guide unit to clear airplane structure.
4. With the APU in place, make sure the seal of the cooling air inlet duct is touching the cooling fan flanges.
5. Close mount caps and install bolts, washers, and nuts. Tighten nuts to a torque range of 30 to 40 pound-inches.

Figure 8-17. *APU engine insulation.*

7. Rotate compressor plenum to match compressor air inlet opening in plenum with air inlet duct in upper shroud.

8. Move compressor air inlet duct lock handle inboard until heel of cam falls behind spring arm. Install locking screws and two nuts to secure locking handle.

9. Slacken hoist cables and disconnect cables from tubes by removing pins.

10. Remove pins securing cradle base to APU powerplant and remove cradle.

11. Remove pins securing hoist to brackets in APU compartment and remove hoists.

12. Slide bleed air duct coupling inboard as far as it will go.

13. Install clamp attaching bleed air duct coupling to turbine plenum bleed air flange. Tighten clamp-coupling nut to a torque range of 45 to 55 pound-inches.

14. Connect fuel hose to elbow on low pressure fuel filter.

15. Connect fire detection sensor element plug to receptacle on upper shroud and safety wire.

16. Connect bleed load control air line to fitting in upper shroud.
17. Connect EGT indicating system plug to receptacle in upper shroud and safety wire.
18. Connect APU generator control plug to receptacle in upper shroud and safety wire.
19. Connect APU harness, APU starter motor, and APU generator plugs to receptacles in upper shroud and safety wire connectors.
20. Connect APU to upper shroud bonding jumper.
21. Depreserve, or purge, the fuel system by motoring.

Turbofan Powerplant QECA Removal

The powerplant may be removed from the aircraft by either of two methods. One method involves lowering the powerplant from the nacelle by using an engine dolly. The other method requires hoists and a special sling to lower the powerplant to a movable engine stand. The following preliminary steps are applicable to either method of removal:

1. Adequately secure the aircraft either with wheel chocks or tiedown provisions; attach ground wire or cable to aircraft.
2. Open the nacelle doors and support them with the struts. Verify that no external power is connected to the aircraft and that the electric power switch is off.
3. Remove the mount access plates from both sides of the nacelle structure.
4. Remove the engine's pneumatic ducts as needed.
5. Disconnect the turbine electrical wiring connections, thermocouple lead. *[Figure 8-18]*
6. Disconnect the fuel line by removing the bolts from the hose flange. *[Figure 8-19]*
7. Disconnect the hydraulic lines and connections. *[Figure 8-20]*

After the engine has been disconnected, except for the engine mounts, and a dolly is being used to remove the engine, position it under the engine. Attach it to the engine and raise the dolly until all the weight is relieved from the wing. If hoists are used, connect the hoists to the engine mounts through the accesses on the pylon. When lowering the engine with hoists, operate them simultaneously to exert tension on the hoist cables at all times. Position a movable engine stand under the engine before lowering it.

With either the hoists or dolly attached and the stand in place, the engine is now ready to be lowered.

Figure 8-18. *Electrical disconnect.*

Figure 8-19. *Fuel line disconnect.*

Remove the rear engine mount bolt and bushing and the front engine mount nuts and washers. Start lowering the engine, constantly observing the engine clearance with the nacelle to prevent damage to the engine or nacelle. Secure the engine to the dolly or stand. If hoists are used, detach them from the engine. Roll the engine clear of the aircraft. Care must be taken while moving the engine clear to prevent damage to the pylon or pod. Cap or plug all lines, hoses, and outlets. With the engine removed, inspect the power control rod bracket and crank assembly for bearing looseness and the nacelle

Figure 8-20. *New hydraulic connections (Boeing).*

area for structural damage. Inspect for cracks or openings in the area where the pylon structure joins the nacelle structure.

Removal of QECA Accessories

When an aircraft engine is to be replaced, the aircraft-furnished accessories and equipment may be removed either for installation on the replacement engine or for overhaul, as required. Note carefully the locations and attachments of all units before removal to aid in the assembly of the replacement powerplant. When accessories are to be sent to overhaul or storage, preserve them in accordance with the manufacturer's instructions and attach all pertinent data and the proper accessory record cards.

After removal of these accessories and equipment, cover all exposed drives and ports. Prepare the engine for shipment, storage, or disassembly as directed in applicable manufacturer's instructions.

Installation of Turbofan Engines

Installation With Dolly

The following procedures are typical of those used to install a turbofan engine using a dolly. Specific ground-handling instructions are normally placarded on the dolly.

1. Operate the dolly and carefully raise the engine to the engine mount attaching fittings.

2. Align the rear engine mount with the mount attaching fittings.

3. Install the engine mount bolts and tighten to the specified torque.

Installation with Cable Hoist

Figure 8-21 shows an engine being installed using a cable hoist. Hoists of this type are commonly used to install turbofan engines.

1. Position the powerplant beneath the nacelle.

2. Attach the engine sling to the engine.

3. Carefully operate all the hoists simultaneously to raise the engine and guide the mounts into position.

Completing the Installation

The following procedures cover the typical final installation instructions:

1. Install the bushing through the engine rear mount and the rear mount attaching fitting. Install the bolt through the bushing; install the nut and secure it with a cotter pin.

2. Through the forward mount accesses, place the chamfered washer, flat washer, and nut on each engine forward mount bolt. Tighten the nut to the required torque and safety.

Figure 8-21. *Hoisting a typical turbine fan (Boeing).*

3. Connect the pneumatic ducts from the pylon to the compressor bleed-air duct from the engine. Tighten the duct connection by applying the proper torque.
4. Remove the dolly or slings and related equipment from the engine.
5. Connect the fuel hose to the fuel line from the pylon. Use a new gasket between the flanges of the fuel hose and the line.
6. Sparingly apply anti-seize compound to the threads of the electrical harness receptacle and adjacent thermocouple receptacles. Connect the leads and secure the harness connector and safety.
7. Connect the turbine control connections, electrical and pneumatic.
8. Connect the power control rod to the fuel control or the electrical connection for this purpose.
9. Inspect the engine installation for completeness.
10. Install the access covers.
11. Adjust the fuel control linkage and trim

Rigging, Inspections, and Adjustments

The following instructions cover some of the basic inspections and procedures for rigging and adjusting fuel controls, fuel selectors, and fuel shutoff valves.

1. Inspect all bellcranks for looseness, cracks, or corrosion.
2. Inspect rod ends for damaged threads and the number of threads remaining after final adjustment.
3. Inspect cable drums for wear and cableguards for proper position and tension.

While rigging the fuel selector, power controls, and shutoff valve linkages, follow the manufacturer's step-by-step procedure for the particular aircraft model being rigged. The cables should be rigged with the proper tension with the rigging pins installed. The pins should be free to be removed without any binding; if they are hard to remove, the cables are not rigged properly and should be rechecked. The power lever should have the proper cushion at the idle and full-power positions. The pointers, or indicators, on the fuel control should be within limits. The fuel selectors must be rigged so that they have the proper travel and do not restrict the fuel flow to the engines.

Rigging Power Controls

Many older conventional turbofan engines use various power lever control systems. One of the common types is the cable and rod system. This system uses bellcranks, push-pull rods, drums, fairleads, flexible cables, and pulleys. All of these components make up the control system and must be adjusted or rigged from time to time. On single-engine aircraft, the rigging of the power lever controls is not very difficult. The basic requirement is to have the desired travel on the power lever and correct travel at the fuel control. On multiengine turbojet aircraft, the power levers must be rigged so that they are aligned at all power settings.

Most computer controlled engines have an electronic connection from the flight deck to the engine. This eliminates the need for any type of cable or linkages. In the computer controlled system, the computer sends electronic information through wires or buses to the fuel control to command it to follow pilot inputs from the flight deck.

On older style aircraft the power lever control cables and push-pull rods in the airframe system to the pylon and nacelle are not usually disturbed at engine change time and usually no rigging is required, except when some component has been changed. The control system from the pylon to the engine must be rigged after each engine change and fuel control change. *Figure 8-22* shows the control system from the bellcrank in the upper pylon to the fuel control.

Before adjusting the power controls at the engine, be sure that the power lever is free from binding and the controls have full throw on the console. If they do not have full throw or are binding, the airframe system should be checked and the discrepancies repaired. After all adjustments have been made, move the power levers through their complete range, carefully inspecting for adequate clearance between the various push-pull rods and tubes. Secure all locknuts, cotter pins, and safety as required.

Figure 8-22. *Power lever control system.*

Adjusting the Fuel Control

The fuel control unit of the typical turbofan on older aircraft can be a hydromechanical device that schedules the quantity of fuel flowing to the engine so that the desired amount of thrust can be obtained. The amount of thrust is dictated by the position of the power lever in the cockpit and the particular operation of the engine. Thus, the thrust of the engine and the consequent rpm of its turbine are scheduled by fuel flow.

The fuel control unit of the engine is adjusted to trim the engine to obtain maximum thrust output of the engine when desired. The engine must be retrimmed after a fuel control unit is replaced, the engine does not develop maximum thrust, engine change, or excessive throttle stagger.

After trimming the engine, the idle rpm can be adjusted. The idle rpm is adjusted by turning the INC. IDLE screw an eighth of a turn at a time, allowing sufficient time for the rpm to stabilize between adjustments. Retard the power lever to idle and recheck the idle rpm.

If wind velocity is a factor, the aircraft should be headed into the wind while trimming or checking the trim on an engine. Since trimming accuracy decreases as windspeed and moisture content increase, the most accurate trimming is obtained under conditions of no wind and clear, moisture-free air. Do not trim when there is a tailwind because hot exhaust gases may be reingested. As a practical matter, the engine should never be trimmed when icing conditions exist because of the adverse effects on trimming accuracy. To obtain the most accurate results, the aircraft should always be headed into the wind while the engine is being trimmed.

With the aircraft headed into the wind, verify that the exhaust area is clear. Install an engine trim gauge to the T-fitting in the turbine discharge pressure line. Start the engine and allow it to stabilize for 5 minutes before attempting to adjust the fuel control. Refer to the applicable manufacturer's instructions for correct trim values. Compensate for temperature and pressure during the trimming process. If a hydromechanical fuel control is not within limits, turn the INC. MAX screw *[Figure 8-23]* about one-eighth turn in the appropriate direction. Repeat, if necessary, until the desired value is attained. If the aircraft is equipped with a pressure ratio gauge, set it to the correct value.

Figure 8-23. *Typical fuel control adjustments.*

An example of a trim check using an electronic controlled fuel control must take into account temperature and pressure for each parameter measured. The parameters checked can include:

1. Minimum idle (percent N_2)
2. Approach idle (percent N_2)
3. 2.5 bleed open (percent N_1)
4. 2.5 bleed closed (percent N_1)
5. Takeoff engine pressure ratio (EPR)
6. 95 percent takeoff thrust (EPR)
7. 90 percent thrust change decal (EPR)

The actual trim check would be done based on a temperature and pressure, such as the example in *Figure 8-24*. For these given temperature and pressures, the target parameter values

ASSUME
1. Ambient temperature: OAT = 12 °F
2. Barometric pressure = 29.0 inches of mercury

SELECT TRIM TARGETS FOR THE FOLLOWING
1. Minimum idle (%N2) is 57.7 (+1.5/ 0.5)%N2
2. Approach idle (%N2) is 67.6 ±0.5 %N2
3. 2.5 bleed open inc (%N1) 60.4 ±0.5 %N1
4. 2.5 bleed closed inc (%N1) is 63.5 ±0.5 %N1
5. Takeoff (EPR) is 1.50 +0.01/ 0.00 EPR
6. 95% takeoff thrust (EPR) is 1.46 EPR
7. 90% thrust change deceleration (EPR) is 1.04 EPR

DAT °F (°C)	Trim targets	Barometer (inches of mercury)									
		31.0	30.0	29.0	28.0	27.0	26.0	25.0	24.0	23.0	22.0
12 (11)	MIN IDLE (%N2)	57.6	57.6	57.7	58.0	58.3	58.6	58.9	59.5	60.2	60.9
	APP IDLE (%N2)	67.5	67.5	67.6	67.7	67.8	67.9	68.0	68.3	68.8	69.0
	2.5 BLEED OPEN INC (%N1)	60.4	60.4	60.4	60.4	60.4	60.4	60.4	60.4	60.4	60.4
	2.5 BLEED CLOSED INC (%N1)	63.5	63.5	63.5	63.5	63.5	63.5	63.5	63.5	63.5	63.5
	TAKEOFF (EPR)	1.45	1.48	1.50	1.51	1.53	1.54	1.56	1.57	1.59	1.61
	95% TAKEOFF THRUST (EPR)	1.42	1.45	1.46	1.47	1.48	1.50	1.51	1.52	1.53	1.54
	90% THRUST CHANGE DECEL (EPR)	1.03	1.03	1.04	1.04	1.04	1.04	1.04	1.04	1.04	1.04
16 (9)	MIN IDLE (%N2)	57.9	57.9	58.0	58.2	58.5	58.8	59.2	59.8	60.4	61.2
	APP IDLE (%N2)	67.8	67.8	67.9	68.0	68.1	68.2	68.3	68.6	68.9	69.3
	2.5 BLEED OPEN INC (%N1)	60.6	60.6	60.6	60.6	60.6	60.6	60.6	60.6	60.6	60.6
	2.5 BLEED CLOSED INC (%N1)	63.8	63.8	63.8	63.8	63.8	63.8	63.8	63.8	63.8	63.8
	TAKEOFF (EPR)	1.45	1.48	1.50	1.51	1.53	1.54	1.56	1.57	1.59	1.61
	95% TAKEOFF THRUST (EPR)	1.42	1.45	1.46	1.47	1.48	1.50	1.51	1.52	1.53	1.54
	90% THRUST CHANGE DECEL (EPR)	1.03	1.03	1.04	1.04	1.04	1.04	1.04	1.04	1.04	1.04
20 (7)	MIN IDLE (%N2)	58.1	58.1	58.2	58.5	58.8	59.1	59.4	60.0	60.7	61.4
	APP IDLE (%N2)	68.1	68.1	68.2	68.3	68.3	68.5	68.6	68.9	69.2	69.6
	2.5 BLEED OPEN INC (%N1)	60.9	60.9	60.9	60.9	60.9	60.9	60.9	60.9	60.9	60.9
	2.5 BLEED CLOSED INC (%N1)	64.0	64.0	64.0	64.0	64.0	64.0	64.0	64.0	64.0	64.0
	TAKEOFF (EPR)	1.45	1.48	1.50	1.51	1.53	1.54	1.56	1.57	1.59	1.61
	95% TAKEOFF THRUST (EPR)	1.42	1.45	1.46	1.47	1.48	1.50	1.52	1.52	1.53	1.54
	90% THRUST CHANGE DECEL (EPR)	1.03	1.03	1.04	1.04	1.04	1.04	1.04	1.04	1.04	1.04

Figure 8-24. *Trim check data (Boeing).*

can be derived from a chart in the manufacturer's manual. The engine is run up, and these values are checked against the tolerances given in the manual.

Turboprop Powerplant Removal and Installation

Since most turboprop powerplant removal and installation instructions are developed for QECA, the following procedures reflect those used for a typical QECA. The procedures for turboprop engine removal and installation are similar to those presented in the section of this chapter for turbojet engines, except for those systems related to the turboprop propeller.

Open the engine side panels, and remove the nacelle access panels. Disconnect the engine thermocouple leads at the terminal board. Before disconnecting any lines, make sure that all fuel, oil, and hydraulic fluid valves are closed. Plug all lines as they are disconnected to prevent entrance of foreign material.

Remove the clamps securing the bleed-air ducts at the firewall. Then, disconnect the electrical connector plugs, engine breather and vent lines, and fuel, oil, and hydraulic lines.

Disconnect the engine power lever and propeller control rods or cables. Remove the covers from the QECA lift points, attach the QECA sling, and remove slack from the cables using a suitable hoist. The sling must be adjusted to position the hoisting eye over the QECA CG. Failure to do so may result in engine damage.

Remove the engine mount bolts. The QECA is then ready to be removed. Recheck all of the disconnect points to make certain they are all disconnected prior to moving the engine. Move the engine forward, out of the nacelle structure, until it clears the aircraft. Lower the QECA into position on the QECA stand, and secure it prior to removing the engine sling.

The installation procedures are essentially the reverse of the removal procedures. Move the QECA straight back into the nacelle structure and align the mount bolt holes and the firewall. Start all the bolts before torquing. With all the bolts started, and using the correct torque wrench adapter, tighten the mount bolts to their proper torque. Remove the sling and install the access covers at the lift point. Using the reverse of the removal procedures, connect the various lines and connectors. New O-ring seals should be used. The manufacturer's instructions should be consulted for the proper torque limits for the various clamps and bolts.

After installation, an engine runup should be made. In general, the runup consists of checking proper operation of the powerplant and related systems. Several functional tests are performed to evaluate each phase of engine operation. The tests and procedures outlined by the engine or airframe manufacturers should he followed,

Reciprocating Helicopter Engine and QECA

The engine is installed facing aft with the propeller shaft approximately 39° above horizontal. The engine is supported by the engine mount, which is bolted to the fuselage structure. The installation of the engine provides for ease of maintenance by allowing easy access to all accessories and components when the engine access doors are opened. The QECA contains the engine, engine mount, engine accessories, engine controls, fuel system, lubrication system, ignition system, cooling system, and hydromechanical clutch and fan assembly.

Removal of Helicopter QECA

Prior to removing the helicopter QECA, the engine should be preserved if it is possible to do so. Then, shut off the fuel supply to the engine and drain the oil. Make the disconnections necessary to remove the QECA, and then perform the following steps:

1. Attach the engine lifting sling to a hoist of at least a two-ton capacity.
2. Raise the hoist to apply a slight lift to the QECA. Loosen both engine mount lower attachment bolt nuts before leaving the upper attachment bolts.
3. Remove the bolts from the sway braces and remove both engine upper attachment bolts. Then, remove both engine mount lower attachment bolts and remove the QECA from the helicopter. Mount the power package in a suitable workstand and remove the sling.

Installation, Rigging, and Adjustment of Helicopter QECA

The installation of a new or an overhauled engine is in reverse of the removal procedure. The manufacturer's instructions for the helicopter must be consulted to ascertain the correct interchange of parts from the old engine to the new engine. The applicable maintenance instructions should be followed.

Refer to the Maintenance Instructions Manual and associated technical publications for detailed information concerning rigging the throttle, mixture control, cable tensions, and related data.

Testing the Engine Installation

Normal engine run-in procedures must be followed in accordance with the manufacturer's instructions. A flight test is usually performed after the engine has been installed and the engine controls have been adjusted.

Engine Mounts

Mounts for Reciprocating Engines

Most aircraft equipped with reciprocating engines use an engine mount structure made of welded steel tubing. The mount is constructed in one or more sections that incorporate the engine mount ring, bracing members (V-struts), and fittings for attaching the mount to the wing nacelle.

The engine mounts are usually secured to the aircraft by special heat-treated steel bolts. The importance of using only these special bolts can be readily appreciated, since they alone support the entire weight of, and withstand all, the stresses imposed by the engine and propeller in flight. The upper bolts support the weight of the engine while the aircraft is on the ground, but when the aircraft is airborne another stress is added. This stress is torsional and affects all bolts, not just the top bolts. A typical engine mount ring shown in *Figure 8-25* discloses fittings and attachment points located at four positions on the engine mount structure. Each fitting houses a dynamic engine mount.

Figure 8-25. *Engine mounting ring.*

8-23

The section of an engine mount where the engine is attached is known as the engine mount ring. It is usually constructed of steel tubing having a larger diameter than the rest of the mount structure. It is circular in shape so that it can surround the engine, which is near the point of balance for the engine. The engine is usually attached to the mount by dynafocal mounts, attached to the engine at the point of balance forward of the mount ring. Other types of mounting devices are also used to secure the different engines to their mount rings.

As aircraft engines became larger and produced more power, some method was needed to absorb their vibration. This demand led to the development of the rubber and steel engine-suspension units called shock mounts. This combination permits restricted engine movement in all directions. These vibration isolators are commonly known as flexible, or elastic, shock mounts. An interesting feature common to most shock mounts is that the rubber and metal parts are arranged so that, under normal conditions, rubber alone supports the engine. Of course, if the engine is subjected to abnormal shocks or loads, the metal snubbers limit excessive movement of the engine. Dynafocal engine mounts, or vibration isolators, are units that give directional support to the engines. Dynafocal engine mounts have the mounting pad angled to point to the CG of the engines mass. *[Figure 8-25]*

Mounts for Turbofan Engines

The engine mounts on most turbofan engines perform the same basic functions of supporting the engine and transmitting the loads imposed by the engine to the aircraft structure. Most turbine engine mounts are made of stainless steel, and are typically located as illustrated in *Figure 8-26*. Some engine mounting systems use two mounts to support the forward end of the engine and a single mount at the rear end.

Turbine Vibration Isolation Engine Mounts

The vibration isolator engine mounts support the power plants and isolate the airplane structure from adverse engine vibrations. Each power plant is generally supported by forward vibration isolator mounts and an aft vibration isolator mount.

The forward vibration isolator engine mounts carry vertical, side, and axial (thrust) loads and allow engine growth due to thermal expansion. The aft mounts take only vertical and side loads; however, they will also accommodate thermal expansion of the engine without applying axial loads to the engine flanges.

The vibration isolators consist of a resilient material permanently enclosed in a metal case. As an engine vibrates, the resilient material deforms slightly, thereby dampening the vibrations before they reach the airplane structure. If complete failure or loss of the resilient material occurs, the isolators will continue to support the engine.

Preservation and Storage of Engines

An engine awaiting overhaul or return to service after overhaul must be given careful attention. It does not receive the daily care and attention necessary to detect and correct early stages of corrosion. For this reason, some definite action must be taken to prevent corrosion from affecting the engine. Engines that are not flown regularly may not achieve normal service life because of corrosion in and around the cylinders. The normal combustion process creates moisture and corrosive by-products that attack the unprotected surfaces of the cylinder walls, valves, and any other exposed areas that are unprotected. In engines that have accumulated 50 hours or more time in service in a short period, the cylinder walls have acquired a varnish that tends to protect them from corrosive action; engines under favorable atmospheric conditions can remain inactive for several weeks without evidence of damage by corrosion. This is the best-case scenario, but aircraft that operate close to oceans, lakes, rivers, and humid regions have a greater need for engine preservation than engines operated in dry low humid areas.

Corrosion-Preventive Materials

An engine in service is in a sense self-purging of moisture, since the heat of combustion evaporates the moisture in and around the engine, and the lubricating oil circulated through the engine temporarily forms a protective coating on the metal it contacts. If the operation of an engine in service is limited or suspended for a period of time, the engine is preserved to a varying extent, depending upon how long it

Figure 8-26. *Turbine engine front mount.*

is to be inoperative. There are three types of engine storage: active engine, temporary, and indefinite. An engine in active storage is defined as having at least one continuous hour of operation with an oil temperature of at least 165 °F to 200 °F and storage time not to exceed 30 days. Temporary storage describes an aircraft and engine that is not flown for 30 to 90 days, and indefinite storage is for an aircraft not to be flown for over 90 days or is removed from the aircraft for extended time.

Corrosion-Preventive Compounds

The preservation materials discussed are used for all types of engine storage. Corrosion-preventive compounds are petroleum-based products that form a waxlike film over the metal to which they are applied. Several types of corrosion-preventive compounds are manufactured according to different specifications to fit the various aviation needs. The type mixed with engine oil to form a corrosion-preventive mixture is a relatively light compound that readily blends with engine oil when the mixture is heated to the proper temperature.

The light mixture is available in three forms: MIL-C-6529C type I, type II, or type III. Type I is a concentrate and must be blended with three parts of MIL-L-22851 or MIL-L-6082C (SAE J1966) grade 1100 oil to one part of concentrate. Type II is a ready-mixed material with MIL-L-22851 or grade 1100 oil and does not require dilution. Type III is a ready-mixed material with grade 1010 oil for use in turbine engines only. The light mixture is intended for use when a preserved engine is to remain inactive for less than 30 days. It is also used to spray cylinders and other designated areas.

The desired proportions of lubricating oil, and either heavy or light corrosion-preventive compound, must not be obtained by adding the compound to the oil already in the engine. The mixture must be prepared separately before applying to the engine or placing in an oil tank.

A heavy compound is used for the dip treating of metal parts and surfaces. It must be heated to a high temperature to be sufficiently liquid to effectively coat the objects to be preserved. A commercial solvent, or kerosene spray, is used to remove corrosion-preventive compounds from the engine or parts when they are being prepared for return to service.

Although corrosion-preventive compounds act as an insulator from moisture, in the presence of excessive moisture, they eventually break down and corrosion begins. Also, the compounds eventually dry because their oil base gradually evaporates. This allows moisture to contact the engine's metal and aids in corroding it. Therefore, when an engine is stored in a shipping case or container, some dehydrating (moisture removing) agent must be used to remove the moisture from the air in and around the engine.

Dehydrating Agents

There are a number of substances (referred to as desiccants) that can absorb moisture from the atmosphere in sufficient quantities to be useful as dehydrators. One of these is silica gel. This gel is an ideal dehydrating agent since it does not dissolve when saturated.

As a corrosion preventive, bags of silica gel are placed around and inside various accessible parts of a stored engine. It is also used in clear plastic plugs, called dehydrator plugs, that can be screwed into engine openings, such as the spark plug holes. Cobalt chloride is added to the silica gel used in dehydrator plugs. This additive makes it possible for the plugs to indicate the moisture content, or relative humidity, of the air surrounding the engine. The cobalt-chloride-treated silica gel remains a bright blue color with low relative humidities; as the relative humidity increases, the shade of the blue becomes progressively lighter, becoming lavender at 30 percent relative humidity and fading through the various shades of pink *[Figure 8-27]*, until at 60 percent relative humidity it is a natural or white color. Some types of dehydrator plugs can be dried by removing the silica gel and heating the gel to dry it out, returning it to its original blue color. *[Figure 8-28]* When the relative humidity is less than 30 percent, corrosion does not normally take place. Therefore, if the dehydrator plugs are bright blue, the air in the engine has so little moisture that internal corrosion is held

Figure 8-27. *Dehydrator plug "pink" showing high humidity (Sacramento Sky Ranch).*

Figure 8-28. *Dehydrator plug "blue" showing low humidity (Sacramento Sky Ranch).*

to a minimum. This same cobalt-chloride-treated silica gel is used in humidity indicator envelopes. These envelopes can be fastened to the stored engine so that they can be inspected through a small window in the shipping case or metal engine container. All desiccants are sealed in containers to prevent their becoming saturated with moisture before they are used. Care should be taken never to leave the container open or improperly closed.

Engine Preservation and Return to Service

Before an engine is placed in temporary or indefinite storage, it should be operated and filled with a corrosion-preventive oil mixture added in the oil system to retard corrosion by coating the engine's internal parts. Drain the normal lubricating oil from the sump or system, and replace with a preservative oil mixture according to the manufacturer's instructions. Operate the engine until normal operating temperatures are obtained for at least one hour.

Always take the appropriate precautions when turning or working around a propeller. After the flight, remove all the spark plug leads and the top spark plugs.

To prevent corrosion, spray each cylinder interior with corrosion-preventive mixture to prevent moisture and oxygen from contacting the deposits left by combustion. Spray the cylinders by inserting the nozzle of the spray gun into each spark plug hole and playing the gun to cover as much area as possible. Before spraying, each cylinder to be treated should be at the bottom center position and the oil at room temperature. This allows the entire inside of the cylinder to become coated with corrosion-preventive mixture. After spraying each engine cylinder at bottom center, respray each cylinder while the crankshaft is stationary with none of the cylinder's pistons at top dead center.

The crankshaft must not be moved after this final spraying, or the seal of corrosion-preventive mixture between the pistons and cylinder walls are broken. Air can then enter past the pistons into the engine. Also, the coating of corrosion-preventive mixture on the cylinder walls is scraped away, exposing the bare metal to possible corrosion. The engine should have a sign attached similar to the following: "DO NOT TURN CRANKSHAFT—ENGINE PRESERVED PRESERVATION DATE _____."

When preparing the engine for storage, dehydrator plugs are screwed into the spark plug opening of each cylinder. If the engine is to be stored in a wooden shipping case, the ignition harness leads are attached to the dehydrator plugs with lead supports. *[Figure 8-29]* Special ventilatory plugs are installed in the spark plug holes of an engine stored horizontally in a storage container. Any engine being prepared for storage must receive thorough treatment around the exhaust ports. Because the residue of exhaust gases is potentially very corrosive, a corrosion-preventive mixture must be sprayed into each exhaust port, including the exhaust valve. After the exhaust ports have been thoroughly coated, a moisture-proof and oil-proof gasket backed by a metal or wooden plate should be secured over the exhaust ports using the exhaust stack mounting studs and nuts. These covers form a seal to prevent moisture from entering the interior of the engine through the exhaust ports. Engines stored in metal containers

Figure 8-29. *Ignition harness lead support installation.*

usually have special ventilatory covers. Another point at which the engine must be sealed is the intake manifold. If the carburetor is to remain on the engine during storage, the throttle valve should be wired open and a seal installed over the air inlet. But, if the carburetor is removed and stored separately, the seal is made at the carburetor mounting pad. The seal used in either instance can be an oil-proof and moisture-proof gasket, backed by a wooden or metal plate securely bolted into place. Silica gel should be placed in the intake manifold to absorb moisture. The silica gel bags are usually suspended from the cover plate. This eliminates the possibility of forgetting to remove the silica gel bags when the engine is eventually removed from storage. A ventilatory cover, without silica gel bags attached, can be used when the engine is stored in a metal container.

After the following details have been taken care of, the engine is ready to be packed into its container. If the engine has not been spray coated with corrosion-preventive mixture, the propeller shaft and propeller shaft thrust bearing must be coated with the compound. Then, a plastic sleeve, or moisture-proof paper, is secured around the shaft, and a threaded protector cap is screwed onto the propeller retaining nut threads.

All engine openings into which dehydrator plugs (or ventilatory plugs if the engine is stored in a metal container) have not been fitted must be sealed. At points where corrosion-preventive mixture can seep from the interior of the engine, such as the oil inlet and outlet, oil-proof and moisture-proof gasket material backed by a metal or wooden plate should be used. At other points moisture-proof tape can be used if it is carefully installed.

Before its installation in a shipping container, the engine should be carefully inspected to determine if the following accessories, which are not a part of the basic engine, have been removed: spark plugs and spark plug thermocouples, remote fuel pump adapters (if applicable), propeller hub attaching bolts (if applicable), starters, generators, vacuum pumps, hydraulic pumps, propeller governors, and engine-driven fuel pumps.

1. Remove seals and all desiccant bags.
2. Remove cylinder dehydrators and plugs or spark plugs from upper and lower spark plug holes.
3. Remove oil sump drain plug and drain the corrosion preventive mixture. Replace drain plug, torque and safety. Remove oil filter. Install new oil filter, torque and safety. Service the engine with oil in accordance with the manufacturer's instructions.

    WARNING: To prevent serious bodily injury or death, accomplish the following before moving the propeller:

    a. Disconnect all spark plug leads.
    b. Verify that magneto switches are connected to magnetos and that they are in the off position and P-leads are grounded.
    c. Throttle position CLOSED.
    d. Mixture control IDLE-CUT-OFF.
    e. Set brakes and block aircraft wheels. Ensure that aircraft tiedowns are installed and verify that the cabin door latch is open.
    f. Do not stand within the arc of the propeller blades while turning the propeller.
4. Rotate propeller by hand several revolutions to remove preservative oil.
5. Service and install spark plugs and ignition leads in accordance with the manufacturer's instructions.
6. Service engine and aircraft in accordance with the manufacturer's instruction.
7. Thoroughly clean the aircraft and engine. Perform visual inspection.
8. Correct any discrepancies.
9. Conduct a normal engine start.
10. Perform operational test in accordance with operational inspection of the applicable Maintenance Manual.
11. Correct any discrepancies.
12. Perform a test flight in accordance with airframe manufacturer's instructions.
13. Correct any discrepancies prior to returning aircraft to service.
14. Change oil and filter after 25 hours of operation.

Engine Shipping Containers

For protection, engines are sealed in plastic or foil envelopes and can be packed in a wooden shipping case or in pressurized metal containers.

The engine is lowered into the shipping container so that the mounting plate can be bolted into position. The protective envelope is attached directly to the base of the shipping case. Then, the engine is lowered vertically onto the base and bolted directly to it. A carburetor not mounted on its reciprocating engine (or no provision is made to seal it in a small container to be placed inside the shipping case) can, in some cases, be fastened to a specially constructed platform bolted to the engine.

Before the protective envelope is sealed, silica gel should be placed around the engine to dehydrate the air sealed into the envelope. The amount of silica gel used is determined by the size of the engine. The protective envelope is then carefully gathered around the engine and partially sealed, leaving an opening at one end from which as much air as possible is exhausted. A vacuum applied to the container is very useful for this purpose and is also an aid in detecting any leaks in the envelope. The envelope is then completely sealed, usually by pressing the edges together and fusing them with heat.

Before lowering the shipping case cover over the engine, a quick inventory should be made. Be sure the humidity indicator card is placed so that it can be seen through the inspection window and that everything required is enclosed in the container. While lowering the wooden shipping case cover into position, be careful that it does not twist and tear the protective envelope. Secure the cover and stencil or mark the date of preservation on the case. Also, indicate whether the engine is repairable or serviceable.

There are several types of shipping containers in use. [Figure 8-30] Another type allows horizontal installation of an engine, thus eliminating the need for an extra hoist. The engine is simply lowered onto the base portion of the container and secured. Then, silica gel bags are packed into the container, usually in a special section. The amount of silica gel required in a metal container is generally greater than that needed in a wooden shipping case, since the volume of air in the metal container is much greater than that in the protective envelope installed around an engine in a wooden shipping case. Also, in the metal container the silica gel bags must dehydrate the interior of the engine, since ventilatory plugs are normally installed in the engine openings in place of dehydrator plugs. All records of the engine should be enclosed inside the shipping container or on the outside for accessibility. A humidity indicator should be fastened inside the containers with an inspection window provided. Then, the rubber seal between the base and the top of the container must be carefully inspected. This seal is usually suitable for re-use several times. After the top of the container has been lowered into position and fastened to the base of the container, dehydrated air at approximately 5 pounds per square inch (psi) pressure is forced into the container. The container should be checked for leaks by occasional rechecks of the air pressure, since radical changes in temperature affect the air pressure in the container.

Inspection of Stored Engines

Most maintenance shops provide a scheduled inspection system for engines in storage. Normally, the humidity indicators on engines stored in shipping cases are inspected every 30 days. When the protective envelope must be opened to inspect the humidity indicator, the inspection period may be extended to once every 90 days, if local conditions permit. The humidity indicator of a metal container is inspected every 180 days under normal conditions.

If the humidity indicator in a wooden shipping case shows by its color that more than 30 percent relative humidity is present in the air around the engine, all desiccants should be replaced. If more than half the dehydrator plugs installed in the spark plug holes indicate the presence of excessive moisture, the interior of the cylinders should be resprayed. If the humidity indicator in a metal container gives a safe blue indication, but air pressure has dropped below 1 psi, the container needs only to be brought to the proper pressure with dehydrated air. However, if the humidity indicator shows an unsafe (pink) condition, the engine should be represerved.

Preservation and Depreservation of Gas Turbine Engines

The procedures for preserving and depreserving gas turbine engines vary depending upon the length of inactivity, the type of preservative used, and whether or not the engine may be rotated during the inactive period. Much of the basic information on corrosion control presented in the section on reciprocating engines is applicable to gas turbine engines. However, the requirements for the types of preservatives and their use are normally different.

The lubrication system is usually drained and may or may not be flushed with preservative oil. The engine fuel system is generally filled with preservative oil, including the fuel control. Before the engine can be returned to service, the preservative oil must be completely flushed from the fuel system by motoring the engine and bleeding the fuel system. Always follow the manufacturer's instructions when performing any preservation or depreservation of gas turbine engines.

Figure 8-30. *Turbine engine shipping container.*

Chapter 9
Engine Fire Protection Systems

Introduction

Because fire is one of the most dangerous threats to an aircraft, the potential fire zones of all multiengine aircraft currently produced are protected by a fixed fire protection system. A "fire zone" is an area or region of an aircraft designated by the manufacturer to require fire detection and/or fire extinguishing equipment and a high degree of inherent fire resistance. The term "fixed" describes a permanently installed system in contrast to any type of portable fire extinguishing equipment, such as a hand-held fire extinguisher.

In accordance with Title 14 of the Code of Federal Regulations (14 CFR) parts 23 and 25, engine fire protection systems are mandatory on: multiengine turbine powered airplanes, multiengine reciprocating engine powered airplanes incorporating turbochargers, airplanes with engine(s) located where they are not readily visible from the cockpit, all commuter and transport category airplanes, and the auxiliary power unit (APU) compartment of any airplane incorporating an APU. Fire protection systems are not mandatory for many single and twin reciprocating engine general aviation (GA) aircraft.

Several general failures or hazards can result in overheat conditions or fires peculiar to turbine engine aircraft because of their operating characteristics. The two major types of turbine failure can be classified as 1) thermodynamic and 2) mechanical.

Thermodynamic causes upset the proportion of air used to cool combustion temperatures to the levels that the turbine materials can tolerate. When the cooling cycle is upset, turbine blades can melt, causing a sudden loss of thrust. The rapid buildup of ice on inlet screens or inlet guide vanes can result in severe overheating, causing the turbine blades to melt or to be severed and thrown outward. Such failure can result in a severed tail cone and possible penetration of the aircraft structure, tanks, or equipment near the turbine wheel. In general, most thermodynamic failures are caused by ice, excess air bleed or leakage, or faulty controls that permit compressor stall or excess fuel.

Mechanical failures, such as fractured or thrown blades, can also lead to overheat conditions or fires. Thrown blades can puncture the tail cone, creating an overheat condition. Failure of forward stages of multi-stage turbines usually is much more severe. Penetration of the turbine case by failed blades is a possible fire hazard, as is the penetration of lines and components containing flammable fluids.

A high flow of fuel through an improperly adjusted fuel nozzle can cause burn-through of the tail cone in some engines. Engine fires can be caused by burning fluid that occasionally runs out through the exhaust pipe.

Components

A complete fire protection system includes both a fire detection and a fire extinguishing system. To detect fires or overheat conditions, detectors are placed in the various zones to be monitored. Fires are detected in aircraft by using one or more of the following: overheat detectors, rate-of-temperature-rise detectors, and flame detectors. In addition to these methods, other types of detectors are used in aircraft fire protection systems, but are not used to detect engine fires.

For example, smoke detectors are better suited to monitor areas such as baggage compartments or lavatories, where materials burn slowly or smolder. Other types of detectors in this category include carbon monoxide detectors.

Fire protection systems on current-production aircraft do not rely on observation by crewmembers as a primary method of fire detection. An ideal fire detector system includes as many of the following features as possible:

1. A system that does not cause false warnings under any flight or ground condition.
2. Rapid indication of a fire and accurate location of the fire.
3. Accurate indication that a fire is out.
4. Indication that a fire has reignited.
5. Continuous indication for duration of a fire.
6. Means for electrically testing the detector system from the aircraft cockpit.
7. Detectors that resist damage from exposure to oil, water, vibration, extreme temperatures, or handling.
8. Detectors that are light in weight and easily adaptable to any mounting position.
9. Detector circuitry that operates directly from the aircraft power system without inverters.
10. Minimum electrical current requirements when not indicating a fire.
11. Each detector system should turn on a cockpit light, indicating the location of the fire, and have an audible alarm system.
12. A separate detector system for each engine.

Engine Fire Detection Systems

Several different types of fire detection system are installed in aircraft to detect engine fires. Two common types used are spot detectors and continuously loop systems. Spot detector systems use individual sensors to monitor a fire zone. Examples of spot detector systems are the thermal switch system, the thermocouple system, the optical fire detection system, and the pneumatic-based thermal fire detection system. Continuous loop systems are typically installed on transport type aircraft and provide more complete fire detection coverage by using several loop type of sensors.

Thermal Switch System

A number of detectors or sensing devices are available. Many older model aircraft still operating have some type of thermal switch system or thermocouple system. A thermal switch system has one or more lights energized by the aircraft power system and thermal switches that control operation of the light(s). These thermal switches are heat-sensitive units that complete electrical circuits at a certain temperature. They are connected in parallel with each other, but in series with the indicator lights *[Figure 9-1]*. If the temperature rises above a set value in any one section of the circuit, the thermal switch closes, completing the light circuit to indicate a fire or overheat condition.

of these units may be divided into the following circuits: (1) the detector circuit, (2) the alarm circuit, and (3) the test circuit. These circuits are shown in *Figure 9-2*.

Figure 9-2. *Thermocouple fire warning circuit.*

The relay box contains two relays, the sensitive relay and the slave relay, and the thermal test unit. Such a box may contain from one to eight identical circuits, depending on the number of potential fire zones. The relays control the warning lights. In turn, the thermocouples control the operation of the relays. The circuit consists of several thermocouples in series with each other and with the sensitive relay.

Figure 9-1. *Thermal switch fire circuit.*

No set number of thermal switches is required; the exact number usually is determined by the aircraft manufacturer. On some installations, all the thermal detectors are connected to one light; others may have a separate thermal switch for each indicator light.

Some warning lights are push-to-test lights. The bulb is tested by pushing it in to check an auxiliary test circuit. The circuit shown in *Figure 9-1* includes a test relay. With the relay contact in the position shown, there are two possible paths for current flow from the switches to the light. This is an additional safety feature. Energizing the test relay completes a series circuit and checks all the wiring and the light bulb.

Also included in the circuit shown in *Figure 9-1* is a dimming relay. By energizing the dimming relay, the circuit is altered to include a resistor in series with the light. In some installations, several circuits are wired through the dimming relay, and all the warning lights may be dimmed at the same time.

Thermocouple Systems

The thermocouple fire warning system operates on an entirely different principle than the thermal switch system. A thermocouple depends on the rate of temperature rise and does not give a warning when an engine slowly overheats or a short circuit develops. The system consists of a relay box, warning lights, and thermocouples. The wiring system

The thermocouple is constructed of two dissimilar metals, such as chromel and constantan. The point where these metals are joined and exposed to the heat of a fire is called a hot junction. There is also a reference junction enclosed in a dead air space between two insulation blocks. A metal cage surrounds the thermocouple to give mechanical protection without hindering the free movement of air to the hot junction.

If the temperature rises rapidly, the thermocouple produces a voltage because of the temperature difference between the reference junction and the hot junction. If both junctions are heated at the same rate, no voltage results. In the engine compartment, there is a normal, gradual rise in temperature from engine operation; because it is gradual, both junctions heat at the same rate and no warning signal is given.

If there is a fire, however, the hot junction heats more rapidly than the reference junction. The ensuing voltage causes a current to flow within the detector circuit. Any time the current is greater than 4 milliamperes (0.004 ampere), the sensitive relay closes. This completes a circuit from the aircraft power system to the coil of the slave relay. The slave relay then closes and completes the circuit to the warning light to give a visual fire warning.

The total number of thermocouples used in individual detector circuits depends on the size of the fire zones and the total circuit resistance, which usually does not exceed 5 ohms. As shown in *Figure 9-2*, the circuit has two resistors. The resistor connected across the slave relay terminals absorbs the coil's self-induced voltage to prevent arcing across the points of the sensitive relay. The contacts of the sensitive relay are so fragile that they burn or weld if arcing is permitted.

When the sensitive relay opens, the circuit to the slave relay is interrupted and the magnetic field around its coil collapses. When this happens, the coil gets a voltage through self-induction, but with the resistor across the coil terminals, there is a path for any current flow as a result of this voltage. Thus, arcing at the sensitive relay contacts is eliminated.

Optical Fire Detection Systems

Optical sensors, often referred to as "flame detectors," are designed to alarm when they detect the presence of prominent, specific radiation emissions from hydrocarbon flames. The two types of optical sensors available are infrared (IR) and ultraviolet, based on the specific emission wave lengths they are designed to detect.

Infrared Optical Fire Protection

IR-based optical flame detectors are used primarily on light turboprop aircraft and helicopter engines. These sensors have proven to be very dependable and economical for the relatively benign environments of these applications.

Principle of Operation

Radiation emitted by the fire crosses the airspace between the fire and the detector and impinges on the detector front face and window. The window allows a broad spectrum of radiation to pass into the detector where it impinges on the face of the sensing device filter. The filter allows only radiation in a tight waveband centered around 4.3 micrometers in the IR to pass on to the radiation-sensitive surface of the sensing device. The radiation striking the sensing device minutely raises its temperature causing small thermoelectric voltages to be generated. These voltages are fed to an amplifier whose output is connected to various analytical electronic processing circuits. The processing electronics is tailored exactly to the time signature of all known hydrocarbon flame sources and ignores false alarm sources, such as incandescent lights and sunlight. Alarm sensitivity level is accurately controlled by a digital circuit. A typical warning system is illustrated in *Figure 9-3*.

Figure 9-3. *Optical fire detection system circuit.*

Pneumatic Thermal Fire Detection

Pneumatic detectors are based on the principles of gas laws. The sensing element consists of a closed helium-filled tube connected at one end to a responder assembly. As the element is heated, the gas pressure inside the tube increases until the alarm threshold is reached. At this point, an internal switch closes and reports an alarm to the cockpit. The pneumatic detector integrity pressure switch opens and triggers the fault alarm if the pneumatic detector losses pressure, as in the case of a leak.

Continuous-Loop Detector Systems

Large commercial aircraft almost exclusively use continuous thermal sensing elements for powerplant protection, since these systems offer superior detection performance and coverage, and they have the proven ruggedness to survive in the harsh environment of modern turbofan engines.

A continuous-loop detector, or sensing system, permits more complete coverage of a fire hazard area than any of the spot-type temperature detectors. Continuous-loop systems are versions of the thermal switch system. They are overheat systems, heat-sensitive units that complete electrical circuits at a certain temperature. There is no rate-of-heat-rise sensitivity in a continuous-loop system. Two widely used types of continuous-loop systems are the Kidde and the Fenwal systems. This text briefly discusses the Fenwall system, while the Kidde system is discussed more in-depth.

Fenwall Continuous-Loop System

The Fenwal system uses a slender inconel tube packed with thermally sensitive eutectic salt and a nickel wire center conductor. *[Figure 9-4]* Lengths of these sensing elements are connected in series to a control unit. The elements may be of equal or varying length and of the same or different temperature settings. The control unit, operating directly from the power source, impresses a small voltage on the sensing elements. When an overheat condition occurs at any point along the element length, the resistance of the eutectic salt within the sensing element drops sharply, causing current to flow between the outer sheath and the center conductor. This current flow is sensed by the control unit, which produces a signal to actuate the output relay.

When the fire has been extinguished or the critical temperature lowered, the Fenwal system automatically returns to standby alert, ready to detect any subsequent fire or overheat condition. The Fenwal system may be wired to employ a "loop" circuit. In this case, should an open circuit occur, the system still signals fire or overheat. If multiple open circuits occur, only that section between breaks becomes inoperative.

Kidde Continuous-Loop System

In the Kidde continuous-loop system, two wires are imbedded in an inconel tube filled with a thermistor core material. *[Figure 9-5]* Two electrical conductors go through the length of the core. One conductor has a ground connection to the tube and the other conductor connects to the fire detection control unit.

As the temperature of the core increases, electrical resistance to ground decreases. The fire detection control unit monitors this resistance. If the resistance decreases to the overheat set point, an overheat indication occurs in the flight deck. Typically, a 10-second time delay is incorporated for the overheat indication. If the resistance decreases more to the fire set point, a fire warning occurs. When the fire or overheat condition is gone, the resistance of the core material increases to the reset point and the flight deck indications go away.

The rate of change of resistance identifies an electrical short or a fire. The resistance decreases more quickly with an electrical short than with a fire. In addition to fire and overheat detection, the Kidde continuous-loop system can supply nacelle temperature data to the airplane condition monitoring function of the Aircraft In-Flight Monitoring System (AIMS).

Sensing Element

The sensing element consists, essentially, of an infinite number of unit thermistors electrically in parallel along its length. The resistance of the sensing element is a function of the length heated, as well as the temperature-heating of less than the full length of element, which requires that portion to be heated to a higher temperature to achieve the same total resistance change. As a result, the system responds not to a fixed alarm temperature but to the sum of the resistances (in parallel) that reflects a nonarithmetic "average." The sensing element may be routed close to nonhazardous hot spots that may have a normal temperature well above the overall alarm

Figure 9-4. *Fenwal sensing element.*

Figure 9-5. *Kidde continuous-loop system.*

temperature, without danger of causing a false alarm. This feature permits the alarm point to be set close to the maximum general ambient temperature, giving greater sensitivity to a general overheat or fire without being subject to false alarms from localized nonhazardous hot spots.

Combination Fire and Overheat Warning

The analog signal from the thermistor sensing element permits the control circuits to be arranged to give a two-level response from the same sensing element loop. The first is an overheat warning at a temperature level below the fire warning, indicating a general engine compartment temperature rise, which could be caused by leakage of hot bleed air or combustion gas into the engine compartment. It could be an early warning of fire, and would alert the crew to appropriate action to reduce the engine compartment temperature. The second-level response would be at a level above that attainable by the leaking hot gas and would be the fire warning.

Temperature Trend Indication

The analog signal produced by the sensing element loop as its temperature changes can readily be converted to signals suitable for meter or cathode ray tube (CRT) display to indicate engine bay temperature increases from normal. A comparison of the readings from each loop system also provides a check on the condition of the fire detection system, because the two loops should normally read alike.

System Test

The integrity of the continuous-loop fire detection system may be tested by actuating a test switch in the flight deck, which switches one end of the sensing element loop from its control circuit to a test circuit, built into the control unit, that simulates the sensing element resistance change due to fire. *[Figure 9-6]* If the sensing element loop is unbroken, the resistance detected "seen" by the control circuit is now that of the simulated fire and so the alarm is signaled. This demonstrates, in addition to the continuity of the sensing element loop, the integrity of the alarm indicator circuit and the proper functioning of the control circuits. The thermistor properties of the sensing element remain unchanged for the life of the element (no chemical or physical changes take place on heating), so that it functions properly as long as it is electrically connected to the control unit.

Figure 9-6. *Continuous-loop fire detection system test circuit.*

Fault Indication

Provision can be made in the control unit to send a fault signal to activate a fault indicator whenever the short discriminator circuit detects a short in the sensing element loop. While this is a requirement in 14 CFR for transport category aircraft because such a short disables the fire detection system, it is offered as an option for other aircraft types in which it may not be a requirement.

Dual-Loop Systems

Dual-loop systems are, in essence, two complete basic fire detection systems with their output signals connected so that both must signal to result in a fire warning. This arrangement, called "AND" logic, results in greatly increased reliability against false fire warnings from any cause. Should one of the two loops be found inoperative at the preflight integrity test, a cockpit selector switch disconnects that loop and allows the signal from the other loop alone to activate the fire warning. Since the single operative loop meets all fire detector requirements, the aircraft can be safely dispatched and maintenance deferred to a more convenient time. However, should one of the two loops become inoperative in flight and a fire subsequently occur, the fire signaling loop activates a cockpit fault signal that alerts the flight crew to select single-loop operation to confirm the possible occurrence of fire.

Automatic Self-Interrogation

Dual-loop systems automatically perform the loop switching and decision-making function required of the flight crew upon appearance of the fault indication in the cockpit. Automatic self-interrogation eliminates the fault indication, and assures the immediate appearance of the fire indication should fire occur while at least one loop of the dual-loop system is operative. Should the control circuit from a single loop signal "fire," the self-interrogation circuit automatically tests the functioning of the other loop. If it tests operative, the circuit suppresses the fire signal (because the operative loop would have signaled if a fire existed). If, however, the other loop tests inoperative, the circuit outputs a fire signal. The interrogation and decision takes place in milliseconds, so that no delay occurs if a fire actually exists.

Support Tube-Mounted Sensing Elements

When you want to mount the sensing elements on the engine, and in some cases, on the aircraft structure, the support tube-mounted element solves the problem of providing sufficient element support points, and greatly facilitates the removal and reinstallation of the sensing elements for engine or system maintenance.

Most modern installations use the support tube concept of mounting sensing elements for better maintainability as well as increased reliability. The sensing element is attached to a prebent stainless steel tube by closely spaced clamps and bushings, where it is supported from vibration damage and protected from pinching and excessive bending. The support tube-mounted elements can be furnished with either single- or dual-sensing elements.

Being prebent to the designed configuration assures its installation in the aircraft precisely in its designed location, where it has the necessary clearance to be free from the possibility of the elements chafing against engine or aircraft structure. The assembly requires only a few attachment points, and removal for engine maintenance is quick and easy. Should the assembly require repair or maintenance, it is easily replaced with another assembly, leaving the repair for the shop. A damaged sensing element is easily replaced in the assembly. The assembly is rugged, easy to handle, and unlikely to suffer damage during handling for installation or removal.

Fire Detection Control Unit (Fire Detection Card)

The control unit for the simplest type of system typically contains the necessary electronic resistance monitoring and alarm output circuits, housed in a hermetically sealed aluminum case and filled with a mounting bracket and circular electrical connector. For more sophisticated systems, control modules may be employed that contain removable control cards having circuitry for individual hazard areas, and/or unique functions. In the most advanced applications, the detection system circuitry controls all aircraft fire protection functions, including fire detection and extinguishing for engines, APUs, cargo bays, and bleed air systems.

Fire Zones

The powerplant installation has several designated fire zones: (1) the engine power section; (2) the engine accessory section; (3) except for reciprocating engines, any complete powerplant compartment in which no isolation is provided between the engine power section and the engine accessory section; (4) any APU compartment; (5) any fuel-burning heater and other combustion equipment installation; (6) the compressor and accessory sections of turbine engines; and (7) combustor, turbine, and tailpipe sections of turbine engine installations that contain lines or components carrying flammable fluids or gases. *Figure 9-7* shows fire protection for a large turbo fan engine.

In addition to the engine and nacelle area zones, other areas on multiengine aircraft are provided with fire detection and protection systems. These areas include baggage compartments, lavatories, APU, combustion heater installations, and other hazardous areas. Discussion of fire protection for these areas is not included in this section, which is limited to engine fire protection.

Figure 9-7. *Large turbofan engine fire zones.*

Engine Fire Extinguishing System

Commuter aircraft certificated under 14 CFR part 23 are required to have, at a minimum, a one-shot fire extinguishing system. All transport category aircraft certificated under 14 CFR part 25 are required to have two discharges, each of which produces adequate agent concentration. An individual one-shot system may be used for APUs, fuel burning heaters, and other combustion equipment. For each "other" designated fire zone, two discharges (two-shot system) must be provided, each of which produces adequate agent concentration. *[Figure 9-8]*

Fire Extinguishing Agents

The fixed fire extinguisher systems used in most engine fire protection systems are designed to dilute the atmosphere with an inert agent that does not support combustion. Many systems use perforated tubing or discharge nozzles to distribute the extinguishing agent. High rate of discharge (HRD) systems use open-end tubes to deliver a quantity of extinguishing agent in 1 to 2 seconds. The most common extinguishing agent still used today is Halon 1301 because of its effective firefighting capability and relatively low toxicity (U.L. classification Group 61). Noncorrosive, Halon 1301 does not affect the material it contacts and requires no clean-up when discharged. Halon 1301 is the current extinguishing agent for commercial aircraft, but a replacement is under development. Because Halon 1301 depletes the ozone layer only recycled Halon 1301 is currently available. Halon 1301 is used until a suitable replacement is developed. Some military aircraft use HCL-125, which the Federal Aviation Administration (FAA) is testing for use in commercial aircraft.

Figure 9-8. *Typical fire extinguishing system.*

Turbine Engine Ground Fire Protection

On many aircraft, means are usually provided for rapid access to the compressor, tailpipe, or burner compartments. Many aircraft systems are equipped with spring-loaded or pop-out access doors in the skin of the various compartments. Internal engine tailpipe fires that take place during engine shutdown or false starts can be blown out by motoring the engine with the starter. A running engine can be accelerated to rated speed to achieve the same result. If such a fire persists, a fire extinguishing agent can be directed into the tailpipe. It should be remembered that excessive use of CO_2, or other agents that have a cooling effect, can shrink the turbine housing on the turbine and cause the engine to disintegrate.

Containers

Fire extinguisher containers (HRD bottles) store a liquid halogenated extinguishing agent and pressurized gas (typically nitrogen) normally manufactured from stainless steel. Depending upon design considerations, alternate materials are available including titanium. Containers are also available in a wide range of capacities and are produced under Department of Transportation (DOT) specifications or exemptions. Most aircraft containers are spherical in design, which provides the lightest weight possible. However, cylindrical shapes are available where space limitations are a factor. Each container incorporates a temperature/pressure sensitive safety relief diaphragm that prevents container pressure from exceeding container test pressure in the event of exposure to excessive temperatures. *[Figure 9-9]*

Discharge Valves

Discharge valves are installed on the containers. A cartridge (squib) and frangible disk type valve are installed in the outlet of the discharge valve assembly. Special assemblies having solenoid-operated or manually-operated seat type valves are also available. Two types of cartridge disk-release techniques are used. Standard release type uses a slug driven by explosive energy to rupture a segmented closure disk. For high temperature or hermetically sealed units, a direct explosive impact type cartridge is used, which applies fragmentation impact to rupture a prestressed corrosion-resistant steel diaphragm. Most containers use conventional metallic gasket seals that facilitate refurbishment following discharge. *[Figure 9-10]*

Pressure Indication

A wide range of diagnostics are utilized to verify the fire extinguisher agent charge status. A simple visually indicated gauge is available, typically a vibration-resistant helical bourdon-type indicator. *[see Figure 9-9]*

A combination gauge switch visually indicates actual container pressure and also provides an electrical signal if container pressure is lost, precluding the need for discharge indicators. A ground checkable diaphragm-type low-pressure switch is commonly used on hermetically sealed containers. The Kidde system also has a temperature compensated pressure switch that tracks the container pressure variations with temperatures by using a hermetically sealed reference chamber.

Two-Way Check Valve

A complete line of two-way check valves is available, manufactured from either lightweight aluminum or steel. These valves are required in a two-shot system to prevent the agent in a reserve container from backing up into the previous emptied main container. Valves are supplied with either MS-33514 or MS-33656 fitting configurations.

Discharge Indicators

Discharge indicators provide immediate visual evidence of container discharge on fire extinguishing systems. Two kinds of indicators can be furnished: thermal and discharge. Both types are designed for aircraft and skin mounting. *[Figure 9-11]*

Figure 9-9. *Fire extinguisher containers (HRD bottles).*

Figure 9-10. *Discharge valve and cartridge (squib).*

Figure 9-11. *Discharge indicators.*

Thermal Discharge Indicator (Red Disk)

The thermal discharge indicator is connected to the fire container relief fitting and ejects a red disk to show when container contents have dumped overboard due to excessive heat. The agent discharges through the opening created when the disk blows out. This gives the flight and maintenance crews an indication that the fire extinguisher container needs to be replaced before the next flight.

Yellow Disk Discharge Indicator

If the flight crew activates the fire extinguisher system, a yellow disk is ejected from the skin of the aircraft fuselage. This is an indication for the maintenance crew that the fire extinguishing system was activated by the flight crew, and that the fire extinguishing container needs to be replaced before the next flight.

Fire Switch

Fire switches are typically installed on the center overhead panel or center console in the flight deck. *[Figure 9-12]* When the fire switch is activated, the following happens: the engine stops because the fuel control shuts off, the engine is isolated from the aircraft systems, and the fire extinguishing system is activated. Some aircraft use fire switches that need to be pulled and turned to activate the system, while others use a push-type switch with a guard. To prevent accidental activation of the fire switch, a lock is installed that releases the fire switch only when a fire has been detected. This lock can

Figure 9-12. *Engine fire switches.*

be manually released by the flight crew if the fire detection system malfunctions. *[Figure 9-13]*

Warning Systems

Visible and audible warning systems are installed in the cockpit to alert the flight crew. A horn sounds and one or several warning lights illuminate to alert the flight crew that an engine fire has been detected. These indications stop when the fire is extinguished.

Fire Detection System Maintenance

Fire detector sensing elements are located in many high-activity areas around aircraft engines. Their location, together with their small size, increases the chance of damage to the sensing elements during maintenance. An inspection and maintenance program for all types of continuous-loop systems should include the following visual checks. These procedures are examples and should not be used to replace the applicable manufacturer's instructions.

Sensing elements of a continuous-loop system should be inspected for the following:

1. Cracked or broken sections caused by crushing or squeezing between inspection plates, cowl panels, or engine components.
2. Abrasion caused by rubbing of the element on cowling, accessories, or structural members.
3. Pieces of safety wire or other metal particles that may short the spot-detector terminals.
4. Condition of rubber grommets in mounting clamps, which may be softened from exposure to oils or hardened from excessive heat.
5. Dents and kinks in sensing element sections. Limits on the element diameter, acceptable dents and kinks, and degree of smoothness of tubing contour are specified by the manufacturer. No attempt should be made to straighten any acceptable dent or kink, since stresses may be set up that could cause tubing failure. (See illustration of kinked tubing in *Figure 9-14*.)

Figure 9-14. *Sensing element defects.*

Figure 9-13. *Engine fire switch operation.*

6. Nuts at the end of the sensing elements *[Figure 9-15]* should be inspected for tightness and the presence of a safety wire. Loose nuts should be retorqued to the value specified by the manufacturer's instructions. Some types of sensing element connection joints require the use of copper crush gaskets, which should be replaced any time a connection is separated.

Figure 9-16. *Rubbing interference.*

Figure 9-15. *Connector joint fitting attached to the structure.*

Figure 9-17. *Inspection of fire detector loop clamp.*

7. If shielded flexible leads are used, they should be inspected for fraying of the outer braid. The braided sheath is composed of many fine metal strands woven into a protective covering surrounding the inner insulated wire. Continuous bending of the cable or rough treatment can break these fine wires, especially those near the connectors.

8. Sensing element routing and clamping should be inspected carefully. *[Figure 9-14]* Long, unsupported sections may permit excessive vibration that can cause breakage. The distance between clamps on straight runs, usually about 8–10 inches, is specified by the manufacturer. At end connectors, the first support clamp is usually located about four to six inches from the end connector fittings. In most cases, a straight run of one inch is maintained from all connectors before a bend is started, and an optimum bend radius of three inches is normally applied.

9. Interference between a cowl brace and a sensing element can cause rubbing. *[Figure 9-16]* This interference may cause wear and short the sensing element.

10. Grommets should be installed on the sensing element so that both ends are centered on its clamp. The split end of the grommet should face the outside of the nearest bend. Clamps and grommets should fit the element snugly. *[Figure 9-17]*

Fire Detection System Troubleshooting

The following troubleshooting procedures represent the most common difficulties encountered in engine fire detection systems:

1. Intermittent alarms are most often caused by an intermittent short in the detector system wiring. Such shorts may be caused by a loose wire that occasionally touches a nearby terminal, a frayed wire brushing against a structure, or a sensing element rubbing against a structural member long enough to wear through the insulation. Intermittent faults often can be located by moving wires to re-create the short.

2. Fire alarms and warning lights can occur when no engine fire or overheat condition exists. Such false alarms can be most easily located by disconnecting the engine sensing loop connections from the control unit. If the false alarm ceases when the engine sensing loop is disconnected, the fault is in the disconnected sensing loop, which should be examined for areas that have been bent into contact with hot parts of the engine. If no bent element can be found, the shorted section can be located by isolating the connecting elements consecutively around the entire loop.

3. Kinks and sharp bends in the sensing element can cause an internal wire to short intermittently to the outer tubing. The fault can be located by checking the sensing element with an ohm meter while tapping the element in the suspected areas to produce the short.
4. Moisture in the detection system seldom causes a false fire alarm. If, however, moisture does cause an alarm, the warning persists until the contamination is removed or boils away, and the resistance of the loop returns to its normal value.
5. Failure to obtain an alarm signal when the test switch is actuated may be caused by a defective test switch or control unit, the lack of electrical power, inoperative indicator light, or an opening in the sensing element or connecting wiring. When the test switch fails to provide an alarm, the continuity of a two-wire sensing loop can be determined by opening the loop and measuring the resistance. In a single-wire, continuous-loop system, the center conductor should be grounded.

Fire Extinguisher System Maintenance Practices.

Regular maintenance of fire extinguisher systems typically includes such items as the inspection and servicing of fire extinguisher bottles (containers), removal and reinstallation of cartridge and discharge valves, testing of discharge tubing for leakage, and electrical wiring continuity tests. The following paragraphs contain details of some of the most typical maintenance procedures.

Fire extinguisher containers are checked periodically to determine that the pressure is between the prescribed minimum and maximum limits. Changes of pressure with ambient temperatures must also fall within prescribed limits. The graph shown in *Figure 9-18* is typical of the pressure temperature curve graphs that provide maximum and minimum gauge readings. If the pressure does not fall within the graph limits, the extinguisher container is replaced. The service life of fire extinguisher discharge cartridges is calculated from the manufacturer's date stamp, which is usually placed on the face of the cartridge. The cartridge service life recommended by the manufacturer is usually in terms of years. Cartridges are available with a service life of 5 years or more. To determine the unexpired service life of a discharge cartridge, it is usually necessary to remove the electrical leads and discharge line from the plug body, which can then be removed from the extinguisher container.

Be careful when replacing cartridge and discharge valves. Most new extinguisher containers are supplied with their cartridge and discharge valve disassembled. Before installation on the aircraft, properly assemble the cartridge in the discharge valve and connect the valve to the container, usually by means of a swivel nut that tightens against a packing ring gasket. *[Figure 9-19]*

Figure 9-18. *Fire extinguisher container pressure-temperature chart.*

Figure 9-19. *Components of fire extinguisher container.*

If a cartridge is removed from a discharge valve for any reason, it should not be used in another discharge valve assembly, since the distance the contact point protrudes may vary with each unit. Thus, continuity might not exist if a used plug that had been indented with a long contact point were installed in a discharge valve with a shorter contact point.

The preceding material in this chapter is general in nature, addressing the principles involved and general procedures to be followed. When actually performing maintenance, always refer to the applicable maintenance manuals and other related publications pertaining to a particular aircraft.

Boeing 777 Aircraft Fire Detection and Extinguishing System

The following section discusses the fire detection and extinguishing system of the B777 aircraft. The information is included only for familiarization purposes.

Each engine has two fire detection loops: loop 1 and loop 2. A fire detection card in the system card file monitors the loops for fires, overheat conditions, and faults. There is a fire detection card for each engine.

Overheat Detection

If the fire detection loops detect an overheat condition, the fire detection card sends a signal to the AIMS and to the warning electronics unit. The following indications occur in the flight deck:

- The master caution lights come on.
- The caution aural operates.
- An engine overheat caution message shows.

Fire Detection

If an engine fire occurs, the fire detection card sends a signal to the AIMS and to the warning electronics unit, and a warning message illuminates. The following indications occur in the flight deck:

- The master warning lights come on.
- The fire warning aural operates.
- An engine fire warning message shows.
- The engine fire warning light comes on.
- The fuel control switch fire warning light comes on.

Nacelle Temperature Recording

The fire detection card measures the average temperature of the loops. This data goes to the AIMS through the system's ARINC 629 buses and is recorded by the airplane condition monitoring function.

Continuous Fault Monitoring

The fire detection card monitors the two loops and their wiring for defects. In normal (dual loop) operation, both loops must have a fire or overheat condition to cause the flight deck indications.

If a failure occurs in a loop, the fire detection card sends the data to the AIMS. A status message shows, and the system changes to single-loop operation. In this mode, fire/overheat indications occur when one loop is defective and the other has a fire or overheat condition.

Single/Dual Loop Operation

The fire detection card monitors the loops for faults. In normal (dual loop) operation, both loops must have a fire or overheat condition to cause the flight deck indications. If one detection loop fails, the card sends data about the failure to the AIMS, and a status message shows. The card changes to single-loop operation, if necessary. If both detection loops fail, an advisory message and status messages is displayed, and the fire detection system does not operate.

System Test

Built-in test equipment (BITE) performs a test of the engine fire detection system for these conditions:

- When the system first gets power
- After a power interrupt
- Every 5 minutes of operation *[Figures 9-20* and *9-21]*

Boeing 777 Fire Extinguisher System

Fire Extinguisher Containers

The B777 airplane has two fire extinguishing bottles that contain Halon fire extinguishing agent pressurized with nitrogen. The engine fire switches in the flight deck are pulled and rotated to release the Halon. Halon from each bottle can be discharged to the right or left engine. Engine indicating and crew alerting system (EICAS) messages, status messages, and indicator lights show when the bottle pressure is low. The two engine fire extinguishing bottles are located behind the right sidewall lining of the forward cargo compartment, aft of the cargo door. *[Figure 9-22]*

The two engine fire extinguishing bottles are identical. Each bottle has these following components:

- A safety relief and fill port
- A handle for removal and installation
- A pressure switch
- Two discharge assemblies

Figure 9-20. *Engine fire detection system.*

Figure 9-21. *Engine fire detection system functional description.*

9-15

- An identification plate
- Four mounting lugs *[Figures 9-23, 9-24, 9-25]*

The bottles contain Halon fire extinguishing agent pressurized with nitrogen. If the pressure in the bottle becomes too high, the safety relief and fill port opens so the bottle does not explode. The discharge assembly has an explosive squib. An electric current from the fire extinguishing circuit fires the squib. This releases the Halon through the discharge port. The pressure switch gives flight deck indications when bottle pressure decreases. The switch monitors the pressure inside the bottle and is normally open. When the pressure decreases because of a leak or bottle discharge, the switch closes an indicating circuit.

Squib

The squib is installed in the discharge assembly at the bottom of the fire container. A fire container has two squibs, one for each engine. The squib is an electrically operated explosive device. When the squib is activated, it fires a slug through the breakable disk, and nitrogen pressure inside the bottle pushes the Halon through the discharge port. The squib fires when the fire switch is pulled and turned to the DISCH 1 or DISCH 2 position. *[Figure 9-22]*

Engine Fire Switches

The engine fire panel is in the flight deck on the P8 aisle stand. The engine fire panel has a fire switch for each engine and a discharge light for each fire bottle. *[Figure 9-26]*

Figure 9-23. *Fire extinguishing bottle.*

The engine fire switch has four functions:

- Gives an indication of an engine fire
- Stops the engine
- Isolates the engine from the airplane systems
- Controls the engine fire extinguishing system

Figure 9-22. *Boeing 777 fire extinguisher container location.*

Figure 9-24. *Location of fire extinguishing bottles.*

Figure 9-25. *Squib or cartridge.*

The fire switch assembly incorporates a solenoid that locks the fire switch so that the flight crew cannot pull it accidently. If an engine has a fire, the fire warning light comes on and the solenoid energizes to release the switch. When the solenoid is energized, the fire switch can be pulled.

When the fire detection system malfunctions or the solenoid is defective and the flight crew wants to extinguish an engine fire, someone must push the fire override switch. The fire override switch allows the fire switch to be pulled when the solenoid is not energized. When the fire switch is pulled, the push-pull switch contacts operate electrical circuits that stop the engine and isolate it from the airplane systems. With the switch pulled, it can be rotated to left or right to a mechanical stop at the discharge position. The rotary switch contacts close and operate the fire extinguishing system.

When the fire switch is pulled, the switch isolates the following aircraft systems from the engine:

- Closes the fuel spar valve
- Deenergizes the engine fuel metering unit (FMU) cutoff solenoid
- Closes the engine hydraulic pump shutoff valve
- Depressurizes the engine driven hydraulic pump valve
- Closes the pressure regulator and shutoff valve
- Removes power from thrust reverser isolation valve
- Trips the generator field
- Trips the backup generator field *[Figure 9-27]*

Engine Fire Operation

If an engine has a fire, the engine fire detection system gives a fire warning in the flight deck. The engine fire warning lights come on to identify which fire switch to use to extinguish the fire. The solenoid in the fire switch energizes and releases the switch so that the fire switch can be pulled. If the solenoid does not energize, push the fire override switch to release the fire switch manually. When the fire switch is pulled, it

Figure 9-26. *Fire switch.*

Figure 9-27. *Engine fire switch circuit.*

stops the engine, and the fire switch isolates the engine from the airplane systems.

If the fire warnings do not go away when the switch is pulled, position the switch to the DISCH 1 or DISCH 2 position, and hold the switch against the stop for one second. This fires the squib in the fire extinguisher container and releases the fire extinguishing agent into the engine nacelle. Ensure that the engine bottle discharge light comes on. If the first bottle does not extinguish the fire, the switch must be placed to the other DISCH position. This fires the squib for the other bottle.

APU Fire Detection and Extinguishing System

The APU fire protection system is similar in design to engine fire protection systems, but there are some differences. The APU is often operated with no personnel in the flight deck and; the APU fire protection system can operate in an unattended mode on the ground with the engines not running. If there is an APU fire in the unattended mode, the fire extinguisher discharges automatically. The APU operates in the attended mode when at least one engine is running. If there is an APU fire in this mode, the crew discharges the bottle manually. Fire switches are located on the cargo fire/engine control panel and the service and APU shutdown panel located outside the airplane on the nose landing gear. *[Figure 9-28]*

APU Fire Warning

If there is an APU fire, the APU fire detection system gives fire warnings and automatically stops the APU. The APU fire warning light comes on to identify the correct fire switch to use to extinguish the fire. The fire switch solenoid releases the switch so that it can be pulled up. If the APU is running, it stops when the fire switch is pulled. The fire switch isolates the APU from the airplane systems.

Fire Bottle Discharge

If the fire warnings do not go away with the switch out, put the switch to the left or right DISCH position. Hold the switch against the discharge stop for one second. This fires the bottle squib and releases the fire extinguishing agent into the APU compartment. Verify that the APU bottle discharge light comes on. *[Figure 9-29]*

Figure 9-28. *P40 service and APU shutdown panel.*

Figure 9-29. *APU fire extinguishing circuit.*

Chapter 10
Engine Maintenance and Operation

Reciprocating Engine Overhaul

Both maintenance and complete engine overhauls are performed normally at specified intervals. This interval is usually governed by the number of hours the powerplant has been in operation. The actual overhaul period for a specific engine is generally determined by the manufacturer's recommendations. Each engine manufacturer sets a total time in service when the engine should be removed from service and overhauled. Depending upon how the engine is used in service, the overhaul time can be mandatory. The overhaul time is listed in hours and is referred to as time before overhaul (TBO). For example, if an engine had a life of 2,000 hours and had operated 500 hours, it would have a TBO of 1,500 hours. Tests and experience have shown that operation beyond this period of time could result in certain parts being worn beyond their safe limits. For an overhauled engine to be as airworthy as a new one, worn parts, as well as damaged parts, must be detected and replaced during overhaul. The only way to detect all unairworthy parts is to perform a thorough and complete overhaul process while the engine is disassembled. The major purpose of overhaul is to inspect, repair, and replace worn engine parts.

A complete overhaul process includes the following ten steps: receiving inspection; disassembly; visual inspection; cleaning; structural inspection; non-destructive testing (NDT) inspection; dimensional inspection; repair and replacement; reassembly; and testing and break in. The inspection phases are the most precise and the most important phases of the overhaul. Inspection cannot be slighted or performed in a careless or incomplete manner. It is always recommended that complete records be made of the inspection process and kept with the engine records.

Each engine manufacturer provides very specific tolerances to which the engine parts must conform, and provides general instructions to aid in determining the airworthiness of the part. However, in many cases, the final determination must be made by the technician. Although the determination must be made if the part is serviceable, repairable, or should be rejected, the technician should follow the manufacturer's manuals and information. When dimensional tolerances are concerned, the manufacturer publishes a new minimum and serviceable dimension for all critical component parts. Knowledge of the operating principles, strength, and stresses applied to a part is essential in making decisions regarding visible wear. When the powerplant technician signs the release for the return to service for an overhauled engine, this certifies that the complete overhaul process has been performed using methods, techniques, and practices acceptable to the Federal Aviation Administration (FAA) Administrator.

Top Overhaul

Reciprocating piston aircraft engines can be repaired by a top overhaul. This means an overhaul of those parts on top of the crankcase, without completely dismantling the engine. It includes removal of the units (i.e., exhaust collectors, ignition harness, intake pipes) necessary to remove the cylinders. The actual top overhaul consists of reconditioning the engine's cylinders by replacing or reconditioning the piston and piston rings, and reconditioning or plating the cylinder wall and valve-operating mechanism, including valve guides if needed. A top overhaul is a little misleading, because it is really an engine repair procedure and not a real overhaul as described earlier. Usually at this time, the accessories require no attention other than that normally required during ordinary maintenance functions. This repair is generally due to valves or piston rings wearing prematurely. Many stress that if an engine requires this much dismantling, it should be completely disassembled and receive a major overhaul.

Major Overhaul and Major Repairs

Major overhaul consists of the complete reconditioning of the powerplant. A reciprocating engine would require that the crankcase be disassembled per the FAA; a major overhaul is not generally a major repair. A certified powerplant-rated technician can perform or supervise a major overhaul of an engine if it is not equipped with an internal supercharger, or has a propeller reduction system other than spur-type gears. At regular intervals, an engine should be completely dismantled, thoroughly cleaned, and inspected. Each part should be overhauled in accordance with the manufacturer's instructions and tolerances for the engine involved. At this time all accessories are removed, overhauled, and tested. Again, instructions from the manufacturer of the accessory concerned should be followed.

General Overhaul Procedures

Because of the continued changes and the many different types of engines in use, it is not possible to treat the specific overhaul of each engine in this text. However, there are various overhaul practices and instructions of a nonspecific nature that apply to all makes and models of engines.

Any engine to be overhauled completely should receive a runout check of its crankshaft or propeller shaft as a first step. Any question concerning crankshaft or propeller shaft replacement is resolved at this time, since a shaft whose runout is beyond limits must be replaced.

Receiving Inspection

The receiving inspection consists of determining the general condition of the total engine as received, along with an inventory of the engine's components. The accessory information should be recorded, such as model and serial numbers, and the accessories should be sent to overhaul if needed. The overhaul records should be organized and the appropriate manuals obtained and reviewed along with a review of the engine's history (log books). The engine's service bulletins, airworthiness directives, and type certificate compliance should be checked. The exterior of the engine should be cleaned after mounting it on an overhaul stand. [Figure 10-1]

Disassembly

As visual inspection immediately follows disassembly, all individual parts should be laid out in an orderly manner on a workbench as they are removed. To guard against damage and to prevent loss, suitable containers should be available in which to place small parts (nuts, bolts, etc.) during the disassembly operation.

Other practices to observe during disassembly include:

1. Drain the engine oil sumps and remove the oil filter. Drain the oil into a suitable container; strain it through a clean cloth. Check the oil and the cloth for metal particles.

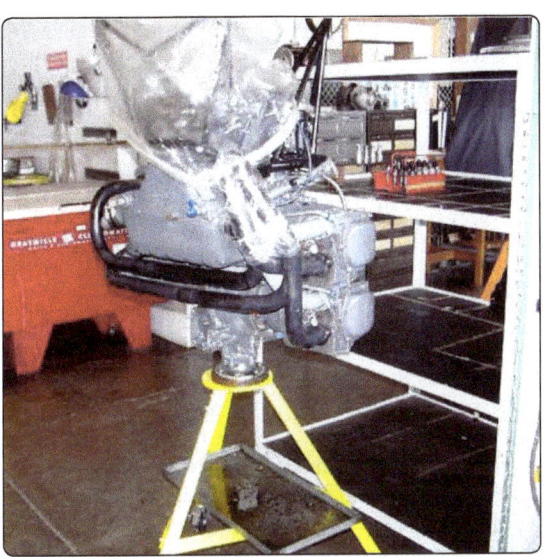

Figure 10-1. *Engine mounted on an overhaul stand.*

2. Dispose of all safety devices (safety wire, cotter pins, etc.) as they are removed. Never use them a second time. Always replace with new safety devices.

3. All loose studs, and loose or damaged fittings, should be carefully tagged to prevent being overlooked during inspection.

4. Always use the proper tool for the job. Use sockets and box end wrenches wherever possible. If special tools are required, use them rather than improvising.

Inspection Process

The inspection of engine parts during overhaul is divided into three categories:

1. Visual
2. Structural NDT
3. Dimensional

Many defects on the engine components can be detected visually, and a determination of airworthiness can be made at this time. If, by visual inspection, the component is determined to be unairworthy, the part is rejected and no further inspection or repair is required. Structural failures can be determined by several different methods. Magnetic parts can readily be examined by the magnetic particle method. Other methods, such as dye penetrate, eddy current, ultra sound, and X-ray, can also be used. The first two methods are aimed at determining structural failures in the parts, while the last method deals with the size and shape of each part. By using very accurate measuring equipment, each engine component can be dimensionally evaluated and compared to service limits and standards (tolerances) set by the manufacturer.

Visual Inspection

Visual inspection should precede all other inspection procedures. Parts should not be cleaned before a preliminary visual inspection, since indications of a failure may often be detected from the residual deposits of metallic particles in some recesses in the engine.

Several terms are used to describe defects detected in engine parts during inspection. Some of the more common terms and definitions are:

1. Abrasion—an area of roughened scratches or marks usually caused by foreign matter between moving parts or surfaces.

2. Brinelling—one or more indentations on bearing races, usually caused by high static loads or application of force during installation or removal. Indentations are rounded or spherical due to the impression left by the contacting balls or rollers of the bearing.

3. Burning—surface damage due to excessive heat. It is usually caused by improper fit, defective lubrication, or over-temperature operation.

4. Burnishing—polishing of one surface by sliding contact with a smooth, harder surface. Usually no displacement nor removal of metal.

5. Burr—a sharp or roughened projection of metal usually resulting from machine processing.

6. Chafing—a condition caused by a rubbing action between two parts under light pressure that results in wear.

7. Chipping—breaking away of pieces of material, that is usually caused by excessive stress concentration or careless handling.

8. Corrosion—loss of metal by a chemical or electrochemical action. The corrosion products are easily removed by mechanical means. Iron rust is an example of corrosion.

9. Crack—a partial separation of material usually caused by vibration, overloading, internal stresses, defective assembly, or fatigue. Depth may be a few thousandths, to the full thickness of the piece.

10. Cut—loss of metal, usually to an appreciable depth over a relatively long and narrow area, by mechanical means, as would occur with the use of a saw blade, chisel, or sharp-edged stone striking a glancing blow.

11. Dent—a small, rounded depression in a surface usually caused by the part being struck with a rounded object.
12. Erosion—loss of metal from the surface by mechanical action of foreign objects, such as grit or fine sand. The eroded area is rough and may be lined in the direction that the foreign material moved relative to the surface.
13. Flaking—the breaking loose of small pieces of metal or coated surfaces, that is usually caused by defective plating or excessive loading.
14. Fretting—a condition of surface erosion caused by minute movement between two parts usually clamped together with considerable unit pressure.
15. Galling—a severe condition of chafing or fretting in which a transfer of metal from one part to another occurs. It is usually caused by a slight movement of mated parts having limited relative motion and under high loads.
16. Gouging—a furrowing condition in which a displacement of metal has occurred (a torn effect). It is usually caused by a piece of metal, or foreign material, between close moving parts.
17. Grooving—a recess, or channel, with rounded and smooth edges usually caused by faulty alignment of parts.
18. Inclusion—presence of foreign or extraneous material entirely within a portion of metal. Such material is introduced during the manufacture of rod, bar, or tubing by rolling or forging.
19. Nick—a sharp-sided gouge or depression with a V-shaped bottom, that is generally the result of careless handling of tools and parts.
20. Peening—a series of blunt depressions in a surface.
21. Pick up or scuffing—a buildup or rolling of metal from one area to another, that is usually caused by insufficient lubrication, clearances, or foreign matter.
22. Pitting—small hollows of irregular shape in the surface, usually caused by corrosion or minute mechanical chipping of surfaces.
23. Scoring—a series of deep scratches caused by foreign particles between moving parts or careless assembly or disassembly techniques.
24. Scratches—shallow, thin lines or marks, varying in degree of depth and width, caused by presence of fine foreign particles during operation or contact with other parts during handling.
25. Stain—a change in color, locally, causing a noticeably different appearance from the surrounding area.
26. Upsetting—a displacement of material beyond the normal contour or surface (a local bulge or bump). Usually indicates no metal loss.

Examine all gears for evidence of pitting or excessive wear. These conditions are of particular importance when they occur on the teeth; deep pit marks in this area are sufficient cause to reject the gear. Bearing surfaces of all gears should be free from deep scratches. However, minor abrasions usually can be dressed out with a fine abrasive cloth.

All bearing surfaces should be examined for scores, galling, and wear. Considerable scratching and light scoring of aluminum bearing surfaces in the engine do no harm and should not be considered a reason for rejecting the part, provided it falls within the clearances set forth in the table of limits in the engine manufacturer's overhaul manual. Even though the part comes within the specific clearance limits, it is not satisfactory for re-assembly in the engine unless inspection shows the part to be free from other serious defects.

Ball bearings should be inspected visually and by feel for roughness, flat spots on balls, flaking or pitting of races, or scoring on the outside of races. All journals should be checked for galling, scores, misalignment, or out-of-round condition. Shafts, pins, etc., should be checked for straightness. This may be done, in most cases, by using V-blocks and a dial indicator.

Pitted surfaces in highly stressed areas, resulting from corrosion, can cause ultimate failure of the part. The following areas should be examined carefully for evidence of such corrosion:

1. Interior surfaces of piston pins
2. The fillets at the edges of crankshaft main and crankpin journal surfaces
3. Thrust bearing races

If pitting exists on any of the surfaces mentioned, to the extent that it cannot be removed by polishing with crocus cloth or other mild abrasive, the part usually must be rejected.

Parts, such as threaded fasteners or plugs, should be inspected to determine the condition of the threads. Badly worn or mutilated threads cannot be tolerated; the parts should be rejected. However, small defects, such as slight nicks or burrs, may be dressed out with a small file, fine abrasive cloth, or stone. If the part appears to be distorted, badly galled, mutilated by overtightening, or from the use of improper tools, replace it with a new one.

Cylinder Head

Inspect the cylinder head for internal and external cracks. Use a bright light to inspect for cracks, and investigate any suspicious areas with a magnifying glass or microscope. Carbon deposits must be cleaned from the inside of the head, and paint must be removed from the outside for this inspection. Exterior cracks show up on the head fins where they have been damaged by tools or contact with other parts because of careless handling. Cracks near the edge of the fins are not dangerous, if the portion of the fin is removed and contoured properly. Cracks at the base of the fin are a reason for rejecting the cylinder. Cracks may also occur on the rocker box or in the rocker bosses. Interior cracks almost always radiate from the valve seat bosses or the spark plug bushing boss. These cracks are usually caused by improper installation of the seats or bushings. They may extend completely from one boss to the other. Inspect the cylinder walls for rust, pitting, or scores. Mild damage of this sort can be removed when the cylinders are deglazed. With more extensive damage, the cylinder has to be reground or honed. If the damage is too deep to be removed by either of these methods, the cylinder usually will have to be rejected. Most engine manufacturers, or engine overhaul repair stations, have an exchange service on cylinders with damaged barrels.

Piston, Valve Train, and Piston Pin

When applicable, check for flatness of the piston head using a straightedge and thickness gauge. *[Figure 10-2]* If a depression is found, check for cracks on the inside of the piston. A depression in the top of the piston usually means that detonation has occurred within the cylinder.

Figure 10-2. *A method for checking cylinder flange warpage.*

Inspect the exterior of the piston for scores and scratches. Scores on the top ring land are not cause for rejection, unless they are excessively deep. Deep scores on the side of the piston are usually a reason for rejection. Examine the piston for cracked skirts, broken ring lands, and scored piston-pin holes. Do not mistake casting marks or laps for a crack. During major overhaul, most pistons are generally replaced, as it requires more labor to clean and inspect the piston than it costs to replace it.

Examine the valve visually for physical damage and damage from burning or corrosion. Do not re-use valves that indicate damage of this nature.

Using a magnifying glass, examine the valve in the stem area and the tip for evidence of cracks, nicks, or other indications of damage. This type of damage seriously weakens the valve, making it susceptible to failure. If superficial nicks and scratches on the valve indicate that it might be cracked, inspect it using a structural inspection method described later. Examine the valve springs for cracks, rust, broken ends, and compression. Cracks can be located by visual inspection or the magnetic particle method.

Inspect the rocker shaft bosses for scoring, cracks, oversize, or out-of-roundness. Scoring is generally caused by the rocker shaft turning in the bosses, which means either the shaft was too loose in the bosses or a rocker arm was too tight on the shaft. Inspect the rocker arm bushing for correct size by sliding the shaft into the bushings to check for proper clearance between the shaft and the bushing. This clearance is also dimensionally checked during the dimensional inspection to confirm the proper clearance. Often, the bushings are scored because of mishandling during disassembly. Check to see that the oil holes line up. At least 50 percent of the hole in the bushing should align with the hole in the rocker arm. On engines that use a bearing rather than a bushing, inspect the bearing to make certain it has not been turning in the rocker arm boss. Also, inspect the bearing to determine its serviceability. Inspect the valve rockers for cracks and worn, pitted, or scored tips. See that all oil passages are free from obstructions.

Inspect all the studs on the cylinder head for looseness, straightness, damaged threads, and proper length. Slightly damaged threads may be chased with the proper die. The length of the stud should be correct within $\pm 1/32$ (0.03125) inch to allow for proper installation of safety devices.

Crankshaft and Connecting Rods

Carefully inspect all surfaces of the crankshaft for cracks. Check the bearing surfaces for evidence of galling, scoring, or other damage. When a shaft is equipped with oil transfer tubes, check them for tightness.

Visual inspection of connecting rods should be done with the aid of a magnifying glass or bench microscope. A rod that is obviously bent or twisted should be rejected without further inspection. Inspect all surfaces of the connecting rods for cracks, corrosion, pitting, galling, or other damage. Galling is caused by a slight amount of movement between the surfaces of the bearing insert and the connecting rod during periods of high loading, such as that produced during overspeed or excessive manifold pressure operation. The visual evidence produced by galling appears as if particles from one contacting surface had welded to the other. Evidence of any galling is sufficient reason for rejecting the complete rod assembly. Galling is a distortion in the metal and is comparable to corrosion in the manner in which it weakens the metallic structure of the connecting rod.

Cleaning

After visually inspecting engine recesses for deposits of metal particles, it is important to clean all engine parts thoroughly to facilitate further inspection. Two processes for cleaning engine parts are:

1. Degreasing to remove dirt and sludge (soft carbon).
2. The removal of hard carbon deposits by decarbonizing, brushing or scraping, and grit-blasting.

Degreasing

Degreasing can be done by immersing or spraying the part in a suitable commercial solvent. *[Figure 10-3]* Extreme care must be used if any water-mixed degreasing solutions containing caustic compounds or soap are used. Such compounds, in addition to being potentially corrosive to aluminum and magnesium, may become impregnated in the pores of the metal and cause oil foaming when the engine is returned to service. Therefore, when using water-mixed solutions, it is imperative that the parts be rinsed thoroughly and completely in clear boiling water after degreasing. Regardless of the method and type of solution used, coat or spray all parts with lubricating oil immediately after cleaning to prevent corrosion.

Removing Hard Carbon

While the degreasing solution removes dirt, grease, and soft carbon, deposits of hard carbon almost invariably remain on many interior surfaces. To remove these deposits, they must first be loosened by immersion in a tank containing a decarbonizing solution (usually heated). A great variety of commercial decarbonizing agents are available. Decarbonizers, like the degreasing solutions previously mentioned, fall generally into two categories, water-soluble and hydrocarbons. The same caution concerning the use of water-soluble degreasers is applicable to water-soluble decarbonizers.

CAUTION: When using a decarbonizing solution on magnesium castings, avoid immersing steel and magnesium parts in the same decarbonizing tank, as this practice often results in damage to the magnesium parts from corrosion.

Decarbonizing will usually loosen most of the hard carbon deposits remaining after degreasing. However, the complete removal of all hard carbon generally requires brushing, scraping, or grit-blasting. In all of these operations, be careful to avoid damaging the machined surfaces. In particular, wire brushes and metal scrapers must never be used on any bearing or contact surface.

Follow the manufacturer's recommendations when grit-blasting parts for the abrasive material being used. Sand, rice, baked wheat, plastic pellets, glass beads, or crushed walnut shells are examples of abrasive substances that are used for grit-blasting parts. A grit-blasting machine is shown in *Figure 10-4*.

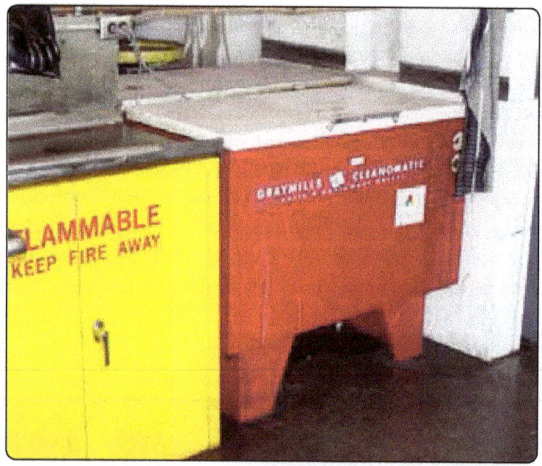

Figure 10-3. *Typical solvent degreasing tank.*

Figure 10-4. *Grit-blasting machine.*

All machined surfaces must be masked properly and adequately, and all openings tightly plugged before blasting. The one exception to this is the valve seats, which may be left unprotected when blasting the cylinder head combustion chamber. It is often advantageous to grit-blast the seats, since this will cut the glaze which tends to form (particularly on the exhaust valve seat), thus facilitating subsequent valve seat reconditioning. Piston ring grooves may be grit-blasted if necessary; however, extreme caution must be used to avoid the removal of metal from the bottom and sides of the grooves. When grit-blasting housings, plug all drilled oil passages with rubber plugs or other suitable material to prevent the entrance of foreign matter.

The decarbonizing solution will generally remove most of the enamel on exterior surfaces. All remaining enamel should be removed by grit-blasting, particularly in the crevices between cylinder cooling fins.

At the conclusion of cleaning operations, rinse the part in petroleum solvent, dry and remove any loose particles of carbon or other foreign matter by air-blasting, and apply a liberal coating of preservative oil to all surfaces.

Magnesium parts should be cleaned thoroughly with a dichromate treatment prior to painting. This treatment consists of cleaning all traces of grease and oil from the part by using a neutral, noncorrosive degreasing medium followed by a rinse, after which the part is immersed for at least 45 minutes in a hot dichromate solution (three-fourths of a pound of sodium dichromate to 1 gallon of water at 180 °F to 200 °F). Then the part should be washed thoroughly in cold running water, dipped in hot water, and dried in an air blast. Immediately thereafter, the part should be painted with a prime coat and engine enamel in the same manner as that suggested for aluminum parts.

Some older engines used sludge chambers in the crankshafts, which were manufactured with hollow crankpins that serve as sludge removers. The sludge chambers require inspection and cleaning at overhaul. Sludge chambers are formed by means of spool-shaped tubes pressed into the hollow crankpins, or by plugs pressed into each end of the crankpin. If an engine has a sludge chamber or tubes, they must be removed for cleaning at overhaul. If these are not removed, accumulated sludge loosened during cleaning may clog the crankshaft oil passages and cause subsequent bearing failures. If the sludge chambers are formed by means of tubes pressed into the hollow crankpins, make certain they are re-installed correctly to avoid covering the ends of the oil passages. Due to improved oils, sludge chambers are no longer used with modern engines.

Structural Inspection

One of the best methods to double check your visual inspection findings is to supplement them with one of the forms of nondestructive testing, such as magnetic particle inspect, dye penetrate inspection, eddy current, ultrasound, and x-ray. Defects in nonmagnetic parts (aluminum parts) can be found by all these methods except for magnetic particle inspect, which is used for magnetic or ferrous materials (steel).

Dye Penetrant Inspection

Dye penetrant inspection is a nondestructive test for defects open to the surface in parts made of any nonporous material. It is used with equal success on such metals as aluminum, magnesium, brass, copper, cast iron, stainless steel, and titanium. Dye penetrant inspection uses a penetrating liquid that enters a surface opening and remains there, making it clearly visible to the inspector. It calls for visual examination of the part after it has been processed, increasing the visibility of the defect so that it can be detected. Visibility of the penetrating material is increased by the addition of one of two types of dye: visible or fluorescent. When using a fluorescent dye, the inspection is accomplished using an ultraviolet (UV) light source (black light).

The steps for performing a dye penetrant inspection are:

1. Thorough cleaning of the metal surface.
2. Applying penetrant.
3. Removing penetrant with remover emulsifier or cleaner.
4. Drying the part.
5. Applying the developer.
6. Inspecting and interpreting results.

Eddy Current Inspection

Eddy currents are composed of free electrons under the influence of an induced electromagnetic field, that are made to drift through metal. Different meter readings are seen when the same metal is in different hardness states. Readings in the affected area are compared with identical materials in known unaffected areas for comparison. A difference in readings indicates a difference in the hardness state of the affected area. Eddy current inspection can frequently be performed without removing the surface coatings, such as primer, paint, and anodized films. It can be effective in detecting surface and subsurface corrosion, pots, and heat treat condition.

Ultrasonic Inspection

Ultrasonic detection equipment makes it possible to locate defects in all types of materials. There are three basic ultrasonic inspection methods:

1. Pulse-echo
2. Through transmission
3. Resonance

Pulse-Echo

Flaws are detected by measuring the amplitude of signals reflected and the time required for these signals to travel between specific surfaces and the discontinuity.

Through Transmission

Through transmission inspection uses two transducers, one to generate the pulse and another placed on the opposite surface to receive it. A disruption in the sound path indicates a flaw and is displayed on the instrument screen. Through transmission is less sensitive to small defects than the pulse-echo method.

Resonance

This system differs from the pulse-echo method, in that the frequency of transmission may be continuously varied. The resonance method is principally used for thickness measurements when the two sides of the material being tested are smooth and parallel, and the backside is inaccessible. The point at which the frequency matches the resonance point of the material being tested is the thickness determining factor.

Magnetic Particle Inspection

Magnetic particle inspection is a method of detecting invisible cracks and other defects in ferromagnetic materials, such as iron and steel. It is not applicable to nonmagnetic materials. The inspection process consists of magnetizing the part, and then applying ferromagnetic particles to the surface area to be inspected. The ferromagnetic particles (indicating medium) may be held in suspension in a liquid that is flushed over the part; the part may be immersed in the suspension liquid; or the particles, in dry powder form, may be dusted over the surface of the part. The wet process is more commonly used in the inspection of aircraft parts.

If a discontinuity is present, the magnetic lines of force are disturbed, and opposite poles exist on either side of the discontinuity. The magnetized particles form a pattern in the magnetic field between the opposite poles. This pattern, known as an indication, assumes the approximate shape of the surface projection of the discontinuity. A discontinuity may be defined as an interruption in the normal physical structure or configuration of a part.

X-ray

X-rays can penetrate material and disclose discontinuities through the metal or non-metal components, making it an excellent inspection process when needed to determine the structural integrity of an engine component. The penetrating radiation is projected through the part to be inspected and produces an invisible or latent image in the film. When processed, the film becomes a radiograph, or shadow picture, of the object. This inspection medium, as a portable unit, provides a fast and reliable means for checking the integrity of engine components.

Additional and more thorough information on NDT inspection is covered in detail in the General Aviation Maintenance Technician Handbook FAA-H-8083-30.

Dimensional Inspection

The dimensional inspection is used to assure that the engine's component parts and clearances meet the manufacturer's specifications. These specs are listed in a table of limits, which lists serviceable limits and the manufacturer's new part maximum and minimum dimensions. Many measuring tools are used to perform the dimensional inspection of the engine. Some examples of these devices are discussed as the procedure for measuring the engine's components for dimensional inspection is explained in the following paragraphs.

Cylinder Barrel

Inspect the cylinder barrel for wear, using a cylinder bore gauge *[Figure 10-5]*, a telescopic gauge, and micrometer or an inside micrometer. Dimensional inspection of the barrel consists of the following measurements:

1. Maximum taper of cylinder walls
2. Maximum out-of-roundness

Figure 10-5. *A cylinder bore gauge.*

3. Bore diameter
4. Step
5. Fit between piston skirt and cylinder

All measurements involving cylinder barrel diameters must be taken at a minimum of two positions 90° apart in the particular plane being measured. It may be necessary to take more than two measurements to determine the maximum wear. Taper of the cylinder walls is the difference between the diameter of the cylinder barrel at the bottom and the diameter at the top. The cylinder is usually worn larger at the top than at the bottom. This taper is caused by the natural wear pattern. At the top of the stroke, the piston is subjected to greater heat and pressure and more erosive environment than at the bottom of the stroke. Also, there is greater freedom of movement at the top of the stroke. Under these conditions, the piston wears the cylinder wall more at the top of the cylinder. In most cases, the taper ends with a ridge, that must be removed during overhaul. *[Figure 10-6]*

Where cylinders are built with an intentional choke, measurement of taper becomes more complicated. Cylinder choke is where the top of the cylinder has been made with the very top diameter of the cylinder smaller, to compensate for wear and expansion during operation. It is necessary to know exactly how the size indicates wear or taper. Taper can be measured in any cylinder by a cylinder dial gauge as long as there is not a sharp step. The dial gauge tends to ride up on the step and causes inaccurate readings at the top of the cylinder.

The measurement for out-of-roundness is usually taken at the top of the cylinder. However, a reading should also be taken at the skirt of the cylinder to detect dents or bends caused by careless handling. A step, or ridge, is formed in the cylinder by the wearing action of the piston rings. *[Figure 10-6]* The greatest wear is at the top of the ring travel limit. The ridge that results is likely to cause damage to the rings or piston. If the step exceeds tolerances, it should be removed by grinding the cylinder oversize, or it should be blended by hand-stoning to break the sharp edge. A step also may be found where the bottom ring reaches the lowest travel. This step is rarely found to be excessive, but it should be checked. Check the cylinder flange for warpage by placing the cylinder on a suitable jig. Check to see that the flange contacts the jig all the way around. The amount of warpage can be checked by using a thickness gauge. *[Figure 10-2]* A cylinder whose flange is warped beyond the limits should be rejected.

Figure 10-6. *Ridge or step formed in an engine cylinder.*

Valves and Valve Springs

The locations for checking runout and edge thickness of the valves are shown in *Figure 10-7*. Measure the edge thickness of valve heads. If, after re-facing, the edge thickness is less than the limit specified by the manufacturer, the valve must not be re-used. The edge thickness can be measured with sufficient accuracy by a dial indicator and a surface plate. Out-of-roundness is usually caused by a stuck valve. If a valve sticks, the rocker shaft tends to work up and down when the valve offers excessive resistance to opening. Inspect for out-of-roundness and oversize using a telescopic gauge and a micrometer.

Figure 10-7. *Valve showing locations for checking runout and section for measuring edge thickness.*

Figure 10-8. *Checking valve stretch with a manufacturer's gauge.*

Inspect the valve for stretch and wear, using a micrometer or a valve radius' gauge. *[Figure 10-8]* If a micrometer is used, stretch is found as a smaller diameter of the valve stem near the neck of the valve. Measure the diameter of the valve stem, and check the fit of the valve in its guide.

Compression is tested with a valve spring compression tester. *[Figure 10-9]* The spring is compressed until its total height is that specified by the manufacturer. The dial on the tester should indicate the pressure, in pounds, required to compress the spring to the specified height. This must be within the pressure limits established by the manufacturer.

Inspect the shaft's diameter for correct size with a micrometer. Rocker shafts are often found to be scored and burned because of excessive turning in the cylinder head. Also, there may be some pickup on the shaft (bronze from the rocker bushing transferred to the steel shaft). Generally, this is caused by overheating and too little clearance between

Figure 10-9. *Valve spring compression tester.*

shaft and bushing. The clearance between the shaft and the bushing is most important.

Crankshaft

Use extreme care in inspecting and checking the crankshaft for straightness. Place the crankshaft in V-blocks, supported at the locations specified in the applicable engine overhaul manual as in *Figure 10-10*. Using a surface plate and a dial indicator, measure the shaft runout. If the total indicator reading exceeds the dimensions given in the manufacturer's table of limits, the shaft must not be re-used. A bent crankshaft should not be straightened. Any attempt to do so results in rupture of the nitrided surface of the bearing journals, a condition that causes eventual failure of the crankshaft. Measure the outside diameter of the crankshaft main and rod-bearing journals using a micrometer. *[Figure 10-11]* Internal measurements can be made by using telescoping gauges, and then measuring the telescoping gauge with a micrometer. *[Figure 10-12]* Compare the resulting measurements with those in the table of limits.

Figure 10-12. *Telescoping gauges and micrometer combination.*

Checking Alignment

Check bushings that have been replaced to determine if the bushing and rod bores are square and parallel to each other. The alignment of a connecting rod can be checked several ways. One method requires a push fit arbor for each end of the connecting rod, a surface plate, and two parallel blocks of equal height.

To measure rod squareness, or twist, insert the arbors into the rod bores. *[Figure 10-13]* Place the parallel blocks on a surface plate. Place the ends of the arbors on the parallel blocks. Using a thickness gauge, check the clearance at the points where the arbors rest on the blocks. This clearance, divided by the separation of the blocks in inches, gives the twist per inch of length.

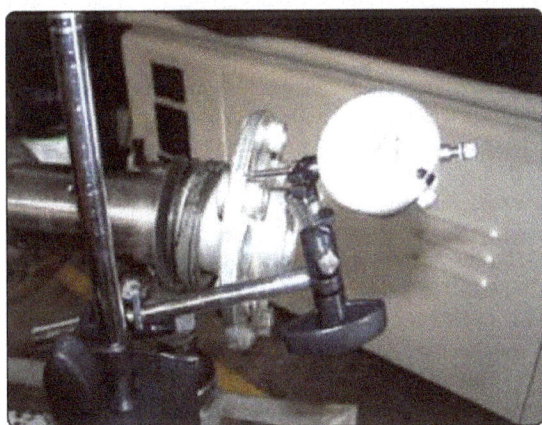

Figure 10-10. *Checking crankshaft runout.*

Figure 10-11. *A micrometer.*

Figure 10-13. *Checking connecting rod squareness.*

To determine bushing or bearing parallelism (convergence), insert the arbors in the rod bores. Measure the distance between the arbors on each side of the connecting rod at points that are equidistant from the rod centerline. For exact parallelism, the distances checked on both sides should be the same. Consult the manufacturer's table of limits for the amount of misalignment permitted.

The preceding operations are typical of those used for most reciprocating engines and are included to introduce some of the operations involved in engine overhaul. It would be impractical to list all the steps involved in the overhaul of an engine. It should be understood that there are other operations and inspections that must be performed. For exact information regarding a specific engine model, consult the manufacturer's overhaul manual.

Repair and Replacement

The engine components that have failed inspection, or are unrepairable, should have been discarded. The component parts that need repair and replacement are now given the attention required. The replacement components (new parts) are organized and laid out for reassembly.

Minor damage to engine parts, such as burrs, nicks, scratches, scoring, or galling, should be removed with a fine oil stone, crocus cloth, or any similar abrasive substance. Following any repairs of this type, the part should be cleaned carefully to be certain that all abrasive has been removed, and then checked with its mating part to assure that the clearances are not excessive. Flanged surfaces that are bent, warped, or nicked can be repaired by lapping to a true surface on a surface plate. Again, the part should be cleaned to be certain that all abrasive has been removed. Defective threads can sometimes be repaired with a suitable die or tap. Small nicks can be satisfactorily removed with Swiss pattern files or small, edged stones. Pipe threads should not be tapped deeper to clean them, because this practice results in an oversized tapped hole. If galling or scratches are removed from a bearing surface of a journal, it should be buffed to a high polished finish.

In general, welding of highly-stressed engine parts can be accomplished only when approved by the manufacturer. However, welding may be accomplished using methods that are approved by the engine manufacturer, and if it can be reasonably expected that the welded repair will not adversely affect the airworthiness of the engine.

Many minor parts not subjected to high stresses may be safely repaired by welding. Mounting lugs, cowl lugs, cylinder fins, rocker box covers, and many parts originally fabricated by welding are in this category. The welded part should be suitably stress-relieved after welding. However, before welding any engine part, consult the manufacturer's instructions for the engine concerned to see if it is approved for repair by welding.

Parts requiring use of paint for protection or appearance should be repainted according to the engine manufacturer's recommendations. Aluminum alloy parts should have original, exterior painted surfaces rubbed smooth to provide a proper paint base. See that surfaces to be painted are thoroughly cleaned. Care must be taken to avoid painting mating surfaces. Exterior aluminum parts should be primed first with a thin coat of zinc chromate primer. After the primer is dry, parts should be painted with engine enamel, that should be air dried until hard, or baked for ½ hour at 82 °C (180 °F). Aluminum parts from which the paint has not been removed may be repainted without the use of a priming coat, provided no bare aluminum is exposed.

Any studs that are bent, broken, damaged, or loose must be replaced. After a stud has been removed, the tapped stud hole should be examined for size and condition of threads. If it is necessary to re-tap the stud hole, it also is necessary to use a suitable oversize stud. Studs that have been broken off flush with the case must be drilled and removed with suitable stud remover. Be careful not to damage any threads. When replacing studs, coat the coarse threads of the stud with an anti-seize compound.

Cylinder Assembly Reconditioning

Cylinder and piston assemblies are inspected according to the procedures contained in the engine manufacturer's manuals, charts, and service bulletins. A general procedure for inspecting and reconditioning cylinders is discussed in the following section to provide an understanding of the operations involved.

Visually inspect the head fins for other damage besides cracks. Dents or bends in the fins should be left alone unless there is danger of cracking. Where pieces of fin are missing, the sharp edges should be filed to a smooth contour. Fin breakage in a concentrated area causes dangerous local hot spots. Fin breakage near the spark plug bushings or on the exhaust side of the cylinder is obviously more dangerous than in other areas. When removing or re-profiling a cylinder fin, follow the instructions and the limits in the manufacturer's manual.

Inspect spark plug inserts for the condition of the threads and for looseness. Run a tap of the proper size through the bushing. Very often, the inside threads of the bushing are burned. If more than one thread is missing, the bushing should be rejected. Tighten a plug in the bushing to check for looseness.

Piston and Piston Pins

If the old piston is to be reused, or a new piston is to be used, measure the outside of the piston by means of a micrometer. Measurements must be taken in several directions and on the skirt, as well as on the lands section. Check these sizes against the cylinder size. Most engines use cam ground pistons to compensate for the greater expansion parallel to the pin during engine operation. The diameter of these pistons measures several thousandths of an inch larger at an angle to the piston pin hole, than parallel to the pin hole. Inspect the ring grooves for evidence of wear. The groove needs to be checked for side clearance with a feeler gauge to determine the amount of wear in the grooves. Examine the piston pin for scoring, cracks, excessive wear, and pitting. Check the clearance between the piston pin and the bore of the piston pin bosses using a telescopic gauge and a micrometer. Use the magnetic particle method to inspect the pin for cracks. Since the pins are often case hardened, cracks show up inside the pin more often than they on the outside. Check the pin for bends using V-blocks and a dial indicator on a surface plate. *[Figure 10-14]* Measure the fit of the plugs in the pin. In many cases, the pistons and piston pins are routinely replaced at overhaul.

Figure 10-14. *Checking a piston pin for bends.*

Valves and Valve Springs

Critical areas of the valve include the face and tip *[Figure 10-15]*, both of which should be examined for pitting and excessive wear. Minor pitting on valve faces can sometimes be removed by grinding. Be sure the valve guides are clean before inspection. Often, carbon covers pits inside the guide. If a guide in this condition is put back in service, carbon again collects in the pits and valve sticking results. Besides pits, scores, and burned areas inside the valve guide, inspect them for wear or looseness. Inspection of valve seat inserts before they are re-faced is mostly a matter of determining if there is enough of the seat left to correct any pitting, burning, scoring, or out-of-trueness.

Figure 10-15. *Valve face surface.*

Refacing Valve Seats

The valve seat inserts of aircraft engine cylinders usually are in need of refacing at every overhaul. They are refaced to provide a true, clean, and correct size seat for the valve. When valve guides or valve seats are replaced in a cylinder, the seats must be made concentric with the valve guide.

Low power engines can use either bronze or steel seats. Bronze seats, although not widely used on current engines, are made of aluminum bronze or phosphor bronze alloys. Steel seats are commonly used for valve seats on higher powered engines and are made of heat-resistant steel with a layer of stellite steel alloy on the valve contact surface. Stellite seats can require a special stone to grind this very hard material.

Steel valve seats are refaced by grinding equipment. *[Figure 10-16]* Bronze seats are refaced preferably by the use of cutters or reamers, but they may be ground when this equipment is not available. The only disadvantage of using a stone on bronze is that the soft metal loads the stone to such an extent that much time is consumed in redressing the stone to keep it clean.

The equipment used on steel seats can be either wet or dry valve seat grinding equipment. The wet grinder uses a mixture of soluble oil and water to wash away the chips and to keep the stone and seat cool; this produces a smoother, more accurate job than the dry grinder. The stones may be either silicon carbide or aluminum oxide.

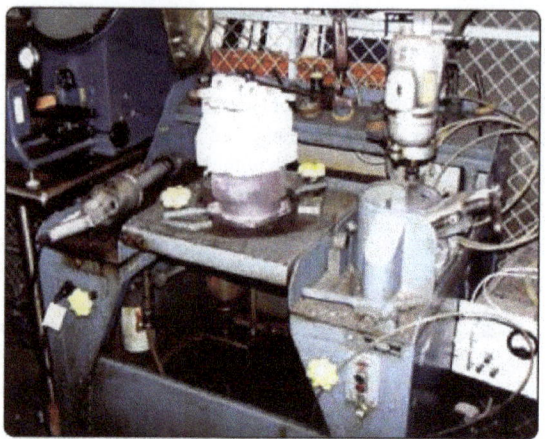

Figure 10-16. *Valve seat grinding equipment.*

Before refacing the seat, make sure that the valve guide is in good condition, clean, and does not have to be replaced. Mount the cylinder firmly in the hold down fixture. An expanding pilot is inserted in the valve guide from the inside of the cylinder, and an expander screw is inserted in the pilot from the top of the guide. *[Figure 10-17]* The pilot must be tight in the guide, because any movement can cause a poor grind. The fluid hose is inserted through one of the spark plug inserts.

Figure 10-17. *Valve seat grinding setup.*

The three grades of stones available for use are classified as rough, finishing, and polishing stones. The rough stone is designed to true and clean the seat. The finishing stone must follow the rough to remove grinding marks and produce a smooth finish. The polishing stone does just as the name implies and is used only where a highly polished seat is desired.

The stones are installed on special stone holders. The face of the stone is trued by a diamond dresser. The stone should be refaced whenever it is grooved or loaded, and when the stone is first installed on the stone holder. The diamond dresser also may be used to cut down the diameter of the stone. Dressing of the stone should be kept to a minimum as a matter of conservation; therefore, it is desirable to have sufficient stone holders for all the stones to be used on the job.

In the actual grinding job, considerable skill is required in handling the grinding gun. The gun must be centered accurately on the stone holder. If the gun is tilted off-center, chattering of the stone results, and a rough grind is produced. It is very important that the stone be rotated at a speed that permits grinding instead of rubbing. This speed is approximately 8,000 to 10,000 revolutions per minute (rpm). Excessive pressure on the stone can slow it down. It is not a good technique to let the stone grind at slow speed by putting pressure on the stone when starting or stopping the gun. The maximum pressure used on the stone at any time should be no more than that exerted by the weight of the gun.

Another practice, conducive to good grinding, is to ease off on the stone every second or so to let the coolant wash away the chips on the seat. This rhythmic grinding action also helps keep the stone up to its correct speed. Since it is quite a job to replace a seat, remove as little material as possible during the grinding. Inspect the job frequently to prevent unnecessary grinding.

The rough stone is used until the seat is true to the valve guide and until all pits, scores, or burned areas are removed. *[Figure 10-18]* After refacing, the seat should be smooth and true. The finishing stone is used only until the seat has a smooth, polished appearance. Extreme caution should be used when grinding with the finishing stone to prevent chattering.

The size and trueness of the seat can be checked by several methods. Runout of the seat is checked with a special dial indicator and should not exceed 0.002 inch. The size of the seat may be determined by using Prussian blue. Prussian blue is used to check for contact transfer from one surface to the other. To check the fit of the seat, spread a thin coat of Prussian blue evenly on the seat. Press the valve onto the seat. The blue transferred to the valve indicates the contact surface. The contact surface should be one-third to two-thirds the width of the valve face and in the middle of the face. In some cases, a-go and no-go gauge is used in place of the valve when making the Prussian blue check. If Prussian blue is not used, the same check may be made by lapping the valve lightly to the seat. Lapping is accomplished by using a small amount of lapping compound placed between the valve face and seat. The valve is then moved in a rotary motion back and forth until the lapping compound grinds slightly into the

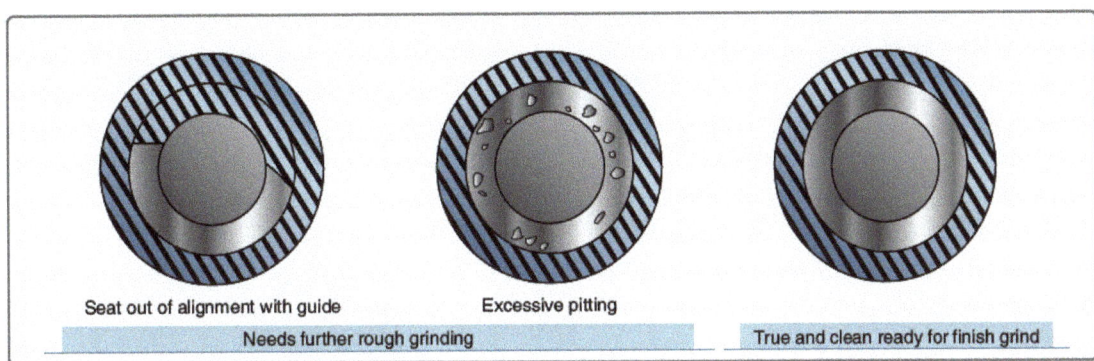

Figure 10-18. *Valve seat grinding.*

surface. After cleaning the lapping contact compound off, a contact area can be seen. Examples of test results are shown in *Figure 10-19.*

If the seat contacts the upper third of the valve face, grind off the top corner of the valve seat. *[Figure 10-20]* Such grinding is called narrowing grinding. This permits the seat to contact the center third of the valve face without touching the upper portion of the valve face.

If the seat contacts the bottom third of the valve face, grind off the inner corner of the valve seat. *[Figure 10-21]* The seat is narrowed by a stone other than the standard angle. It is common practice to use a 15° angle and 45° angle cutting stone on a 30° angle valve seat, and a 30° angle and 75° angle stone on a 45° angle valve seat. *[Figure 10-22]*

If the valve seat has been cut or ground too much, the valve contacts the seat too far up into the cylinder head, and the

Figure 10-19. *Fitting the valve and seat.*

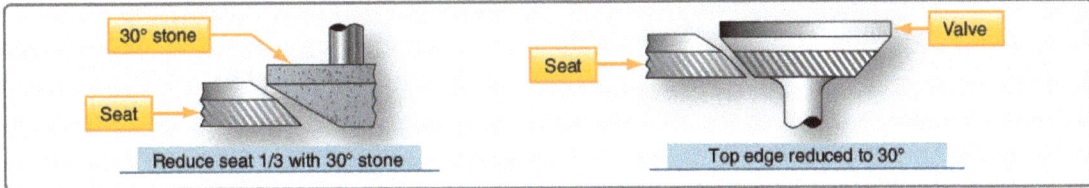

Figure 10-20. *Grinding top surface of the valve seat.*

Figure 10-21. *Grinding the inner corner of the valve seat.*

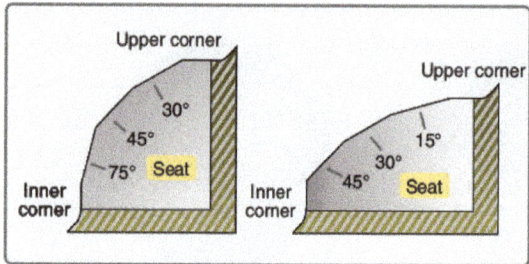

Figure 10-22. *Valve seat angles.*

valve clearance, spring tension, and the fit of the valve to the seat is affected. To check the height of a valve, insert the valve into the guide, and hold it against the seat. Check the height of the valve stem above the rocker box or some other fixed position.

Before refacing a valve seat, consult the overhaul manual for the particular model engine. Each manufacturer specifies the desired angle for grinding and narrowing the valve seat.

Valve Reconditioning

One of the most common jobs during engine overhaul is grinding the valves. The equipment used should preferably be a wet valve grinder. With this type of machine, a mixture of soluble oil and water is used to keep the valve cool and carry away the grinding chips.

Like many machine jobs, valve grinding is mostly a matter of setting up the machine. The following points should be checked or accomplished before starting a grind. True the stone by means of a diamond nib. The machine is turned on, and the diamond is drawn across the stone, cutting just deep enough to true and clean the stone. Determine the face angle of the valve being ground, and set the movable head of the machine to correspond to this valve angle. Usually, valves are ground to the standard angles of 30° or 45°. However, in some instances, an interference fit of 0.5° or 1.5° less than the standard angle may be ground on the valve face.

The interference fit is used to obtain a more positive seal by means of a narrow contact surface. *[Figure 10-23]* Theoretically, there is a line contact between the valve and seat. With this line contact, the load that the valve exerts against the seat is concentrated in a very small area, thereby increasing the unit load at any one spot. The interference fit is especially beneficial during the first few hours of operation after an overhaul. The positive seal reduces the possibility of a burned valve or seat that a leaking valve might produce. After the first few hours of running, these angles tend to pound down and become identical.

Figure 10-23. *Interference fit of valve and valve seat.*

Notice that the interference angle is ground into the valve, not the seat. It is easier to change the angle of the valve grinder work head than to change the angle of a valve seat grinder stone. Do not use an interference fit unless the manufacturer approves it.

Install the valve into the chuck, and adjust the chuck so that the valve face is approximately 2 inches from the chuck. *[Figure 10-24]* If the valve is chucked any further out, there is danger of excessive wobble and also a possibility of grinding into the stem.

There are various types of valve grinding machines. In one type, the stone is moved across the valve face; in another, the valve is moved across the stone. Whichever type is used, the following procedures are typical of those performed when refacing a valve.

Check the travel of the valve face across the stone. The valve should completely pass the stone on both sides, yet not travel far enough to grind the stem. There are stops on the machine that can be set to control this travel.

With the valve set correctly in place, turn on the machine and the grinding fluid so that it splashes on the valve face. Back the grinding wheel off all the way. Place the valve directly in front of the stone. *[Figure 10-25]* Slowly bring the wheel forward until a light cut is made on the valve. The intensity of the grind is measured by sound more than anything else. Slowly draw the valve back and forth across the stone without increasing the cut. Move the work head table back and forth using the full face of the stone, but always keep the valve face on the stone. When the sound of the grind diminishes,

Figure 10-24. *Valve installed in grinding machine.*

Figure 10-25. *Valve in chuck ready to grind.*

Figure 10-26. *Engine valves showing normal margin and a feather edge.*

indicating that some valve material has been removed, move the workhead table to the extreme left to stop rotation of the valve. Inspect the valve to determine if further grinding is necessary. If another cut must be made, bring the valve in front of the stone, then advance the stone out to the valve. Do not increase the cut without having the valve directly in front of the stone.

An important precaution in valve grinding, as in any kind of grinding, is to make light cuts only. Heavy cuts cause chattering, that may make the valve surface so rough that much time is lost in obtaining the desired finish.

After grinding, check the valve margin to be sure that the valve edge has not been ground too thin. A thin edge is called a feather edge and can lead to preignition; the valve edge would burn away in a short period of time, and the cylinder would have to be overhauled again. *Figure 10-26* shows a valve with a normal margin and one with a feather edge.

The valve tip may be resurfaced on the valve grinder. The tip is ground to remove cupping or wear, and also to adjust valve clearances on some engines.

The valve is held by a clamp on the side of the stone. *[Figure 10-27]* With the machine and grinding fluid turned on, the valve is pushed lightly against the stone and swung back and forth. Do not swing the valve stem off either edge of the stone. Because of the tendency for the valve to overheat during this grinding, be sure plenty of grinding fluid covers the tip.

Grinding of the valve tip may remove, or partially remove, the bevel on the edge of the valve. To restore this bevel, mount a V-way approximately 45° to the grinding stone. Hold the valve onto the V-way and twist the valve tip onto the stone. With a light touch, grind all the way around the tip. This bevel prevents scratching the valve guide when the valve is installed.

Figure 10-27. *Grinding a valve tip.*

Valve Lapping and Leak Testing

After the grinding procedure is finished, it is sometimes necessary that the valve be lapped to the seat. This is done by applying a small amount of lapping compound to the valve face, inserting the valve into the guide, and rotating the valve with a lapping tool until a smooth, gray finish appears at the contact area. The appearance of a correctly lapped valve is shown in *Figure 10-28.*

Figure 10-28. *A correctly lapped valve.*

After the lapping process is finished, be sure that all lapping compound is removed from the valve face, seat, and adjacent areas. The final step is to check the mating surface for leaks to see if it is sealing properly. This is done by installing the valve in the cylinder, holding the valve by the stem with the fingers, and pouring kerosene or solvent into the valve port. While holding finger pressure on the valve stem, check to see if the kerosene is leaking past the valve into the combustion chamber. If it is not, the valve re-seating operation is finished. If kerosene is leaking past the valve, continue the lapping operation until the leakage is stopped. The incorrect indications are of value in diagnosing improper valve and valve seat grinding. Incorrect indications, their cause, and remedy are shown in *Figure 10-29.*

Piston Repairs

Piston repairs are not required as often as cylinder repairs since most of the wear is between the piston ring and cylinder wall, valve stem and guide, and valve face and seat. A lesser amount of wear is encountered between the piston skirt and cylinder, ring and ring groove, or piston pin and bosses.

The most common repair is the removal of scores. Usually, these may be removed only on the piston skirt if they are very light. On engines where the entire rotating and reciprocating assembly is balanced, the pistons must weigh within one-fourth ounce of each other. When a new piston is installed, it must be within the same weight tolerance as the one removed. It is not enough to have the pistons matched alone; they must be matched to the crankshaft, connecting rods, piston pins, etc. To make weight adjustments on new pistons, the manufacturer provides a heavy section at the base of the skirt. To decrease weight, file metal evenly off the inside of this heavy section. The piston weight can be decreased easily, but welding, metalizing, or plating cannot be done to increase the piston weight.

If ring grooves are worn or stepped, the pistons are normally replaced. Small nicks on the edge of the piston pin boss may be sanded down. Deep scores inside the boss, or anywhere around the boss, are definite reasons for rejection. It has become more economical to replace pistons rather than reconditioning and reusing old ones, especially during overhaul.

Cylinder Grinding and Honing

If a cylinder has excessive taper, out-of-roundness, step, or its maximum size is beyond limits, it can be reground to the next allowable oversize. If the cylinder walls are lightly rusted, scored, or pitted, the damage may be removed by honing or lapping.

Regrinding a cylinder is a specialized job that the powerplant mechanic is not usually expected to be able to do. However, the mechanic must be able to recognize when a cylinder needs regrinding, and he or she must know what constitutes a good or bad job.

Generally, standard aircraft cylinder oversizes are 0.010 inch, 0.015 inches, 0.020 inch, or 0.030 inch. Aircraft cylinders have relatively thin walls and may have a nitrided surface, that must not be ground away. Nitriding is a surface hardening process that hardens the steel surface to a depth of several thousandths of an inch. Any one manufacturer usually does not allow all of the above oversizes. Some manufacturers do not allow regrinding to an oversize at all. The manufacturer's overhaul manual, or parts catalog, usually lists the oversizes allowed for a particular make and model engine.

Figure 10-29. *Incorrectly lapped valves.*

To determine the regrind size, the standard bore size must be known. This usually can be determined from the manufacturer's specifications or manuals. The regrind size is figured from the standard bore. For example, a certain cylinder has a standard bore of 3.875 inches. To have a cylinder ground to 0.015 inches oversize, it is necessary to grind to a bore diameter of 3.890 inch (3.875 + 0.015). A tolerance of ±0.0005 inches is usually accepted for cylinder grinding.

Another factor to consider when determining the size to which a cylinder must be reground is the maximum wear that has occurred. If there are spots in the cylinder wall that are worn larger than the first oversize, then obviously it is necessary to grind to the next oversize to clean up the entire cylinder.

The type of finish desired in the cylinder is an important consideration when ordering a regrind. Some engine manufacturers specify a fairly rough finish on the cylinder walls, that allows the rings to seat even if they are not lapped to the cylinder. Other manufacturers desire a smooth finish to which a lapped ring seats without much change in ring or cylinder dimensions. The latter type of finish is more expensive to produce.

The standard used when measuring the finish of a cylinder wall is known as micro-inch root-meansquare (micro-inch rms). In a finish where the depth of the grinding scratches are one-millionth (0.000001) of an inch deep, it is specified as 1 microinch rms. Most aircraft cylinders are ground to a finish of 15 to 20 microinch rms. Several low-powered engines have cylinders that are ground to a relatively rough 20- to 30-microinch rms finish. On the other end of the scale, some manufacturers require a superfinish of approximately 4- to 6-microinch rms.

Cylinder grinding is accomplished by a firmly mounted stone that revolves around the cylinder bore, as well as up and down the length of the cylinder barrel. *[Figure 10-30]* The cylinder, the stone, or both may move to get this relative movement.

The size of the grind is determined by the distance the stone is set away from the centerline of the cylinder. Some cylinder bore grinding machines produce a perfectly straight bore, while others are designed to grind a choked bore. A choked bore grind refers to the manufacturing process in which the cylinder walls are ground to produce a smaller internal diameter at the top than at the bottom. The purpose of this type grind or taper is to maintain a straight cylinder wall during operation. As a cylinder heats up during operation, the head and top of the cylinder are subjected to more heat than the bottom. This causes greater expansion at the top than at the bottom, thereby maintaining the desired straight wall.

After grinding a cylinder, it may be necessary to hone the cylinder bore to produce the desired finish. In this case, specify the cylinder regrind size to allow for some metal removal during honing. The usual allowance for honing is 0.001 inch. If a final cylinder bore size of 3.890 inches is desired, specify the regrind size of 3.889 inches, and then hone to 3.890 inches.

There are several different makes and models of cylinder hones. The burnishing hone is used only to produce the desired finish on the cylinder wall. The more elaborate micromatic hone can also be used to straighten out the cylinder walls. A burnishing hone should not be used in an attempt to straighten cylinder walls. *[Figure 10-31]* Since the stones are only spring loaded, they follow the contour of the cylinder wall and may aggravate a tapered condition.

Deglazing the cylinder walls is accomplished with the use of a deglazing hone. A cross-hatch pattern must be placed on the cylinder wall to allow for piston ring break-in. This is accomplished by a deglazing hone turned by a drill being moved in and out of the cylinder rapidly. *[Figure 10-32]*

After the cylinders have been reground or deglazed, or both, check the size and wall finish, and check for evidence of overheating or grinding cracks before installing on an engine.

Figure 10-30. *Cylinder bore grinding.*

Figure 10-31. *Cylinder honing.*

Figure 10-32. *Cross-hatch pattern on cylinder wall.*

Reassembly

Before starting reassembly, all serviceable and new engine components need to be cleaned, organized, and laid out in the order they are to be assembled. A popular method of engine assembly is for the engine to be assembled at one work station with the same technicians completing the total assembly of the engine. It is also important to refer to the parts catalog to ensure that the correct hardware is used during the assembly of the engine. The engine overhaul manual should be referred to for information on the use of safety wire, self-locking nuts, and torque values. During assembly, the components should be pre-lubricated as the overhaul manual sets forth. It is important to follow the manufacturer's overhaul assembly procedures completely, and perform all checks and procedures that are called for in the manual.

Installation and Testing

Engine Testing of Reciprocating Engines

The procedures and equipment used in determining that an engine is ready for airworthy service and is in excellent mechanical condition, normally requires the use of a test stand, or test cell, although the aircraft can be used. *[Figure 10-33]* The method of engine testing or run-in that takes place during overhaul prior to delivery of the engine is critical to the airworthiness of the engine. It must be emphasized that engine run-in is as vital as any other phase of engine overhaul, for it is the means by which the quality of a new or newly overhauled engine is checked, and it is the final step in the preparation of an engine for service. Thus, the reliability and potential service life of an engine is in question until it has satisfactorily passed the cell test.

The test serves a dual purpose. First, it accomplishes piston ring run-in and bearing burnishing. Second, it provides valuable information that it used to evaluate engine

Figure 10-33. *Test stand.*

Figure 10-34. *Test club.*

performance and determine engine condition. To provide proper oil flow to the upper portion of the cylinder barrel walls with a minimum loss of oil, it is important that piston rings be properly seated in the cylinder in which they are installed. The process is called piston ring run-in (break-in) and is accomplished chiefly by controlled operation of the engine in the high-speed range. Improper piston ring conditioning, or run-in, may result in unsatisfactory engine operation with high oil consumption. A process called bearing burnishing creates a highly polished surface on new bearings and bushings installed during overhaul. The burnishing is usually accomplished during the first periods of the engine run-in at comparatively slow engine speeds.

The failure of any part during engine testing or run-in requires that the engine be returned, repaired, and completely retested. After an engine has successfully completed test requirements, it is then specially treated to prevent corrosion, if it is shipped or stored before being installed in an aircraft. During the final run-in period during testing, the engines are operated on the proper grade of fuel prescribed for the particular kind of engine. The oil system is serviced with a mixture of corrosion-preventive compound and engine oil. The temperature of this mixture is maintained at 105 °C to 121 °C. Near the end of final run-in, corrosion-preventive mixture (CPM) is used as the engine lubricant. The engine induction passages and combustion chambers are also treated with CPM by an aspiration method. CPM is drawn or breathed into the engine.

Test Cell Requirements

The test cell requires an area to mount and hold the engine for testing. The cell needs to have the controls, instruments, and any special equipment to evaluate the total performance of the engine. A test club should be used for testing instead of a flight propeller. *[Figure 10-34]* A test club provides more cooling air flow and the correct amount of load. The operational tests and test procedures vary with individual engines, but the basic requirements are generally closely related.

Engine Instruments

The test cell control room contains the controls used to operate the engine and the instruments used to measure various temperatures and pressures, fuel flow, and other factors. These devices are necessary in providing an accurate check and an evaluation of the operating engine. The control room is separate from, but adjacent to, the space (test cell) that houses the engine being tested. The safe, economical, and reliable testing of modern aircraft engines depends largely upon the use of instruments. In engine run-in procedures, the same basic engine instruments are used as when the engine is installed in the aircraft, plus some additional connections to these instruments, and some indicating and measuring devices that cannot be practically installed in the aircraft. Instruments used in the testing procedures are inspected and calibrated periodically, as are instruments installed in the aircraft; thus, accurate information concerning engine operation is ensured.

Engine instruments can operate using different methods, some mechanically, some electrically, and some by sensing the direct pressure of air or liquid. Some of the basic instruments are:

1. Carburetor air temperature gauge
2. Fuel pressure gauge
3. Fuel flowmeter
4. Manifold pressure gauge
5. Oil temperature gauge
6. Oil pressure gauge
7. Tachometer
8. Exhaust gas temperature gauge

9. Cylinder head temperature gauge
10. Torquemeter

Instrument markings, ranges of operation, minimum and maximum limits, and the interpretation of these markings are general to all the instruments. Generally, the instrument marking system consists of three colors: red, yellow, and green. A red line, or mark, indicates a point beyond which a dangerous operating condition exists. A red arc indicates a dangerous operating range due generally to an engine propeller vibration range. This arc can be passed through, but the engine cannot be operated in this area. Of the two, the red mark is used more commonly and is located radially on the cover glass or dial face. The yellow arc covers a given range of operation and is an indication of caution. Generally, the yellow arc is located on the outer circumference of the instrument cover glass or dial face. The green arc shows a normal and safe range of operation. When the markings appear on the cover glass, a white line is used as an index mark, often called a slippage mark. The white radial mark indicates any movement between the cover glass and the case, a condition that would cause mislocation of the other range and limit markings.

Carburetor Air Temperature (CAT) Indicator

Measured at the carburetor entrance, carburetor air temperature (CAT) is regarded by many as an indication of induction system ice formation. Although it serves this purpose, it also provides many other important items of information.

The powerplant is a heat machine, and the temperature of its components, or the fluids flowing through it, affects the combustion process either directly or indirectly. The temperature level of the induction air affects not only the charge density, but also the vaporization of the fuel. CAT is also useful for checking induction system condition. Backfiring is indicated as a momentary rise on the gauge, provided it is of sufficient severity for the heat to be sensed at the carburetor air-measuring point. A sustained induction system fire shows a continuous increase of CAT.

The CAT should be noted before starting and just after shutdown. The temperature before starting is the best indication of the temperature of the fuel in the carburetor body, and tells whether vaporization is sufficient for the initial firing, or whether the mixture must be augmented by priming. If an engine has been shut down for only a short time, the residual heat in the carburetor may make it possible to rely on the vaporizing heat in the fuel and powerplant. Priming would then be unnecessary.

After shutdown, a high CAT is a warning that the fuel trapped in the carburetor will expand, producing high internal pressure. When a high temperature is present at this time, the fuel line and manifold valves should be open so that the pressure can be relieved by allowing fuel passage back to the tank. The CAT gauge indicates the temperature of the air before it enters the carburetor. The temperature reading is sensed by a bulb or electric sensor. In the test cell, the sensor is located in the air intake passage to the engine and, in an aircraft it is located in the ram-air intake duct. The CAT gauge is calibrated in the centigrade scale. *[Figure 10-35]* This gauge, like many other multi-engine aircraft instruments, is a dual gauge; two gauges, each with a separate pointer and scale, are used in the same case.

Figure 10-35. *Carburetor air temperature gauge.*

Notice the range markings used. The yellow arc indicates a range from −10 °C to +15 °C, since the danger of icing occurs between these temperatures. The green range indicates the normal operating range from +15 °C to +40 °C. The red line indicates the maximum operating temperature of 40 °C; any operation at a temperature over this value places the engine in danger of detonation.

Fuel Pressure Indicator

The fuel pressure gauge is calibrated in pounds per square inch (psi) of pressure. It is used during the test run-in to measure engine fuel pressure at the carburetor inlet, the fuel feed valve discharge nozzle, and the main fuel supply line. Fuel gauges are located in the operator's control room and are connected by flexible lines to the different points at which pressure readings are desired during the testing procedures.

In some aircraft installations, the fuel pressure is sensed at the carburetor or fuel injection unit inlet of each engine, and the pressure is indicated on individual gauges on the instrument panel. *[Figure 10-36]* The dial is calibrated in graduations and is extended and numbered. The numbers range from 0 to 10 in this example. The red line on the dial at the 2 pounds psi graduation shows the minimum fuel pressure

Figure 10-36. *Engine instrument clusters.*

readings, it can be determined if the engine heat transferred to the oil is low, normal, or excessive. This information is of extreme importance during the breaking-in process of large reciprocating engines. The oil temperature gauge line in the aircraft is connected at the oil inlet to the engine.

Three range markings are used on the oil temperature gauge. The green arc in *Figure 10-36*, on the dial, shows the minimum oil temperature permissible for ground operational checks or during flight. The green mark between 25 °F and below 245 °F shows the desired oil temperature for continuous engine operation. The red mark at 245 °F indicates the maximum permissible oil temperature.

Fuel Flow Meter
The fuel flow meter measures the amount of fuel delivered to the engine. During engine testing procedures, the fuel flow to the engine can be measured by three different methods: a direct flow meter, a pressure-based flow meter, or a turbine senor-based flow meter. The direct reading flow meter uses a series of calibrated tubes located in the control room. The tubes are of various sizes to indicate different volumes of fuel flow. Each tube contains a float that can be seen by the operator, and as the fuel flow through the tube varies, the float is either raised or lowered, indicating the amount of fuel flow. From these indications, the operator can determine whether an engine is operating at the correct fuel/air mixture for a given power setting. Reciprocating engines on light aircraft usually use a fuel pressure gauge that is also used for the flowmeter. This is because the fuel flow is proportional to the fuel pressure in this system. Fuel flow is measured normally in gallons per hour.

In most turbine aircraft installations, the fuel flow indicating system consists of a transmitter and an indicator for each engine. The fuel flow transmitter is conveniently mounted in the engine's accessory section and measures the fuel flow between the engine-driven fuel pump and the fuel control device. The transmitter is an electrical device that contains a turbine that turns faster as the flow increases, which increases the electrical signal to the indicator. The fuel flow transmitter is connected electrically to the indicator located on the aircraft flight deck, or on the test cell operator's panel. The reading on the indicator on turbine aircraft is calibrated to record the amount of fuel flow in pounds of fuel per hour.

Manifold Pressure Indicator
The preferred type of instrument for measuring the manifold pressure on reciprocating engines is a gauge that records the pressure as an absolute pressure reading. Absolute pressure takes into account the atmospheric pressure plus the pressure in the intake manifold. To read the manifold pressure of the engines, a specially designed manifold pressure gauge that

allowed during flight. The green arc shows the desired range of operation, which is 2 to 9 psi. The red line at the 9 psi graduation indicates the maximum allowable fuel pressure. Fuel pressures vary with the type of fuel system installation and the size of the engine. When fuel injection systems are used, the fuel pressure range is much higher; the minimum allowable pressure is approximately 10 psi, and the maximum is generally 25 psi.

Oil Pressure Indicator
The main oil pressure reading is taken at the pressure side of the oil pump. Generally, there is only one oil pressure gauge for each aircraft engine. The oil pressure gauge dial does not show the pressure range or limits for all installations. *[Figure 10-36]* The actual markings for specific aircraft may be found in the aircraft specifications or Type Certificate Data Sheets. The lower red line at 25 psi indicates the minimum oil pressure permissible in flight. The green arc between 60 to 85 psi illustrates the desired operating oil pressure range. The red line at 100 psi indicates maximum permissible oil pressure.

The oil pressure gauge indicates the pressure, in psi, that the oil of the lubricating system is being supplied to the moving parts of the engine. The engine should be shut down immediately if the gauge fails to register pressure when the engine is operating. Excessive oscillation of the gauge pointer indicates that there is air in the lines leading to the gauge, or that some unit of the oil system is functioning improperly.

Oil Temperature Indicator
During engine run-in in the test cell, engine oil temperature readings are taken at the oil inlet and outlet. From these

indicates absolute manifold pressure in inches of mercury ("Hg) is used. The red line indicates the maximum manifold pressure permissible during takeoff.

The manifold pressure gauge range markings and indications vary with different kinds of engines and installations. *Figure 10-37* illustrates the dial of a typical manifold pressure gauge and shows how the range markings are positioned. The green arc starts at 35 "Hg and continues to the 44 "Hg. The red line on the gauge, at 49 "Hg shows the manifold pressure recommended for takeoff. This pressure should not be exceeded.

Figure 10-37. *Manifold pressure gauge.*

Tachometer Indicator

The tachometer for reciprocating engines shows the engine crankshaft rpm. The system used for testing the engine is the same as the system in the aircraft installation. The tachometer, often referred to as TACH, is calibrated in hundreds with graduations at every 100-rpm interval. The dial shown in *Figure 10-38* starts at 0 rpm and goes to 35 (3,500 rpm). The green arc indicates the rpm range within operation that is permissible. The red line indicates the maximum rpm permissible during takeoff; any rpm beyond this value is an overspeed condition.

Turbine engines use percent rpm indicators due to the high rpm that the engines generally operate. Each rotating assembly in an engine has its own percent rpm indicator. The 100 percent position on the indicator is the highest rpm the engine can operate. Red lines and green arcs operate the same as with reciprocating engines.

Figure 10-38. *Tachometer.*

Cylinder Head Temperature Indicator

During the engine test procedures, the cylinder head temperatures of various cylinders on the reciprocating engine are normally tested. Thermocouples are connected to several cylinders and, by a selector switch, any cylinder head temperature can be indicated on the indicators. When installed in the aircraft, there is sometimes only one thermocouple lead and indicator for each engine installed in an aircraft.

Cylinder head temperatures are indicated by a gauge connected to a thermocouple attached to the cylinder, that tests show to be the hottest on an engine in a particular installation. The thermocouple may be placed in a special gasket located under a rear spark plug, or in a special well in the top or rear of the cylinder head.

The temperature recorded at either of these points is merely a reference or control temperature; but as long as it is kept within the prescribed limits, the temperatures inside the cylinder dome, exhaust valve, and piston is within a satisfactory range. Since the thermocouple is attached to only one cylinder, it can do no more than give evidence of general engine temperature. While normally it can be assumed that the remaining cylinder temperatures are lower, conditions such as detonation are not indicated unless they occur in the cylinder that has the thermocouple attached.

The cylinder head temperature gauge range marking is similar to that of the manifold pressure and tachometer indicator. The cylinder head temperature gauge is a dual gauge that incorporates two separate temperature scales.

[Figure 10-39] The scales are calibrated in increments of 10°, with numerals at the 0°, 100°, 200°, and 300° graduations. The space between any two graduation marks represents 10 °C.

Figure 10-39. *Cylinder head temperature gauge.*

Torquemeter

Most torque systems use an oil pressure output from a torque valve to indicate actual engine power output at various power settings. The torquemeter indicates the amount of torque being produced at the propeller shaft. A helical gear moves back and forth as the torque on the propeller shaft varies. This gear, acting on a piston, positions a valve that meters the oil pressure proportionally to the torque being produced. A change in pressure from the valve that is connected to a transducer is then converted to an electrical signal and is transmitted to the flight deck. The torquemeter can read out in pounds-feet of torque, percent of horsepower, or horsepower. The earlier systems read out in psi, and the flight engineer converted this to the correct power setting. *[Figure 10-40]* Some systems use strain gauges to attach to the ring gear to provide an electrical signal directly to the readout.

Figure 10-40. *Torquemeter readout.*

Warning Systems

Many of the miscellaneous gauges and devices indicate only that a system is functioning or has failed to function. On some aircraft, a warning light illuminates when the fuel pressure or oil pressure is low.

Reciprocating Engine Operation

The operation of the powerplant is controlled from the cockpit or flight deck. Some installations have numerous control handles and levers connected to the engine by rods, cables, bellcranks, pulleys, etc. In most cases, the control handles are conveniently mounted on quadrants in the flight deck. Placards, or markings, are placed on the quadrant to indicate the functions and positions of the levers. In some installations, friction clutches are installed to hold the controls in place.

Engine Instruments

The term engine instruments usually includes all instruments required to measure and indicate the functioning of the powerplant. The engine instruments are generally installed on the instrument panel so that all of them can easily be observed at one time. Manifold pressure, rpm, engine temperature, oil temperature, CAT, and the fuel-air ratio can be controlled by manipulating the flight deck controls. Coordinating the movement of the controls with the instrument readings protects against exceeding operating limits.

Engine operation is usually limited by specified operating ranges of the following:

1. Crankshaft speed (rpm)
2. Manifold pressure
3. Cylinder head temperature
4. CAT
5. Oil temperature
6. Oil pressure
7. Fuel pressure
8. Fuel flow meter
9. Fuel/air mixture setting

The procedures, pressures, temperatures, and rpm used throughout this section are solely for the purpose of illustration and do not have general application. The operating procedures and limits used on individual makes and models of aircraft engines vary considerably from the values shown here. For exact information regarding a specific engine model, consult the applicable instructions.

Engine Starting

Before starting the engine, observe the manifold pressure gauge that should read approximate atmospheric (barometric) pressure when the engine is not running. At sea level, this is approximately 30 "Hg, and at fields above sea level, the atmospheric pressure is less, depending on the height above sea level. Also, observe all engine gauges for the correct reading for engine off settings.

Correct starting technique is an important part of engine operation. Improper procedures often are used, because some of the basic principles involved in engine operation are misunderstood. Read more about typical procedures for starting reciprocating engines in the Airframe and Powerplant Mechanics General Handbook.

Pre-Oiling

Engines that have undergone overhaul or major maintenance can have air trapped in some of the oil passages that must be removed before the first start. This is done by pre-oiling the engine by cranking, with the spark plugs removed, the engine with the starter or by hand (turning) until oil pressure is indicated. A second method is to pump oil under pressure through the oil system using an external pump until oil comes out of the oil outlet of the engine.

Hydraulic Lock

Whenever a radial engine remains shut down for any length of time beyond a few minutes, oil or fuel may drain into the combustion chambers of the lower cylinders or accumulate in the lower intake pipes ready to be drawn into the cylinders when the engine starts. *[Figure 10-41]* As the piston approaches top center of the compression stroke (both valves closed), this liquid being incompressible, stops piston movement. If the crankshaft continues to rotate, something must give. Therefore, starting or attempting to start an engine with a hydraulic lock of this nature may cause the affected cylinder to blow out or, more likely, may result in a bent or broken connecting rod.

To eliminate a lock, remove either the front or rear spark plug of the lower cylinders and pull the propeller through in the direction of rotation. The piston expels any liquid that may be present. If the hydraulic lock occurs as a result of over-priming prior to initial engine start, eliminate the lock in the same manner (i.e., remove one of the spark plugs from the cylinder and rotate the crankshaft through two turns). Never attempt to clear the hydraulic lock by pulling the propeller through in the direction opposite to normal rotation. This tends to inject the liquid from the cylinder into the intake pipe with the possibility of a complete or partial lock occurring on the subsequent start.

Figure 10-41. *Initial step in developing a hydraulic lock.*

Engine Warm-Up

Proper engine warm-up is important, particularly when the condition of the engine is unknown. Improperly adjusted idle mixture, intermittently firing spark plugs, and improperly adjusted engine valves all have an overlapping effect on engine stability. Therefore, the warm-up should be made at the engine speed where maximum engine stability is obtained. Experience has shown that the optimum warm-up speed is from 1,000 to 1,600 rpm. The actual speed selected should be the speed at which engine operation is the smoothest, since the smoothest operation is an indication that all phases of engine operation are the most stable.

Some engines incorporate temperature-compensated oil pressure relief valves. This type of relief valve results in high engine oil pressures immediately after the engine starts, if oil temperatures are very low. Consequently, start the warm-up of these engines at approximately 1,000 rpm and then move to the higher, more stable engine speed as soon as oil temperature reaches a warmer level.

During warm-up, watch the instruments associated with engine operation. This aids in making sure that all phases of engine operation are normal. For example, engine oil pressure should be indicated within 30 seconds after the start. Furthermore, if the oil pressure is not up to or above normal within 1 minute after the engine starts, the engine should be shut down. Cylinder head or coolant temperatures should be observed continually to see that they do not exceed the maximum allowable limit.

A lean mixture should not be used to hasten the warm-up. Actually, at the warm-up rpm, there is very little difference in the mixture supplied to the engine, whether the mixture is in a rich or lean position, since metering in this power range is governed by throttle position.

Carburetor heat can be used as required under conditions leading to ice formation. For engines equipped with a float-type carburetor, it is desirable to raise the CAT during warm-up to prevent ice formation and to ensure smooth operation.

The magneto safety check can be performed during warm-up. Its purpose is to ensure that all ignition connections are secure and that the ignition system permits operation at the higher power settings used during later phases of the ground check. The time required for proper warm-up gives ample opportunity to perform this simple check, which may disclose a condition that would make it inadvisable to continue operation until after corrections have been made.

The magneto safety check is conducted with the propeller in the high rpm (low pitch) position, at approximately 1,000 rpm. Move the ignition switch from "both" to "right" and return to "both;" from "both" to "left" and return to "both;" from "both" to "off" momentarily and return to "both."

While switching from "both" to a single magneto position, a slight but noticeable drop in rpm should occur. This indicates that the opposite magneto has been properly grounded out. Complete cutting out of the engine when switching from "both" to "off" indicates that both magnetos are grounded properly. While in the single magneto position, failure to obtain any rpm drop, or failure of the engine to cut out while switching to off, indicates that one or both ground connections are faulty. This indicates a safety problem; the magnetos are not secured at shut down and may fire if the propeller is turned.

Ground Check

The ground check is performed to evaluate the functioning of the engine by comparing power input, as measured by manifold pressure, with power output, as measured by rpm or torque.

The engine may be capable of producing a prescribed power, even rated takeoff, and not be functioning properly. Only by comparing the manifold pressure required during the check against a known standard is an unsuitable condition disclosed. The magneto check can also fail to show shortcomings, since the allowable rpm dropoff is only a measure of an improperly functioning ignition system and is not necessarily affected by other factors. Conversely, it is possible for the magneto check to prove satisfactory when an unsatisfactory condition is present elsewhere in the engine.

The ground check is made after the engine is thoroughly warm. It consists of checking the operation of the powerplant and accessory equipment by ear, by visual inspection, and by proper interpretation of instrument readings, control movements, and switch reactions. During the ground check, the aircraft should be headed into the wind, if possible, to take advantage of the cooling airflow. A ground check procedure is outlined below:

1. Control position check
2. Cowl flaps (if equipped)—open
3. Mixture—rich
4. Propeller—high rpm
5. Carburetor heat—cold
6. Check propeller according to propeller manufacturer's instruction.
7. Open throttle to the run-up rpm setting as per manufacturer's instructions (specified RPM and manifold pressure).
8. Ignition system operational check.

In performing the ignition system operational check (magneto check), the power-absorbing characteristics of the propeller in the low fixed-pitch position are utilized. In switching to individual magnetos, cutting out the opposite plugs results in a slower rate of combustion, which gives the same effect as retarding the spark advance. The drop in engine speed is a measure of the power loss at this slower combustion rate.

When the magneto check is performed, a drop in torquemeter pressure indication is a good supplement to the variation in rpm. In cases where the tachometer scale is graduated coarsely, the torquemeter variation may give more positive evidence of the power change when switching to the individual magneto condition. A loss in torquemeter pressure not to exceed 10 percent can be expected when operating on a single magneto. By comparing the rpm drop with a known standard, the following are determined:

1. Proper timing of each magneto.
2. General engine performance as evidenced by smooth operation.
3. Additional check of the proper connection of the ignition leads.

Any unusual roughness on either magneto is an indication of faulty ignition caused by plug fouling or by malfunctioning of the ignition system. The operator should be very sensitive to engine roughness during this check. Lack of dropoff in rpm may be an indication of faulty grounding of one side of the ignition system. Complete cutting out when switching to one magneto is definite evidence that its side of the ignition system is not functioning. Excessive difference in rpm drop off between the left and right switch positions can indicate a difference in time between the left and right magnetos.

Sufficient time should be given to the check on each single switch position to permit complete stabilization of engine speed and manifold pressure. There is a tendency to perform this check too rapidly with resultant wrong indications. Operation as long as 1 minute on a single ignition system is not excessive.

Another point that must be emphasized is the danger of sticking tachometer. The tachometer should he tapped lightly to make sure the indicator needle moves freely. In some cases using older mechanical tachometers, sticking has caused errors in indication to the extent of 100 rpm. Under such conditions, the ignition system could have had as much as a 200 rpm drop with only a 100 rpm drop indicated on the instrument. In most cases, tapping the instrument eliminates the sticking and results in accurate readings.

In recording the results of time ignition system check, record the amount of the total rpm drop that occurs rapidly and the amount that occurs slowly. This breakdown in rpm drop provides a means of pinpointing certain troubles in the ignition system. This can reduce unnecessary work by confining maintenance to the specific part of the ignition system that is responsible for the trouble.

Fast rpm drop is usually the result of either faulty spark plugs or faulty ignition harness. This is true because faulty plugs or leads, take effect at once. The cylinder goes dead or starts firing intermittently the instant the switch is moved from "both" to the "right" or "left" position.

Slow rpm drop usually is caused by incorrect ignition timing or faulty valve adjustment. With late ignition timing, the charge is fired too late (in relation to piston travel) for the combustion pressures to build up to the maximum at the proper time. The result is a power loss greater than normal for single ignition because of the lower peak pressures obtained in the cylinder. However, this power loss does not occur as rapidly as that which accompanies a dead spark plug. This explains the slow rpm drop as compared to the instantaneous drop with a dead plug or defective lead. Incorrect valve clearances, through their effect on valve overlap, can cause the mixture to be too rich or too lean. The too rich or too lean mixture may affect one plug more than another, because of the plug location and show up as a slow rpm drop on the ignition check. Switch from "both" to "right" and return to "both." Switch from "both" to "left" and return to "both." Observe the rpm drop while operating on the right and left positions. The maximum drop should not exceed that specified by the engine manufacturer.

Fuel Pressure and Oil Pressure Check

Fuel pressure and oil pressure must be within the established tolerance (green arc) for the engine.

Propeller Pitch Check

The propeller is checked to ensure proper operation of the pitch control and the pitch-change mechanism. The operation of a controllable pitch propeller is checked by the indications of the tachometer and manifold pressure gauge when the propeller governor control is moved from one position to another. Because each type of propeller requires a different procedure, the applicable manufacturer's instructions should be followed.

Power Check

Specific rpm and manifold pressure relationship should be checked during each ground check. This can be done at the time the engine is run-up to make the magneto check. The purpose of this check is to measure the performance of the engine against an established standard. Calibration tests have determined that the engine is capable of delivering a given power at a given rpm and manifold pressure. The original calibration, or measurement of power, is made by means of a dynamometer in a test cell. During the ground check, power is measured with the propeller. With constant conditions of air density, the propeller, at any fixed-pitch position, always requires the same rpm to absorb the same horsepower from the engine. This characteristic is used in determining the condition of the engine.

With the governor control set for full low pitch, the propeller operates as a fixed-pitch propeller, because the engine is static. Under these conditions, the manifold pressure for any specific engine, with the mixture control in rich, indicates whether all the cylinders are operating properly. With one or more dead or intermittently firing cylinders, the operating cylinders must provide more power for a given rpm. Consequently, the carburetor throttle must be opened further, resulting in higher manifold pressure. Different engines of the same model using the same propeller installation, and at the same barometer and temperature readings, should require the same manifold pressure to within 1 "Hg. A higher than normal manifold pressure usually indicates a dead cylinder or late ignition timing. An excessively low manifold pressure for a particular rpm usually indicates that the ignition timing is early. Early ignition can cause detonation and loss of power at takeoff power settings.

The accuracy of the power check may be affected by the following variables:

1. Wind—any appreciable air movement (5 mph or more) changes the air load on the propeller blade when it is in the fixed-pitch position. A head wind increases the rpm obtainable with a given manifold pressure. A tail wind decreases the rpm.
2. Atmospheric temperatures—the effects of variations in atmospheric temperature tend to cancel each other. Higher carburetor intake and cylinder temperatures tend to lower the rpm, but the propeller load is lightened because of the less dense air.
3. Engine and induction system temperature—if the cylinder and carburetor temperatures are high because of factors other than atmospheric temperature, a low rpm results since the power is lowered without a compensating lowering of the propeller load.
4. Oil temperature—cold oil tends to hold down the rpm, since the higher viscosity results in increased friction horsepower losses.

Idle Speed and Idle Mixture Checks

Plug fouling difficulty is the inevitable result of failure to provide a proper idle mixture setting. The tendency seems to be to adjust the idle mixture on the extremely rich side and to compensate for this by adjusting the throttle stop to a relatively high rpm for minimum idling. With a properly adjusted idle mixture setting, it is possible to run the engine at idle rpm for long periods. Such a setting results in a minimum of plug fouling and exhaust smoking, and it pays dividends from the savings on the aircraft brakes after landing and while taxiing.

If the wind is not too strong, the idle mixture setting can be checked easily during the ground check as follows:

1. Close throttle.
2. Move the mixture control to the idle cutoff position and observe the change in rpm. Return the mixture control back to the rich position before engine cutoff.

As the mixture control lever is moved into idle cutoff, and before normal dropoff, one of two things may occur momentarily:

1. The engine speed may increase. An increase in rpm, but less than that recommended by the manufacturer (usually 20 rpm), indicates proper mixture strength. A greater increase indicates that the mixture is too rich.
2. The engine speed may not increase or may drop immediately. This indicates that the idle mixture is too lean. The idle mixture should be set to give a mixture slightly richer than best power, resulting in a 10- to 20-rpm rise after idle cutoff.

Engine Stopping

With each type of engine installation, specific procedures are used in stopping the engine. The general procedure, outlined in the following paragraphs, reduces the time required for stopping, minimizes backfiring tendencies, and prevents overheating of tightly baffled air-cooled engine during operation on the ground.

In stopping any aircraft engine, the controls are set as follows, irrespective of the type or fuel system installation.

1. Cowl flaps and any other shutters or doors are always placed in the full open position to avoid overheating the engine and are left in that position after the engine is stopped to prevent engine residual heat from deteriorating the ignition system.
2. Carburetor air-heater control is left in the cold position to prevent damage that may occur from backfire.
3. Constant speed propeller is usually stopped with the control set in the high pitch (decrease rpm) position.

No mention is made of the throttle, mixture control, fuel selector valve, and ignition switches in the preceding set of directions because the operation of these controls varies with the type of carburetor used with the engine. An engine equipped with a carburetor incorporating an idle cutoff mixture control is stopped as follows:

1. Idle the engine by setting the throttle for 800 to 1,000 rpm.
2. Move the mixture control to the idle cutoff position. In a float-type carburetor, it equalizes the pressure in the float chamber and at the discharge nozzle.
3. After the propeller has stopped rotating, place the ignition switch in the off position.

In addition to the operations outlined previously, check the functioning of various items of aircraft equipment, such as generator systems, hydraulic systems, etc.

Basic Engine Operating Principles

Combustion Process

Normal combustion occurs when the fuel/air mixture ignites in the cylinder and burns progressively at a fairly uniform rate across the combustion chamber. When ignition is properly timed, maximum pressure is built up just after the piston has passed top dead center at the end of the compression stroke.

The flame fronts start at each spark plug and burn in more or less wavelike forms. [Figure 10-42] The velocity of the flame travel is influenced by the type of fuel, the ratio of the fuel/air mixture, and the pressure and temperature of the fuel mixture. With normal combustion, the flame travel is about 100 feet/second. The temperature and pressure within the cylinder rises at a normal rate as the fuel/air mixture burns.

Figure 10-42. *Normal combustion within a cylinder.*

Detonation

There is a limit, however, to the amount of compression and the degree of temperature rise that can be tolerated within an engine cylinder and still permit normal combustion. All fuels have critical limits of temperature and compression. Beyond this limit, they ignite spontaneously and burn with explosive violence. This instantaneous and explosive burning of the fuel/air mixture or, more accurately, of the latter portion of the charge is called detonation.

Detonation is the spontaneous combustion of the unburned charge ahead of the flame fronts after ignition of the charge. [Figure 10-43] During normal combustion, the flame fronts progress from the point of ignition across the cylinder. These flame fronts compress the gases ahead of them. At the same time, the gases are being compressed by the upward movement of the piston. If the total compression on the remaining unburned gases exceeds the critical point, detonation occurs.

Figure 10-43. *Detonation within a cylinder.*

The explosive burning during detonation results in an extremely rapid pressure rise. This rapid pressure rise and the high instantaneous temperature, combined with the high turbulence generated, cause a scrubbing action on the cylinder and the piston. This can burn a hole completely through the piston.

The critical point of detonation varies with the ratio of fuel to air in the mixture. Therefore, the detonation characteristic of the mixture can be controlled by varying the fuel/air ratio. At high power output, combustion pressures and temperatures are higher than they are at low or medium power. Therefore, at high power, the fuel/air ratio is made richer than is needed for good combustion at medium or low power output. This is done because, in general, a rich mixture does not detonate as readily as a lean mixture.

Unless detonation is heavy, there is no flight deck evidence of its presence. Light to medium detonation does not cause noticeable roughness, temperature increase, or loss of power. As a result, it can be present during takeoff and high-power climb without being known to the flight crew.

In fact, the effects of detonation are often not discovered until after teardown of the engine. When the engine is overhauled, however, the presence of severe detonation during its operation is indicated by dished piston heads, collapsed valve heads, broken ring lands, or eroded portions of valves, pistons, or cylinder heads.

The basic protection from detonation is provided in the design of the engine carburetor setting, which automatically supplies the rich mixtures required for detonation suppression at high power; the rating limitations, which include the maximum operating temperatures; and selection of the correct grade of fuel. The design factors, cylinder cooling, magneto timing, mixture distribution, degree of supercharging, and carburetor setting are taken care of in the design and development of the engine and its method of installation in the aircraft.

The remaining responsibility for prevention of detonation rests squarely in the hands of the ground and flight crews. They are responsible for observance of rpm and manifold pressure limits. Proper use of supercharger and fuel mixture, and maintenance of suitable cylinder head and carburetor-air-temperature (CAT) must be adhered to.

Pre-Ignition

Pre-ignition, as the name implies, means that combustion takes place within the cylinder before the timed spark jumps across the spark plug terminals. This condition can often be traced to excessive carbon or other deposits that cause local hot spots. Detonation often leads to pre-ignition. However, pre-ignition may also be caused by high-power operation on excessively lean mixtures. Pre-ignition is usually indicated in the flight deck by engine roughness, backfiring, and by a sudden increase in cylinder head temperature.

Any area within the combustion chamber that becomes incandescent serves as an igniter in advance of normal timed ignition and causes combustion earlier than desired. Pre-ignition may be caused by an area roughened and heated by detonation erosion. A cracked valve or piston, or a broken spark plug insulator, may furnish a hot point, that serves as a glow plug.

The hot spot can be caused by deposits on the chamber surfaces resulting from the use of leaded fuels. Normal carbon deposits can also cause pre-ignition. Specifically, pre-ignition is a condition similar to early timing of the spark. The charge in the cylinder is ignited before the required time for normal engine firing. However, do not confuse pre-ignition with the spark that occurs too early in the cycle. Pre-ignition is caused by a hot spot in the combustion chamber, not by incorrect ignition timing. The hot spot may be due to either an overheated cylinder or a defect within the cylinder.

The most obvious method of correcting pre-ignition is to reduce the cylinder temperature. The immediate step is to retard the throttle. This reduces the amount of fuel charge and the amount of heat generated. If a supercharger is in use, reduce manifold pressure as much as possible to reduce the charge temperature. Following this, the mixture should be enriched, if possible, to lower combustion temperature. If the engine is at high power when pre-ignition occurs, retarding the throttle for a few seconds may provide enough cooling to chip off some of the lead, or other deposit, within the combustion chamber. These chipped-off particles pass out through the exhaust.

Backfiring

When a fuel/air mixture does not contain enough fuel to consume all the oxygen, it is called a lean mixture. Conversely, a charge that contains more fuel than required is called a rich mixture. An extremely lean mixture either does not burn at all or burns so slowly that combustion is not complete at the end of the exhaust stroke. The flame lingers in the cylinder and then ignites the contents in the intake manifold or the induction system when the intake valve opens. This causes an explosion known as backfiring, which can damage the carburetor and other parts of the induction system.

Incorrect ignition timing, or faulty ignition wires, can cause the cylinder to fire at the wrong time, allowing the cylinder to fire when the intake valve is open, which can cause backfiring. A point worth stressing is that backfiring rarely involves the whole engine. Therefore, it is seldom the fault of the carburetor. In practically all cases, backfiring is limited to one or two cylinders. Usually, it is the result of faulty valve clearance setting, defective fuel injector nozzles, or other conditions that cause these cylinders to operate leaner than the engine as a whole. There can be no permanent cure until these defects are discovered and corrected. Because these backfiring cylinders fire intermittently and, therefore, run cool, they can be detected by the cold cylinder check. The cold cylinder check is discussed later in this chapter.

In some instances, an engine backfires in the idle range but operates satisfactorily at medium and high power settings. The most likely cause, in this case, is an excessively lean idle mixture. Proper adjustment of the idle fuel/air mixture usually corrects this difficulty.

Afterfiring

Afterfiring, sometimes called afterburning, often results when the fuel/air mixture is too rich. Overly rich mixtures are also slow burning, therefore, charges of unburned fuel are present in the exhausted gases. Air from outside the exhaust stacks mixes with this unburned fuel that ignites. This causes an explosion in the exhaust system. Afterfiring is perhaps more common where long exhaust ducting retains greater amounts of unburned charges. As in the case of backfiring, the correction for afterfiring is the proper adjustment of the fuel/air mixture.

Afterfiring can also be caused by cylinders that are not firing because of faulty spark plugs, defective fuel-injection nozzles. or incorrect valve clearance. The unburned mixture from these dead cylinders passes into the exhaust system, where it ignites and burns. Unfortunately, the resultant torching or afterburning can easily be mistaken for evidence of a rich carburetor. Cylinders that are firing intermittently can cause a similar effect. Again, the malfunction can be remedied only by discovering the real cause and correcting the defect. Dead or intermittent cylinders can be located by the cold cylinder check.

Factors Affecting Engine Operation

Compression

To prevent loss of power, all openings to the cylinder must close and seal completely on the compression and power strokes. In this respect, there are three items in the proper operation of the cylinder that must be operating correctly for maximum efficiency. First, the piston rings must be in good condition to provide maximum sealing during the stroke of the piston. There must be no leakage between the piston and the walls of the combustion chamber. Second, the intake and exhaust valves must close tightly so that there is no loss of compression at these points. Third, and very important, the timing of the valves (opening and closing) must be such that highest efficiency is obtained when the engine is operating at its normal rated rpm. A failure at any of these points results in greatly reduced engine efficiency.

Fuel Metering

The induction system is the distribution and fuel-metering part of the engine. Obviously, any defect in the induction system seriously affects engine operation. For best operation, each cylinder of the engine must be provided with the proper fuel/air mixture, usually metered by the carburetor. On some fuel-injection engines, fuel is metered by the fuel injector flow divider and fuel-injection nozzles.

The relation between fuel/air ratio and power is illustrated in *Figure 10-44*. Note that, as the fuel mixture is varied from lean to rich, the power output of the engine increases until it reaches a maximum. Beyond this point, the power output falls off as the mixture is further enriched. This is because the fuel mixture is now too rich to provide perfect combustion. Note that maximum engine power can be obtained by setting the carburetor for one point on the curve.

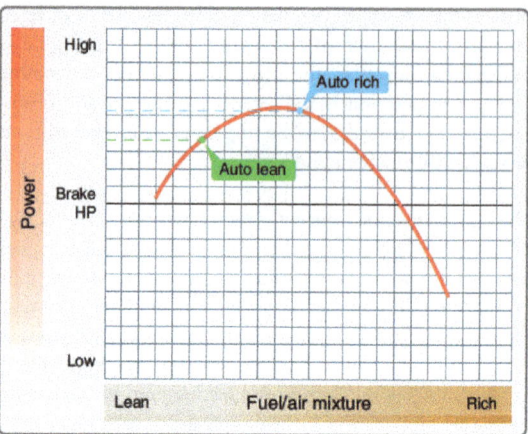

Figure 10-44. *Power versus fuel/air mixture curve.*

In establishing the carburetor settings for an aircraft engine, the design engineers run a series of curves similar to the one shown. A curve is run for each of several engine speeds. If, for example, the idle speed is 600 rpm, the first curve might be run at this speed. Another curve might be run at 700 rpm, another at 800 rpm, and so on, in 100-rpm increments, up to takeoff rpm. The points of maximum power on the curves are then joined to obtain the best power curve of the engine for all speeds. This best power curve establishes the rich setting of the carburetor.

In establishing the detailed engine requirements regarding carburetor setting, the fact that the cylinder head temperature varies with fuel/air ratio must be considered. This variation is illustrated in the curve shown in *Figure 10-45*. Note that the cylinder head temperature is lower with the auto-lean setting than it is with the auto-rich mixture. This is exactly opposite

Figure 10-45. *Variation in head temperature with fuel/air mixture (cruise power).*

common belief, but it is true. Furthermore, knowledge of this fact can be used to advantage by flight crews. If, during cruise, it becomes difficult to keep the cylinder head temperature within limits, the fuel/air mixture may be leaned out to get cooler operation. The desired cooling can then be obtained without going to auto-rich with its costly waste of fuel. The curve shows only the variation in cylinder head temperature. For a given rpm, the power output of the engine is less with the best-economy setting (auto-lean) than with the best-power mixture.

The decrease in cylinder head temperature with a leaner mixture holds true only through the normal cruise range. At higher power settings, cylinder temperatures are higher with the leaner mixtures. The reason for this reversal hinges on the cooling ability of the engine. As higher powers are approached, a point is reached where the airflow around the cylinders do not provide sufficient cooling. At this point, a secondary cooling method must be used. This secondary cooling is done by enriching the fuel/air mixture beyond the best-power point. Although enriching the mixture to this extent results in a power loss, both power and economy must be sacrificed for engine cooling purposes.

Many older, large, high-powered radial engines were influenced by the cooling requirements on fuel/air mixture, by effects of water injection. *Figure 10-46* shows a fuel/air curve for a water-injection engine. The dotted portion of the curve shows how the fuel-air mixture is leaned out during water injection. This leaning is possible because water, rather than extra fuel, is used as a cylinder coolant. These types of systems are not used on modern aircraft.

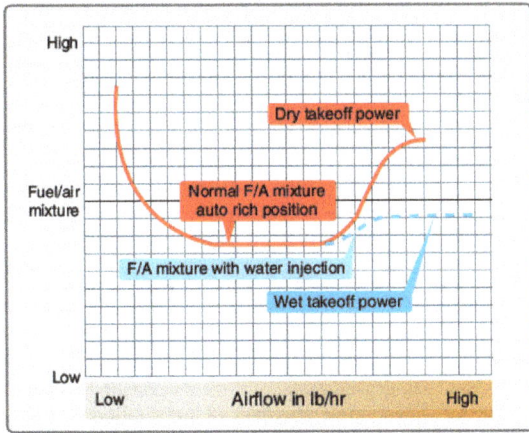

Figure 10-46. *Fuel/air curve for a water-injection engine.*

This permits leaning out to approximately best-power mixture without danger of overheating or detonation. This leaning out gives an increase in power. The water does not alter the combustion characteristics of the mixture. Fuel added to the auto-rich mixture in the power range during dry operation is solely for cooling. A leaner mixture would give more power. Actually, water or, more accurately, the antidetonant (water/alcohol) mixture is a better coolant than extra fuel. Therefore, water injection permits higher manifold pressures and a still further increase in power.

In establishing the final curve for engine operation, the engine's ability to cool itself at various power settings is, of course, taken into account. Sometimes the mixture must be altered for a given installation to compensate for the effect of cowl design, cooling airflow, or other factors on engine cooling. The final fuel/air mixture curves take into account economy, power, engine cooling, idling characteristics, and all other factors that affect combustion.

Figure 10-47 shows a typical final curve for a float-type carburetor. Note that the fuel/air mixture at idle is the same in rich and in manual lean. The mixture remains the same until the low cruise range is reached. At this point, the curves separate and then remain parallel through the cruise and power ranges.

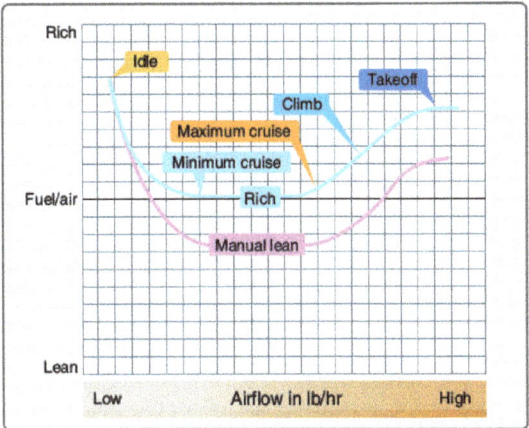

Figure 10-47. *Typical fuel-air mixture curve for a float-type carburetor.*

Note the spread between the rich and lean setting in the cruise range of both curves. Because of this spread, there is a decrease in power when the mixture control is moved from auto-rich to auto-lean with the engine operating in the cruise range. This is true because the auto-rich setting in the cruise range is very near the best power mixture ratio. Therefore, any leaning out gives a mixture that is leaner than best power.

Idle Mixture

The idle mixture curve shows how the mixture changes when the idle mixture adjustment is changed. *[Figure 10-48]* Note that the greatest effect is at idling speeds. However, there is some effect on the mixture at airflows above idling. The airflow at which the idle adjustment effect cancels out varies from minimum cruise to maximum cruise. The exact point depends on the type of carburetor and the carburetor setting. In general, the idle adjustment affects the fuel/air mixture up to low cruise on engines equipped with float-type carburetors. This means that incorrect idle mixture adjustments can easily give faulty cruise performance, as well as poor idling.

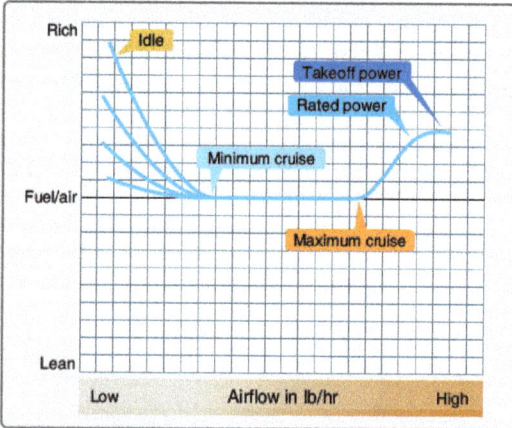

Figure 10-48. *Idle mixture curve.*

There are variations in mixture requirements between one engine and another because of the fuel distribution within the engine and the ability of the engine to cool. Remember, a carburetor setting must be rich enough to supply a combustible mixture for the leanest cylinder. If fuel distribution is poor, the overall mixture must be richer than would be required for the same engine if distribution were good. The engine's ability to cool depends on such factors as cylinder design (including the design of the cooling fins), compression ratio, accessories on the front of the engine that cause individual cylinders to run hot, and the design of the baffling used to deflect airflow around the cylinder. At takeoff power, the mixture must be rich enough to supply sufficient fuel to keep the hottest cylinder cool.

Induction Manifold

The induction manifold provides the means of distributing air, or the fuel/air mixture, to the cylinders. Whether the manifold handles a fuel/air mixture or air alone depends on the type of fuel metering system used. On an engine equipped with a carburetor, the induction manifold distributes a fuel/air mixture from the carburetor to the cylinders. On a fuel-injection engine, the fuel is delivered to injection nozzles, one in each cylinder, that provide the proper spray pattern for efficient burning. Thus, the mixing of fuel and air takes place at the inlet port to the cylinder. On a fuel-injection engine the induction manifold handles only air.

The induction manifold is an important item because of the effect it can have on the fuel/air mixture that finally reaches the cylinder. Fuel is introduced into the airstream by the carburetor in a liquid form. To become combustible, the fuel must be vaporized in the air. This vaporization takes place in the induction manifold, which includes the internal supercharger, if one is used. Any fuel that does not vaporize clings to the walls of the intake pipes. Obviously, this affects the effective fuel/air ratio of the mixture that finally reaches the cylinder in vapor form. This explains the reason for the apparently rich mixture required to start a cold engine. In a cold engine, some of the fuel in the airstream condenses out and clings to the walls of the manifold. This is in addition to that fuel that never vaporized in the first place. As the engine warms up, less fuel is required because less fuel is condensed out of the airstream and more of the fuel is vaporized, thus giving the cylinder the required fuel/air mixture for normal combustion.

Any leak in the induction system has an effect on the mixture reaching the cylinders. This is particularly true of a leak at the cylinder end of an intake pipe. At manifold pressures below atmospheric pressure, such a leak leans out the mixture. This occurs because additional air is drawn in from the atmosphere at the leaky point. The affected cylinder may overheat, fire intermittently, or even cut out altogether.

Operational Effect of Valve Clearance

While considering the operational effect of valve clearance, keep in mind that all aircraft reciprocating engines of current design use valve overlap. Valve overlap is when the intake and exhaust valves are open at the same time. This takes advantage of the momentum of the entering and exiting gases to improve the efficiency of getting fuel/air in and exhaust gases out. *Figure 10-49* shows the pressures at the intake and exhaust ports under two different sets of operating conditions. In one case, the engine is operating at a manifold pressure of 35 "Hg. Barometric pressure (exhaust back pressure) is 29 "Hg. This gives a pressure acting in the direction indicated by the arrow of differential of 6 "Hg (3 psi).

During the valve overlap period, this pressure differential forces the fuel/air mixture across the combustion chamber toward the open exhaust. This flow of fuel/air mixture forces ahead of it the exhaust gases remaining in the cylinder, resulting in complete scavenging of the combustion chamber. This, in turn, permits complete filling of the cylinder with a fresh charge on the following intake event. This is the situation in which valve overlap gives increased power.

Figure 10-49. *Effect of valve overlap.*

There is a pressure differential in the opposite direction of 9 "Hg (4.5 psi) when the manifold pressure is below atmospheric pressure, for example, 20 "Hg. These cause air or exhaust gases to be drawn into the cylinder through the exhaust port during valve overlap.

In engines with collector rings, this inflow through the exhaust port at low power settings consists of burned exhaust gases. These gases are pulled back into the cylinder and mix with the incoming fuel/air mixture. However, these exhaust gases are inert; they do not contain oxygen. Therefore, the fuel/air mixture ratio is not affected much. With open exhaust stacks, the situation is entirely different. Here, fresh air containing oxygen is pulled into the cylinders through the exhaust. This leans out the mixture. Therefore, the carburetor must be set to deliver an excessively rich idle mixture so that, when this mixture is combined with the fresh air drawn in through the exhaust port, the effective mixture in the cylinder will be at the desired ratio.

At first thought, it does not appear possible that the effect of valve overlap on fuel/air mixture is sufficient to cause concern. However, the effect of valve overlap becomes apparent when considering idle fuel-air mixtures. These mixtures must be enriched 20 to 30 percent when open stacks, instead of collector rings (radial engines) are used on the same engine. *[Figure 10-50]* Note the spread at idle between an open stack and an exhaust collector ring installation for engines that are otherwise identical. The mixture variation decreases as the engine speed or airflow is increased from idle into the cruise range.

Figure 10-50. *Comparison of fuel/air mixture curves for open-stack and collector-ring installations.*

Engine, airplane, and equipment manufacturers provide a powerplant installation that gives satisfactory performance. Cams are designed to give best valve operation and correct overlap. But valve operation is correct only if valve clearances are set and remain at the value recommended by the engine manufacturer. If valve clearances are set wrong, the valve overlap period is longer or shorter than the manufacturer intended. The same is true if clearances get out of adjustment during operation.

Where there is too much valve clearance, the valves do not open as wide or remain open as long as they should. This reduces the overlap period. At idling speed, it affects the fuel/air mixture, since a less-than-normal amount of air or exhaust gases is drawn back into the cylinder during the shortened overlap period. As a result, the idle mixture tends to be too rich.

When valve clearance is less than it should be, the valve overlap period is lengthened. A greater than normal amount of air, or exhaust gases, is drawn back into the cylinder at idling speeds. As a result, the idle mixture is leaned out at the cylinder. The carburetor is adjusted with the expectation that a certain amount of air or exhaust gases is drawn back into the cylinder at idling. If more or less air, or exhaust gases, are drawn into the cylinder during the valve overlap period, the mixture is too lean or too rich.

When valve clearances are wrong, it is unlikely that they are all wrong in the same direction. Instead, there is too much clearance on some cylinders and too little on others. Naturally, this gives a variation in valve overlap between cylinders. This results in a variation in fuel/air ratio at idling and lower-power settings, since the carburetor delivers the same mixture to all cylinders. The carburetor cannot tailor the mixture to each cylinder to compensate for variation in valve overlap. The effect of variation in valve clearance and valve overlap on the fuel/air mixture between cylinders is illustrated in *Figure 10-51*. Note how the cylinders with too little clearance run rich, and those with too much clearance run lean. Note also the extreme mixture variation between cylinders.

Valve clearance also effects volumetric efficiency. Any variations in fuel/air into, and exhaust gases out of, the cylinder affects the volumetric efficiency of the cylinder. With the use of hydraulic valve lifters that set the valve clearance automatically engine operation has been greatly improved. Hydraulic lifters do have a limited range in which they can control the valve clearance, or they can become stuck in one position that can cause them to be a source of engine trouble. Normally engines equipped with hydraulic lifters require little to no maintenance.

Engine Troubleshooting

Troubleshooting is a systematic analysis of the symptoms that indicate engine malfunction. It would be impractical to list all the malfunctions that could occur in a reciprocating engine, so only the most common malfunctions are discussed. A thorough knowledge of the engine systems, applied with logical reasoning, solves most problems that may occur.

Figure 10-52 lists general conditions or troubles that may be encountered on reciprocating engines, such as engine fails to start. They are further divided into the probable causes contributing to such conditions. Corrective actions are indicated in the remedy column. The items are presented with consideration given to frequency of occurrence, ease of accessibility, and complexity of the corrective action indicated.

The need for troubleshooting normally is dictated by poor operation of the complete powerplant. Power settings for the type of operation at which any difficulty is encountered, in many cases, indicate that part of the powerplant that is the basic cause of difficulty.

The cylinders of an engine, along with any type of supercharging, form an air pump. Furthermore, the power developed in the cylinders varies directly with the rate that air can be consumed by the engine. Therefore, a measure of air consumption or airflow into the engine is a measure of power input. Ignoring for the moment such factors as humidity and exhaust back pressure, the manifold pressure gauge and the engine tachometer provide a measure of engine air consumption. Thus, for a given rpm, any change in power input is reflected by a corresponding change in manifold pressure.

The power output of an engine is the power absorbed by the propeller. Therefore, propeller load is a measure of power output. Propeller load, in turn, depends on the propeller rpm, blade angle, and air density. For a given angle and air density, propeller load (power output) is directly proportional to engine speed. The basic power of an engine is related to

Figure 10-51. *Effect of variation in valve overlap on fuel/air mixture between cylinders.*

Trouble	Probable causes	Remedy
Engine fails to start	• Lack of fuel	• Check fuel system for leaks fill fuel tank. • Clean dirty lines, strainers, or fuel valves.
	• Underpriming	• Use correct priming procedure.
	• Overpriming	• Open throttle and "unload" engine by rotating the propeller.
	• Incorrect throttle setting	• Open throttle to one-tenth of its range.
	• Defective spark plugs	• Clean and re-gap or replace spark plugs.
	• Defective ignition wire	• Test and replace any defective wires.
	• Defective or weak battery.	• Replace with charged battery.
	• Improper operation of magneto or breaker points.	• Check internal timing of magnetos.
	• Water in carburetor	• Drain carburetor and fuel lines.
	• Internal failure	• Check oil sump strainer for metal particles.
	• Magnetized impulse coupling, if installed.	• Demagnetize impulse coupling.
	• Frozen spark plug electrodes.	• Replace spark plugs or dry out plugs.
	• Mixture control in idle cutoff.	• Open mixture control.
	• Shorted ignition switch or loose ground.	• Check and replace or obtain correct idle.
Engine fails to idle properly	• Incorrect carburetor idle speed adjustment.	• Adjust throttle stop to obtain correct idle.
	• Incorrect idle mixture.	• Adjust mixture. (refer to engine manufacturer's handbook for proper procedure.)
	• Leak in the induction system.	• Tighten all connections in the induction system. Replace any defective parts.
	• Low cylinder compression	• Check cylinder compression.
	• Faulty ignition system.	• Check entire ignition system.
	• Open or leaking primer.	• Lock or repair primer.
	• Improper spark plug setting for altitude	• Check spark plug gap.
	• Dirty air filter.	• Clean or replace.
Low power and engine running uneven	• Mixture too rich; indicated by sluggish engine operation, red exhaust flame, and black smoke.	• Check primer. Re-adjust carburetor mixture.
	• Mixture too lean; indicated by overheating or backfiring.	• Check fuel lines for dirt or other restrictions. Check fuel supply.
	• Leaks in induction system.	• Tighten all connections. Replace defective parts.
	• Defective spark plugs.	• Clean or replace spark plugs.
	• Improper grade of fuel.	• Fill tank with recommended grade.
	• Magneto breaker points not working properly.	• Clean points. Check internal timing of magneto.
	• Defective ignition wire.	• Test and replace any defective wires.
	• Defective spark plug terminal connectors.	• Replace connectors on spark plug wire.
	• Incorrect valve clearance.	• Adjust valve clearance. • Check and replace or repair.

Figure 10-52. *Troubleshooting opposed engines.*

manifold pressure, fuel flow, and rpm. Because the rpm of the engine and the throttle opening directly control manifold pressure, the primary engine power controls are the throttle and the rpm control. An engine equipped with a fixed-pitch propeller has only a throttle control. In this case, the throttle setting controls both manifold pressure and engine rpm.

With proper precautions, manifold pressure can be taken as a measure of power input, and rpm can be taken as a measure of power output. However, the following factors must be considered:

Trouble	Probable causes	Remedy
Low power and engine running uneven	• Restriction in exhaust system.	• Remove restriction.
	• Improper ignition timing.	• Check magnetos for timing and synchronization.
Engine fails to develop full power	• Throttle lever out of adjustment.	• Adjust throttle lever.
	• Leak in induction system.	• Tighten all connections and replace defective parts.
	• Restriction in carburetor airscoop.	• Examine airscoop and remove restriction.
	• Improper fuel.	• Fill tank with recommended fuel.
	• Propeller governor out of adjustment.	• Adjust governor.
	• Faulty ignition.	• Tighten all connections. Check system. Check ignition timing.
Rough running engine	• Cracked engine mount(s).	• Repair or replace engine mount(s).
	• Unbalanced propeller.	• Remove propeller and have it checked for balance.
	• Defective mounting bushings.	• Install new mounting bushings.
	• Lead deposit on spark plugs.	• Clean or replace plugs.
	• Primer unlocked.	• Lock primer.
Low oil pressure	• Insufficient oil.	• Check oil supply.
	• Dirty oil strainers.	• Remove and clean oil strainers.
	• Defective pressure gauge.	• Replace gauge.
	• Air lock or dirt in relief valve.	• Remove and clean oil pressure relief valve.
	• Leak in suction line or pressure line.	• Check gasket between accessory housing crankcase.
	• High oil temperature.	• See "high oil temperature" in trouble column.
	• Stoppage in oil pump intake passage.	• Check line for obstruction. Clean suction strainer.
	• Worn or scored bearings.	• Overhaul engine.
High oil temperature	• Insufficient air cooling.	• Check air inlet and outlet for deformation or obstruction.
	• Insufficient oil supply.	• Fill oil tank to proper level.
	• Clogged oil lines or strainers.	• Remove and clean oil line or strainers.
	• Failing or failed bearings.	• Examine sump for metal particles and, if found, overhaul engine.
	• Defective thermostats.	• Replace thermostats.
	• Defective temperature gauge.	• Usually caused by weak or stuck rings.
	• Exceddive blow-by.	• Overhaul engine.
Excessive oil consumption	• Failing or failed bearing.	• Check sump for metal particles and if found, an an overhaul of engine is indicated.
	• Worn or broken piston rings.	• Install new rings.
	• Incorrect installation of piston rings.	• Install new rings.
	• External oil leakage.	• Check engine carefully for leaking gaskets or O-rings.
	• Leakage through engine fuel pump vent.	• Replace fuel pump seal.
	• Engine breather or vacuum pump breather.	• Check engine, and overhaul or replace vacuum pump.

Figure 10-52. *Troubleshooting opposed engines (continued).*

1. Atmospheric pressure and air temperature must be considered, since they affect air density.
2. These measures of power input and power output should be used only for comparing the performance of an engine with its previous performance, or for comparing identical powerplants.
3. With a controllable propeller, the blades must be against their low-pitch stops, since this is the only blade position in which the blade angle is known and does not vary. Once the blades are off their low-pitch stops, the propeller governor takes over and maintains a constant rpm, regardless of power input or engine condition. This precaution means that the propeller control must be set to maximum or takeoff rpm, and the checks made at engine speeds below this setting.

Having relative measures of power input and power output, the condition of an engine can be determined by comparing input and output. This is done by comparing the manifold pressure required to produce a given rpm with the manifold pressure required to produce the same rpm at a time when the engine (or an identical powerplant) was known to be in top operating condition.

An example shows the practical application of this method of determining engine condition. With the propeller control set for takeoff rpm (full low blade angle), an engine may require 32 inches of manifold pressure to turn 2,200 rpm for the ignition check. On previous checks, this engine required only 30 inches of manifold pressure to turn 2,200 rpm at the same station (altitude) and under similar atmospheric conditions. Obviously, something is wrong; a higher power input (manifold pressure) is now required for the same power output (rpm). There is a good chance that one cylinder has a malfunction.

There are several standards against which engine performance can be compared. The performance of a particular engine can be compared with its past performance, provided adequate records are kept. Engine performance can be compared with that of other engines on the same aircraft or aircraft having identical installations.

If a fault does exist, it may be assumed that the trouble lies in one of the following systems:

1. Ignition system
2. Fuel-metering system
3. Induction system
4. Power section (valves, cylinders, etc.)
5. Instrumentation

If a logical approach to the problem is taken and the instrument readings properly utilized, the malfunctioning system can be pinpointed, and the specific problem in the defective system can be singled out.

The more information available about any particular problem, the better the opportunity for a rapid repair. Information that is of value in locating a malfunction includes:

1. Was any roughness noted? Under what conditions of operation?
2. What is the time on the engine and spark plugs? How long since last inspection?
3. Was the ignition system operational check and power check normal?
4. When did the trouble first appear?
5. Was backfiring or afterfiring present?
6. Was the full throttle performance normal?

From a different point of view, the powerplant is, in reality, a number of small engines turning a common crankshaft and being operated by two common phases: fuel metering and ignition. When backfiring, low power output or other powerplant difficulty is encountered, first find out which system, fuel metering or ignition, is involved and then determine whether the entire engine or only one cylinder is at fault. For example, backfiring normally is caused by:

1. Valves holding open or sticking open in one or more of the cylinders
2. Lean mixture
3. Intake pipe leakage
4. An error in valve adjustment that causes individual cylinders to receive too small a charge or one too large, even though the mixture to the cylinders has the same fuel/air ratio

Ignition system reasons for backfiring might be a cracked distributor block or a high-tension leak between two ignition leads. Either of these conditions could cause the charge in the cylinder to be ignited during the intake stroke. Ignition system troubles involving backfiring normally are not centered in the basic magneto, since a failure of the basic magneto would result in the engine not running, or it would run well at low speeds but cut out at high speeds. On the other hand, replacement of the magneto would correct a difficulty caused by a cracked distributor where the distributor is a part of the magneto.

If the fuel system, ignition system, and induction system are functioning properly, the engine should produce the correct bhp unless some fault exists in the basic power section.

Valve Blow-By

Valve blow-by is indicated by a hissing or whistle when pulling the propeller through prior to starting the engine, when turning the engine with the starter, or when running and blow-by past the intake valve is audible through the carburetor.

Correct valve blow-by immediately to prevent valve failure and possible engine failure by taking the following steps:

1. Perform a cylinder compression test to locate the faulty cylinder.
2. Check the valve clearance on the affected cylinder. If the valve clearance is incorrect, the valve may be sticking in the valve guide. To release the sticking valve, place a fiber drift on the rocker arm immediately over the valve stem and strike the drift several times with a mallet. Sufficient hand pressure should be exerted on the fiber drift to remove any space between the rocker arm and the valve stem prior to hitting the drift.
3. If the valve is not sticking and the valve clearance is incorrect, adjust it as necessary.
4. Determine whether blow-by has been eliminated by again pulling the engine through by hand or turning it with the starter. If blow-by is still present, it may be necessary to replace the cylinder.

Cylinder Compression Tests

The cylinder compression test determines if the valves, piston rings, and pistons are adequately sealing the combustion chamber. If pressure leakage is excessive, the cylinder cannot develop its full power. The purpose of testing cylinder compression is to determine whether cylinder replacement is necessary. The detection and replacement of defective cylinders prevents a complete engine change because of cylinder failure. It is essential that cylinder compression tests be made periodically. Low compression, for the most part, can be traced to leaky valves.

Conditions that affect engine compression are:

1. Incorrect valve clearances
2. Worn, scuffed, or damaged piston
3. Excessive wear of piston rings and cylinder walls
4. Burned or warped valves
5. Carbon particles between the face and the seat of the valve or valves
6. Early or late valve timing

Perform a compression test as soon as possible after the engine is shut down so that piston rings, cylinder walls, and other parts are still freshly lubricated. However, it is not necessary to operate the engine prior to accomplishing compression checks during engine buildup or on individually replaced cylinders. In such cases, before making the test, spray a small quantity of lubricating oil into the cylinder(s), and turn the engine over several times to seal the piston and rings in the cylinder barrel.

Be sure that the ignition switch is in the OFF position so that there is no accidental firing of the engine. Remove necessary cowling and the most accessible spark plug from each cylinder. When removing the spark plugs, identify them to coincide with the cylinder. Close examination of the plugs aid in diagnosing problems within the cylinder. Review the maintenance records of the engine being tested. Records of previous compression checks help in determining progressive wear conditions and in establishing the necessary maintenance actions.

Differential Pressure Tester

The differential pressure tester checks the compression of aircraft engines by measuring the leakage through the cylinders. The design of this compression tester is such that minute valve leakages can be detected, making possible the replacement of cylinders where valve burning is starting. The operation of the compression tester is based on the principle that, for any given airflow through a fixed orifice, a constant pressure drop across the orifice results.

As the airflow and pressure changes, pressure varies accordingly in the same direction. If air is supplied under pressure to the cylinder with both intake and exhaust valves closed, the amount of air that leaks by the valves or piston rings indicates their condition; the perfect cylinder would have no leakage. The differential pressure tester requires the application of air pressure to the cylinder being tested with the piston at top-center compression stroke. *[Figure 10-53]*

Guidelines for performing a differential compression test are:

1. Perform the compression test as soon as possible after engine shutdown to provide uniform lubrication of cylinder walls and rings.
2. Remove the most accessible spark plug from the cylinder, or cylinders, and install a spark plug adapter in the spark plug insert.
3. Connect the compression tester assembly to a 100 to 150 psi compressed air supply. *[Figure 10-54]* With the shutoff valve on the compression tester closed, adjust the regulator of the regulated pressure gauge compression tester to obtain 80 psi.

Figure 10-53. *Differential compression tester diagrams.*

Figure 10-54. *Compression tester and adapter.*

4. Open the shutoff valve and attach the air hose quick-connect fitting to the spark plug adapter. The shutoff valve, when open, automatically maintains a pressure in the cylinder of 15 to 20 psi when both the intake and exhaust valves are closed.

5. By hand, turn the engine over in the direction of rotation until the piston in the cylinder being tested comes up on the compression stroke against the 15 psi. Continue turning the propeller slowly in the direction of rotation until the piston reaches top dead center. Top dead center can be detected by a decrease in force required to move the propeller. If the engine is rotated past top dead center, the 15 to 20 psi tends to move the propeller in the direction of rotation. If this occurs, back the propeller up at least one blade prior to turning the propeller again in the direction of rotation. This backing up is necessary to eliminate the effect of backlash in the valve-operating mechanism and to keep the piston rings seated on the lower ring lands.

6. Close the shutoff valve in the compression tester and re-check the regulated pressure to see that it is 80 psi with air flowing into the cylinder. If the regulated pressure is more or less than 80 psi, readjust the regulator in the test unit to obtain 80 psi. When closing the shutoff valve, make sure that the propeller path is clear of all objects. There is sufficient air pressure in the combustion chamber to rotate the propeller if the piston is not on top dead center.

7. With regulated pressure adjusted to 80 psi, if the cylinder pressure reading indicated on the cylinder pressure gauge is below the minimum specified for the engine being tested, move the propeller in the direction of rotation to seat the piston rings in the grooves. Check all the cylinders and record the readings.

If low compression is obtained on any cylinder, turn the engine through with the starter, or re-start, and run the engine to takeoff power and re-check the cylinder, or cylinders, having low compression.

If the low compression is not corrected, remove the rocker-box cover and check the valve clearance to determine if the difficulty is caused by inadequate valve clearance. If the low compression is not caused by inadequate valve clearance, place a fiber drift on the rocker arm immediately over the valve stem and tap the drift several times with a 1 to 2 pound hammer to dislodge any foreign material that may be lodged between the valve and valve seat.

After staking the valve in this manner, rotate the engine with the starter and re-check the compression. Do not make a compression check after staking a valve until the crankshaft has been rotated either with the starter or by hand to re-seat the valve in normal manner. The higher seating velocity obtained when staking the valve will indicate valve seating, even though valve seats are slightly egged or eccentric. This procedure should only be performed if approved by the manufacturer.

Cylinders having compression below the minimum specified should be further checked to determine whether leakage is past the exhaust valve, intake valve, or piston. Excessive leakage can be detected (during the compression check):

1. At the exhaust valve by listening for air leakage at the exhaust outlet;
2. At the intake valve by escaping air at the air intake; and
3. Past the piston rings by escaping air at the engine breather outlets.

Next to valve blow-by, the most frequent cause of compression leakage is excessive leakage past the piston. This leakage may occur because of lack of oil. To check this possibility, apply engine oil into the cylinder and around the piston. Then, re-check the compression. If this procedure raises compression to or above the minimum required, continue the cylinder in service. If the cylinder pressure readings still do not meet the minimum requirement, replace the cylinder. When it is necessary to replace a cylinder as a result of low compression, record the cylinder number and the compression value of the newly installed cylinder on the compression check sheet.

Cylinder Replacement

Reciprocating engine cylinders are designed to operate for a specified time before normal wear requires their overhaul. If the engine is operated as recommended and proficient maintenance is performed, the cylinders normally last until the engine has reached its TBO. It is known from experience that materials fail and engines are abused through incorrect operation; this has a serious effect on cylinder life. Another reason for premature cylinder change is poor maintenance. Therefore, exert special care to ensure that all the correct maintenance procedures are adhered to when working on the engine. Some of the reasons for cylinder replacement are:

1. Low compression
2. High oil consumption in one or more cylinders
3. Excessive valve guide clearance
4. Loose intake pipe flanges
5. Loose or defective spark plug inserts
6. External damage, such as cracks

The cylinder is always replaced as a complete assembly, which includes piston, rings, valves, and valve springs. Obtain the cylinder by ordering the cylinder assembly under the part number specified in the engine parts catalog. Parts, such as valve springs, rocker arms, and rocker box covers, may be replaced individually.

Normally, all the cylinders in an engine are similar, all are standard size or all a certain oversize, and all are steel bore or all are chrome-plated. The size of the cylinder is indicated by a color code around the barrel between the attaching flange and the lower barrel cooling fin. In some instances, air-cooled engines are equipped with chrome-plated cylinders. Chrome-plated cylinders are usually identified by a paint band around the barrel between the attaching flange and the lower barrel cooling fin. This color band is usually international orange.

When installing a chrome-plated cylinder, do not use chrome-plated piston rings. The matched assembly includes the correct piston rings. However, if a piston ring is broken during cylinder installation, check the cylinder marking to determine what ring, chrome-plated or otherwise, is correct for replacement. Similar precautions must be taken to be sure that the correct size rings are installed.

Correct procedures and care are important when replacing cylinders. Careless work or the use of incorrect tools can damage the replacement cylinder or its parts. Incorrect procedures in installing rocker-box covers may result in troublesome oil leaks. Improper torque on cylinder hold down nuts or cap-screws can easily result in a cylinder malfunction and subsequent engine failure.

Cylinder Removal

Since these instructions are meant to cover all air-cooled engines, they are of a very general nature. The applicable manufacturer's maintenance manual should be consulted for torque values and special precautions applying to a particular aircraft and engine. However, always practice neatness and cleanliness, and always protect openings so that nuts, washers, tools, and miscellaneous items do not enter the engine's internal sections.

Assuming that all obstructing cowling and brackets have been removed, first remove the intake pipe and exhaust pipes. Plug or cover openings in the intake or diffuser section. Then, remove cylinder deflectors and any attaching brackets that would obstruct cylinder removal. Loosen the spark plugs and remove the spark plug lead clamps. Do not remove the spark plugs until ready to pull the cylinder off. Remove the rocker box covers. First, remove the nuts and then tap the cover lightly with a rawhide mallet or plastic hammer. Never pry the cover off with a screwdriver or similar tool.

Loosen the pushrod packing gland nuts or hose clamps, top and bottom. Pushrods are removed by depressing the rocker arms with a special tool, or by removing the rocker arm. Before removing the pushrods, turn the crankshaft until the piston is at top dead center on the compression stroke. This relieves the pressure on both intake and exhaust rocker arms. It is also wise to back off the adjusting nut as far as possible, because this allows maximum clearance for pushrod removal when the rocker arms are depressed.

On some model engines, or if the engine is rotated, tappets and springs of lower cylinders can fall out. Provision must be made to catch them as the pushrod and housing are removed.

After removing the pushrods, examine them for markings or mark them so that they may be replaced in the same location as they were before removal. The ball ends are usually worn to fit the sockets in which they have been operating. Furthermore, on some engines, pushrods are not all of the same length. A good procedure is to mark the pushrods near the valve tappet ends No. 1 IN, No. 1 EX, No. 2 IN, No. 2 EX., etc. On fuel injection engines, disconnect the fuel injection line and any line clamps that interfere with cylinder removal.

The next step in removing the cylinder is to cut the lock wire or remove the cotter pin, and pry off the locking device from the cylinder-attaching cap-screws or nuts. Remove all the screws or nuts except two located 180° apart. Use the wrench specified for this purpose in the special tools section of the applicable manual.

Finally, while supporting the cylinder, remove the two remaining screws or nuts and gently pull the cylinder away from the crankcase. Two technicians working together during this step, as well as during the remaining procedure for cylinder replacement, helps prevent damage or dropping of the cylinder. After the cylinder skirt has cleared the crankcase, but before the piston protrudes from the skirt, provide some means (usually a shop cloth) for preventing pieces of broken rings from falling into the crankcase. After the piston has been removed, remove the cloths and carefully check that all pieces were prevented from falling into the crankcase.

Place a support on the cylinder mounting pad and secure it with two cap-screws or nuts. Then, remove the piston and ring assembly from the connecting rod. A pin pusher or puller tool can be used when varnish makes it hard to remove the pin. If the special tool is not available and a drift is used to remove the piston pin, the connecting rod should be supported so that it does not have to take the shock of the blows. If this is not done, the rod may be damaged.

After the removal of a cylinder and piston, the connecting rod must be supported to prevent damage to the rod and crankcase. This can be done by supporting each connecting rod with the removed cylinder base oil seal ring looped around the rod and cylinder base studs.

Using a wire brush, clean the studs or cap-screws and examine them for cracks, damaged threads, or any other visible defects. If one cap-screw is found loose or broken at the time of cylinder removal, all the cap-screws for the cylinder should be discarded, since the remaining cap-screws may have been seriously weakened. A cylinder hold down stud failure places the adjacent studs under a greater operating pressure, and they are likely to be stretched beyond their elastic limit. The engine manufacturer's instruction must be followed for the number of studs that have to be replaced after a stud failure. When removing a broken stud, take proper precautions to prevent metal chips from entering the engine crankcase section. In all cases, both faces of the washers and the seating faces of stud nuts or cap-screws must be cleaned and any roughness or burrs removed.

Cylinder Installation

See that all preservative oil accumulation on the cylinder and piston assembly is washed off with solvent and thoroughly dried with compressed air. Install the piston and ring assembly on the connecting rod. Be sure that the piston faces in the right direction. The piston number stamped on the bottom of the piston head should face toward the front of the engine. Lubricate the piston pin before inserting it. It should fit with a push fit. If a drift must be used, follow the same precaution that was taken during pin removal.

Oil the exterior of the piston assembly generously, forcing oil around the piston rings and in the space between the rings and grooves. Stagger the ring gaps around the piston and check to see that rings are in the correct grooves, and whether they are positioned correctly, as some are used as oil scrapers, others as pumper rings. The number, type, and arrangement of the compression and oil-control rings vary with the make and model of engine.

Perform any and all visual, structural, and dimensional inspection checks before installing the cylinder. Check the flange to see that the mating surface is smooth and clean. Coat the inside of the cylinder barrel generously with oil. Be sure that the cylinder oil-seal ring is in place and that only one seal ring is used.

Using a ring compressor, compress the rings to a diameter equal to that of the piston. With the piston at TDC, start the cylinder assembly down over the piston, making certain that the cylinder and piston plane remain the same. Ease the cylinder over the piston with a straight, even movement that moves the ring compressor as the cylinder slips on. Do not rock the cylinder while slipping it on the piston, since any rocking is apt to release a piston ring or a part of a ring from the ring compressor prior to the ring's entrance into the cylinder bore. A ring released in this manner expands and prevents the piston from entering the cylinder. Any attempt to force the cylinder onto the piston is apt to cause cracking or chipping of the ring or damage to the ring lands.

After the cylinder has slipped on the piston, so that all piston rings are in the cylinder bore, remove the ring compressor and the connecting rod guide. Then, slide the cylinder into place on the mounting pad. If cap-screws are used, rotate the cylinder to align the holes. While still supporting the cylinder, install two cap-screws or stud nuts 180° apart.

Install the remaining nuts or cap-screws, and tighten them until they are snug. The hold down nuts, or cap-screws, must now be torqued to the value specified in the table of torque values in the engine manufacturer's service or overhaul manual. Apply the torque with a slow, steady motion until the prescribed value is reached. Hold the tension on the wrench for a sufficient length of time to ensure that the nut or cap-screw tightens no more at the prescribed torque value. In many cases, additional turning of the cap-screw, or nut, as much as one-quarter turn can be done by maintaining the prescribed torque on the nut for a short period of time. After the stud nuts, or cap-screws, have been torqued to the prescribed value, safety them in the manner recommended in the engine manufacturer's service manual.

Reinstall the push rods, push rod housings, rocker arms, barrel deflectors, intake pipes, ignition harness lead clamps and brackets, fuel injection line clamps and fuel injection nozzles (if removed), exhaust stack, cylinder head deflectors, and spark plugs. Remember that the push rods must be installed in their original locations and must not be turned end to end. Make sure that the push rod ball end seats properly in the tappet. If it rests on the edge or shoulder of the tappet during valve clearance adjustment and later drops into place, valve clearance is off.

Furthermore, rotating the crankshaft with the push rod resting on the edge of the tappet may bend the push rod. After installing the push rods and rocker arms, set the valve clearance. Before installing the rocker-box covers, lubricate the rocker arm bearings and valve stems. Check the rocker-box covers for flatness; re-surface them if necessary. After installing the gaskets and covers, tighten the rocker-box cover nuts to the specified torque. Always follow the recommended safety procedures.

Cold Cylinder Check

The cold cylinder check determines the operating characteristics of each cylinder of an air-cooled engine. The tendency for any cylinder, or cylinders, to be cold, or to be only slightly warm, indicates lack of combustion or incomplete combustion within the cylinder. This must be corrected if best operation and power conditions are to be obtained. The cold cylinder check is made with a cold cylinder indicator.

Engine difficulties that can be analyzed by use of the cold cylinder indicator are *[Figure 10-55]*:

1. Rough engine operation
2. Excessive rpm drop during the ignition system check
3. High manifold pressure for a given engine rpm during the ground check when the propeller is in the full low-pitch position
4. Faulty mixture ratios caused by improper valve clearance

In preparation for the cold cylinder check, head the aircraft into the wind to minimize irregular cooling of the individual cylinders and to ensure even propeller loading during engine operation.

Figure 10-55. *Cold cylinder indicator.*

Operate the engine on its roughest magneto at a speed between 1,200 and 1,600 rpm until the cylinder head temperature reading is stabilized. If engine roughness is encountered at more than one speed, or if there is an indication that a cylinder ceases operating at idle or higher speeds, run the engine at each of these speeds, and perform a cold cylinder check to pick out all the dead or intermittently operating cylinders. When low power output or engine vibration is encountered at speeds above 1,600 rpm when operating with the ignition switch on both, run the engine at the speed where the difficulty is encountered until the cylinder head temperatures have stabilized.

When cylinder head temperatures have reached the stabilized values, stop the engine by moving the mixture control to the idle cutoff or full lean position. When the engine ceases firing, turn off both ignition and master switches. Record the cylinder head temperature reading registered on the flight deck gauge. As soon as the propeller has ceased rotating, apply the instrument to each cylinder head, and record the relative temperature of each cylinder. Start with number one and proceed in numerical order around the engine, as rapidly as possible. To obtain comparative temperature values, a firm contact must be made at the same relative location on each cylinder. Note any outstandingly low (cold) values. Compare the temperature readings to determine which cylinders are dead (cold cylinders) or are operating intermittently.

Difficulties that may cause a cylinder to be inoperative (dead) when isolated to one magneto, either the right or left positions, are:

1. Defective spark plugs
2. Incorrect valve clearances
3. Leaking intake pipes
4. Lack of compression
5. Defective spark plug lead
6. Defective fuel-injection nozzle

Repeat the cold cylinder test for the other magneto positions on the ignition switch, if necessary. Cooling the engine between tests is unnecessary. The airflow created by the propeller, and the cooling effect of the incoming fuel/air mixture is sufficient to cool any cylinders that are functioning on one test and not functioning on the next.

In interpreting the results of a cold cylinder check, remember that the temperatures are relative. A cylinder temperature taken alone means little, but when compared with the temperatures of other cylinders on the same engine, it provides valuable diagnostic information. The readings shown in *Figure 10-56* illustrate this point. On this check,

Cylinder No.	Temperature readings	
	Right magneto	Left magneto
1	180	170
2	170	175
3	100	170
4	145	60
5	70	155
6	60	45

Figure 10-56. *Readings taken during a cold cylinder check.*

the cylinder head temperature gauge reading at the time the engine was shut down was 160 °C on both tests.

A review of these temperature readings reveals that, on the right magneto, cylinder number 3 runs cool and cylinders 5 and 6 run cold. This indicates that cylinder 3 is firing intermittently, and cylinders 5 and 6 are dead during engine operation on the plugs fired by the right magneto. Cylinders 4 and 6 are dead during operation on the plugs fired by the left magneto. Cylinder 6 is completely dead. An ignition system operational check would not disclose this dead cylinder, since the cylinder is inoperative on both right and left switch positions.

A dead cylinder can be detected during run-up, since an engine with a dead cylinder requires a higher than normal manifold pressure to produce any given rpm below the cut-in speed of the propeller governor. A dead cylinder could also be detected by comparing power input and power output with the aid of a torquemeter.

Defects within the ignition system that can cause a cylinder to go completely dead are:

1. Both spark plugs inoperative
2. Both ignition leads grounded, leaking, or open
3. A combination of inoperative spark plugs and defective ignition leads
4. Faulty fuel-injection nozzles, incorrect valve clearances, and other defects outside the ignition system

In interpreting the readings obtained on a cold cylinder check, the amount the engine cools during the check must be considered. To determine the extent to which this factor should be considered in evaluating the readings, re-check some of the first cylinders tested, and compare the final readings with those made at the start of the check. Another factor to be considered is the normal variation in temperature between cylinders and between rows. This variation results from those design features that affect the airflow past the cylinders.

Turbine Engine Maintenance

Turbine powerplant maintenance procedures vary widely according to the design and construction of the particular engine being serviced. The detailed procedures recommended by the engine manufacturer should be followed when performing inspections or maintenance. Maintenance information presented in this section is not intended to specify the exact manner in which maintenance operations are to be performed, but is included to convey a general idea of the procedures involved. For inspection purpose, the turbine engine is divided into two main sections: the cold and hot.

Compressor Section

Maintenance of the compressor, or cold section, is one of concern because damage to blades can cause engine failure. Much of the damage to the blades arises from foreign matter being drawn into the turbine engine air intakes. The atmosphere near the ground is filled with tiny particles of dirt, oil, soot, and other foreign matter. A large volume of air is introduced into the compressor, and centrifugal force throws the dirt particles outward so that they build up to form a coating on the casing, the vanes, and the compressor blades. Accumulation of dirt on the compressor blades reduces the aerodynamic efficiency of the blades with resultant deterioration in engine performance. The efficiency of the blades is impaired by dirt deposits in a manner similar to that of an aircraft wing under icing conditions. Unsatisfactory acceleration and high exhaust gas temperature can result from foreign deposits on compressor components.

An end result of foreign particles, if allowed to accumulate in sufficient quantity, would be inefficiency. The condition can be remedied by periodic inspection, cleaning, and repair of compressor components.

Inspection and Cleaning

Minor damage to axial-flow engine compressor blades may be repaired if the damage can be removed without exceeding the allowable limits established by the manufacturer. Typical compressor blade repair limits are shown in *Figure 10-57*. Well-rounded damage to leading and trailing edges that is evident on the opposite side of the blade is usually acceptable without re-work, provided the damage is in the outer half of the blade only, and the indentation does not exceed values specified in the engine manufacturer's service and overhaul instruction manuals. When working on the inner half of the blade, damage must be treated with extreme caution. Repaired compressor blades are inspected by either magnetic particle or fluorescent penetrant inspection methods to ensure that all traces of the damage have been removed. All repairs must be well blended so that surfaces are smooth. *[Figure 10-58]* No cracks of any extent are tolerated in any area.

Whenever possible, stoning and local re-work of the blade should be performed parallel to the length of the blade. Re-work must be accomplished by hand, using stones, files, or emery cloth. Do not use a power tool to buff the entire area of the blade. The surface finish in the repaired area must be comparable to that of a new blade. On centrifugal flow engines, it is difficult to inspect the compressor inducers without first removing the air-inlet screen. After removing the screen, clean the compressor inducer and inspect it with a strong light. Check each vane for cracks by slowly turning the compressor. Look for cracks in the leading edges. A crack is usually cause for component rejection. The compressor inducers are normally the parts that are damaged by the impingement of foreign material during engine operation.

Compressor inducers are repaired by stoning out and blending the nicks and dents in the critical band (1½ to 2½ inches from the outside edge), if the depth of such nicks or dents does not exceed that specified in the engine manufacturer's service or overhaul instruction manuals. Repair nicks by stoning out material beyond the depth of damage to remove the resulting cold-worked metal. A generous radius must be applied at the edges of the blend. After blending the nick, it should be smoothed over with a crocus cloth. Pitting nicks or corrosion found on the sides of the inducer vanes are similarly removed by blending.

Causes of Blade Damage

Loose objects often enter an engine either accidentally or through carelessness. Foreign object damage (FOD), such as pencils, tools, and flashlights, are often drawn into the engine and can cause damage to the fan blades. *[Figure 10-59]* Do not carry any objects in pockets when working around operational turbine engines.

A compressor rotor can be damaged beyond repair by tools that are left in the air intake, where they are drawn into the engine on subsequent starts. A simple solution to the problem is to check the tools against a tool checklist. Prior to starting a turbine engine, make a minute inspection of engine inlet ducts to assure that items, such as nuts, bolts, lock wire, or tools, were not left there after work had been performed.

Figure 10-60 shows some examples of blade damage to an axial-flow engine. The descriptions and possible causes of blade damage are given in *Figure 10-61*. Corrosion pitting is not considered serious on the compressor stator vanes of axial-flow engines if the pitting is within the allowed tolerance. Do not attempt to repair any vane by straightening, brazing, welding, or soldering. Crocus cloth, fine files, and stones are used to blend out damage by removing a minimum of material and leaving a surface finish comparable to that

Figure 10-57. *Typical compressor blade repair limits.*

Figure 10-58. *Examples of repairs to damaged blades.*

10-47

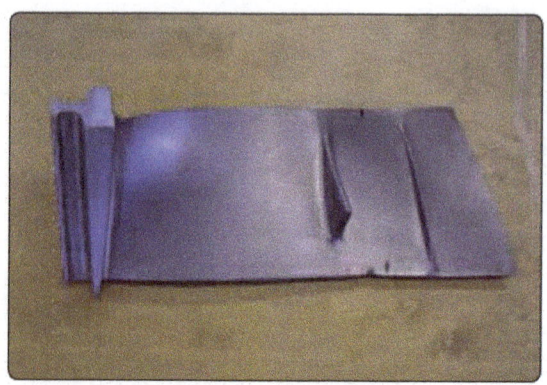

Figure 10-59. *Fan blade damage.*

of a new part. The purpose of this blending is to minimize stresses that concentrate at dents, scratches, or cracks.

The inspection and repair of air intake guide vanes, swirl vanes, and screens on centrifugal-flow engines necessitates the use of a strong light. Inspect screen assemblies for breaks, rips, or holes. Screens may be tin-dipped to tighten the wire mesh, provided the wires are not worn too thin. If the frame strip or lugs have separated from the screen frames, re-brazing may be necessary.

outer edges of the guide vanes, paying particular attention to the point of contact between the guides and swirl vanes for cracks and dents due to the impingement of foreign particles. Inspect the edges of the swirl vanes. Inspect the downstream edge of the guide vanes very closely, because cracks are generally more prevalent in this area. Cracks that branch or fork out so that a piece of metal could break free and fall into the compressor are cause for vane rejection.

Blending and Replacement

Because of the thin-sheet construction of hollow vanes, blending on the concave and convex surfaces, including the leading edge, is limited. Small, shallow dents are acceptable if the damage is of a rounded or gradual contour type and not a sharp or V-type, and if no cracking or tearing of vane material is evident in the damaged area.

Trailing edge damage may be blended, if one-third of the weld seam remains after repair. *[Figure 10-62]* Concave surfaces of rubber-filled vanes may have allowable cracks extending inward from the outer airfoil, provided there is no suggestion of pieces breaking away. Using a light and mirror, inspect each guide vane trailing edge and vane body for cracks or damage caused by foreign objects.

Figure 10-60. *Compressor blade damage.*

Inspect the guide and swirl vanes for looseness. Inspect the

Term	Appearance	Usual Causes
• Blend	• Smooth repair of ragged edge or surface into the contour of surrounding area.	
• Bow	• Bent blade.	• Foreign objects.
• Burning	• Damage to surfaces evidenced by discoloration or, in severe cases, by flow of material.	• Excessive heat.
• Burr	• A ragged or turned out edge.	• Grinding or cutting operation.
• Corrosion (pits)	• Breakdown of the surface; pitted appearance.	• Corrosive agents—moisture, etc.
• Cracks	• A partial fracture (separation).	• Excessive stress due to shock, overloading, or faulty processing; defective materials; overheating.
• Dent	• Small, smoothly rounded hollow.	• Striking of a part with a dull object.
• Gall	• A transfer of metal from one surface to another.	• Severe rubbing.
• Gouging	• Displacement of material from a surface; a cutting or tearing effect.	• Presence of a comparatively large foreign body between moving parts.
• Growth	• Eleongation of blade.	• Continued and/or excessive heat and centrifugal force.
• Pit	• (See corrosion).	
• Profile	• Contour of a blade or surface.	
• Score	• Deep scratches.	• Presence of chips between surfaces.
• Scratch	• Narrow shallow marks.	• Sand or fine foreign particles; careless handling.

Figure 10-61. *Blade maintenance terms.*

Any inspection and repair of turbine compressor section components require that the technician always use the specific manufacturer's current information for evaluation and limits of repairs.

Combustion Section Inspection

One of the controlling factors in the service life of the turbine engine is the inspection and cleaning of the hot section. Emphasis must be placed on the importance of careful inspection and repair of this section.

The following are general procedures for performing a hot section (turbine and combustion section) inspection. It is not intended to imply that these procedures are to be followed when performing repairs or inspections on turbine engines. However, the various practices are typical of those used on many turbine engines. Where a clearance or tolerance is shown, it is for illustrative purposes only. Always follow the instructions contained in the applicable manufacturer's maintenance and overhaul manuals.

The entire external combustion case should be inspected for evidence of hotspots, exhaust leaks, and distortions before the case is opened. After the combustion case has been opened, the combustion chambers can be inspected for localized overheating, cracks, or excessive wear. *[Figure 10-63]* Inspect the first stage turbine blades and nozzle guide vanes for cracks, warping, or FOD. Also inspect the combustion chamber outlet ducts and turbine nozzle for cracks and for evidence of FOD.

One of the most frequent discrepancies that are detected while inspecting the hot section of a turbine engine is cracking. These cracks may occur in many forms, and the only way to determine that they are within acceptable limits or if they are allowed at all, is to refer to the applicable engine manufacturer's service and overhaul manuals.

Cleaning the hot section is not usually necessary for a repair in the field, but in areas of high salt water or other chemicals a turbine rinse should be accomplished.

Engine parts can be degreased by using the emulsion-type cleaners or chlorinated solvents. The emulsion-type cleaners are safe for all metals, since they are neutral and noncorrosive. Cleaning parts by the chlorinated solvent method leaves the parts absolutely dry. If they are not to be subjected to further cleaning operations, they should be sprayed with a corrosion-preventive solution to protect them against rust or corrosion.

Figure 10-62. *Guide vane trailing edge damage.*

The hot section, which generally includes the combustion section and turbine sections, normally require inspections at regular intervals. The extent of disassembly of the engine to accomplish this inspection varies from different engine types. Most engines require that the combustion case be open for the inspection of the hot section. However, in performing this disassembly, numerous associated parts are readily accessible for inspection. The importance of properly supporting the engine and the parts being removed cannot be overstressed.

Figure 10-63. *Combustion case inspection.*

The alignment of components being removed and installed is also of the utmost importance. After all the inspections and repairs are made, the manufacturer's detailed assembly instructions should be followed. These instructions are important in efficient engine maintenance, and the ultimate life and performance of the engine. Extreme care must be taken during assembly to prevent dirt, dust, cotter pins, lock wire, nuts, washers, or other foreign material from entering the engine.

Marking Materials for Combustion Section Parts

Certain materials may be used for temporary marking during assembly and disassembly. Always refer to manufacturer's information for marking parts. Layout dye (lightly applied) or chalk may be used to mark parts that are directly exposed to the engine's gas path, such as turbine blades and disks, turbine vanes, and combustion chamber liners. A wax marking pencil may be used for parts that are not directly exposed to the gas path. Do not use a wax marking pencil on a liner surface or a turbine rotor. The use of carbon alloy or metallic pencils is not recommended because of the possibility of causing intergranular corrosion attack, that could result in a reduction in material strength and cracking.

Inspection and Repair of Combustion Chambers

Inspect the combustion chambers and covers for cracks by using visible dye or fluorescent penetrant inspection method. Any cracks, nicks, or dents are usually cause for rejecting the component. Inspect the covers, noting particularly the area around the fuel drain bosses for any pits or corrosion. When repairing the combustion chamber liner, the procedures given in the appropriate engine manufacturer's overhaul instruction manual should be followed. If there is doubt that the liner is serviceable, it should be replaced.

Combustion chambers should be replaced or repaired if two cracks are progressing from a free edge so that their meeting is imminent and could allow a piece of metal that could cause turbine damage to break loose. Separate cracks in the baffle are acceptable. Cracks in the cone are rare but, at any location on this component, is cause for rejection of the liner. Cracks in the swirl vanes are cause for rejection of the liner. Loose swirl vanes may be repaired by silver brazing. Cracks in the front liner emanating from the air holes are acceptable, provided they do not exceed allowable limits. If such cracks fork or link with others, the liner must be repaired. If two cracks originating from the same air hole are diametrically opposite, the liner is acceptable. Radial cracks extending from the interconnector and spark igniter boss are acceptable, if they do not exceed allowable limits and if such cracks do not fork or link with others. Circumferential cracks around the boss pads should be repaired prior to re-use of the liner. Baffle cracks connecting more than two holes should be repaired.

After long periods of engine operation, the external surfaces of the combustion chamber liner location pads often show signs of fretting. This is acceptable, provided no resultant cracks or perforation of the metal is apparent. Any cover or chamber inadvertently dropped on a hard surface or mishandled should be thoroughly inspected for minute cracks that may elongate over a period of time and then open, creating a hazard.

Parts may be found where localized areas have been heated to an extent to buckle small portions of the chamber. Such parts are considered acceptable if the burning of the part has not progressed into an adjacent welded area, or to such an extent as to weaken the structure of the liner weldment. Buckling of the combustion chamber liner can be corrected by straightening the liner. Moderate buckling and associated cracks are acceptable in the row of cooling holes. More severe buckling that produces a pronounced shortening or tilting of the liner is cause for rejection. Upon completion of the repairs by welding, the liner should be restored as closely as possible to its original shape.

Fuel Nozzle and Support Assemblies

Clean all carbon deposits from the nozzles by washing with a cleaning fluid approved by the engine manufacturer, and remove the softened deposits with a soft bristle brush. It is desirable to have filtered air passing through the nozzle during the cleaning operation to carry away deposits as they are loosened. Make sure all parts are clean. Dry the assemblies with clean, filtered air. Because the spray characteristics of the nozzle may become impaired, no attempt should be made to clean the nozzles by scraping with a hard implement or by rubbing with a wire brush. Inspect each component part of the fuel nozzle assembly for nicks and burrs. Many fuel nozzles can be checked by flowing fluid through the nozzle under pressure and closely checking the flow pattern coming for the nozzle.

Turbine Disk Inspection

The inspection for cracks is very important because cracks are not normally allowed. Crack detection, when dealing with the turbine disk and blades, is mostly visual, although structural inspection techniques can be used, such as penetrant methods and others to aid in the inspection. Cracks on the disk necessitate the rejection of the disk and replacement of the turbine rotor. Slight pitting caused by the impingement of foreign matter may be blended by stoning and polishing.

Turbine Blade Inspection

Turbine blades are usually inspected and cleaned in the same manner as compressor blades. However, because of the extreme heat under which the turbine blades operate, they are more susceptible to damage. Using a strong light and a magnifying glass, inspect the turbine blades for stress rupture cracks and deformation of the leading edge. *[Figures 10-64* and *10-65]*

Stress rupture cracks usually appear as minute hairline cracks on or across the leading or trailing edge at a right angle to the edge length. Visible cracks may range in length from one-sixteenth inch upward. Deformation, caused by over-temperature, may appear as waviness and/or areas of varying airfoil thickness along the leading edge. The leading edge must be straight and of uniform thickness along its entire length, except for areas repaired by blending. Do not confuse stress rupture cracks or deformation of the leading edge with foreign material impingement damage or with blending repairs to the blade. When any stress rupture cracks or deformation of the leading edges of the first-stage turbine blades are found, an over-temperature condition must be suspected. Check the individual blades for stretch and the turbine disk for hardness and stretch. Blades removed for a detailed inspection or for a check of turbine disk stretch must be re-installed in the same slots from which they were removed. Number the blades prior to removal.

The turbine blade outer shroud should be inspected for air seal wear. If shroud wear is found, measure the thickness of the shroud at the worn area. Use a micrometer or another suitable and accurate measuring device that ensures a good reading in the bottom of the comparatively narrow wear groove. If the remaining radial thickness of the shroud is less than that specified, the stretched blade must be replaced. Typical blade inspection requirements are indicated in *Figure 10-66*. Blade tip curling within a one-half inch square area on the leading edge of the blade tip is usually acceptable if the curling is not

Figure 10-64. *Stress rupture cracks.*

Figure 10-65. *Turbine blade waviness.*

sharp. Curling is acceptable on the trailing edge if it does not extend beyond the allowable area. Any sharp bends that may result in cracking or a piece breaking out of the turbine blade is cause for rejection, even though the curl may be within the allowable limits. Each turbine blade should be inspected for cracks.

Turbine Blade Replacement Procedure

Turbine blades are generally replaceable, subject to moment-weight limitations. These limitations are contained in the engine manufacturer's applicable technical instructions. If visual inspection of the turbine assembly discloses several broken, cracked, or eroded blades, replacing the entire turbine assembly may be more economical than replacing the damaged blades. *[Figure 10-67]*

In the initial buildup of the turbine, a complete set of 54 blades made in coded pairs (two blades having the same code letters) is laid out on a bench in the order of diminishing moment-weight. The code letters, indicating the moment-weight balance in ounces, are marked on the rear face of the fir-tree section of the blade (viewing the blade as installed at final assembly of the engine). The pair of blades having the heaviest moment-weight is numbered 1 and 28; the next heaviest pair of blades is numbered 2 and 29; the third heaviest pair is numbered 3 and 30. This is continued until all the blades have been numbered. Mark a number 1 on the face of the hub on the turbine disk. The number 1 blade is then installed adjacent to the number 1 on the disk. *[Figure 10-68]* The remaining blades are then installed consecutively in a clockwise direction, viewed from the rear face of the turbine disk. If there are several pairs of blades having the same code letters, they are installed consecutively before going to the next code letters. If a blade requires replacement, the diametrically opposite blade must also be replaced. Computer programs generally determine the location for turbine blades for turbine wheels on modern engines.

Turbine Nozzle Inlet Guide Vane Inspection

After removing the required components, the first stage turbine blades and turbine nozzle vanes are accessible for inspection. The blade limits specified in the engine manufacturer's overhaul and service instruction manual

Figure 10-66. *Typical turbine blade inspection.*

Figure 10-67. *Typical turbine rotor blade moment-weight distribution.*

Figure 10-68. *Turbine blades.*

should be adhered to. *Figure 10-69* shows where cracks usually occur on a turbine nozzle assembly. Slight nicks and dents are permissible if the depth of damage is within limits. Inspect the nozzle vanes for nicks or cracks. Small nicks are not cause for vane rejection, provided such nicks blend out smoothly.

Inspect the nozzle vane supports for defects caused by the impingement of foreign particles. Use a stone to blend any doubtful nicks to a smooth radius. Like turbine blades, it is

Figure 10-69. *Turbine nozzle assembly defects.*

possible to replace a maximum number of turbine nozzle vanes in some engines. If more than the maximum vanes are damaged, a new turbine nozzle vane assembly must be installed. With the tailpipe (exhaust nozzle) removed, the rear turbine stage can be inspected for any cracks or evidence of blade stretch. Additional nozzle stages can also be inspected with a strong light by looking through the rear-stage turbine.

Clearances

Checking the clearances is one of the procedures in the maintenance of the turbine section of a turbine engine. The manufacturer's service and overhaul manual gives the procedures and tolerances for checking the turbine. Turbine clearances being measured at various locations are shown in *Figures 10-70* and *10-71*. To obtain accurate readings, special tools provided by each manufacturer must be used as described in the service instructions for specific engines.

Figure 10-71. *Measuring turbine wheel to exhaust cone clearance.*

by the different manufacturers. Other differences include the manner of disassembly, the tooling necessary, and the repair methods and limits.

Engine Ratings

The flat rating of a turbine engine is the thrust performance that is guaranteed by the manufacturer for a new engine under specific operating conditions, such as takeoff, maximum continuous climb, and cruise power settings. The turbine inlet temperature is proportional to the energy available to turn the turbine. This means that the hotter the gases are that are entering the turbine section of the engine, the more power is available to turn the turbine wheel. The exhaust temperature is proportional to the turbine inlet temperature. Regardless of how or where the exhaust temperature is taken on the engine for the flight deck reading, this temperature is proportional to the temperature of the exhaust gases entering the first stage of inlet guide vanes. A higher EGT corresponds to a larger amount of energy to the turbine so it can turn the compressor faster. This works fine until the temperature reaches a point when the turbine inlet guide vanes start to be damaged. EGT must be held constant, or lowered as the result of a prolonged hot section life and, at the same time, provide the thrust to meet the certification requirements.

Figure 10-70. *Measuring the turbine blades to shroud (tip) clearances.*

Exhaust Section

The exhaust section of the turbine engine is susceptible to heat cracking. This section must be thoroughly inspected along with the inspection the combustion section and turbine section of the engine. Inspect the exhaust cone and exhaust nozzle for cracks, warping, buckling, or hotspots. Hotspots on the tail cone are a good indication of a malfunctioning fuel nozzle or combustion chamber.

The inspection and repair procedures for the hot section of any one gas turbine engine share similarities to those of other gas turbine engines. One usual difference is the nomenclature applied to the various parts of the hot section

Before high bypass turbofan engines, some older types of engines used water injection to increase thrust for takeoff (wet). This is the maximum allowable thrust for takeoff. The rating is obtained by actuating the water-injection system and setting the computed wet thrust with the throttle, in terms of a predetermined turbine discharge pressure or engine pressure ratio for the prevailing ambient conditions. The rating is restricted to takeoff, is time-limited, and has an altitude limitation. Water injection is not used very much on turbine engines any more.

Turbine Engine Instruments

Engine Pressure Ratio Indicator

Engine pressure ratio (EPR) is an indication of the thrust being developed by a turbofan engine and is used to set power for takeoff on many types of aircraft. It is instrumented by total pressure pickups in the engine inlet (Pt2) and in the turbine exhaust (Pt7). The reading is displayed in the flight deck by the EPR gauge, which is used in making engine power settings. *[Figure 10-72]*

Figure 10-72. *Engine pressure ratio indications.*

Torquemeter (Turboprop Engines)

Only 10 to 15 percent of the thrust produced by a turboprop engine is from propulsive force derived from the jet thrust exiting the exhaust. Engine pressure ratio is not used as an indicator of the power produced by a turboprop engine. Turboprops are usually fitted with a torquemeter that measures torque applied to a shaft turned by the gas generator and power turbines of the turbine engine. The torquemeter can be operated by engine oil pressure metered through a valve that is controlled by a helical ring gear that moves in response to the applied torque. *[Figure 10-73]* This gear moves against a piston that controls the opening of a valve, which controls the oil pressure flow. This action makes the oil pressure proportional to torque being applied at the propeller shaft. Generally, transducer is used to transfer the oil pressure into an electrical signal to be read by the flight deck instrument.

The read out in the flight deck is normally in lb/ft of torque, or percent horsepower. The torquemeter is very important as it is used to set power settings. This instrument must be calibrated at intervals to assure its accuracy.

Tachometer

Gas turbine engine speeds are measured by the engines rpm, which are also the compressor/turbine combination rpm of each rotating spool. Most turbofan engines have two or more spools, compressor, and turbine sections that turn independently at different speeds. Tachometers are usually calibrated in percent rpm so that various types of engines can be operated on the same basis of comparison. *[Figure 10-73]* Also, turbine speeds are generally very high and the large numbers of rpm would make it very confusing. Turbofan engines with two spools or separate shafts, high pressure and low pressure spools, are generally referred to as N1 and N2, with each having their own indicator. The main purpose of the tachometer is to be able to monitor rpm under normal conditions, during an engine start, and to indicate an overspeed condition, if one occurs.

Exhaust Gas Temperature Indicator (EGT)

Exhaust gas temperature (EGT), turbine inlet temperature, (TIT), turbine gas temperature (TGT), interstage turbine temperature (ITT), and turbine outlet temperature (TOT) are all relative temperatures used to monitor the temperature of the exhaust gases entering the first stage turbine inlet guide vanes. Even though these temperatures are taken at different locations on the engine (each engine having one location), they are all relative to the temperature of the gases entering the first stage turbine inlet guide vanes.

Temperature is an engine operating limit and is used to monitor the mechanical integrity of the turbines, as well as to check engine operating conditions. Actually, the temperature of the gases entering the first stage turbine inlet guide vanes is the important consideration, since it is the most critical of all the engine variables. However, it is impractical to measure turbine inlet temperature in most engines, especially large engines. Consequently, temperature thermocouples are inserted at the turbine discharge, where the temperature provides a relative indication of that at the inlet. Although the temperature at this point is much lower than at the inlet, it provides surveillance over the engine's internal operating conditions. Several thermocouples are usually used, that are spaced at intervals around the perimeter of the engine exhaust duct near the turbine exit. The EGT indicator in the flight deck shows the average temperature measured by the individual thermocouples. *[Figure 10-73]*

Figure 10-73. *Typical turbine engine instruments.*

Fuel-Flow Indicator

Fuel-flow instruments indicate the fuel flow in pounds per hour (lb/hr) from the engine fuel control. Fuel flow in turbine aircraft is measured in lb/hr instead of gallons, because the fuel weight is a major factor in the aerodynamics of large turbine aircraft. Fuel flow is of interest in monitoring fuel consumption and checking engine performance. *[Figure 10-73]*

Engine Oil Pressure Indicator

To guard against engine failure resulting from inadequate lubrication and cooling of the various engine parts, the oil supply to critical areas must be monitored. The oil pressure indicator usually shows the engine oil pump discharge pressure.

Engine Oil Temperature Indicator

The ability of the engine oil to lubricate and cool depends on the temperature of the oil, as well as the amount of oil supplied to the critical areas. An oil inlet temperature indicator frequently is provided to show the temperature of the oil as it enters the oil pressure pump. Oil inlet temperature is also an indication of proper operation of the engine oil cooler.

Turbine Engine Operation

The engine operating procedures presented here apply generally to turbofan, turboprop, turboshaft, and auxiliary power units (APU). The procedures, pressures, temperatures, and rpm that follow are intended primarily to serve as a guide. It should be understood that they do not have general application. The manufacturer's operating instructions should be consulted before attempting to start and operate any turbine engine.

A turbofan engine has only one power control lever. Adjusting the power lever, or throttle lever, sets up a thrust condition for which the fuel control meters fuel to the engine. Engines equipped with thrust reversers go into reverse thrust at throttle positions below idle. A separate fuel shutoff lever is usually provided on engines equipped with thrust reversers.

Prior to start, particular attention should be paid to the engine air inlet, the visual condition and free movement of the compressor and turbine assembly, and the parking ramp area fore and aft of the aircraft. The engine is started by using an external air power source, APU, or an already operating engine. Starter types and the engine starting cycle have been discussed previously. On multi-engine aircraft, the engines are usually started by an onboard APU that supplies the air pressure for a pneumatic starter on each engine. Air bled from the APU is used as a source of power for starting the engines.

During the start, it is necessary to monitor the tachometer, the oil pressure, and the exhaust gas temperature. The normal starting sequence is:

1. Rotate the compressor with the starter;
2. Turn the ignition on; and
3. Open the engine fuel valve, either by moving the throttle to idle or by moving a fuel shutoff lever or turning a switch.

Adherence to the procedure prescribed for a particular engine is necessary as a safety measure and to avoid a hot or hung start. A successful start is noted first by a rise in exhaust gas temperature. If the engine does not light up, meaning that fuel starts to burn inside of the engine within a prescribed period of time, or if the exhaust gas starting temperature limit is exceeded, a hot start, the starting procedure should be aborted. Hot starts are not common, but when they do occur, they can usually be stopped in time to avoid excessive temperature by observing the exhaust gas temperature constantly during the start. When necessary, the engine is cleared of trapped fuel or gases by continuing to rotate the compressor with the starter, but with the ignition and fuel turned off. If the engine did not light off during start after the allotted time, about 10 seconds although this time varies from engine to engine, the fuel must be shut off as the engine is being filled with unburned fuel. A hung start is when the engine lights off, but the engine will not accelerate to idle rpm.

Ground Operation Engine Fire

Move the fuel shutoff lever to the off position if an engine fire occurs, or if the fire warning light is illuminated during the starting cycle. Continue cranking or motoring the engine until the fire has been expelled from the engine. If the fire persists, CO_2 can be discharged into the inlet duct while it is being cranked. Do not discharge CO_2 directly into the engine exhaust, because it may damage the engine. If the fire cannot be extinguished, secure all switches and leave the aircraft. If the fire is on the ground under the engine overboard drain, discharge the CO_2 on the ground rather than on the engine. This also is true if the fire is at the tailpipe and the fuel is dripping to the ground and burning.

Engine Checks

Checking turbofan engines for proper operation consists primarily of simply reading the engine instruments and then comparing the observed values with those known to be correct for any given engine operating condition. After the engine has started, idle rpm has been attained, and the instrument readings have stabilized, the engine should be checked for satisfactory operation at idling speed. The oil pressure indicator, tachometer, and the exhaust gas temperature readings should be compared with the allowable ranges.

Checking Takeoff Thrust

Takeoff thrust is checked by adjusting the throttle to obtain a single, predicted reading on the engine pressure ratio indicator in the aircraft. The value for engine pressure ratio, which represents takeoff thrust for the prevailing ambient atmospheric conditions, is calculated from a takeoff thrust setting curve or, on newer aircraft, is a function of the onboard computer. This curve has been computed for static conditions. *[Figure 10-74]* Therefore, for all precise thrust checking, the aircraft should be stationary, and stable engine operation should be established. If it is needed for calculating thrust during an engine trim check, turbine discharge pressure (P_{t7}) is also shown on these curves. Appropriate manuals should be consulted for the charts for a specific make and model engine. Engine trimming procedure is also covered in Chapter 3, Engine Fuel and Fuel Metering Systems. The engine pressure ratio computed from the thrust setting curve represents thrust or a lower thrust call part power thrust used for testing. The aircraft throttle is advanced to obtain this predicted reading on the engine pressure ratio indicator, or the part power stop is engaged in the aircraft. If an engine develops the predicted thrust and if all the other engine instruments are reading within their proper ranges, engine operation is considered satisfactory. Full authority digital engine controls (FADEC) engine controls (computer controls) also have means of checking the engine with the results displayed on the flight deck.

Ambient Conditions

The sensitivity of gas turbine engines to compressor inlet air temperature and pressure necessitates that considerable care be taken to obtain correct values for the prevailing ambient air conditions when computing takeoff thrust. Some things to remember are:

1. The engine senses the air temperature and pressure at the compressor inlet. This is the actual air temperature just above the runway surface. When the aircraft is stationary, the pressure at the compressor inlet is the static field or true barometric pressure, and not the barometric pressure corrected to sea level that is normally reported by airport control towers as the altimeter setting. On FADEC engines, the computer reads this information and sends it to the engine controls.

2. Temperature sensed is the total air temperature (TAT) that is used by several onboard computers. The engine controls set the engine computers according to the TAT.

Figure 10-74. *Typical takeoff thrust setting curve for static conditions.*

3. Relative humidity, which affects reciprocating engine power appreciably, has a negligible effect on turbine engine thrust, fuel flow, and rpm. Therefore, relative humidity is not usually considered when computing thrust for takeoff or determining fuel flow and rpm for routine operation.

Engine Shutdown

On turbine engines that have a thrust reverser, retarding the aircraft throttle to idle or power lever to OFF cuts the fuel supply to the engine and shuts down the engine. On engines equipped with thrust reversers, this is accomplished by means of a separate fuel shutoff lever or switch. When an engine has been operated at high power levels for extended periods of time, a cool down time should be allowed before shut down. It is recommended the engine be operated at below a low power setting, preferably at idle for a period of 5 minutes to prevent possible seizure of the rotors. This applies, in particular, to prolonged operation at high rpm on the ground, such as during engine trimming. The turbine case and the turbine wheels operate at approximately the same temperature when the engine is running. However, the turbine wheels are relatively massive, compared with the case, and are not cooled so readily. The turbine case is exposed to cooling air from both inside and outside the engine. Consequently, the case and the wheels lose their residual heat at different rates after the engine has been shut down. The case, cooling faster, tends to shrink upon the wheels, that are still rotating. Under extreme conditions, the turbine blades may squeal or seize; thus a cooling period is required if the engine has been operating at prolonged high speed. Should the turbine wheels seize, no harm normally results, provided no attempt is made to turn the engine over until it has cooled sufficiently to free the wheels. In spite of this, every effort should be made to avoid seizure.

To ensure that fuel remains in the lines and that the engine-driven fuel pumps are not starved for fuel that lubricates the pumps, the aircraft fuel boost pump must be turned off after, not before, the throttle or the fuel shutoff lever is placed in the OFF position.

Generally, an engine should not be shut down by the fuel shutoff lever until after the aircraft throttle has been retarded to idle. Because the fuel shutoff valve is located on the fuel control discharge, a shutdown from high thrust settings results in high fuel pressures within the control that can harm the fuel system parts.

When an accurate reading of the oil level in the oil tank is needed following an engine shutdown, the engine should be operated and shut down with the oil check taking place within not more than 30 minutes after shutdown. Check the engine manuals for the specific procedure.

Troubleshooting Turbine Engines

Included in this section are typical guidelines for locating engine malfunctions on most turbine engines. Since it would be impractical to list all the malfunctions that could occur, only the most common malfunctions are covered. A thorough knowledge of the engine systems, applied with logical reasoning, solves most problems that may occur.

Figure 10-75 enumerates some malfunctions that may be encountered. Possible causes and suggested actions are given in the adjacent columns. The malfunctions presented herein are solely for the purpose of illustration and should not be construed to have general application. For exact information about a specific engine model, consult the applicable manufacturer's instructions.

Turboprop Operation

Turboprop engine operation is quite similar to that of a turbojet engine, except for the added feature of a propeller. The starting procedure and the various operational features are very much alike. The turboprop chiefly requires attention to engine operating limits, the throttle or power lever setting, and the torquemeter pressure gauge. Although torquemeters indicate only the power being supplied to the propeller and not the equivalent shaft horsepower, torquemeter pressure is approximately proportional to the total power output and, thus, is used as a measure of engine performance. The torquemeter pressure gauge reading during the takeoff engine check is an important value. It is usually necessary to compute the takeoff power in the same manner as is done for a turbojet engine. This computation is to determine the maximum allowable exhaust gas temperature and the torquemeter pressure that a normally functioning engine should produce for the outside, or ambient, air temperature and barometric pressure prevailing at the time.

Troubleshooting Procedures for Turboprop Engines

All test run-ups, inspections, and troubleshooting should be performed in accordance with the applicable engine manufacturer's instructions. In *Figure 10-76*, the troubleshooting procedure for the turboprop reduction gear, torquemeter, and power section are combined because of their inter-relationships. The table includes the principal troubles, together with their probable causes and remedies.

Indicated Malfunction	Probable Causes	Suggested Action
Engine has low rpm, exhaust gas temperature, and fuel flow when set to expected engine pressure ratio.	• Engine pressure ratio indication has high reading error.	• Check inlet pressure line from probe to transmitter for leaks. • Check engine pressure ratio transmitter and indicator for accuracy.

Engine has high rpm, exhaust gas temperature, and fuel flow when set to expect engine pressure ration.	• Engine pressure ratio indication has low reading error due to:
	  - Misaligned or cracked turbine discharge probe.
	  - Leak in turbine discharge pressure line from probe to transmitter.
	  - Inaccurate engine pressure ratio transmitter or indicator.
	  - Carbon particles collected in turbine discharge pressure line or restrictor orifices.
		• Check probe condition.
		• Pressure-test turbine discharge pressure line for leaks.
		• Check engine pressure ratio transmitter and indicator for accuracy.

Engine has high exhaust gas temperature, low rpm, and high fuel flow at all engine pressure ratio settings.	• Possible turbine damage and/or loss of turbine efficiency.	• Confirm indication of turbine damage by:
		  - Checking engine coast-down for abnormal noise and reduced time.
		  - Visually inspect turbine area with strong light.

NOTE: Engines with damage in turbine section may have tendency to hang up during starting.	• If only exhaust gas temperature is high, other parameters normal, the problem may be thermocouple leads or instrument.	• Re-calibrate exhaust gas temperature instrumentation.
Engine vibrates throughout rpm range, but indicated amplitude reduces as rpm is reduced.	• Turbine damage.	• Check turbine as outlined in preceding item.
Engine vibrates at high rpm and fuel flow when compared to constant engine pressure ratio.	• Damage in compressor section.	• Check compressor section for damage.
Engine vibrates throughout rpm range, but is more pronounced in cruise or idle rpm range.	• Engine-mounted accessory such as constant-speed drive, generator, hydraulic pump, etc.	• Check each component in turn.
No change in power setting parameters, but oil temperature high.	• Engine main bearings.	• Check scavenge oil filters and magnetic plugs.
Engine has higher than normal exhaust gas temperature during takeoff, climb, and cruise. Rpm and fuel flow higher than normal.	• Engine bleed-air valve malfunction. • Turbine discharge pressure probe or line to transmitter leaking.	• Check operation of bleed valve. • Check condition of probe and pressure line to transmitter.
Engine has high exhaust gas temperature at target engine pressure ratio for takeoff.	• Engine out of trim.	• Check engine with jetcal. Re-trim as desired.

Figure 10-75. *Troubleshooting turbojet engines.*

10-61

Indicated Malfunction	Probable Causes	Suggested Action
Engine rumbles during starting and at low power cruise conditions.	• Pressurizing and drain valve malfunction. • Cracked air duct. • Fuel control malfunction.	• Replace pressurizing and drain valves. • Repair or replace duct. • Replace fuel control.
Engine rpm hangs up during starting.	• Subzero ambient temperatures. • Compressor section damage. • Turbine section damage.	• If hang-up is due to low ambient temperature, engine usually can be started by turning on fuel booster pump or by positioning start lever to run earlier in the starting cycle. • Check compressor for damage. • Inspect turbine for damage.
High oil temperature.	• Scavenge pump failure. • Fuel heater malfunction.	• Check lubricating system and scavenge pumps. • Replace fuel heater.
High oil consumption.	• Scavenge pump failure. • High sump pressure. • Gearbox seal leakage.	• Check scavenge pumps. • Check sump pressure as outlined in manufacturer's maintenance manual. • Check gearbox seal by pressurizing overboard vent.
Overboard oil loss.	• Can be caused by high airflow through the tank, foaming oil, or unusual amounts of oil returned to the tank through the vent system.	• Check oil for foaming. • Vacuum-check sumps. • Check scavenge pumps.

Figure 10-75. *Troubleshooting turbojet engines (continued).*

Turbine Engine Calibration and Testing

Some of the most important factors affecting turbine engine life are EGT, engine cycles (a cycle is generally a takeoff and landing) and engine speed. Excess EGT of a few degrees reduces turbine component life. Low EGT materially reduces turbine engine efficiency and thrust. So, to make the engine highly efficient, the exhaust temperatures need to be as high as possible, while maintaining an EGT operating temperature that does not damage the turbine section of the engine. If the engine is operated at excess exhaust temperatures, engine deterioration occurs. Since the EGT temperature is set by the EGT temperature gauge, it is imperative that it is accurate. Excessive engine speed can cause premature engine wear and, if extreme, can cause engine failure.

One older type of calibration test unit used to analyze the turbine engine is the jetcal analyzer. *[Figure 10-77]* A jetcal analyzer is a portable instrument made of aluminum, stainless steel, and plastic. The major components of the analyzer are the thermocouple, rpm, EGT indicator, resistance, and insulation check circuits, as well as the potentiometer, temperature regulators, meters, switches, and all the necessary cables, probes, and adapters for performing all tests.

Turbine Engine Analyzer Uses

Many different types of analyzers are used each with its own function, including onboard systems that use computers to test aircraft systems. Depending upon the specific analyzer used, procedures vary somewhat, but the basic test are outlined here. Always refer to the specific instructions associated with the analyzer being used.

Most analyzers may be used to:

1. Functionally check the aircraft EGT system for error, without running the engine or disconnecting the wiring.
2. Check individual thermocouples before placement in a parallel harness.
3. Check each engine thermocouple in a parallel harness for continuity.
4. Check the thermocouples and parallel harness for accuracy.
5. Check the resistance of the EGT circuit.
6. Check the insulation of the EGT circuit for shorts to ground, or for shorts between leads.
7. Check EGT indicators, either in or out of the aircraft, for error.

Trouble	Probable causes	Remedy
Power unit fails to turn over during attempted start.	• No air to starter. • Propeller brake locked.	• Check started air valve solenoid and air supply. • Unlock brake by turning propeller by hand in direction of normal rotation.
Power unit fails to start.	• Starter speed low because of inadequate air supply to starter. • If fuel is not observed leaving the exhaust pipe during start, fuel selector valve may be inoperative because of low power supply or may be locked in "OFF." • Fuel pump inoperative. • Aircraft fuel filter dirty. • Fuel control cutoff valve closed.	• Check starter air valve solenoid and air supply. • Check power supply or electrically operated valves. Replace valves if defective. • Check pump for sheared drives or internal damage. Check for air leaks at outlet. • Clean filter and replace filtering elements if necessary. • Check electrical circuit to ensure that actuator is being energized. Replace actuator or control.
Engine fires, but will not accelerate to correct speed.	• Insufficient fuel supply to control unit. • Fuel control main metering valve sticking. • Fuel control bypass valve sticking open. • Drain valve stuck open. Starting fuel enrichment pressure switch setting too high.	• Check fuel system to ensure all valves are open and pumps are operative. • Flush system. Replace control. • Flush system. Replace control. • Replace drain valve. Replace pressure switch.
Acceleration temperature too high during starting.	• Fuel control bypass valve sticking closed. • Fuel control acceleration cam incorrectly adjusted. • Defective fuel nozzle. • Fuel control thermostat failure.	• Flush system. Replace control. • Replace control. • Replace nozzle with a known satisfactory unit. • Replace control.
Acceleration temperature during starting too low.	• Acceleration cam of fuel control incorrectly adjusted.	• Replace control.
Engine speed cycles after start.	• Unstable fuel control governor operation.	• Continue engine operation to allow control to condition itself.
Power unit oil pressure drops off severely.	• Oil supply low. • Oil pressure transmitter or indicator giving false indication.	• Check oil supply and refill as necessary. • Check transmitter or indicator and repair or replace if necessary.
Oil leakage at accessory drive seals.	• Seal failure.	• Replace seal or seals.
Engine unable to reach maximum controlled speed of 100 percent.	• Faulty propeller governor. • Faulty fuel control or air sensing tip.	• Replace propeller control assembly. • Replace faulty control. If dirty, use air pressure in reverse direction of normal flow through internal engine passage and sensing tip.
Vibration indication high.	• Vibration pickup or vibration meter malfunction.	• Calibrate vibration meter. • Start engine and increase power gradually. • Observe vibration indicator. If indications prove pickup to be at fault, replace it. If high vibration remains as originally observed, remove power unit for overhaul.

Figure 10-76. *Troubleshooting turboprop engines.*

Figure 10-77. *Jetcal analyzer instrument compartment.*

8. Determine engine rpm accuracy during engine testing. Added to this is the checking and troubleshooting of the aircraft tachometer system.

9. Establish the proper relationship between the EGT and engine rpm during engine run-up.

Analyzer Safety Precautions

Observe the following safety precautions while operating the engine analyzer or other types of test equipment:

1. Never use a voltammeter to check the potentiometer for continuity. If a voltammeter is used, damage to the galvanometer and standard battery cell results.

2. Check the thermocouple harness before engine run-up. This must be done because the circuit must be correct before the thermocouples can be used for true EGT pickup.

3. For safety, ground the jetcal analyzer when using an AC power supply. Any electrical equipment operated on AC power and utilizing wire-wound coils, such as the probes with the jetcal analyzer, has an induced voltage on the case that can be discharged if the equipment is not grounded. This condition is not apparent during dry weather, but on damp days the operator can be shocked slightly. Therefore, for the operator's protection, the jetcal analyzer should be grounded using the pigtail lead in the power inlet cable.

4. Use heater probes designed for use on the engine thermocouples to be tested. Temperature gradients are very critical in the design of heater probes. Each type of aircraft thermocouple has its own specially designed probe. Never attempt to modify heater probes to test other types of thermocouples.

5. Do not leave heater probe assemblies in the exhaust nozzle during engine run-up.

6. Never allow the heater probes to go over 900 °C (1,652 °F). Exceeding these temperatures results in damage to the jetcal analyzer and heater probe assemblies.

Continuity Check of Aircraft EGT Circuit

To eliminate any error caused by one or more inoperative aircraft thermocouples, a continuity check is performed. The check is made by heating one heater probe to between 500 and 700 °C and placing the hot probe over each of the aircraft thermocouples, one at a time. The EGT indicator must show a temperature rise as each thermocouple is checked. When large numbers (eight or more) of thermocouples are used in the harness, it is difficult to see a rise on the aircraft instrument because of the electrical characteristics of a parallel circuit. Therefore, the temperature indication of the aircraft thermocouples is read on the potentiometer of the analyzer by using the check cable and necessary adapter.

Functional Check of Aircraft EGT Circuit

During the EGT system functional test and the thermocouple harness checks, the analyzer has a specific degree of accuracy at the test temperature, which is usually the maximum operating temperature of the turbine engine. *[Figure 10-78]* Each engine has its own maximum operating temperature, that can be found in applicable technical instructions.

Figure 10-78. *EGT analyzer.*

The test is made by heating the engine thermocouples in the exhaust nozzle or turbine section to the engine test temperature. The heat is supplied by heater probes through the necessary cables. With the engine thermocouples hot, their temperature is registered on the aircraft EGT indicator. At the same time, the thermocouples embedded in the heater probes, which are completely isolated from the aircraft system, are picking up and registering the same temperature on the test analyzer.

The temperature registered on the aircraft EGT indicator should be within the specified tolerance of the aircraft system and the temperature reading on the temperature analyzer. When the temperature difference exceeds the allowable tolerance, troubleshoot the aircraft system.

EGT Indicator Check

The EGT indicator is tested after being removed from the aircraft instrument panel and disconnected from the aircraft EGT circuit leads. Attach the instrument cable and EGT indicator adapter leads to the indicator terminals, and place the indicator in its normal operating position. Adjust the analyzer switches to the proper settings. The indicator reading should correspond to the readings of the analyzer within the allowable limits of the EGT indicator.

Correction for ambient temperature is not required for this test, as both the EGT indicator and analyzer are temperature compensated. The temperature registered on the aircraft EGT indicator should be within the specified tolerance of the aircraft system and the temperature reading on the analyzer readout. When the temperature difference exceeds the allowable tolerance, troubleshoot the aircraft system.

Resistance and Insulation Check

The thermocouple harness continuity is checked while the EGT system is being checked functionally. The resistance of the thermocouple harness is held to very close tolerances, since a change in resistance changes the amount of current flow in the circuit. A change of resistance gives erroneous temperature readings. The resistance and insulation check circuits make it possible to analyze and isolate any error in the aircraft system. How the resistance and insulation circuits are used is discussed with troubleshooting procedures.

Tachometer Check

To read engine speed with an accuracy of ±0.1 percent during engine run, the frequency of the tachometer-generator (older style) is measured by the rpm check analyzer. The scale of the rpm check circuit is calibrated in percent rpm to correspond to the aircraft tachometer indicator, which also reads in percent rpm. The aircraft tachometer and the rpm check circuit are connected in parallel, and both are indicating during engine run-up. The rpm check circuit readings can be compared with the readings of the aircraft tachometer to determine the accuracy of the aircraft instrument.

Many newer engines use a magnetic pickup that counts passing gear teeth edges, which are seen electrically as pulses of electrical power as they pass by the pickup. *[Figure 10-79]* By counting the amount of pulses, the rpm of the shaft is obtained. This type of system requires little maintenance, other than setting the clearance between the gear teeth and the magnetic pickup.

Troubleshooting EGT System

An appropriate analyzer is used to test and troubleshoot the aircraft thermocouple system at the first indication of trouble, or during periodic maintenance checks.

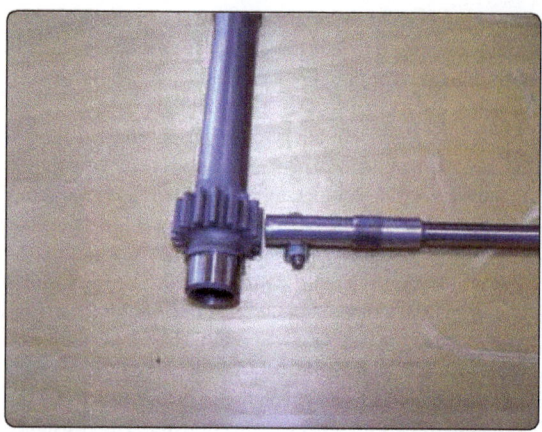

Figure 10-79. *Magnetic pickup and gear.*

The test circuits of the analyzer make it possible to isolate the troubles listed below. Following the list is a discussion of each trouble mentioned.

1. One or more inoperative thermocouples in engine parallel harness
2. Engine thermocouples out of calibration
3. EGT indicator error
4. Resistance of circuit out of tolerance
5. Shorts to ground
6. Shorts between leads

One or More Inoperative Thermocouples in Engine Parallel Harness

This error is found in the regular testing of aircraft thermocouples with a hot heater probe and is a broken lead wire in the parallel harness, or a short to ground in the harness. In the latter case, the current from the grounded thermocouple can leak off and never be shown on the indicator. However, this grounded condition can be found by using the insulation resistance check.

Engine Thermocouples Out of Calibration

When thermocouples are subjected for a period of time to oxidizing atmospheres, such as encountered in turbine engines, they drift appreciably from their original calibration. On engine parallel harnesses, when individual thermocouples can be removed, these thermocouples can be bench-checked, using one heater probe. The temperature reading obtained from the thermocouples should be within manufacturer's tolerances.

EGT Circuit Error

This error is found by using the EGT and comparing the reading of the aircraft EGT indicator with the analyzer temperature reading. *[Figure 10-78]* The analyzer and aircraft temperature readings are then compared.

Resistance of Circuit Out of Tolerance

The engine thermocouple circuit resistance is a very important adjustment since a high-resistance condition gives a low indication on the aircraft EGT indicator. This condition is dangerous, because the engine is operating with excess temperature, but the high resistance makes the indicator read low. It is important to check and correct this condition.

Shorts to Ground/Shorts Between Leads

These errors are found by doing the insulation check using an ohmmeter. Resistance values from zero to 550,000 ohms can be read on the insulation check ohmmeter by selecting the proper range.

Troubleshooting Aircraft Tachometer System

A function of the rpm check is troubleshooting the aircraft tachometer system. The rpm check circuit in the analyzer is used to read engine speed during engine run-up with an accuracy of ±0.1 percent. The connections for the rpm check are the instrument cable and aircraft tachometer system lead to the tachometer indicator. After the connections have been made between the analyzer rpm check circuit and the aircraft tachometer circuit, the two circuits, now classed as one, are a parallel circuit. The engine is then run-up as prescribed in applicable technical instructions. Both systems can be read simultaneously.

If the difference between the readings of the aircraft tachometer indicator and the analyzer rpm check circuit exceeds the tolerance prescribed in applicable technical instructions, the engine must be stopped, and the trouble located and corrected.

Chapter 11
Light-Sport Aircraft Engines

Engine General Requirements

Engines used for light-sport aircraft and other types of aircraft, such as some experimental aircraft, ultralight aircraft, and powered parachutes, must be very light for the power they develop. Each aircraft requires thrust to provide enough forward speed for the wings to provide lift to overcome the weight of the aircraft. An aircraft that meets the requirements of the light-sport categories must meet the following requirements.

NOTE: All of the following requirements and regulations are subject to change. Always refer to the latest Federal Aviation Regulations for current information.

A light-sport aircraft means an aircraft, other than a rotorcraft or powered-lift, since its original certification, has continued to meet the following:

1. A maximum takeoff weight of not more than 1,320 pounds (lb) (600 kilograms (kg)) for aircraft not intended for operation on water; or 1,430 lb (650 kg) for an aircraft intended for operation on water.
2. A maximum airspeed in level flight with maximum continuous power (V_H) of not more than 120 knots calibrated airspeed (CAS) under standard atmospheric conditions at sea level.
3. A maximum never-exceed speed (V_{NE}) of not more than 120 knots CAS for a glider.
4. A maximum stalling speed or minimum steady flight speed without the use of lift-enhancing devices (V_{S1}) of not more than 45 knots CAS at the aircraft's maximum certificated takeoff weight and most critical center of gravity.
5. A maximum seating capacity of no more than two persons, including the pilot.
6. A single, reciprocating engine, if powered.
7. A fixed or ground-adjustable propeller, if a powered aircraft other than a powered glider.
8. A fixed or auto-feathering propeller system, if a powered glider.
9. A fixed-pitch, semirigid, teetering, two-blade rotor system, if a gyroplane.
10. A non-pressurized cabin, if equipped with a cabin.
11. Fixed landing gear, except for an aircraft intended for operation on water or a glider.
12. Fixed or retractable landing gear, or a hull, for an aircraft intended for operation on water.
13. Fixed or retractable landing gear for a glider.

Powered parachute means a powered aircraft comprised of a flexible or semirigid wing connected to a fuselage so that the wing is not in position for flight until the aircraft is in motion. The fuselage of a powered parachute contains the aircraft engine, a seat for each occupant, and is attached to the aircraft's landing gear.

Weight shift control aircraft means a powered aircraft with a framed pivoting wing and a fuselage controllable only in pitch and roll by the pilot's ability to change the aircraft's center of gravity with respect to the wing. Flight control of the aircraft depends on the wing's ability to flexibly deform rather than the use of control surfaces.

As the weight of an engine is decreased, the useful load that an aircraft can carry and the performance of the aircraft are obviously increased. Every excess pound of weight carried by an aircraft engine reduces its performance. Since light-sport aircraft have a narrow margin of useful load, engine weight is a very important concern with all of the light, low airspeed aircraft. Tremendous gains in reducing the weight of the aircraft engine through improvements in design, operating cycles, and metallurgy have resulted in engines with a much improved power to weight ratio.

A light-sport aircraft engine is reliable when it can perform at the specified ratings in widely varying flight attitudes and in extreme weather conditions. The engine manufacturer ensures the reliability and durability of the product by design, research, and testing. Although most of these engines are not certificated by the Federal Aviation Administration (FAA), close control of manufacturing and assembly procedures is generally maintained, and normally each engine is tested before it leaves the factory and meets certain American Society for Testing and Materials (ASTM) standards. Some engines used on light-sport aircraft are certificated by the FAA and these engines are maintained as per the manufacturer's instructions and Title 14 of the Code of Federal Regulations (14 CFR).

Most light-sport engines require a definite time interval between overhauls. This is specified or implied by the engine manufacturer. The time between overhauls (TBO) varies with the type of engine (cycle), operating conditions, such as engine temperatures, amount of time the engine is operated at high-power settings, and the maintenance received. After reaching the time limit, the engine has to be overhauled. Sometimes this requires the engine to be shipped to an authorized manufacturer's overhaul facility. *[Figure 11-1]*

One consideration when selecting a light-sport engine is the shape, size, and number of cylinders of the engine. Since these engines range from single cylinder to multicylinder engines, the mounting in the airframe is important to maintain the view of the pilot, aircraft center of gravity, and to reduce aircraft drag.

Personnel Authorized to Perform Inspection and Maintenance on Light-sport Engines

Given they meet all applicable regulations, the holder of a powerplant certificate can perform maintenance and inspections on light-sport engines. The holder of at least a sport pilot certificate may approve any aircraft owned and

Designation of Engine Type	For Engine S/N	Time Between Overhaul (TBO)	SB To Be Carried Out To Increase TBO
914 F	to 4,420.313	1,000 hours or 10 years, whichever comes first	SB-914-027 1,000 hours to 1,200 hours or 12 years, whichever comes first
914 F	from 4,420.314	1,200 hours or 12 years, whichever comes first	None
914 UL	to 4,418.103	1,000 hours or 10 years, whichever comes first	SB-914-027 1,000 hours to 1,200 hours or 12 years, whichever comes first
914 UL	from 4,418.104	1,200 hours or 12 years, whichever comes first	None

Figure 11-1. *Examples of TBO and calendar life for engines.*

operated by that pilot and issue a special Airworthiness Certificate in the light-sport category for return to service after performing preventive maintenance under the provisions of 14 CFR part 43, section 43.3 (g). All maintenance must be performed in accordance with 14 CFR part 65, section 65.81, which describes specific experience requirements and current instructions for performing maintenance.

The following is used to determine eligibility for a repairman certificate (light-sport aircraft) and appropriate rating. To be eligible for a repairman certificate (light-sport aircraft), you must:

- Be at least 18 years old.
- Be able to read, speak, write, and understand English. If for medical reasons you cannot meet one of these requirements, the FAA may place limits on the repairman certificate necessary to safely perform the actions authorized by the certificate and rating.
- Demonstrate the requisite skill to determine whether a light-sport aircraft is in a condition for safe operation.
- Be a citizen of the United States, or a citizen of a foreign country who has been lawfully admitted for permanent residence in the United States.
- To be eligible for a repairman certificate (light-sport aircraft) with an inspection rating, the applicant must:
    o Meet the requirements stated above for a repairman's certificate.
    o Complete a 16-hour training course acceptable to the FAA on inspecting the particular class of experimental light-sport aircraft for which these privileges are intended to be exercised.
- To be eligible for a repairman certificate (light-sport aircraft) with a maintenance rating, the applicant must:
    o Meet the requirements stated above for a repairman's certificate.
    o Complete a training course acceptable to the FAA on maintaining the particular class of light-sport aircraft upon which the privileges are intended to be exercised. The training course must, at a minimum provide the following number of hours of instruction:
        - For airplane class privileges: 120 hours.
        - Weight-shift control aircraft class privileges: 104 hours.
        - Powered parachute class privileges: 104 hours.
        - Lighter-than-air class privileges: 80 hours.
        - Glider class privileges: 80 hours.

The holder of a repairman certificate (light-sport aircraft) with an inspection rating may perform the annual condition inspection on a light-sport aircraft that is owned by the holder, has been issued an experimental certificate for operating a light-sport aircraft under 14 CFR part 21, section 21.191(i), and is in the same class of light-sport aircraft for which the holder has completed the training specified in the above paragraphs.

The holder of a repairman certificate (light-sport aircraft) with a maintenance rating may approve and return to service an aircraft that has been issued a special Airworthiness Certificate in the light-sport category under 14 CFR part 21, section 21.190, or any part thereof, after performing or inspecting maintenance (to include the annual condition inspection and the 100-hour inspection required by 14 CFR part 91, section 91.327), preventive maintenance, or an alteration (excluding a major repair or a major alteration on a product produced under an FAA approval). They may perform the annual condition inspection on a light-sport aircraft that has been issued an experimental certificate for operating a light-sport aircraft under 14 CFR part 21, section 21.191(i).

However, they may only perform maintenance, preventive maintenance, and an alteration on a light-sport aircraft for which the holder has completed the training specified in the preceding paragraphs. Before performing a major repair, the holder must complete additional training acceptable to the FAA and appropriate to the repair performed.

The holder of a repairman certificate (light-sport aircraft) with a maintenance rating may not approve for return to service any aircraft or part thereof unless that person has previously performed the work concerned satisfactorily. If that person has not previously performed that work, the person may show the ability to do the work by performing it under the direct supervision of a certificated and appropriately rated mechanic, or a certificated repairman who has had previous experience in the specific operation concerned. The repairman may not exercise the privileges of the certificate unless the repairman understands the current instructions of the manufacturer and the maintenance manuals for the specific operation concerned.

Authorized Personnel That Meet FAA Regulations

All applicable aviation regulatory authority regarding maintenance procedures must be met. Maintenance organizations and personnel are encouraged to contact the manufacturer for more information and guidance on any of the maintenance procedures.

It is a requirement that every individual or maintenance provider possess the required special tooling, training, or experience to perform all tasks outlined. Maintenance providers that meet the following conditions outlined below may perform engine maintenance providing they meet all of the following FAA requirements:

- Knowledge of the specific task as a result of receiving authorized training from a training provider.

- Previous experience in performing the task and formal instruction from a manufacturer's authorized training facility or "on-the-job" instruction by a manufacturer's representative.

- A suitable work environment to prevent contamination or damage to engine parts or modules is needed.

- Suitable tools and fixtures as outlined in the manufacturers' Maintenance Manual should be used while performing maintenance requiring such tooling.

- Reasonable and prudent maintenance practices should be utilized.

Types of Light-Sport and Experimental Engines

Note: All information in this text is for educational illustrational purposes and is not to be used for actual aircraft maintenance. This information is not revised at the same rate as the maintenance manual; always refer to the current maintenance information when performing maintenance on any engine.

Light-Sport Aircraft Engines

Light-sport/ultralight aircraft engines can be classified by several methods, such as by operating cycles, cylinder arrangement, and air or water cooled. An inline engine generally has two cylinders, is two-cycle, and is available in several horsepower ranges. These engines may be either liquid cooled, air cooled, or a combination of both. They have only one crankshaft that drives the reduction gear box or propeller directly. Most of the other cylinder configurations used are horizontally opposed, ranging from two to six cylinders from several manufacturers. These engines are either gear reduction or direct drive.

Two-Cycle, Two Cylinder Rotax Engine
Single Capacitor Discharge Ignition (SCDI)
Dual Capacitor Discharge Ignition (DCDI)
Rotax 447 UL (SCDI) and Rotax 503 UL (DCDI)

The Rotax inline cylinder arrangement has a small frontal area and provides improved streamlining. *[Figure 11-2]* The two cylinder, inline two-stroke engine, which is piston ported with air cooled cylinder heads and cylinders, is available in a fan or free air cooled version. Being a two-stroke cycle engine, the oil and fuel must be mixed in the fuel tank on some models. Other models use a lubrication system, such as the 503 oil injection lubrication system. This system does not mix the fuel and oil as the oil is stored in a separate tank.

Figure 11-2. *Rotax inline cylinder arrangement.*

As the engine needs lubrication, the oil is injected directly from this tank. The typical ignition system is a breakerless ignition system with a dual ignition system used on the 503, and a single ignition system used on the 447 engine series. Both systems are of a magneto capacitor discharge design.

The engine is equipped with a carburetion system with one or two piston-type carburetors. One pneumatic driven fuel pump delivers the fuel to the carburetors. The propeller is driven via a flange connected gearbox with an incorporated shock absorber. The exhaust system collects the exhaust gases and directs them overboard. These engines come with an integrated alternating current (AC) generator (12V 170W) with external rectifier-regulator as an optional extra.

Rotax 582 UL DCDI

The Rotax 582 is a two-stroke engine, two cylinder inline with rotary valve inlet, has liquid cooled cylinder heads and cylinders that use an integrated water pump. *[Figure 11-3]* The lubrication system can be a fuel/oil mixture or oil injection lubrication. The ignition system is a dual ignition using a breakerless magneto capacitor discharge design. Dual piston type carburetors and a pneumatic fuel pump deliver the fuel to the cylinders. The propeller is driven via the prop flange connected gearbox with an incorporated torsional vibration shock absorber. This engine also uses a standard version exhaust system with an electric starter or manual rewind starter.

Description of Systems for Two-Stroke Engines
Cooling System of Rotax 447 UL SCDI and Rotax 503 UL DCDI

Two versions of air cooling are available for these engines. The first method is free air cooling, which is a process of engine cooling by an air-stream generated by aircraft speed and propeller. The second is fan cooling, which is cooling by an air-stream generated by a fan permanently driven from the crankshaft via a V-belt.

Cooling System of the Rotax 582 UL DCDI

Engine cooling for the Rotax 582 is accomplished by liquid cooled cylinders and cylinder heads. *[Figure 11-4]* The cooling system is in a two circuit arrangement. The cooling

Figure 11-3. *Rotax 582 engine.*

Figure 11-4. *Rotax 582 cooling system.*

11-5

liquid is supplied by an integrated pump in the engine through the cylinders and the cylinder head to the radiator. The cooling system has to be installed, so that vapor coming from the cylinders and the cylinder head can escape to the top via a hose, either into the water tank of the radiator or to an expansion chamber. The expansion tank is closed by a pressure cap (with excess pressure valve and return valve). As the temperature of the coolant rises, the excess pressure valve opens, and the coolant flows via a hose at atmospheric pressure to the transparent overflow bottle. When cooling down, the coolant is sucked back into the cooling circuit.

Lubrication Systems

Oil Injection Lubrication of Rotax 503 UL DCDE, 582 UL DCDI, and 582 UL DCDI

Generally, the smaller two cycle engines are designed to run on a mixture of gasoline and 2 percent oil that is premixed in the fuel tank. The engines are planned to run on an oil-gasoline mixture of 1:50. Other engines use oil injection systems that use an oil pump driven by the crankshaft via the pump gear that feeds the engine with the correct amount of fresh oil. The oil pump is a piston type pump with a metering system. Diffuser jets in the intake inject pump supplied two-stroke oil with the exact proportioned quantity needed. The oil quantity is defined by the engine rotations per minute and the oil pump lever position. This lever is actuated via a cable connected to the throttle cable. The oil comes to the pump from an oil tank by gravity.

NOTE: In engines that use oil injection, the carburetors are fed with pure gasoline (no oil/gasoline mixture). The oil quantity in the oil tank must be checked before putting the engine into service as the oil is consumed during operation and needs to be replenished.

Electric System

The 503 UL DCDI, 582 UL DCDI engine types are equipped with a breakerless, single capacitor discharge ignition unit with an integrated generator. *[Figure 11-5]* The 447 UL SCDI engine is equipped with a breakerless, single capacitor discharge ignition unit with integrated generator. The ignition unit is completely free of maintenance and needs no external power supply. Two charging coils fitted on the generator stator, independent from each other, each feed one ignition circuit. The energy supplied is stored in the ignition capacitor. At the moment of ignition, the external triggers supply an impulse to the control circuits and the ignition capacitors are discharged via the primary winding of the ignition coil. The secondary winding supplies the high voltage for the ignition spark.

Fuel System

Due to higher lead content in aviation gas (AVGAS), operation can cause wear and deposits in the combustion chamber to increase. Therefore, AVGAS should only be used if problems are encountered with vapor lock or if the other fuel types are not available. Caution must be exercised to use only fuel suitable for the relevant climatic conditions, such as using winter fuel for summer operation.

Fuel/Oil Mixing Procedure

The following describes the process for fuel/oil mixing. Use a clean approved container of known volume. To help predilute

Figure 11-5 *Rotax 503 and 582 electrical system.*

the oil, pour a small amount of fuel into the container. Fill known amount of oil (two-stroke oil ASTM/Coordinating European Council (CEC) standards, API-TC classification (e.g., Castrol TTS) mixing ratio 1:50 (2 percent)), into container. Oil must be approved for air-cooled engines at 50:1 mixing ratio. Agitate slightly to dilute oil with gasoline. Add gasoline to obtain desired mixture ratio; use fine mesh screen. Replace the container cap and shake the container thoroughly. Then, using a funnel with a fine mesh screen to prevent the entry of water and foreign particles, transfer mixture from container into the fuel tank.

WARNING: To avoid electrostatic charging at refueling, use only metal containers and ground the aircraft in accordance with the grounding specifications.

Opposed Light-Sport, Experimental, and Certified Engines

Many certified engines are used with light-sport and experimental aircraft. Generally, cost is a big factor when considering this type of powerplant. The certified engines tend to be much more costly than the non-certified engines, and are not ASTM approved.

Rotax 912/914

Figure 11-6 shows a typical four cylinder, four-stroke Rotax horizontally opposed engine. The opposed-type engine has two banks of cylinders directly opposite each other with a crankshaft in the center. The pistons of both cylinder banks are connected to the single crankshaft. The engine cylinder heads are both liquid cooled and air cooled; the aircooling is mostly used on the cylinder. It is generally mounted with the cylinders in a horizontal position. The opposed-type engine has a low weight to horsepower ratio, and its narrow silhouette makes it ideal for horizontal installation on the aircraft wings (twin-engine applications). Another advantage

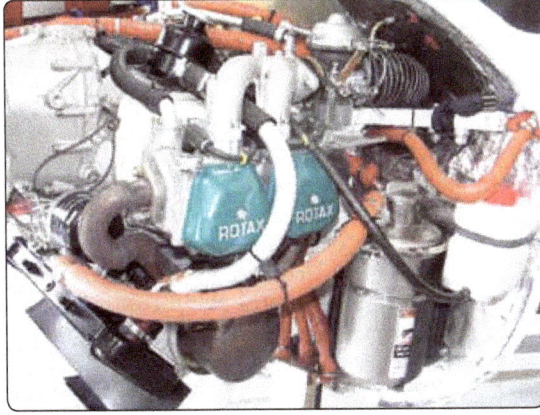

Figure 11-6. *Typical four cylinder, four-stroke horizontally opposed engine.*

is its low vibration characteristics. It is an ideal replacement for the Rotax 582 two-cylinder, two-stroke engine, which powers many of the existing light aircraft, as it is the same weight as the Rotax 582. These engines are ASTM approved for installation into light-sport category aircraft, with some models being FAA certified engines.

Description of Systems
Cooling System

The cooling system of the Rotax 914, shown in *Figure 11-7*, is designed for liquid cooling of the cylinder heads and ram-air cooling of the cylinders. The cooling system of the cylinder heads is a closed circuit with an expansion tank. *[Figure 11-8]* The coolant flow is forced by a water pump driven from the camshaft, from the radiator, to the cylinder heads. From the top of the cylinder heads, the coolant passes on to the expansion tank (1). Since the standard location of the radiator (2) is below engine level, the expansion tank located on top of the engine allows for coolant expansion. The expansion tank is closed by a pressure cap (3) (with excess pressure valve and return valve). As the temperature of the coolant rises, the excess pressure valve opens and the coolant flows via a hose at atmospheric pressure to the transparent overflow bottle (4). When cooling down, the coolant is sucked back into the cooling circuit. Coolant temperatures are measured by means of temperature probes installed in the cylinder heads 2 and 3. The readings are taken on measuring the hottest point of cylinder head depending on engine installation. *[Figure 11-7]*

Fuel System

The fuel flows from the tank (1) via a coarse filter/water trap (2) to the two electric fuel pumps (3) connected in series. *[Figure 11-9]* From the pumps, fuel passes on via the fuel pressure control (4) to the two carburetors (5). Parallel to each fuel pump is a separate check valve (6) installed via the return line (7) that allows surplus fuel to flow back to the fuel tank. Inspection for possible constriction of diameter or obstruction must be accomplished to avoid overflowing of fuel from the carburetors. The return line must not have any resistance to flow. The fuel pressure control ensures that the fuel pressure is always maintained approximately 0.25 bar (3.63 pounds per square inch (psi)) above the variable boost pressure in the airbox and thus, ensures proper operation of the carburetors.

Lubrication System

The Rotax 914 engine is provided with a dry, sump-forced lubrication system with a main oil pump with integrated pressure regulator and an additional suction pump. *[Figure 11-10]* The oil pumps are driven by the camshaft. The main oil pump draws oil from the oil tank (1) via the

Figure 11-7. *Rotax 914 cooling system.*

Figure 11-8. *Water-cooled heads.*

Figure 11-9. *Fuel system components.*

oil cooler (2) and forces it through the oil filter to the points of lubrication. It also lubricates the plain bearings of the turbocharger and the propeller governor. The surplus oil emerging from the points of lubrication accumulates on the bottom of crankcase and is forced back to the oil tank by the blow-by gases. The turbocharger is lubricated via a separate oil line (from the main oil pump). The oil emerging from the lower placed turbocharger collects in the oil sump by a separate pump and is pumped back to the oil tank via the oil line (3). The oil circuit is vented via bore (5) in the oil tank. There is an oil temperature sensor in the oil pump flange for reading of the oil inlet temperature.

Electric System

The Rotax 914 engine is equipped with a dual ignition unit that uses a breakerless, capacitor discharge design with an integrated generator. *[Figure 11-11]* The ignition unit is completely free of maintenance and needs no external power supply. Two independent charging coils (1) located on the generator stator supply one ignition circuit each. The energy is stored in capacitors of the electronic modules (2). At the moment of ignition, two each of the four external trigger coils (3) actuate the discharge of the capacitors via the primary circuit of the dual ignition coils (4). The firing order is as follows: 1-4-2-3. The fifth trigger coil (5) is used to provide the revolution counter signal.

Figure 11-10. *Lubrication system.*

Figure 11-11. *Electric system.*

11-9

Turbocharger and Control System

The Rotax 914 engine is equipped with an exhaust gas turbocharger making use of the energy in the exhaust gas for compression of the intake air or for providing boost pressure to the induction system. The boost pressure in the induction system (airbox) is controlled by means of an electronically controlled valve (wastegate) in the exhaust gas turbine. The wastegate regulates the speed of the turbocharger and consequently the boost pressure in the induction system. The required nominal boost pressure in the induction system is determined by the throttle position sensor mounted on the carburetor 2/4. The sensor's transmitted position is linear from 0 to 115 percent, corresponding to a throttle position from idle to full power. *[Figure 11-12]* For correlation between throttle position and nominal boost pressure in the induction, refer to *Figure 11-13*. As shown in the diagram, with the throttle position at 108–110 percent results in a rapid rise of nominal boost pressure.

To avoid unstable boost, the throttle should be moved smoothly through this area either to full power (115 percent) or at a reduced power setting to maximum continuous power. In this range (108–110 percent throttle position), small changes in throttle position have a big effect on engine performance and speed. These changes are not apparent to the pilot from the throttle lever position. The exact setting for a specific performance is virtually impossible in this range and has to be prevented, as it might cause control fluctuations or surging. Besides the throttle position, overspeeding of the engine and too high intake air temperature have an effect on the nominal boost pressure. If one of the stated factors exceeds the specified limits, the boost pressure is automatically reduced, thus protecting the engine against over boost and detonation.

The turbo control unit (TCU) is furnished with output connections for an external red boost lamp and an orange caution lamp for indications of the functioning of the TCU. When switching on the voltage supply, the two lamps are automatically subject to a function test. Both lamps illuminate for one to two seconds, then they extinguish. If they do not, a check per the engine maintenance manual is necessary. If the orange caution lamp is not illuminated, then this signals that TCU is ready for operation. If the lamp is blinking, this indicates a malfunction of the TCU or its periphery systems. Exceeding of the admissible boost pressure activates and illuminates the red boost lamp continuously. The TCU registers the time of full throttle operation (boost pressure). Full throttle operation for longer than 5 minutes, with the red boost light illuminated, makes the red boost lamp start blinking. The red boost lamp helps the pilot to avoid full power operation for longer than 5 minutes or the engine could be subject to thermal and mechanical overstress.

HKS 700T Engine

The HKS 700T engine is a four-stroke, two cylinder turbocharged engine equipped with an intercooler. *[Figure 11-14]* The horizontally opposed cylinders house four valves per cylinder, with a piston displacement of 709 cc. It uses an electronic control fuel injection system. A reduction gearbox is used to drive the propeller flange at a speed reduction ratio of 2.13 to 1. The engine is rated at 77 horsepower continuous and 80 horsepower takeoff (3 minutes) at 4,900 rpm and 5,300 rpm, respectively. A total engine weight of 126 pounds provides a good power to weight ratio. The 700T has a TBO of 500 hours.

Jabiru Light-Sport Engines

Jabiru engines are designed to be manufactured using the latest manufacturing techniques. *[Figure 11-15]* All Jabiru engines are manufactured, assembled, and ran on a Dynometer, then calibrated before delivery. The crankcase

Figure 11-12. *Turbocharger control system throttle range and position.*

Figure 11-13. *Correlation between throttle position and nominal boost pressure.*

Figure 11-14. *HKS 700T engine.*

Figure 11-15. *Jabiru engines.*

halves, cylinder heads, crankshaft, starter motor housings, gearbox cover (the gearbox powers the distributor rotors), together with many smaller components are machined from solid material. The sump (oil pan) is the only casting. The cylinders are machined from bar 4140 chrome molybdenum alloy steel, with the pistons running directly in the steel bores. The crankshaft is also machined from 4140 chrome molybdenum alloy steel, the journals of which are precision ground prior to being Magnaflux inspected. The camshaft is manufactured from 4140 chrome molybdenum alloy steel with nitrided journals and cams.

The propeller is direct crankshaft driven and does not use a reduction gearbox. This facilitates its lightweight design and keeps maintenance costs to a minimum. The crankshaft features a removable propeller flange that enables the easy replacement of the front crankshaft seal and provides for a propeller shaft extension to be fitted, should this be required for particular applications. Cylinder heads are machined from a solid aluminum billet that is purchased directly from one company, thereby providing a substantive quality control trail to the material source. Connecting rods are machined from 4140 alloy steel and the 45 millimeters big end bearings are of the automotive slipper type. The ignition coils are sourced from outside suppliers and are modified by Jabiru for their own particular application.

An integral alternator provides AC rectification for battery charging and electrical accessories. The alternator is attached to the flywheel and is driven directly by the crankshaft. The ignition system is a transistorized electronic system; two fixed coils mounted adjacent to the flywheel are energized by magnets attached to the flywheel. The passing of the coils by the magnets creates the high voltage current, that is transmitted by high tension leads to the center post of two automotive type distributors, which are simply rotors and caps, before distribution to automotive spark plugs (two in the top of each cylinder head). The ignition system is fixed timing and, therefore, removes the need for timing adjustment. It is suppressed to prevent radio interference.

The ignition system is fully redundant, self-generating, and does not depend on battery power. The crankshaft is designed with a double bearing at the propeller flange end and a main bearing between each big end. Thrust bearings are located fore and aft of the front double bearing, allowing either tractor or pusher installation. Pistons are remachined to include a piston pin, circlip, and groove. They are all fitted with three rings, the top rings being cast iron to complement the chrome molybdenum cylinder bores. Valves are 7mm (stem diameter) and are manufactured specifically for the Jabiru engine. The valve drive train includes pushrods from the camshaft from the camshaft followers to valve rockers. The valves are Computer Numerical Control (CNC) machined from steel billet, induction hardened, polished on contact surfaces, and mounted on a shaft through Teflon coated bronze-steel bush. Valve guides are manufactured from aluminum/bronze. Replaceable valve seats are of nickel steel and are shrunk into the aluminum cylinder heads. The valve train is lubricated from the oil gallery. Engines use hydraulic lifters that automatically adjust valve clearance. An internal gear pump is driven directly by the camshaft and provides engine lubrication via an oil circuit that includes an automotive spin-on filter, oil cooler and built-in relief valve.

The standard engines are supplied with two ram-air cooling ducts, that have been developed by Jabiru to facilitate the cooling of the engine by directing air from the propeller to the critical areas of the engine, particularly the cylinder heads and barrels. The use of these ducts remove the need to design and manufacture baffles and the establishment of a plenum chamber, which is the traditional method of cooling air-cooled, aircraft engines. The fact that these baffles and plenum chamber are not required also ensures a cleaner engine installation, which in turn facilitates maintenance and inspection of the engine and engine components.

The engine is fitted with a 1.5 kilowatt starter motor that is also manufactured by Jabiru and provides very effective starting. The engine has very low vibration level; however, it is also supported by four large rubber shock mounts attached to the engine mounts at the rear of the engine. The fuel induction system uses a pressure compensating carburetor. Following the carburetor, the fuel/air mixture is drawn through a swept plenum chamber bolted to the sump casting, in which the mixture is warmed prior to entering short induction tubes attached to the cylinder heads.

An effective stainless steel exhaust and muffler system is fitted as standard equipment ensuring very quiet operations. For owners wanting to fit vacuum instruments to their aircraft, the Jabiru engines are designed with a vacuum pump drive direct mounted through a coupling on the rear of the crankshaft.

Jabiru 2200 Aircraft Engine

The Jabiru 2200cc aircraft engine is a four-cylinder, four-stroke horizontally opposed air cooled engine. At 132 pounds (60kgs) installed weight, it is one of the lightest four-cylinder, four-stroke aircraft engines. Small overall dimensions give it a small frontal area width (23.46 in, 596mm) that makes it a good engine for tractor applications. The Jabiru engine is designed for either tractor or pusher installation. The Jabiru engine specifications are listed in *Figure 11-16*.

The Jabiru 3300 (120 hp) engine features *[Figure 11-17]*:

- 4-stroke
- 3300cc engine (200 cubic inches)
- 6-cylinder horizontally opposed
- 1 central camshaft
- Fully machined aluminum alloy crankcase
- Overhead valves (OHV) - push rod operated
- Ram-air cooled
- Wet sump lubrication - 4 liter capacity
- Direct propeller drive
- Dual transistorized magneto ignition
- Integrated AC generator
- Electric starter
- Mechanical fuel pump
- Naturally aspirated - 1 pressure compensation carburetor

Aeromax Aviation 100 (IFB) Aircraft Engine

Aeromax Aviation produces a version of a 100 hp engine called the Integral Front Bearing. The engine features a special made integral front bearing. *[Figure 11-18]* The engine uses an integral permanent magnet 35 amp alternator, lightweight starter, and dual ignition. The compact alternator and starter allow for a streamlined and aerodynamic cowl which improves the fuel efficiency of an experimental aircraft. The Aeromax aircraft engine is an opposed six-cylinder, air-cooled, and direct drive. Being a six-cylinder engine, it has smooth operation. The Aeromax engines are known for their heat dissipation qualities, provided the proper amount of cooling air is provided.

It features a crank extension supported by a massive integral front bearing (IFB) and bearing housing. These engines start out as a GM Corvair automobile core engine. These basic core engines are disassembled and each component that is reused is refurbished and remanufactured. The crankshaft in the Areomax 100 IFB aircraft engine is thoroughly inspected, including a magnaflux inspection. After ensuring the crank is free of any defects, it is extended by mounting the crank extension hub on its front. Then, the crank is ground true, with all five bearings' surfaces (four original and the new extended crank's front bearing), being true to each other and perpendicular to the crank's prop flange. *[Figure 11-19]*

All radiuses are smooth with no sharp corners where stress could concentrate. Every crankshaft is nitrated, which is a heat/chemical process that hardens the crank surfaces. The crank reinforcement coupled with the IFB is required to counter the additional dynamic and bending loads introduced on the crank in an aircraft application. The engine case is totally refurbished and checked for wear. Any studs or bolts that show wear are replaced. The engine heads are machined to proper specifications and all new valves, guides, and valve train components are installed. A three-angle valve grind and lapping ensure a good valve seal.

Once the engine is assembled, it is installed on a test stand, pre-lubricated, and inspected. The engine is, then, run several times for a total of two hours. The engine is carefully inspected after each run to ensure it is in excellent operating condition. At the end of test running the engine, the oil filter is removed and cut for inspection. Its internal

Specifications: Jabiru 2200cc 85 HP Aircraft Engine	
Engine Features	Four-stroke
	Four-cylinder horizontally opposed
Opposed	One central camshaft
	Push rods
	Overhead valves (OHV)
(OHV)	Ram-air cooled
	Wet sump lubrication
	Direct propeller drive
	Dual transistorized magneto ignition
Magneto Ignition	Integrated AC generator 20 amp
Generator 20 Amp	Electric starter
	Mechanical fuel pump
	Naturally aspirated - 1 pressure compensating carburetor
Pressure Compensating Carburetor	Six bearing crankshaft
Displacement	2200 cc (134 cu.in.)
Bore	97.5 mm
Stroke	74 mm
Compression Ratio	8:1
Directional Rotation of Prop Shaft	Clockwise - pilot's view tractor applications
Ramp Weight	132 lb complete including exhaust, carburetor, starter motor, alternator, and ignition system
Ignition Timing	25° BTDC
Firing Order	1-3-2-4
Power Rating	85 hp @ 3300 rpm
Fuel Consumption at 75% power	4 US gal/hr
Fuel	AVGAS 100LL or auto gas 91 octane minimum
Oil	Aeroshell W100 or equivalent
Oil Capacity	2.3 quarts
Spark Plugs	NGK D9EA - automotive

Figure 11-16. *Jabiru 2200cc specifications.*

condition is recorded. This process is documented and kept on file for each individual engine. Once the engine's proper performance is assured, it is removed and packaged in a custom built crate for shipping. Each engine is shipped with its engine service and operations manual. This manual contains information pertaining to installation, break–in, testing, tune-up, troubleshooting, repair, and inspection procedures. The specifications for the Aeromax 100 engine are outlined in *Figure 11-20*.

Direct Drive VW Engines

Revmaster R-2300 Engine

The Revmaster R-2300 engine maintains Revmaster's systems and parts, including its RM-049 heads that feature large fins and a hemispherical combustion chamber. *[Figure 11-21]* It maintains the earlier R-2200 engine's top horsepower (82) at 2950 rpm continuous. *[Figure 11-22]* Takeoff power is rated at 85 at 3350 rpm. The additional power comes from a bore of 94mm plus lengthening of the

Jabiru 3300cc Aircraft Engine	
Displacement	3300 cc (202cu.in.)
Bore	97.5 mm (3.838")
Stroke	74 mm (2.913")
Aircraft Engine	Jabiru 3300cc 120hp
Compression Ratio	8:1
Directional Rotation of Prop Shaft	Clockwise - Pilot's view tractor applications
Ramp Weight	178 lbs (81kg) complete including exhaust, carburetor, starter motor, alternator and ignition system
Ignition Timing	25° BTDC fixed timing
Firing order	1–4–5–2–3–6
Power Rating	120 hp @ 3300 rpm
Fuel Consumption at 75% power	26 l/hr (6.87 US gal/hr)
Fuel	AVGAS 100LL or auto gas 91 octane minimum
Oil	Aeroshell W100 or equivalent
Oil Capacity	3.5l (3.69 quarts)
Spark Plugs	NGK D9EA - automotive

Figure 11-17. *Jabiru 3300cc aircraft engine.*

Figure 11-18. *Aeromax direct drive, air-cooled, six-cylinder engine.*

Figure 11-19. *Front-end bearing on the 1000 IFB engine.*

R-2200's connecting rods, plus increasing the stroke from 78 to 84 mm. The longer stroke results in more displacement, and longer connecting rods yield better vibration and power characteristics. The lower cruise rpm allows the use of longer propellers, and the higher peak horsepower can be felt in shorter takeoffs and steeper climbs.

The Revmaster's four main bearing crankshaft runs on a 60 mm center main bearing, is forged from 4340 steel, and uses nitrided journals. Thrust is handled by the 55 mm #3 bearing at the propeller end of the crank. Fully utilizing its robust #4 main bearing, the Revmaster crank has built in oil-controlled propeller capability, a feature unique in this horsepower range; non-wood props are usable with these engines.

Moving from the crankcase and main bearings, the cylinders are made by using centrifugally cast chilled iron. The pistons are forged out of high quality aluminum alloy, machined and balanced in a set of four. There are two sizes of pistons, 92mm and 94mm, designed to be compatible with a 78mm to 82mm stroke crankshafts. The cylinder set also contains piston rings, wrist pins, and locks. The direct-drive R-2300 uses a dual CDI ignition with eight coil spark to eight spark plugs, dual 20-amp alternators, oil cooler, and its proprietary Rev-Flo

Aeromax 100 Engine Specifications	
Power Output: 100 hp continuous at 3200 rpm	Air cooled
Displacement: 2.7 L	Six cylinders
Compression: 9:1	Dual ignition–single plug
Weight: 210 lb	Normally aspirated
Direct Drive	CHT max: 475 F
Rear Light weight. Starter and 45 amp alternator	New forged pistons
Counterclockwise rotation	Balanced and nitrated crank shaft
Harmonic balancer	New hydraulic lifters
Remanufactured case	New main/rod bearings
Remanufactured heads with new guides, valves, valve train, intake	New all replaceable parts
Remanufactured cylinders	New spark plug wiring harness
New light weight aluminum cylinder - optional	Remanufactured dual ignition distributor with new points set and electronic module
New high torque cam	New oil pump
New CNC prop hub and safety shaft	New oil pan
New Aeromax top cover and data plate	Engine service manual

Figure 11-20. *Aeromax 100 engine specifications.*

Figure 11-21. *Revmaster R-2300 engine.*

Figure 11-22. *Hemispherical combustion chamber within the Revmaster R-2300 Heads.*

carburetor, while introducing the longer cylinders that do not require spacers. The automotive-based bearings, valves, valve springs, and piston rings (among others) make rebuilds easy and inexpensive.

Great Plains Aircraft Volkswagen (VW) Conversions

Great Plains Aircraft is one company that offers several configurations of the Volkswagen (VW) aircraft engine conversion. One very popular model is the front drive long block kits that offer a four-cycle, four-cylinder opposed engine with horsepower ranges from approximately 60-100. *[Figure 11-23]* The long block engine kits, which are the complete engine kits that are assembled, in the field or can be shipped completely assembled, are available from 1600 cc up through 2276 cc. All the engine kits are built from proven time tested components and are shipped with a Type One VW Engine Assembly Manual. This manual was written by the manufacturer, specifically for the assembly of their engine kits. Also included are how to determine service and maintenance procedures and many tips on how to set up and operate the engine correctly. The crankshaft used in the 2180

Figure 11-23. *Great Plain's Volkswagen conversion.*

cc to 2276 cc engines is a 82 mm crankshaft made from a forged billet of E4340 steel, machined and magnafluxed twice. The end of the crankshaft features a ½-inch fine thread versus a 20 mm thread found on the standard automotive crank.

Teledyne Continental O-200 Engine

The O-200 Series engine has become a popular engine for use in light-sport aircraft. The O-200-A/B is a four-cylinder, carbureted engine producing 100 brake hp and has a crankshaft speed of 2750 rpm. *[Figure 11-24]* The engine has horizontally opposed air cooled cylinders. The engine cylinders have an overhead valve design with updraft intake inlets and downdraft exhaust outlets mounted on the bottom of the cylinder. The O-200-A/B engines have a 201 cubic inch displacement achieved by using a cylinder design with a 4.06-inch diameter bore and a 3.88-inch stroke. The dry weight of the engine is 170.18 pounds without accessories. The weight of the engine with installed accessories is approximately 215 pounds. The engine is provided with four integral rear engine mounts. A crankcase breather port is located on the 1-3 side of the crankcase forward of the number 3 cylinder. The engine lubrication system is a wet sump, high-pressure oil system. The engine lubrication system includes the internal engine-driven pressure oil pump, oil pressure relief valve, pressure oil screen mounted on the rear of the accessory case and pressure instrumentation. A fitting is provided at the 1-3 side of the crankcase for oil pressure measurement. The oil sump capacity is six quarts maximum. The O-200-A/B induction system consists of an updraft intake manifold with the air intake and throttle mounted below the engine. Engine manifold pressure is measured at a port located on the 2-4 side of the intake air manifold. The O-200-A/B is equipped with a carburetor that meters fuel flow as the flightdeck throttle and mixture controls are changed.

Lycoming 0-233 Series Light-Sport Aircraft Engine

Lycoming Engines, a Textron Inc. company, produces an experimental non-certified version of its 233 series light-sport aircraft engine. *[Figure 11-25]* The engine is light and capable of running on unleaded automotive fuels, as well as AVGAS. The engine features dual CDI spark ignition, an optimized oil sump, a streamlined accessory housing, hydraulically adjusted tappets, a lightweight starter, and a lightweight alternator with integral voltage regulator. It has a dry weight of 213 pounds (including the fuel pump) and offers continuous power ratings up to 115 hp at 2800 rpm. In addition to its multi-gasoline fuel capability, it has proven to be very reliable with a TBO of 2,400 hours. The initial standard version of the engine is carbureted, but fuel injected configurations of the engine are also available.

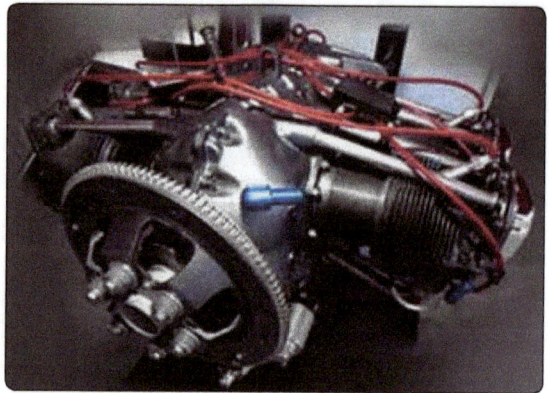

Figure 11-25. *Lycoming 0-233 engine.*

General Maintenance Practices on Light-Sport Rotax Engines

Some specific maintenance practices that differ from conventional certified engines is covered for background and educational acquaintance purposes only. Always refer to the current manufacturer's information when performing maintenance on any engine.

Figure 11-24. *0-200 Continental Engine.*

Safety regulations must be adhered to ensure maintenance personnel safety when performing maintenance and service work on any engine installation. The following information should be followed while performing maintenance.

The ignition should be off and the ignition system grounded with the battery disconnected. Secure the engine against unintentional operation. During maintenance work that requires ignition on and battery connected, secure the propeller against unintentional turning by hand, and secure and observe a propeller safety zone. This precautionary measure serves to avoid any injuries in case of an unintentional start of the engine, which can result in injuries or death. Remember, as long as the ground-cable (plead) is not properly connected to ground, the ignition is switched ON (hot).

Prevent contamination, such as metal chips, foreign material, and/or dirt, from entering the cooling, lubricating, and fuel system during maintenance. Severe burns and scalds may result if the engine is not allowed to cool down to outside air temperature before starting any work. Before reusing disassembled parts, clean with a suitable cleaning agent, check, and refit per instructions. Before every re-assembly, check for missing components. Only use adhesives, lubricants, cleaning agents, and solvents listed for use in the maintenance instructions. Observe the tightening torques for screws and nuts; overtorque or too loose connection could cause serious engine damage or failure.

The following are some general maintenance practices that provide for safety and good technique:

- Work only in a non-smoking area and not close to sparks or open flames.
- Always use the specified tools.
- During disassembling/reassembling the removal of any safety items (e.g., safety wiring, self-locking fastener) must always be followed with replacement of a new one.
- Once loosened, always replace self-securing (locking) nuts.
- Use clean screws and nuts only and inspect face of nuts and thread for damage.
- Check the contact faces and threads for damage and replace if any damaged is detected.
- At reassembly of the engine, replace all sealing rings, gaskets, securing elements, O-rings, and oil seals.
- At disassembly of the engine, mark the engine's components as necessary to provide for locating the original position of the part.
- Parts should be replaced in the same position upon reassembly.
- Any used components have wear patterns that should be replaced or matched if reused. Ensure that these marks are not erased or washed off.

To perform maintenance, the technician must follow the manufacturer's instructions. Obtain, read, and understand the information pertaining to servicing of the light-sport or experimental engine.

Maintenance Schedule Procedures and Maintenance Checklist

All stated checks are visual inspections for damage and wear, unless otherwise stated. All listed work must be carried out within the specified period. For the intervals between maintenance work, a tolerance of + or – 0 hour is permissible, but these tolerances must not be exceeded. This means that if a 100 hour check is actually carried out at 110 hour, the next check is due at 200 hour + or – 10 hour and not at 210 hour + or – 10 hour. If maintenance is performed before the prescribed interval, the next maintenance check is to be done at the same interval (e.g., if first 100-hour check is done after 87 hours of operation, the next 100-hour check must be carried out after 187 hours of operation).

Checks are carried out per the maintenance checklists, where type and volume of maintenance work is outlined in key words. The lists must be photocopied and filled out for each maintenance check. The respective check (e.g., 100-hour check) must be noted on the top of each page of the maintenance checklist. All the maintenance work carried out must be initialed in the signature area by the aircraft mechanic performing the task. After maintenance, the completed checklists must be entered in the maintenance records. The maintenance must be confirmed in the log book. All discrepancies and remedial action must be recorded in a report of findings to be generated and maintained by the company authorized to carry out maintenance work. It is the responsibility of the aircraft operator to store and keep the records. Replacement of equipment (e.g., carburetor, fuel pump, governor) and execution of Service Bulletins must be entered in the log book, stating required information.

Carburetor Synchronization

For smooth idling, synchronization of the throttle valves is necessary. When synchronizing, slacken both Bowden cables, and detach the resonator hose (3) of the compensating tube (2) to separate the two air intake systems. *[Figure 11-26]* In this condition, no significant difference in the engine running should be noticeable. If adjustment is needed for synchronous basic throttle adjustments (mechanical synchronization), proceed as follows. *[Figures 11-27 and 11-28]*

Figure 11-26. *Resonator hose and compensating tube.*

Figure 11-28. *Idle mixture screw.*

(6) clockwise until it is fully inserted and, then, open by 1½ turns counterclockwise. Hook the return spring (5) back up to the throttle lever (1) in its original position. Check that the throttle valve opens fully, automatically. Carry out the above procedure on both carburetors.

NOTE: The mechanical carburetor synchronization is sufficiently exact.

At this point, place the throttle lever in the flightdeck to the idle stop position. Ensure that the throttle lever remains in this position during the next steps of the synchronization process. With the throttle lever in the idle stop position, move the throttle lever (1) to the carburetor idle stop position, using the cable fixation (4), and secure the Bowden cable accordingly. As soon as the two carburetor Bowden cables are installed (throttle lever idle position), check that the idle speed adjustment screw (2) rests fully on the idle stop (3) without pressure.

Figure 11-27. *Carburetor throttle lever.*

Adjust the two Bowden cables for simultaneous opening of the throttle valves. Remove the cable fixation (4) on the throttle lever (1). Next, release the return spring (5) from its attachment on the throttle lever (1), and return the throttle lever (1) to its idle stop position (3) by hand. There should be no resistance during this procedure. Unscrew the idle speed adjustment screw (2) until it is free of the stop. Insert a 0.1 mm (0.004 in) feeler gauge (gap X) between the idle speed adjustment screw (2) and the carburetor idle stop (3), then gently turn the idle screw clockwise until contact is made with the 0.1 mm (0.004 in) feeler gauge. Pull out the feeler gauge and turn each idle speed adjustment screw (2) 1.5 turns in clockwise direction. Gently turn each idle mixture screw

CAUTION: An idle speed that is too low results in gearbox damage, and if an idle speed is too high, the engine is harder to start. Start the engine and verify the idle speed. If the idle speed is too high or too low, adjust accordingly with idle speed adjustment screw (2). Check the operational idle mixture of the engine. If necessary, adjust with the idle mixture screw (6).

Pneumatic Synchronization

Mechanical synchronization should have already been accomplished. The two carburetors are adjusted to equal flow rate at idling by use of a suitable flow meter or vacuum gauges (1).

There are two possible methods to connect test equipment. One option is to remove hex screw (6) M6 x 6 from the intake manifold (7) and connect the vacuum gauge(s). *[Figure 11-26* and *Figure 11- 29]* Remove the compensating tube (2) with attached hoses (12) (connection between intake manifolds) and plug the connections in the intake manifolds. The other hook up option is to remove the compensating tube hose (2) from the push-on connection (5) after removing the tension clamp (4). Using the push-on connection (5), install a flexible rubber hose (8) leading to the vacuum gauge (1), using the balance tube (4). Install the other flexible rubber hose leading to the vacuum gauge. *[Figure 11-29]* Before proceeding any further, secure the aircraft on the ground using wheel chocks and ropes.

WARNING: Secure and observe the propeller zone during engine operation.

Start the engine, verify the idle speed, and make any necessary corrections. If a setting correction of more than ½ turn is required, repeat mechanical synchronization to prevent too high a load on the idle stops. If the idle speed is too high, the maximum the idle screw can be unscrewed is a complete turn. If no satisfactory result can be achieved, inspect the idle jets for contamination and clean if necessary.

Caution: Also check for translucent, jelly-like contamination. Inspect for free flow.

Once the proper idling speed has been established, it is necessary to check the operating range above the idle speed. First, establish that the engine is developing full takeoff performance or takeoff rpm when selected in the flightdeck. Then, the setting of the operating range (idle to full throttle) can be checked or adjusted.

Start and warm up engine as per the operator's manual. Select full power and check that both pressure gauges are registering the same readings. If the same reading is not made on both gauges, shut down the engine and check that carburetor actuation has full travel and that the chokes are in the full off-position. If necessary, fit/modify the carburetor actuation as required to achieve full power on both carburetors. Once full power has been established on both carburetors, retard the throttle and observe the pressure gauge settings. The pressure gauges should show the same reading for both carburetors. Discrepancies must be compensated for by adjusting the off idle adjustment (7). *[Figure 11-27]* The carburetor with the lower indication must be advanced to match the higher one. This is done by shutting down the engine and loosening the locknut on the

Figure 11-29. *Gauges attached to the engine.*

Bowden cable and screwing the off idle adjustment in by ½ turn, then tightening the locknut and retesting the engine. Final idle speed adjustment may be required by resetting the idle speed adjustment screws (2). *[Figure 11-27]* Equal adjustment must be made on both carburetors.

Any major adjustments require retesting to verify all parameters mentioned in this procedure are within limits. Install compensation tube assembly on the engine in reverse sequence of removal. Any minor differences in balance at idle speed is compensated for. Always follow the instructions of the instrument manufacturer.

Idle Speed Adjustment

If satisfactory idle speed adjustment cannot be achieved, inspection of the idle jet or additional pneumatic synchronization is necessary. Always carry out idle speed adjustment when the engine is warm. Basic adjustment of the idle speed is first accomplished by using the idle speed adjustment screw (2) of the throttle valve. *[Figure 11-27]*

Optimizing Engine Running

Optimizing the engine run is necessary only if not accomplished at carburetor synchronization. Close the idle mixture screw (6) by turning clockwise to screw in fully and, then, opening again by 1½ turns counterclockwise. *[Figures 11-27 and 11-28]* Starting from this basic adjustment, the idle mixture screw (6) is turned until the highest motor speed is reached. The optimum setting is the middle between the two positions, at which an rpm drop is noticed. Readjustment of the idle speed is carried out using the idle speed adjustment screw (2) and, if necessary, by slightly turning the idle mixture screw again. Turning the idle mixture control screw in a clockwise direction results in a leaner mixture and turning counterclockwise in a richer mixture.

Checking the Carburetor Actuation

The Bowden cables should be routed in such a way that carburetor actuation is not influenced by any movement of the engine or airframe, thus possibly falsifying idle speed setting and synchronization. *[Figure 11-30]* Each carburetor is actuated by two Bowden cables. At position 1, connection for throttle valve and at position 2, make the connection for the choke actuator. The Bowden cables must be adjusted so that the throttle valve and the choke actuation of the starting carburetor can be fully opened and closed. Bowden cables and lever must operate freely and not jam.

WARNING: With carburetor actuation not connected, the throttle valve is fully open. The initial position of the carburetor is full throttle. Never start the engine with the actuation disconnected. Inspect Bowden cables and levers for free movement. Cables must allow for full travel of lever

Figure 11-30. *Bowden cable routing.*

from stop to stop. Adjust throttle cables to a clearance of 1 mm (0.04 in). Inspect and lubricate linkage on carburetor and carburetor joints with engine oil. Inspect return springs (3) and engagement holes for wear.

Lubrication System

Oil Level Check

Always allow engine to cool down to ambient temperature before starting any work on the lubrication system. Severe burns and scalds may result from hot oil coming into contact with the skin. Switch off ignition and remove ignition key. To assure that the engine does not turn by the starter, disconnect the negative terminal of aircraft battery. Before checking the oil level, make sure that there is not excess residue oil in the crankcase. Prior to oil level check, turn the propeller several times by hand in the direction of engine rotation to pump all the oil from the engine to the oil tank. This process is completed when air flows back to the oil tank. This air flow can be perceived as a gurgling noise when the cap of the oil tank is removed. The oil level in the oil tank should be between the two marks (maximum/minimum) on the oil dipstick, but must never fall below the minimum mark. *[Figure 11-31]* Replenish oil as required, but for longer flights, replenish oil to maximum mark to provide for more of an oil reserve. During standard engine operation, the oil level should be mid-way between the maximum and minimum marks a higher oil level (over servicing). Oil can escape through the venting (breather) passage.

Figure 11-31. *Oil dipstick minimum and maximum marks.*

Oil Change

It is advisable to check the oil level prior to an oil change, as it provides information about oil consumption. Run engine to warm the oil before beginning the procedure. Taking proper precautions, crank the engine by hand to transfer the oil from the crankcase. Remove the safety wire and oil drain screw (1) from the oil tank, drain the used oil, and dispose of as per environmental regulations. *[Figure 11-32]* Remove and replace oil filter at each oil change. It is not necessary to remove oil lines and other oil connections. Draining the suction lines, oil cooler, and return line is not necessary and must be avoided, as it results in air entering the oil system. Replacement of the oil filter and the oil change should be accomplished quickly and without interruption to prevent a draining of the oil system and the hydraulic tappets. Compressed air must not be used to blow through the oil system (or oil lines, oil pump housing, oil bores in the housing). Replace the oil drain screw torque and safety wire. Only use the appropriate oil in accordance with the latest operator's manual and service instruction. The engine must not be cranked when the oil system is open. After the oil change is accomplished, the engine should be cranked by hand in the direction of engine rotation (approximately 20 turns) to completely refill the entire oil circuit.

Cleaning the Oil Tank

Cleaning the oil is optional and requires venting of the oil system. It is only necessary to clean the oil tank and the inner parts if there is heavy oil contamination. The procedure for cleaning the oil tank is shown in *Figure 11-32.* Detach the

CODE		
1	Oil drain screw	5 Baffle insert
2	Profile clamp	6 Partition
3	Oil tank cover	7 Sealing ring
4	O-ring	8 Oil tank

Figure 11-32. *Oil tank.*

profile clamp (2) and remove the oil tank cover (3), together with the O-ring (4) and the oil lines. Remove the inner parts of the oil tank, such as the baffle insert (5) and the partition (6). Clean oil tank (8) and inner parts (5, 6), and check for damage. Be aware that incorrect assembly of the oil tank components can cause engine faults or engine damage. Replace the drain screw with a new sealing ring (7) and tighten to 25 Newton meters (Nm) (18.5 ft/lb) and safety wire. Reassemble the oil tank by following the same steps in reverse order.

Inspecting the Magnetic Plug

Remove the magnetic plug and inspect it for accumulation of chips. *[Figure 11-33]* The magnetic plug (torx screw) is located on the crankcase between cylinder 2 and the gearbox. This inspection is important because it allows conclusions to be drawn on the internal condition of the gearbox and engine, and reveals information about possible damage. If a significant amount of metal chips are detected, the engine must be inspected, repaired, or overhauled. Steel chips in low numbers can be tolerated if the accumulation is below 3 mm (0.125 in). *[Figure 11-33]* In the case of unclear findings, flush the oil circuit and fit a new oil filter. Afterwards, conduct an engine test run and inspect the oil filter once more. If there are larger accumulations of metal chips on the magnetic plug, the engine must be repaired or overhauled in accordance with

Figure 11-33. *Inspecting the magnetic plug.*

the manufacturer's instructions for continued airworthiness. A detailed inspection of affected engine components must be performed. If the oil circuit is contaminated, replace the oil cooler and flush the oil circuit, then trace the cause and remedy the situation. If the magnetic chip is found to have no metal, then clean and reinstall. Tighten the plug to a torque of 25 Nm (18.5 ft/lb). Safety wire the plug and inspect all systems for correct function.

Checking the Propeller Gearbox

The following free rotation check and friction torque check are necessary only on certified engines and on engines with the overload clutch as an optional extra. Engines without the overload clutch (slipper clutch) still incorporate the torsional shock absorption. This design is similar to the system with overload clutch, but without free rotation. For this reason, the friction torque method cannot be applied on engines without the overload clutch.

Checking the Friction Torque in Free Rotation

Fit the crankshaft with a locking pin. *[Figure 11-34]* With the crankshaft locked, the propeller can be turned by hand 15 or 30 degrees, depending on the profile of the dog gears

Figure 11-34. *Checking propeller gearbox.*

installed. This is the maximum amount of movement allowed by the dog gears in the torsional shock absorption unit.

WARNING: Ignition OFF and system grounded. Disconnect negative terminal of aircraft battery.

Turn the propeller by hand back and forth between ramps, taking into consideration the friction torque. No odd noises or irregular resistance must be noticeable during this movement. Attach a calibrated spring scale to the propeller at a certain distance (L) from the center of the propeller. Measure the force required to pull the propeller through the 15 or 30 degree range of free rotation. Calculate friction torque Nm by multiplying the force Newton's (N) or pounds (lb) obtained on the spring scale by the distance the scale is attached from the center of the propeller (L). The distance measurement and torque measurement must be in the same units either standard or metric and cannot be mixed up. The friction torque must be between a minimum of 25 Nm and maximum of 60 Nm (18.5 to 44.3 ft/lb). A calculation example is as follows:

Friction Torque (FT) = Length (meters) × Newtons (torque)
FT = .5 meters × 60 Newtons
FT = 30Nm

Remove crankshaft locking pin and reinstall plug with new gasket. Reconnect negative terminal of aircraft battery. If the above mentioned friction torque is not achieved, inspect, repair, or overhaul the gearbox in accordance with the manufacturer's instructions for continued airworthiness. Testing the propeller flange is not normal maintenance but can be carried out if defects or cracks are suspected.

Daily Maintenance Checks

The following checklist should be used for daily maintenance checks. Repair, as necessary, all discrepancies before flight.

1. Verify ignition OFF.
2. Drain water from fuel tank sump and/or water trap (if fitted).
3. Inspect carburetor rubber socket or flange for cracks and verify secure attachment.
4. Inspect carburetor float chamber for water and dirt.
5. Verify security and condition of intake silencer and air filter.
6. Verify security of radiator mounting. Inspect radiators for damage and leaks.
7. Verify coolant level in overflow bottle and security of cap.
8. Verify coolant hoses for security, and inspect for leaks and chafing.

9. Inspect engine for coolant leaks (cylinder head, cylinder base, and water pump).
10. Verify oil content for rotary valve gear lubrication and security of oil cap.
11. Verify oil hoses for security, and inspect for leaks and chafing (rotary valve gear lubrication system and oil injection system).
12. Verify ignition coils/electronic boxes for secure mounting, and check ignition leads and all electrical wiring for secure connections and chafing.
13. Verify electric starter for secure mounting, and inspect cover for cracks.
14. Verify engine to airframe mounting for security and inspect cracks.
15. Verify fuel pump mounting for security, and inspect all fuel hose connections (filters, primer bulbs, and taps for security, leakage, chafing and kinks).
16. Verify fuel pump impulse hose for secure connections, and inspect for chafing and kinks.
17. Verify safety wiring of gearbox drain and level plugs.
18. Inspect rubber coupling for damage and aging (C type gearbox only).
19. Rotate engine by hand and listen for unusual noises (first, double verify ignition OFF).
20. Check propeller shaft bearing for clearance by rocking propeller.
21. Inspect throttle choke and oil pump lever cables for damage (end fittings, outer casing, and kinks).

Pre-flight Checks

The following checklist should be performed for all pre-flight checks. Repair, as necessary, all discrepancies and shortcoming before flight.

1. Verify ignition OFF.
2. Check fuel content.
3. Inspect for coolant leaks.
4. Verify oil tank content (oil injection engines).
5. Verify spark plug connectors for security.
6. Inspect engine and gearbox for oil leaks.
7. Inspect engine and gearbox for loose or missing nuts, bolts, and screws, and verify security of gearbox to engine mounting.
8. Inspect propeller for splits and chips. If any damage, repair and/or rebalance before use.
9. Verify security of propeller mounting.
10. Check throttle, oil injection pump, and choke actuation for free and full movement.
11. Verify that cooling fan turns when engine is rotated (air cooled engines).
12. Inspect exhaust for cracks, security of mounting, springs, and hooks for breakage and wear, and verify safety wiring of springs.
13. Start engine after assuring that area is clear of bystanders.
14. Single ignition engines: check operation of ignition switch (flick ignition off and on again at idling).
15. Dual ignition engines: check operation of both ignition circuits.
16. Check operation of all engine instruments during warm up.
17. If possible, visually check engine and exhaust for excessive vibration during warm up (indicates propeller out of balance).
18. Verify that engine reaches full power rpm during takeoff roll.

Troubleshooting and Abnormal Operation

The information in this section is for training purposes and should never be used for maintenance on the actual aircraft. Only qualified personnel (experienced two-stroke technicians) trained on this particular type of engine are allowed to carry out maintenance and repair work. If the following information regarding the remedy of the malfunction does not solve the malfunction, contact an authorized facility. The engine must not be returned to service until the malfunction is rectified. As described earlier in the text, engines require basically two essentials to run: spark and correct fuel/air mixture. The majority of problems quite often are a simple lack of one or the other.

Troubleshooting

Follow an organized method of troubleshooting. This facilitates the identification of discrepancies or malfunctions.

- Fuel—start by checking the supply (tank), fittings (loose), filter (plugged), and float chamber (fouled).
- Spark—check for spark at the spark plugs.

Problems of a more complex nature are best left to an engine technician. The following are examples of engine troubles and potential fixes.

Engine Keeps Running With Ignition OFF
Possible cause: Overheating of engine.
Remedy: Let engine cool down at idling at approximately 2,000 engine rpm.

Knocking Under Load
Possible cause: Octane rating of fuel too low.
Remedy: Use fuel with higher octane rating.
Possible cause: Fuel starvation, lean mixture.
Remedy: Check fuel supply.

Abnormal Operating
Exceeding the Maximum Admissible Engine Speed
Reduce engine speed. Any overage of the maximum admissible engine speed must be entered by the pilot into the logbook, stating duration and extent of over-speed.

Exceeding of Maximum Admissible Cylinder Head Temperature
Reduce engine power, setting to the minimum necessary, and carry out precautionary landing. Any exceeding of the maximum admissible cylinder head temperature must be entered by the pilot into the logbook, stating duration and extent of excess-temperature condition.

Exceeding of Maximum Admissible Exhaust Gas Temperature
Reduce engine power, setting to the minimum necessary, and carry out precautionary landing. Any exceedence of the maximum admissible exhaust gas temperature must be entered by the pilot into the logbook, stating duration and extent of excess-temperature condition.

Engine Preservation
If the engine is not going to be used for an extended period of time, certain measures must be taken to protect engine against heat, direct sun light, corrosion, and formation of residues. In particular, the water bonded by the alcohol in the fuel causes increased corrosion problems during storage. After each flight, activate choke for a moment before stopping engine. Close all engine openings like exhaust pipe, venting tube, and air filter to prevent entry of contamination and humidity. For engine storage of one to four weeks, proceed with preservation prior to engine stop or on the engine at operating temperature. Let the engine run at increased idle speed. Shut the engine down and secure against inadvertent engine start. Remove air filters and inject approximately 3 cubic cm of preservation oil or equivalent oil into the air intake of each carburetor. Restart the engine and run at increased idle speed for 10–15 seconds. Shut engine down and secure against inadvertent engine start. Close all engine openings, such as exhaust pipe, venting tube, and air filter, to prevent entry of contamination and humidity.

For engine storage of engine for longer than four weeks and up to one year, proceed with preservation prior to engine stop and on the engine at operating temperature. Let the engine run at increased idle speed. Remove air filters and inject approximately 6 cubic cm of preservative oil or equivalent oil into the air intake of each carburetor. Stop the engine. Remove spark plugs and inject approximately 6 cubic cm preservation oil or equivalent oil into each cylinder and slowly turn crankshaft 2 to 3 turns by hand to lubricate top end parts. Replace and re-torque the spark plugs. Drain gasoline from float chambers, fuel tank, and fuel lines. Drain coolant on liquid cooled engines to prevent any damage by freezing. Lubricate all carburetor linkages using the proper lubricates. Close all openings of the engine, such as exhaust pipe openings, venting tube, and air intake, to prevent entry of any foreign material and humidity. Protect all external steel parts by spraying with engine oil.

General Maintenance Practices for the Light-Sport Jabiru Engines
NOTE: Some specific maintenance practices that differ from conventional certified engines is covered for background and educational acquaintance purposes only. Always refer to the current manufacturer's information when performing maintenance on any engine.

Engine and Engine Compartment Inspection
Check for oil, fuel exhaust, and induction leaks and clean the entire engine and compartment before inspection. Check flywheel screw tensions to 24 foot pounds. Check the carburetor air filter and clean it by removing it from the intake housing and blowing compressed air against the direction of the intake flow. For operation in heavy dust conditions, clean air filter at shorter intervals than recommended for normal conditions. A clogged filter reduces engine performance, as well as promotes premature engine wear. The engine baffles and air ducts should be checked for condition and functionality.

Two methods can be used to check the cylinders compression. The compression gauge method is used to measure compression using a compression tracer. Readings are taken with a fully open throttle valve at engine oil temperature between 30 °C and 70 °C (90 °F to 160 °F). If readings are below 6 bar (90 psi) a check of the pistons, cylinders, valves, and cylinder heads must be undertaken.

The second method uses the pressure differential test. Check using a maximum allowable pressure loss is 25 percent. As an alternative to a compression test, a pressure differential test (leak down) can be accomplished. This is a much better test of the condition of rings, bore, head sealing, and valves. This is the normal test used in aviation and requires specific equipment. The test is carried out with the engine in warm to hot condition. Input pressure is best set at 80 psi; a second gauge reads the differential. This is done with piston on TDC on the firing stroke.

NOTE: The propeller needs to be restrained. A differential of lower than 80/60 (generally a 25 percent loss) indicates a problem.

Problems can be better identified by observing where air is escaping from the cylinder, blow-by. Some examples are as follows:

1. Blow-by through the crankcase vent indicates worn rings or bore.
2. Leaking from carby indicates a poor intake valve seal.
3. Leaking from exhaust indicates a poor exhaust valve seal.
4. Head leak indicates poor head to cylinder seal.

With the problem identified, the malfunction can then be corrected. Poor compression can be an indication of a serious problem. For example, continued operation with poor compression due to a poorly sealing valve can lead to eventual valve failure and heavy damage to the piston, connecting-rod, barrel, and head.

Lubrication System

The oil should be changed as required by the manufacturer. When changed, the oil filter should also be changed. Change the oil filter at every 50 hourly inspection. Drain the oil while engine is still warm and visually check for leaks. Fill the engine with oil (approximately 2.3 liters) and check oil level. Never exceed the maximum mark. Use only registered brand oils meeting the correct specifications. Do not drain the oil cooler during a normal oil change. The cooler holds only a small amount of old oil that has negligible effect on the new oil. Taking the hoses on and off the cooler can prematurely age the oil lines and lead to hoses slipping off the cooler.

Carburetor Adjustment and Checks

To adjust the engine's idle speed, adjust the idle stop screw (7 mm screw) against throttle lever. Standard idle mixture screw position is 1¼ turns out from the seated position. Fine adjustment may be necessary to give a smooth idle.

The mixture is set by selecting jet sizes. As supplied, the engine has jets to suit a majority of installations; however, the mixture may be affected by operation with a propeller that does not meet the requirements listed in the installation manual or by ambient temperature extremes. If an engine is to be used in these situations, an exhaust gas temperature (EGT) gauge should be fitted and monitored against the limits specified above. Do not change carburetor settings if EGT readings fall outside the range given without consulting with Jabiru Aircraft or our local authorized representative. The carburetor automatically adjusts the mixture to account for altitude. Visual inspection should include checks for carburetor joint degradation and carburetor linkage for full and free movement, correct positioning of stops and security.

Spark Plugs

When plugs are removed from a warm engine, the inspection of the tip of the spark plug can be used to indicate the health of the engine. If the tip of the plug is a light brown color, the plug is operating correctly. A black velvet, sooty looking plug tip generally is an indication of an overly rich mixture (check the choke and the air filter and intake). If the firing end tip is covered with oil, it is an indication of too much oil in the combustion chamber (check for worn piston rings and cylinder walls). When servicing the spark plugs, do not use steel or brass brushes for cleaning and never sandblast plugs. Clean the spark plugs with plastic brush in a solvent. Check electrode gap and, if necessary, adjust to 0.55–0.6mm (0.022 in–0.024 in) by carefully bending the electrode. Use the recommended Plugs (NGK D9EA) and place a suitable anti-seize compound on threads of the plug before installing them in the engine. Tighten spark plugs when the engine is cold and adjust engine to the correct torque value. Reconnect the ignition lead.

Exhaust System

Visually check the exhaust system for security of mounting, damage, rubbing, leaks, and general condition. Check nuts and bolts for tightness and condition; re-torque and replace if necessary.

Head Bolts

Check the head bolt torque after five hours of operation, and again after ten hours of operation. The bolts should, thereafter, be checked annually. Head bolts torque when cold to 20 ft/lb.

Tachometer and Sender

Many apparent engine problems can be caused through inaccurate tachometers. Where engine performance is observed to be outside limits, the tachometer should be checked against a calibrated instrument. Tachometer sender gap is 0.4mm (0.016 inches). The sender must have at least 60 percent covered by the tags fitted to the gearbox side of the flywheel. Ensure both tags are equal distance from sender.

Engine Inspection Charts

NOTE: Read all inspection requirement paragraphs prior to using these charts. *[Figure 11-35]*

Propeller	Engine and Engine Compartment
Spinner * *	Check flywheel screw tensions to 24 foot pounds*
Spinner flange * *	Carburetor air filter * *
Spinner screws * *	Engine baffles and air ducts *
Propeller * *	Cylinders *
Propeller bolts/nuts - Tension *	Crankcase & front crankcase seal *
Spinner/prop tracking * *	Hoses, lines and fittings * *
	Intake and exhaust systems *
	Ignition harness, distributor caps & rotors *
	NOTE: Check for oil, fuel exhaust and induction leaks, then clean entire engine and compartment before inspection.
Annual Inspection** Each 100 Hours*	

Figure 11-35. *Engine inspection charts.*

Glossary

Abradable strip. A strip of material in the compressor housing of some axial-flow gas turbine engines. The tip of the compressor blade touches the abradable strip, and wears, or abrades a groove in it. This groove ensures the minimum tip clearance.

Abradable tip (compressor blade tip). The tip of some axial-flow compressor blades constructed so that it will abrade, or wear away, upon contact with the compressor housing, which ensures the minimum tip clearance between the blade and the housing.

Absolute pressure. Pressure referenced from zero pressure or a vacuum.

AC. Alternating current. Electrical current in which the electrons continually change their rate of flow and periodically reverse their direction.

ACC. Active clearance control. A system for controlling the clearance between tips of the compressor and turbine blades and the case of high-performance turbofan engines. When the engine is operating at maximum power, the blade tip clearance should be minimum, and the ACC system sprays cool fan discharge air over the outside of the engine case. This causes the case to shrink enough to decrease the tip clearance. For flight conditions that do not require such close clearance, the cooling air is turned off, and the case expands to its normal dimensions. The control of the ACC system is done by the FADEC, or full-authority digital electronic control.

Acceleration. The amount the velocity of an object is increased by a force during each second it is acted upon by that force. Acceleration is usually measured and expressed in terms of feet per second, per second (fps^2).

Accessory end. The end of a reciprocating engine on which many of the accessories are mounted. Also, called the anti-propeller end.

Accumulator. A hydraulic component that stores a non-compressible fluid, such as oil, under pressure. An accumulator has two compartments separated by a flexible or movable partition with one compartment containing compressed air. When oil is pumped into the other compartment, the partition moves over, further compressing the air which holds pressure on the oil.

AD (ashless dispersant) oil. A mineral-based lubricating oil used in reciprocating engines. This oil does not contain any metallic ash-forming additives, but has additives that disperse the contaminants and hold them in suspension until they can be removed by filters.

ADC. Air data computer. An electronic computer in an aircraft that senses pitot pressure, static pressure, and total air temperature. It produces an indication of altitude, indicated airspeed, true airspeed, and Mach number. The output of ADC is usable by any of the engine or flight control computers.

ADI (antidetonation injection) system. A system used with some large reciprocating engines in which a mixture of water and alcohol is sprayed into the engine with the fuel when operating at extremely high power. The fuel-air mixture is leaned to allow the engine to develop its maximum power, and the ADI fluid absorbs excessive heat when it vaporizes.

Adiabatic change. A physical change that takes place within a material in which heat energy is neither added to the material, nor taken away. If a container of gas is compressed, with no heat energy added to or taken from it, the gas will become hotter; its temperature will rise.

Aerodrome. The name given by Dr. Samuel Langley to the flying machines built under his supervision between the years of 1891 and 1903.

Aeromatic propeller. A patented variable-pitch propeller that has counterweights around the blade shanks and the blades angled back from the hub to increase the effects of aerodynamic and centrifugal twisting forces. This propeller automatically maintains a relatively constant rpm for any throttle setting.

Aft-fan engine. A turbofan engine with the fan mounted behind the compressor section. The blades of an aft-fan are normally extensions of the free turbine blades.

Afterburner. A component in the exhaust system of a turbojet or turbofan engine used to increase the thrust for takeoff and for special flight conditions. Since much of the air passing through a gas turbine engine is used only for cooling, it still contains a great deal of oxygen. Fuel is sprayed into the hot, oxygen-rich exhaust in the afterburner, where it is ignited and burned to produce additional thrust.

Air bleed (carburetor component). A small hole in the fuel passage between the float bowl and the discharge nozzle of a float carburetor. Air drawn into the liquid fuel through the air bleed breaks the fuel up into an emulsion, making it easy to atomize and vaporize.

Air cooling. The removal of unwanted heat from an aircraft engine by transferring the heat directly into the air flowing over the engine components.

Air-fuel mixture ratio. The ratio of the weight of the air to that of the fuel in the mixture fed into the cylinders of an engine.

Air impingement starter. A turbine engine starter that basically consists of a nozzle that blows a stream of compressed air against the turbine blades to rotate the compressor for starting the engine.

Air-oil separator. A component in a turbine engine lubrication system that removes the air from the scavenged oil before it is returned to the oil tank.

Airworthiness Directive. A regulatory notice sent out by the FAA to the registered owner of an aircraft informing him or her of the discovery of a condition that keeps the aircraft from continuing to meet its conditions for airworthiness. Also called AD notes, they are covered by Federal Aviation Regulations part 39 Airworthiness Directives. They must be complied with within the specified time, and the fact, date, and method of compliance must be recorded in the aircraft maintenance records.

All-weather spark plug. A shielded spark plug designed for high altitude operation. The ceramic insulator is recessed into the shell to allow a resilient grommet on the ignition harness to provide a watertight seal. All weather spark plugs, also called high-altitude spark plugs, are identified by their 3/4-20 shielding threads.

Alpha control range (alpha mode). The flight operating mode from takeoff through landing for a turbo-prop engine. Alpha mode includes operations from 95% to 100% of the engine's rated rpm.

Altitude engine. An aircraft reciprocating engine equipped with a supercharger that allows it to maintain its rated sea-level horsepower to an established higher altitude.

Amateur-built aircraft. Aircraft built by individuals as a hobby rather than by factories as commercial products. Amateur-built or homebuilt aircraft do not fall under the stringent requirements imposed by the FAA on commercially built aircraft.

Ambient air pressure. The pressure of the air that surrounds an object.

Analog indicator. An indicator that shows the value of the parameter being measured by a number marked on a graduated dial aligned with a movable pointer.

Angle of attack. The acute angle between the chord line of a propeller blade and the relative wind. The angle of attack is affected by both the engine rpm and the forward speed of the aircraft.

Annual inspection. A complete inspection of the air-frame and powerplant required for FAA-certificated aircraft operating under 14 CFR part 91 General Operating and Flight Rules, and not on one of the authorized special inspection programs. An annual inspection must be conducted every 12 calendar months, and it must be conducted by an aviation maintenance technician who holds an Airframe and Powerplant rating and an Inspection Authorization. The scope of an annual inspection is the same as that of a 100-hour inspection.

Annular duct. A duct, or passage, that surrounds an object. The annular fan-discharge duct surrounds the core engine.

Annular orifice. A ring-shaped orifice, normally one that surrounds another orifice.

Annulus. A ring or groove around the outside of a circular body or shaft, or around the inside of a cylindrical hole.

Annunciator panel. A panel of warning lights visible to the flight crew. The lights are identified by the name of the system they represent and are often covered with colored lenses. Red lights indicate a dangerous condition, amber indicates a system is armed, and green indicate a safe condition.

Anodizing. A hard, airtight, unbroken oxide film electrolytically deposited on an aluminum alloy surface to protect it from corrosion.

Anti-icing. Prevention of the formation of ice on a surface. anti-propeller end. The end of a reciprocating engine that does not attach to the propeller. Also called the accessory end.

APC. Absolute pressure controller.

APU. Auxiliary power unit. A small turbine- or reciprocating-engine-powered generator, hydraulic pump, and air pump. APUs are installed in the aircraft and are used to supply electrical power, air, and hydraulic pressure when the main engines are not running.

Aramid fiber. Fiber made from an organic compound of carbon, hydrogen, oxygen, and nitrogen. It has high strength and low density. It is flexible under load and is able to withstand impact, shock, and vibration. Kevlar is a well-known aramid fiber.

Aromatic compound. A chemical compound such as toluene, xylene, and benzene that is blended with gasoline to improve its anti-detonation characteristics.

Articulating rod. See link rod.

Aspect ratio. The ratio of the length of an airfoil, such as a compressor blade, to its width.

Asymmetrical loading. The loading of a propeller disk that causes one side to produce more thrust than the other side.

ATF. Aerodynamic twisting force. The aerodynamic force that acts on a rotating propeller blade to increase its blade angle. The axis of rotation of a blade is near the center of its chord line, and the center of pressure is between the axis and the leading edge. Aerodynamic lift acting through the center of pressure tries to rotate the blade to a higher pitch angle.

Atomize. The process of breaking a liquid down into tiny droplets or a fine spray. Atomized liquids vaporize easily.

Augmentor tube. A long, specially shaped stainless steel tube mounted around the exhaust tail pipe of a reciprocating engine. As exhaust gases flow through the augmentor tube, they produce a low pressure in the engine compartment that draws in cooling air through the cylinder fins.

Automatic intake valve. An intake valve opened by low pressure created inside the cylinder as the piston moves down. There is no mechanical means of opening it.

Automatic mixture control (AMC). The device in a fuel metering system, such as a carburetor or fuel injection system, that keeps the fuel-air mixture ratio constant as the density of air changes with altitude.

Autosyn system. The registered trade name of a remote indicating instrument system. An Autosyn system uses an electromagnet rotor, excited with 400-hertz AC, and a three-phase distributed-pole stator.

Axial bearing load. The load on a bearing parallel to the shaft on which the bearing is mounted. Thrust produces an axial load on a bearing.

Axial turbine. A turbine that is turned by a fluid flowing through it in a direction that is approximately parallel to the shaft on which the turbine wheel is mounted.

Axial-flow compressor. A type of compressor used in gas turbine engines. Air passes through the compressor in essentially a straight line, parallel to the axis of the compressor. The compressor is made of a number of stages of rotating compressor blades between stages of stationary stator vanes.

Axis of rotation. The center line about which a propeller rotates.

Babbitt. A soft silvery metal used for main bearing inserts in aircraft reciprocating engines. Babbitt is made of tin with small amounts of copper and antimony.

Back (propeller nomenclature). The curved surface of a propeller blade. The back of a propeller blade corresponds to the upper surface of an airplane wing.

Back-suction mixture control. A type of mixture control used in some float carburetors that regulates the fuel-air mixture by varying the air pressure above the fuel in the float bowl.

Baffle. A thin sheet metal shroud or bulkhead used to direct the flow of cooling air between and around the cylinder fins of an air-cooled reciprocating engine.

Bayonet stack. An exhaust stack with an elongated and flattened end. The gases leave the stack through a slot perpendicular to its length. Bayonet stacks decrease both exhaust back pressure and noise.

BDC. Bottom dead center. The position of a piston in a reciprocating engine when the piston is at the bottom of its stroke, and the wrist pin, crankpin, and center of the crankshaft are all in line.

Bell mouth. The shape of the inlet of an augmentor tube that forms a smooth converging duct. The bell mouth shape allows the maximum amount of air to be drawn into the tube.

Bell mouth inlet duct. A form of convergent inlet-air duct used to direct air into the compressor of a gas turbine engine. It is extremely efficient, and is used where there is little ram pressure available to force air into the engine. Bell mouth ducts are used in engine test cells and on engines installed in helicopters.

Benzene. A colorless, volatile, flammable, aromatic hydrocarbon liquid which has the chemical formula C_6H_6. Benzene, which is sometimes called benzoil, is used as a solvent, a cleaning fluid, and a fuel for some special types of reciprocating engines.

Bernoulli's principle. A physical principle that explains the relationship between kinetic and potential energy in a stream of moving fluid. When energy is neither added to nor taken from the fluid, any increase in its velocity (kinetic energy) will result in a corresponding decrease in its pressure (potential energy).

Beta control range (Beta mode). The range of operation of a turboprop powerplant used for in-flight approach and ground handling of the engine and aircraft. Typically, the Beta mode includes operations from 65% to 95% of the engine's rated rpm.

Beta tube. A tube in a Garrett TPE331 turboprop powerplant that extends into the propeller pitch control to act as a follow-up device. It provides movement of the propeller blades in proportion to movement of the power lever.

Bezel. The rim which holds the glass cover in the case of an aircraft instrument.

BHP. Brake horsepower. The actual horsepower delivered to the propeller shaft of a reciprocating or turboprop engine.

Bidirectional fibers. Fibers in a piece of composite material arranged to sustain loads in two directions.

Bimetallic hairspring. A flat, spiral-wound spring made of two strips of metal laid side-by-side and welded together. The two metals have different coefficients of expansion, and as the temperature changes, the spiral either tightens or loosens. A bimetallic hair spring is used in a thermocouple temperature changes at the reference junction.

Bimetallic strip. A metal strip made of two different types of metal fastened together side by side. When heated, the two metals expand different amounts and the strip warps or bends.

BITE. Built-in test equipment. A troubleshooting system installed in many modern jet aircraft. BITE equipment monitors engine and airframe systems, and when a fault is found, isolates it and provides maintenance personnel with a code that identifies the LRU (line replaceable unit) that contains the fault.

Blade. The component of a propeller that converts the rotation of the propeller shaft into thrust. The blade of a propeller corresponds to the wing of an airplane.

Blade angle. The acute angle between the chord line of a propeller blade and the plane of rotation.

Blade butt. The end of a propeller blade that fits into the hub.

Blade root. The ridges or upset portion of a propeller blade that holds it in the hub.

Blade shank. The rounded portion of a propeller blade between the root and the airfoil section.

Blade station. A reference position on a propeller blade that is a specified number of inches from the center of the propeller hub.

Blade tip. The opposite end from the root of a propeller blade.

Blending. A method of repairing damaged compressor and turbine blades. The damage is removed and the area is cleaned out with a fine file to form a shallow depression with generous radii. The file marks are then removed with a fine abrasive stone so the surface of the repaired area will match the surface of the rest of the blade.

Blisk. A turbine wheel machined from a single slab of steel. The disk and blades are an integral unit.

Blow-in doors. Spring-loaded doors in the inlet duct of some turbojet or turbofan engine installations that are opened by differential air pressure when inlet air pressure drops below that of the ambient air. Air flowing through the doors adds to the normal inlet air passing through the engine and helps prevent compressor stall.

Bluckets. The portions of aft-fan blades that are in the exhaust of the core engine. Bluckets drive the fan from energy received from hot gases leaving the core engine.

BMEP. Brake mean effective pressure. The average pressure inside the cylinder of a reciprocating engine during the power stroke. BMEP, measured in pounds per square inch, relates to the torque produced by the engine and can be calculated when you know the brake horsepower.

Boost. A term for manifold pressure that has been increased above the ambient atmospheric pressure by a supercharger.

Bootstrapping. An action that is self-initiating or self-sustaining. In a turbocharger system, bootstrapping describes a transient increase in engine power that causes the turbocharger to speed up, which in turn causes the engine to produce more power.

Bore. The diameter of a reciprocating engine cylinder.

Borescope. An inspection tool for viewing the inside of a turbine engine without disassembling it. The instrument consists of a light, mirror, and magnifying lens mounted inside a small-diameter tube that is inserted into a turbine engine through borescope inspection ports.

Boss. An enlarged area in a casting or machined part. A boss provides additional strength to the part where holes for mounting or attaching parts are drilled.

Bottom. (verb) A condition in the installation of a propeller on a splined shaft when either the front or rear cone contacts an obstruction that prevents the cone from properly seating inside the propeller hub.

Bourdon tube. The major component in a gage-pressure measuring instrument. It is a thin-wall metal tube that has an elliptical cross section and is formed into a curve. One end of the tube is sealed and connected to an arm that moves the pointer across the instrument dial, and the open end is anchored to the instrument case. The pressure to be measured is directed into the open end, which causes the elliptical cross section to become more circular. As the cross section changes, the curve straightens and moves the pointer over the dial by an amount proportional to the amount of pressure.

Brayton cycle. The constant-pressure cycle of energy transformation used by gas turbine engines. Fuel is sprayed into the air passing through the engine and burned. Heat from the burning fuel-air mixture expands the air and accelerates it as it moves through the engine. The Brayton cycle is an open cycle in that the intake, compression, combustion, expansion, and exhaust events all take place at the same time, but in different locations within the engine.

British thermal unit (Btu). The basic unit of heat energy in the English system. One Btu is the amount of heat energy needed to raise the temperature of one pound of pure water from 60 °F to 61°F.

BSFC. Brake specific fuel consumption. A measure of the amount of fuel used for a given amount of power produced by a heat engine. BSFC is expressed in pounds of fuel burned per hour for each brake horse-power the engine is producing.

Bungee cord. An elastic cord made of small strips of rubber encased in a loosely braided cloth tube that holds and protects the rubber, yet allows it to stretch. The energy in a stretched bungee cord may be used to crank a large aircraft engine.

Burner. See combustor.

Burnish. To smooth the surface of a metal part that has been damaged by a deep scratch or gouge. Metal piled at the edge of the damage is pushed back into the damage with a smooth, hard steel burnishing tool.

Butterfly valve. A flat, disk-shaped valve used to control the flow of fluid in a round pipe or tube. When the butterfly valve is across the tube, the flow is shut off, and when it is parallel with the tube, the obstruction caused by the valve is minimum, and the flow is at its greatest. Butterfly-type throttle valves are used to control the airflow through the fuel metering system.

Bypass engine. Another name for a turbofan engine. See turbofan engine.

Bypass ratio. The ratio of the mass of air moved by the fan to the mass of air moved by the core engine.

Calendar month. The measurement of time used by the FAA for inspection and certification purposes. One calendar month from a given date extends from that date until midnight of the last day of that month.

Cam. An eccentric, or lobe, on a rotating shaft that changes rotary motion into linear motion. A cam is mounted on the magnet shaft in a magneto to push upward on the insulated breaker point to separate, or open, the points when the magnet is in a particular location.

Cam engine. A reciprocating engine with axial cylinders arranged around a central shaft. Rollers on the pistons in the cylinders press against a sinusoidal cam mounted on the shaft to produce rotation of the shaft.

Cam-ground piston. A reciprocating engine piston that is not round, but is ground so that its diameter parallel to the wrist pin is slightly smaller than its diameter perpendicular to the pin. The mass of metal used in the wrist pin boss, the enlarged area around the wrist pin hole, expands when heated, and when the piston is at its operating temperature, it is perfectly round.

Can-annular combustor. A type of combustor used in some large turbojet and turbofan engines. It consists of individual cans into which fuel is sprayed and ignited. These cans mount on an annular duct which collects the hot gases and directs them uniformly into the turbine.

Capacitance afterfiring. The continuation of the spark across the gap in a shielded spark plug after the fuel-air mixture in the cylinder is ignited. Afterfiring is caused by the return of electrical energy stored in the capacitance of the shielded ignition leads. Capacitance afterfiring is eliminated by the use of a resistor in the spark plug.

Capacitor. An electrical component, formerly called a condenser, that consists of two large-area conductors, called plates, separated by an insulator. Electrons stored on one of the plates produces an electrostatic pressure difference between the plates.

Capillary tube. A glass or metal tube with a tiny inside diameter. Capillary action causes the fluid to move within the tube.

Carbon pile voltage regulator. A voltage regulator for a high output DC generator that uses a stack of pure carbon disks for the variable resistance element. A spring holds pressure on the stack to reduce its resistance when the generator output voltage is low. This allows maximum field current to flow. The field from an electro-magnet, whose strength varies directly with the generator voltage, opposes the spring to loosen the stack and increase its resistance when the generator voltage needs to be decreased. The increased resistance decreases the field current and reduces the output voltage.

Carbon track. A trail of carbon deposited by an arc across a high-voltage component such as a distributor block. Carbon tracks have a relatively low resistance to the high voltage and can cause misfiring and loss of engine power.

Cartridge starter. A self-contained starter used on some military aircraft. A cartridge similar in size to a shotgun shell is ignited in the starter breech. The expanding gases drive a piston attached to a helical spline that converts the linear movement of the piston into rotary motion to rotate the crankshaft.

Cascade effect. The cumulative effect that occurs when the output of one series of components serves as the input to the next series.

Catalyst. A substance used to change the speed, or rate, of a chemical action without being chemically changed itself.

Cavitating. The creation of low pressure in an oil pump when the inlet system is not able to supply all of the oil the pump requires. Prolonged cavitation can damage pump components.

Center of pressure. The point on the chord line of an airfoil where all aerodynamic forces are concentrated.

Center-line thrust airplane. A twin-engine airplane with both engines mounted in the fuselage. One is installed as a tractor in the front of the cabin. The empennage is mounted on booms.

Centrifugal compressor. A type of compressor that uses a vaned plate like impeller. Air is taken into the center, or eye, of the impeller and slung outward by centrifugal force into a diffuser where its velocity is decreased and its pressure increased.

Ceramic. Any of several hard, brittle, heat-resistant, noncorrosive materials made by shaping and then firing a mineral, such as clay, at a high temperature.

Channel-chromed cylinders. Reciprocating engine cylinders with hard chromium-plated walls. The surface of this chrome plating forms a spider web of tiny stress cracks. Deplating current enlarges the cracks and forms channels that hold lubricating oil on the cylinder wall.

Cheek (crankshaft). The offset portion of a crankshaft that connects the crankpin to the main bearing journals.

Chip detector. A component in a lubrication system that attracts and holds ferrous metal chips circulating with the engine oil. Some chip detectors are part of an electrical circuit. When metal particles short across the two contacts in the detector, the circuit is completed, and an annunciator light is turned on to inform the flight crew that metal particles are loose in the lubrication system.

Choke of a cylinder. The difference in the bore diameter of a reciprocating engine cylinder in the area of the head and in the center of the barrel.

Choke-ground cylinder. A cylinder of a reciprocating engine that is ground so that its diameter at the top of the barrel is slightly smaller than the diameter in the center of the stroke. The large mass of metal in the cylinder head absorbs enough heat to cause the top end of the barrel to expand more than the rest of the barrel. At normal operating temperature, the diameter of a choke-ground cylinder is uniform throughout.

Choke nozzle. A nozzle in a gas turbine engine that limits the speed of gases flowing through it. The gases accelerate until they reach the speed of sound, and a normal shock wave forms that prevents further acceleration.

Chord line. An imaginary line, passing through a propeller blade, joining the leading and trailing edges.

Cigarette. A commonly used name for a spark plug terminal connector used with a shielded spark plug.

Circular magnetism. A method of magnetizing a part for magnetic particle inspection. Current is passed through the part, and the lines of magnetic flux surround it. Circular magnetism makes it possible to detect faults that extend lengthwise through the part.

Circumferential coil spring (garter spring). A coil spring formed into a ring. This type of spring is used to hold segmented ring-type carbon seals tightly against a rotating shaft.

Claret red. A dark purplish pink to a dark gray purplish red color.

Class A fire. A fire with solid combustible materials such as wood, paper, and cloth as its fuel.

Class B fire. A fire that has combustible liquids as its fuel.

Class C fire. A fire which involves energized electrical equipment.

Class D fire. A fire in which a metal such as magnesium burns.

Closed-loop control. A type of control in which part of the output is fed back to the input. This allows the input to continually compare the command signals with the output to determine the extent to which the commands have been complied with.

Coke. The solid carbon residue left when all volatile parts of a mineral oil have been evaporated by heat.

Cold-cranking simulation. A method used for specifying the characteristics of a lubricating oil at low temperature. Oils rated by this test have the letter W (standing for Winter) in their designation. For example, SAE 15W50.

Cold section. The portion of a gas turbine engine ahead of the combustion section. The cold section includes the inlet, compressor, and diffuser.

Cold-tank lubrication system. A turbine engine lubricating system in which the oil cooler is in the scavenge subsystem.

Collector ring. A ring made of thin corrosion-resistant steel tubing that encircles a radial engine and collects exhaust gases from each cylinder. The ring ends with a connection to the exhaust tail pipe.

Combustor (combustion chamber). The section of a gas turbine engine in which fuel is injected. This fuel mixes with air from the compressor and burns. The intense heat from the combustion expands the air flowing through the combustor and directs it our through the turbine. Combustors are also called burners.

Commutator. A mechanical rectifier mounted on the armature shaft of a DC generator or motor. It consists of a cylindrical arrangement of insulated copper bars connected to the armature coils. Carbon brushes ride on the copper bars to carry current into or out of the commutator, providing a unidirectional current from a generator or a reversal of current in the motor coils.

Compensating winding. A series winding in a compound-wound DC generator. The compensating windings are embedded in the faces of the field poles and their varying magnetic field works with the fields from the interpoles to effectively cancel the field distortion caused by armature current.

Composite propeller blade. A propeller blade made from several materials such as metal, graphite, glass or aramid fibers, and foam.

Compression ratio (reciprocating engine). The ratio of the volume of a cylinder of a reciprocating engine with the piston at the bottom of its stroke engine to the volume of the cylinder with the piston at the top of its stroke.

Compression ratio (turbine engine). The ratio of the pressure of the air at the discharge of a turbine engine compressor to the pressure of the air at its inlet.

Compressor bleed air. Air that is tapped off from a turbine engine compressor. Compressor bleed air is used for anti-icing the inlet ducts and for cooling the turbine inlet guide vanes and first stage turbine blades. Bleed air is also used for certain airframe functions. See customer bleed air.

Compressor pressure ratio. See compression ratio (turbine engine).

Compressor stall. A condition in a turbine engine axial-flow compressor in which the angle of attack of one or more blades is excessive and the smooth airflow through the compressor is disrupted.

Compressor surge. A stall that affects the entire compressor and seriously restricts the airflow through the engine.

Con-di ducts. The British name for a convergent-divergent duct. See convergent-divergent duct.

Condenser. See capacitor.

"Contact." The term used between a person hand-propping an aircraft engine and the person in the flightdeck. When the person is ready to spin the propeller, he calls "contact". The person in the flightdeck turns on the fuel, slightly opens the throttle, applies the brakes, and replies "contact", and then turns the ignition switch to BOTH. The propeller is then pulled through to start the engine.

Constant-displacement pump. A fluid pump that moves a specific volume of fluid each time it rotates.

Constant-pressure cycle of energy release. The cycle of energy transformation of a gas turbine engine. See Brayton cycle.

Constant-volume cycle of energy release. The cycle of energy transformation of a reciprocating engine. See Otto cycle.

Continuous magnetic particle inspection. A method of magnetic particle inspection in which the part is inspected by flowing a fluid containing particles of iron oxide over the part while the magnetizing current is flowing.

Contrarotating. Rotating in opposite directions. Turbine rotors are contrarotating when the different stages have a common center, but turn in opposite directions.

Convergent-divergent duct. A duct that has a decreasing cross section in the direction of flow (convergent) until a minimum area is reached. After this point, the cross section increases (divergent). Convergent-divergent ducts are called CD ducts or con-di ducts.

Convergent duct. A duct that has a decreasing cross section in the direction of flow.

Core engine. The gas generator portion of a turboshaft, turboprop, or turbofan engine. The core engine consists of the portion of the compressor used to supply air for the engine operation, diffuser, combustors, and turbine(s) used to drive the compressor. The core engine provides the high-velocity gas to drive the fan and/or any free turbines that provide power for propellers, rotors, pumps, or generators.

Cowling. The removable cover that encloses an aircraft engine.

Crankcase. The housing that encloses the crankshaft, camshaft, and many of the accessory drive gears of a reciprocating engine. The cylinders are mounted on the crankcase, and the engine attaches to the airframe by the crankcase.

Crankshaft. The central component of a reciprocating engine. This high-strength alloy steel shaft has hardened and polished bearing surfaces that ride in bearings in the crankcase. Offset throws, formed on the crankshaft, have ground and polished surfaces on which the connecting rods ride. The connecting rods change the in-and-out motion of the pistons into rotation of the crankshaft.

Creep. The deformation of a metal part that is continually exposed to high centrifugal loads and temperatures.

Critical altitude. The altitude above which a reciprocating engine will no longer produce its rated horsepower with its throttle wide open.

Critical engine. The engine of a twin-engine airplane whose loss would cause the greatest yawing effect.

Critical Match number. The flight match number at which there is the first indication of air flowing over any part of the structure at a speed of Mach one, the local speed of sound.

CRT. Cathode ray tube. An electronic display tube in which a stream of electrons is attracted to the charged inner surface of the tube face. Acceleration grids and inner surface of the tube face. Acceleration grids and focusing grids speed the movement of the electrons and shape the beam to a pinpoint size. Electrostatic or electromagnetic forces caused by deflection plates or coils move the beam over the face of the tube. The inside of the tube face is treated with a phosphor material that emits light when the electrons strike it.

Cryogenic fluid. A liquid which boils at a temperature lower than about 110 °K (-163 °C) under normal atmospheric pressure.

CSD. Constant-speed drive. A component used with either aircraft gas turbine or reciprocating engines to drive AC generators. The speed of the output shaft of the CSD is held constant while the speed of its input shaft caries. The CSD holds the speed of the generator, and the frequency of the AC constant as the engine speed varies through its normal operating range.

CTF. Centrifugal twisting force. The force acting about the longitudinal axis of a propeller blade, and which tries to rotate the blade to a low-pitch angle. As the propeller rotates, centrifugal force tries to flatten the blade so all of its mass rotates in the same plane.

Curtiss Jenny (Curtiss JN4-D). A World War I training airplane powered by a Curtiss OX-5 engine. It was widely available after the war and helped introduce aviation to the general public.

Customer bleed air. Air that is tapped off a turbine engine compressor and used for such airframe functions as the operation of air conditioning and pressurization systems.

Cylinder. The component of a reciprocating engine which houses the piston, valves, and spark plugs and forms the combustion chamber.

Data. The input for computer processing in the form of numerical information that represents characters or analog quantities.

Dataplate specifications. Specification of each gas turbine engine determined in the manufacturer's test cell when the engine was calibrated. This data includes the engine serial number with the EPR that produced a specific RPM. The technician refers to this information when trimming the engine.

Dataplate performance. The performance specifications of a turbine engine observed and recorded by the engine manufacturer or overhauler and recorded on the engine dataplate. This data includes the engine speed at which a specified EPR is attained. When trimming the engine, the technician uses this data as the goal.

DC. Direct current. Electrical current in which the electrons always flow in the same direction.

Deaerator. A component in a turbine engine lubrication system that removes air from the scavenged oil before it is returned to the tank.

Deceleration. The amount the velocity of an object, measured in feet per second, is decreased by a force during each second it is acted upon by that force. Deceleration is usually expressed in terms of feet per second, per second (fps^2).

DeHaviland DH-4. An English designed observation airplane built in large quantities in the united States during World War I. After the war, surplus DH-4s were used for carrying the U.S. Mail.

Deicing. The removal of ice that has formed on a surface.

Density altitude. The altitude in standard air at which the density is the same as that of the existing air.

Detergent oil. A type of mineral oil with metallic-ash-forming additives that protects the inside of an engine from sludge and varnish buildup. Used in automotive engines, it has proven unsuitable for use in aircraft engines.

Detonation. An uncontrolled explosion inside the cylinder of a reciprocating engine. Detonation occurs when the pressure and temperature of the fuel inside the cylinder exceeds the critical pressure and temperature of the fuel. Detonation may be caused by using fuel that has a lower octane rating or performance number than is specified for the engine.

Dewar bottle. A special container used to store liquid oxygen and liquid nitrogen. A Dewar bottle has an inner and an outer container, and the space between them forms a vacuum. The two surfaces within the vacuum are silvered to reflect heat away from the container walls.

Differential pressure. A single pressure that is the difference between two opposing pressures.

Diffuser. A component in a gas turbine engine that decreases the velocity of air flowing through it and increases its pressure.

Digitized image. A modified image picked up by the miniature TV camera in the end of a fiber-optic probe. This image is converted into a digital electronic signal that eliminates unwanted portions of the viewed area and allows the desired image to be enhanced for a clearer view of the inside of a turbine engine.

Dipstick. A gage, in the form of a thin metal rod, used to measure the level of liquid in a reservoir. The dipstick is pushed into the reservoir until it contacts a built-in stop; then it is removed and visually inspected. The level of liquid in the reservoir is indicated by the amount of the dipstick wet by the liquid.

Dirigible. A large, cigar shaped, lighter-than-air flying machine. Dirigibles differ from balloons in that they are powered and can be steered.

Distributed pole stator winding. Alternator stator windings wound in a series of slots in the stator frame. A distributed pole stator is distinguished from a salient pole stator whose coils are wound around separate pole shoes that project inward from the field frame toward the rotor.

Distributor. A high-voltage selector switch that is gear-driven from the shaft of the rotating magnet in a magneto. The distributor rotor picks up the high voltage from the secondary winding of the coil and directs it to high-voltage terminals. From here, it is carried by high-tension ignition leads to the spark plugs.

Divergent duct. A duct that has an increased cross-sectional area in the direction of flow.

Downdraft carburetor. A carburetor that mounts on the top of a reciprocating engine. Air entering the engine flows downward through the carburetor.

∆P (delta P). Differential pressure.

Droop. A progressive decrease in RPOM with load in a gas turbine engine whose speed is governed with a fly-weight-type governor in the fuel control. As the load increases, the pilot valve drops down to meter more fuel. The lower position of the valve decreases the compression of the speeder spring and allows the flyweights to assume an on-speed position at a lower rpm.

Dry-sump engine. An engine that carries its lubricating oil supply in a tank external to the engine.

Dual ignition. An ignition system of an aircraft reciprocating engine that has two of every critical unit, including two spark plugs in each cylinder. Dual ignition provides safety in the event of one system malfunctioning, but more important, igniting the fuel-air mixture inside the cylinder at two locations provides more efficient combustion of the fuel-air mixture in the cylinder.

Dual-spool gas turbine engine. An axial-flow turbine engine that has two compressors, each driven by its own stage or stages of turbines.

Duct heater. A thrust augmentation system, similar to an afterburner, where fuel is added to the fan-discharge air and burned.

Duct losses. A decrease in pressure of the air flowing into a gas turbine engine caused by friction.

Durability. A measure of engine life. Durability is usually measured in TBO hours.

Duty cycle. A schedule that allows a device to operate for a given period of time, followed by a cooling down period before the device can be operated again.

Dwell chamber. A chamber in a turbine engine into which the scavenged oil is returned. Entrained air separates from the oil in the dwell chamber before it is picked up by the pressure pump.

Dynamometer. A device used to measure the amount of torque being produced by an engine. The drive shaft of the engine is loaded with either an electric generator or a fluid pump, and the output of the generator or pump is measured and converted into units of torque. Torque at a specific rpm can be converted into brake horsepower.

Dyne. The unit of force that imparts an acceleration of one centimeter per second, per second to a mass of one gram. One dyne is equal to $2.248 \cdot 10-6$ pounds.

Eddy current. Current induced into a conductor due to a mobbing or non-uniform magnetic field.

EEC. Electronic engine control. An electronic fuel control for a gas turbine engine. The EEC senses the power-lever angle (PLA), engine RPM, bleed valve, and variable stator vane position, and the various engine pressures and temperatures. It meters the correct amount of fuel to the nozzles for all flight conditions, to prevent turbine over-speed and over-temperature.

Effective pitch. The actual distance a propeller advances in one revolution through the air.

E-gap angle. The position of the rotating magnet in a magneto when the breaker points are timed to open. The E-gap (efficiency gap) angle is several degrees of magnet rotation beyond the magnet's neutral position. At this point, the magnetic field stress is the greatest, and the change in flux is the greatest, inducing the maximum voltage in the secondary winding.

EGT. Exhaust gas temperature. The temperature of the gases as they leave the cylinder of a reciprocating engine or the turbine of a gas turbine engine.

EICAS. Engine indicating and crew alerting system. An electronic instrumentation system that monitors airframe and engine parameters and displays the essential information on a video display on the instrument panel. Only vital information is continually displayed, but when any sensed parameters fall outside of their allowable range of operation, they are automatically displayed.

Elastic limit. The maximum amount of tensile load, in pounds per square inch, that a material is able to withstand without permanent deformation.

Electrical potential. The electrical force caused by a deficiency of electrons in one location and an excess of electrons in another. Electrical potential is measured in volts.

Electrical steel. A low-carbon iron alloy that contains some silicon It is used as the core for transformers, field frames for generators and alternators, and the magnetic circuit of magnetos.

Electromagnet. A magnet produced by an electrical current flowing through a coil of wire. The coil is normally wound around a core of soft iron which has an extremely low retentivity, allowing it to lose its magnetism as soon as the current stops flowing.

Electromagnetic radiation. A method of transmitting energy from one location to another. Current caused by high voltage in the secondary winding of a magneto produces electric and magnetic fields which oscillate back and forth at a high frequency and extend out into space in the form of waves. These waves of electromagnetic radiation are received as interference by the radio receivers in the aircraft.

Electromotive force. A force that causes electrons to move from one atom to another within an electrical circuit. An electromotive force, or EMF, is the difference in the electrical pressure, or potential, that exists between two points. An EMF may be produced by converting mechanical movement, pressure, chemical, light, or heat energy into electrical energy. The basic unit of EMF is the volt.

Emulsion. A suspension of small globules of one material in another when the two materials will not mix. Oil and water will not mix, but they can be formed into an emulsion. An emulsion will separate into its components when it is allowed to sit.

Engine trimming. A maintenance procedure in which the fuel control on a gas turbine engine is adjusted to cause the engine to produce the required EGT or EPR at a specified rpm.

Entrained water. Water suspended in jet fuel. The amount of entrained water that can be held in the fuel is determined by the temperature of the fuel. When the fuel becomes cold, the water precipitates out and forms ice crystals on the fuel filter element.

Epicyclic reduction gears. A gear train in which a series of small planetary gears rotate around a central gear. More commonly called a planetary gear train.

EPR. Engine pressure ratio. The ratio of the turbine discharge total pressure to the compressor inlet total pressure. EPR is normally used as the parameter to determine the amount of thrust an axial-flow turbojet or turbofan engine is producing.

ESHP. Equivalent shaft horsepower. A measure of the power produced by a turboprop engine. ESHP takes into consideration both the shaft horsepower delivered to the propeller and the thrust developed at the engine exhaust. Under static conditions, one shaft horsepower is approximately equal to 2.5 pounds of thrust.

Ethanol. Alcohol made from cereal grains such as corn.

Ether. A volatile, highly flammable liquid that may be used to prime the cylinders of an aircraft engine when starting under extremely cold conditions.

Ethylene dibromide. A colorless, poisonous liquid $BrCH_2CH_2Br$ that is blended with leaded gasoline to help scavenge lead oxides.

Ethylene glycol. A form of alcohol used as a coolant for liquid-cooled aircraft engines. It is also used in automobile engines as a permanent antifreeze.

Eutectic. An alloy or solution that has the lowest possible constant melting point.

Evaporative cooling. See steam cooling.

Exceedance condition. A condition in which a parameter sensed by the EICAS exceeds the limits for which it is programmed.

Exhaust cone. The fixed conical fairing centered in the turbine wheel. The exhaust cone straightens the flow and prevents the hot gases from circulating over the rear face of the turbine wheel.

Exhaust nozzle. The opening at the rear of the exhaust pipe.

Expansion wave. The change in pressure and velocity of supersonic air as it passes over a surface that drops away from the flow. As the surface drops away, the air tries to follow it, and in changing its direction, the air speeds up to a higher supersonic speed, and its static pressure decreases. There is no change in the total amount of energy as air passes through an expansion wave.

External-combustion engine. A form of heat engine in which the fuel releases its energy outside of the engine. This released heat expands air which is used to perform useful work. Steam engines are a popular type of external combustion engine.

Extreme pressure (EP) lubricant. A lubricant that reacts with iron to form iron chlorides, sulfides, or phosphides on the surface of a steel part. These compounds reduce wear and damage to surfaces in heavy rubbing contact. EP lubricants are specially suited for lubricating gear trains.

FAA Form 337. The *Major Repair and Alteration* form that must be completed when an FAA-certificated aircraft or engine has been given a major repair or major alteration.

Face (propeller nomenclature). The flat surface of a propeller that strikes the air as the propeller rotates. The face of a propeller corresponds to the bottom of an airplane wing.

FADEC. Full-authority digital electronic control. A digital electronic fuel control for a gas turbine engine that is functioning during all engine operations, hence full authority. It includes the EEC (see EEC) and functions with the flight management computer. FADEC schedules the fuel to the nozzles in such a way that prevents overshooting power changes and over-temperature conditions. FADEC furnishes information to the EICAS (engine indication and crew alerting system).

Fan pressure ratio. The ratio of the fan-discharge pressure to the fan inlet pressure.

Feathering propeller. A controllable-pitch propeller whose blades can be moved into a high pitch angle of approximately 90°. Feathering the propeller of an inoperative engine prevents it from wind-milling and greatly decreases drag.

Feeler gages. A type of measuring tool consisting of strips of precision-ground steel of accurately measured thickness. Feeler gages are used to measure the distance between close-fitting parts, such as the clearances of a mechanical system or the distance by which moving contacts are separated.

FHP. Friction horsepower. The amount of horsepower used to turn the crankshaft, pistons, gears, and accessories in a reciprocating engine and to compress the air inside the cylinders.

Fiber optics. The technique of transmitting light or images through long, thin, flexible fibers of plastic or glass. Bundles of fibers are used to transmit complete images.

Fire sleeve. A covering of fire-resistant fabric used to protect flexible fluid lines that are routed through areas subject to high temperature.

Flame tubes. Small-diameter metal tubes that connect can-type combustors in a turbine engine to carry the ignition flame to all of the combustion chambers. The British call combustion liners flame tubes.

Flameout. A condition of turbine engine operation when the fire unintentionally goes out. Improper fuel-air mixture or interruption of the air flow through the engine can cause a flameout.

Flash point. The temperature to which a liquid must be raised for it to ignite, but not continue to burn when a flame is passed above it.

Flashing the field. A maintenance procedure for a DC generator that restores residual magnetism to the field frame, A pulse of current from a battery is sent through the field coils in the direction in which current normally flows. The magnetic field produced by this current magnetizes the steel frame of the generator.

Flashover. An ignition system malfunction in which the high voltage in the magneto distributor jumps to the wrong terminal. Flashover causes the wrong spark plug to fire. This reduces the engine power and produces vibration and excessive heat.

Flat-rated engine. A turboprop engine whose allowable output power is less than the engine is physically capable of producing.

Float carburetor. A fuel metering device that uses a float-actuated needle valve to maintain fuel level slightly below the edge of the discharge nozzle.

Flock. Pulverized wood or cotton fibers mixed with an adhesive. Flock, attached to a wire screen, acts as an effective induction air filter for small reciprocating engines.

Flow divider (reciprocating engine). The valve in an RSA fuel injection system that divides the fuel from the fuel control unit and distributes it to all of the cylinders. It compares with the manifold valve in a Teledyne-Continental fuel injection system.

Flow divider (turbine engine). A component in a turbine engine fuel system that routes all of the fuel to the primary nozzles or primary orifices when starting the engine or when the rpm is low. When the engine speed builds up, the flow divider shifts and opens a passage to send the majority of the fuel to the secondary nozzles or orifices.

FMC. Flight management computer. An electronic flight instrumentation system that enables the flight crew to initiate and implement a given flight plan and monitor its execution.

FOD. Foreign object damage. Damage to components in the gas path of a turbine engine, caused by ingested objects. Debris from the runway or ramp cause FOD on the ground. Ice and birds cause most in-flight FOD.

Four-stroke cycle. A constant-volume cycle of energy transformation that has separate strokes for intake, compression, power, and exhaust.

Fractional distillation. Procedure used for separating various components from a physical mixture of liquids. Crude oil is a mixture of many different types of hydrocarbon fuels which can be separated by carefully raising its temperature. The first products to be released, those having the lowest boiling points, are some of the gaseous fuels; next are gasoline, kerosene, diesel fuel, heavy fuel oils, lubricating oils, and finally, tar and asphalt.

Frangible. Capable of being broken.

Free-turbine engine. A gas turbine engine with a turbine stage on a shaft independent of the shaft used to drive the compressor. Free turbines are used to drive the propeller reduction gear in a turboprop engine and the rotor transmission in a helicopter.

Freezing point. The temperature at which solids, such as wax crystals, separate from a hydrocarbon fuel as it is cooled.

Fuel-air mixture ratio. Ratio of the number of pounds of fuel to the number of pounds of air in the mixture burned in cylinders of a reciprocating engine.

Full-register position. The position of a magnet in a magneto when its poles are aligned with the pole shoes and the maximum amount of magnetic flux is flowing through the magnetic circuit.

Gauge pressure. Pressure referenced from existing atmospheric pressure.

Gas generator. The basic gas turbine engine. It consists of the compressor, diffuser, combustor, and turbine. The gas generator is also called the core engine.

Gas turbine engine. An internal combustion engine that burns its fuel in a constant-pressure cycle and uses the expansion of the air to drive a turbine which, in turn, rotates a compressor. Energy beyond that needed to rotate the compressor is used to produce torque or thrust.

General Aviation Airworthiness Alerts. Documents published by the FAA as Advisory Circulars 43.16. These are used to alert technicians of problems that have been found in specific models of aircraft, and reported on Malfunction and Defect Reports. Airworthiness Alerts suggest corrective action, but compliance with the suggestion is not mandatory. general aviation. A term used to describe the total field of aviation operation except the military and airlines.

Geometric pitch. The distance a propeller would advance in one revolution if it were rotating in a solid.

Geopotential of the tropopause. The point in the standard atmosphere where the temperature stops dropping and becomes constant. This is the tropopause, or the dividing line between the troposphere and the stratosphere.

Gerotor pump. A form of constant-displacement pump that uses an external-tooth drive gear that meshes with and drives an internal-tooth gear that has one more space for a tooth than there are teeth on the drive gear. Both gears turn inside a close-tolerance housing. As the gears rotate, fluid flows between the teeth that are beginning to un-mesh, and is carried around the pump as the space continues to open up. On the discharge side of the pump, the teeth becomes smaller, fluid is forced out of the pump.

Glass cockpit. An aircraft instrument system that uses a few color cathode-ray-tube displays to replace a large number of mechanically actuated instruments.

Governor. A control used to automatically change the pitch of a constant speed propeller to maintain a constant engine rpm as air loads vary in flight.

GPU. Ground power unit. A service component used to supply electrical power and compressed air to an aircraft when it is operating on the ground.

Gross thrust. The thrust produced by a turbojet or turbofan engine when the engine is static or not moving. The air is considered to have no inlet velocity, and the velocity of the gas leaving the engine is considered to be the acceleration factor.

Ground-boosted engine. An aircraft reciprocating engine with a built-in supercharger that boosts the sea-level rated horsepower of the engine.

Gudgeon pin. The British name for a wrist pin, or piston pin. See wrist pin.

Half-wave rectifier. An electrical rectifier circuit that converts AC into pulsating DC. Only one alternation of each cycle is present in the output.

Halogenated hydrocarbon. A hydrocarbon compound in which one or more hydrogen atoms have been replaced with atoms of one of the halogen elements such as fluorine, chlorine, or bromine.

Head of pressure. Pressure exerted by a column of fluid and created by the height of the column.

Heat engine. A mechanical device that converts the chemical energy in a fuel into heat energy. The heat energy is then converted into mechanical energy and useful work.

Heli-Coil insert. The registered trade name of a special helical insert used to restore threads stripped from a bolt hole, or to reinforce the threads in an aluminum casting. The damaged threads are drilled out and new threads are cut with a special oversize tap. A coil of stainless steel wire, with a cross section in the shape of a diamond, is screwed into the hole and serves as the new threads. Heli-Coil inserts are also used to provide durable threads in soft metal castings. Some spark plug holes in aluminum alloy cylinder heads are fitted with Heli-Coil inserts to minimize the wear caused by repeated removal and installation of the spark plugs.

Helical spline. A spline that twists, or winds, around the periphery of a shaft. Helical splines are used to change linear motion into rotary motion of the shaft on which the splines are cut.

Helical spring. A spring wound in the form of a helix, or coil.

Helix. A spiral.

Heptanes. An organic compound, $CH_3(CH_2)_5CH_3$, that is used as the low reference fuel for rating the antidetonation characteristics of aviation gasoline.

Hermetically sealed. A complete seal, especially against the escape or entry of air.

Hertz. A unit of frequency equal to one cycle per second.

High-bypass ratio engine. A turbofan engine whose bypass ratio is 4:1 or greater.

High-pressure compressor. The second-stage compressor in a dual-spool gas turbine engine. The high pressure compressor is called the N2 compressor and is the one that is rotated by the starter for starting, and the one whose rpm is controlled by the fuel control.

High unmetered fuel pressure. Pressure in a Teledyne-Continental fuel injector pump that is adjusted by the variable orifice.

Homebuilt aircraft. See amateur-built aircraft.

Honing (cylinder wall treatment). Scratching the surface of the cylinder wall with an abrasive to produce a series of grooves of microscopic depth and uniform pattern. The honed pattern holds oil to lubricate the cylinder walls.

Horsepower. The most commonly used unit of mechanical power. One horsepower is equal to 33,000 foot-pounds of work done in one second.

Hot section. The portion of a gas turbine engine that operates at a high temperature. The hot section includes the combustion, turbine, and exhaust sections.

Hot-tank lubricating system. A turbine engine lubricating system in which the oil cooler is located in the pressure subsystem. The oil is returned to the tank without being cooled.

HRD fire extinguisher. A fire extinguisher that carries the extinguishing agent in a sealed sphere or cylinder. When the agent-discharged switch is closed, an ignited powder charge drives a cutter through a frangible disk which releases the agent. The entire contents of the container is emptied in much less than a second.

Hub (propeller component). The high-strength component inside a propeller that attaches the blades to the engine propeller shaft.

Hybrid compressor engine. A gas turbine engine that has both centrifugal and axial-flow compressors.

Hybrid spark plug. A fine-wire spark plug that has a platinum center electrode and iridium ground electrodes.

Hydraulic lock. A condition in which oil drains into the lower cylinders of a reciprocating engine and leaks past the piston rings to fill the combustion chamber. If the oil is not removed before the engine is started, it can cause serious damage.

Hydromechanical. Any device that combines fluid pressures with mechanical actions to achieve a desired result. In a hydromechanical fuel control used for a turbine engine, hydraulic servos are used in conjunction with the mechanical linkages.

Ice bridging. A spark plug failure that occurs when starting a reciprocating engine in extremely cold weather. When a cylinder fires, the fuel-air mixture is converted into carbon dioxide and water vapor. The water vapor condenses on the spark plug electrodes and forms ice that bridges the electrode gap and prevents the plug firing until the ice is melted. This normally requires removing the spark plugs from the engine.

IDG. Integrated drive generator. An AC generator installed on turbine engines. An IDG incorporates a brushless, three-phase AC generator and a constant-speed drive in a single component.

Igniter. The component in a turbine-engine ignition system that provides a high-energy spark for igniting the fuel-air mixture in the combustion chamber for starting.

IHP. Indicated horsepower. The theoretical horse-power a reciprocating engine develops.

IMEP. Indicated mean effective pressure. The average pressure existing inside the cylinder of a reciprocating engine during its power stroke.

Impulse coupling. A spring-loaded coupling between a magneto shaft and the drive gear inside the engine. When the engine is rotated for starting, the impulse coupling locks the magnet so it cannot turn. The spring in the coupling winds up as the crankshaft continues to turn, and when the piston is near top center, the coupling releases and spins the magnet, producing a hot and retarded spark.

In-line engine. A reciprocating engine with all of the cylinders arranged in a straight line.

Incandescent. Glowing because of intense heat.

Inconel. The registered trade name for an alloy of chromium, iron, and nickel. Inconel is similar to stainless steel, but cannot be hardened by heat treatment.

Inductive reactance. An opposition to the flow of AC or changing DC caused by inductance in the circuit. Inductive reactance, whose symbol is XL, causes a voltage drop, but it does not use power nor produce heat.

Inertia. The tendency of a body to resist acceleration. A body at rest will remain at rest or a body in motion will stay in motion in a straight line unless acted on by an outside force.

Inertia starter. A starter for a large reciprocating engine that uses energy stored in a rapidly spinning flywheel to turn the crankshaft.

Inlet guide vanes. A set of stator vanes in front of the first stage of compression in a gas turbine engine. The inlet guide vanes deflect the air entering the compressor in the correct direction for optimum operation. Inlet guide vanes may be fixed, or their angle may be controlled hydraulically by fuel from the fuel control.

Integral fuel tank. An aircraft fuel tank made by sealing off part of the structure so fuel can be carried in the structure itself.

Intercooler. An air-to-air heat exchanger installed between a turbosupercharger and the carburetor. Intercoolers decrease the temperature of compressed air to prevent detonation.

Interference angle (poppet valve dimension). The difference between the valve seat and the valve face angles. Normally, the valve seats are ground with between 0.5° and 1° greater angle than the valve face. This allows the face to touch the seat with a line contact that provides the best sealing.

Interference fit. A type of fit used when assembling certain mechanical devices. The hole is made smaller than the part that fits into it. The material containing the hole is heated to expand the hole, and the part that fits into the hole is chilled to shrink it. The parts are assembled, and when they reach the same temperature their fit is so tight they will not loosen in service.

Internal-combustion engine. A form of heat engine in which the fuel and air mixture is burned inside the engine to heat and expand the air so it can perform useful work.

Internal timing. The adjustment of the breaker points of a magneto so they will begin to open at the time the magnet is in its E-gap position.

Interpole. A field pole in a compound-wound DC generator used to minimize armature reaction. Interpoles are located between each of the regular field poles, and their coils are in series with the armature winding so all of the armature current flows through them. The magnetic field produced by the interpole coils cancels the distortion caused by the armature field and allows the brushed to remain in the neutral plane where there is no potential difference between the commutator segments. Keeping the brushes in the neutral plane minimizes sparking.

Inverted engine. An in-line or V-engine in which the cylinders are mounted below the crankshaft.

Iridium. A very hard, brittle, highly corrosion-resistant, whitish-yellow, metallic chemical element. Iridium is used for the fine-wire electrodes in spark plugs that must operate in engines using fuel with an exceptionally high lead content. iso-octane. An organic compound used as the high reference fuel for rating the antidetonation characteristics of aviation gasoline $(CH_3)_2CHCH_2C(CH_3)_3$.

Isothermal change. A physical change that takes place within a material in which heat energy is added to or taken from the material as needed to keep its temperature constant.

Jet fuel. Fuel designed and produced to be used in aircraft gas turbine engines.

Jet propulsion. A method of propulsion by accelerating a relatively small mass of air through a large change in velocity.

Jeweler's file. A small, fine-cut, metalworking file used by jewelry manufacturers.

Joule. A measure of energy. In terms of electrical energy, one joule is equal to one watt-second.

Journal (bearing). A hardened and polished surface on a rotating shaft that rides in a plain bearing.

Kerosene. A light, almost colorless, hydrocarbon liquid obtained from crude oil through the fractional distillation process. Kerosene is the base for turbine engine fuel.

Kevlar. The registered trade name by DuPont for a patented aramid fiber.

Kinematic viscosity. The ratio of the absolute viscosity of a fluid to its density. Kinematic viscosity is measured in centistokes.

Labyrinth seal. A type of air and/or seal used around the main –shaft bearings in a gas turbine engine. The seal consists of a series of rotating blades that almost contact the seal land. A small amount of air flows between the seal and the land to prevent oil flowing past the seal.

Land (piston) The portion of a piston between the ring grooves.

Land (splined shaft). The portion of a splined shaft between the grooves.

Laser tachometer. A highly accurate tachometer that shines a laser beam on a rotating element that has reflective tape or a contrasting mark. The reflected laser beam is converted into electrical pulses which are counted and displayed on a monitoring instrument.

Last-chance oil filter. A small filter installed in the oil line to the bearing jet in a gas turbine engine. This filter traps any contaminants that have passed the main filter and holds them until the engine is disassembled for overhaul.

LCD. Liquid crystal display. A digital display that consists of two sheets of glass separated by a sealed-in, normally transparent liquid crystal material. The outer surface of each glass sheet has a transparent conductive coating with the viewing side etched into character-forming segments with leads going to the edges of the display. A voltage applied between the front and back coatings disrupts the orderly arrangement of molecules and causes the liquid to darken so that light cannot pass through it. The segment to which the voltage is applied appears as black against a reflected background.

Leading edge. The thick edge at the front of a propeller blade.

Lean die-out. A condition in which the fire in a gas turbine engine goes out because the fuel-air mixture ratio is too lean to sustain combustion.

Lean mixture. A fuel-air mixture that contains more than 15 parts of air to 1 part of fuel, by weight.

Liaison aircraft. A type of light military aircraft made popular during World War II because of its ability to land and takeoff from unimproved terrain. Liaison aircraft have been replaced with helicopters.

Line boring. A method of assuring concentricity of bored holes. A boring bar extends through all of the holes and cuts the inside diameters so they all have the same center.

Link rod. The rod in a radial engine that connects one of the piston wrist pins to a knuckle pin on the master rod. Also called articulating rods.

Liquid cooling. The removal of unwanted heat from an aircraft engine by transferring the heat into a liquid and then passing the heated liquid through a liquid-to-air heat exchanger (radiator) to transfer the heat into the ambient air.

Longitudinal magnetism. A method of magnetizing through a solenoid, or coil, that encircles the part so the lines of magnetic flux pass lengthwise through the part. Longitudinal magnetism makes it possible to detect faults that extend across the part.

Low bypass ratio engine. A turbofan engine whose bypass ratio is less than 2:1.

Low-pressure compressor. The first-stage compressor in a dual-spool gas turbine engine. The low-pressure compressor is called the N1 compressor and its speed is not governed. It seeks its own best speed as the atmospheric conditions change so it can furnish a relatively constant mass of air to the inlet of the second-stage compressor.

Low unmetered fuel pressure. Pressure in a Teledyne-Continental fuel injector pump that is adjusted by the relief valve.

LRU. Line replaceable unit. Aircraft components designed to be replaced as a unit while the aircraft is on the flight line.

M&D (Malfunction and Defect) report. A small postcard-like form (FAA Form 8330) used by repair stations, maintenance shops, and technicians to report an unacceptable condition to the FAA. Information on these forms provides the basis for the General Airworthiness Alerts and subsequent Airworthiness Directives.

Mach number. The ratio of the speed of an object through the air to the speed of sound under the same atmospheric conditions. An object traveling at the speed of sound is traveling at Mach one (M1.0).

Magnesyn system. The registered trade name of a remote indicating instrument system. A Magnesyn system uses a permanent magnet as its rotor and a toroidal coil excited by 400-hertz AC as its stator. A small magnet in the center of the indicator coil follows the movement of a larger magnet in the transmitter coil.

Magnetic field. The invisible, but measurable, force surrounding a permanent magnet or current-carrying conductor. This field is produced when the orbital axes of the electrons of the atoms in the material are all in alignment.

Magnetic flux. Lines of magnetic force that are assumed to leave a magnet at its north end and return to its south end. Lines of flux tend to be as short as possible and cannot cross each other.

Magnetic particle inspection. A method of non-destructive inspection for ferrous metal components. The part being inspected is magnetized and then flooded with a solution of iron oxide suspended in a light oil, much like kerosene. Any flaw, either on the surface or just below the surface, forms a north and south pole, and the iron oxide attracted to these poles helps locate the flaw. The iron oxide is normally treated with a fluorescent dye, and the inspection is conducted in a darkened booth. When an ultraviolet light (black light) is shone on the part, the treated iron oxide shows up as a brilliant line.

Major alteration. An alteration not listed in the aircraft, aircraft engine, or propeller specifications that might appreciably affect weight, balance, structural strength, powerplant operation, flight characteristics, or other qualities affecting airworthiness; an alteration not done according to accepted practices, or one that cannot be done by elementary operations.

Major overhaul. The disassembly, cleaning, and inspection of an engine and the repair and replacement of all parts that do not meet the manufacturer's specification.

Major repair. A repair to a component that if improperly done might appreciably affect weight, balance, structural strength, performance, powerplant operation, flight characteristics, or other qualities affecting airworthiness; a repair not done according to accepted practices, or one that cannot be done by elementary operations.

Mandrel. A precision steel bar on which a propeller is mounted for balancing. The mandrel is placed across two perfectly level knife-edge plates, and the propeller is allowed to rotate until it stops with its heavy point at the bottom.

Manifold pressure. The absolute pressure of the air inside the induction system of a reciprocating engine.

Manifold valve. See flow divider (reciprocating engine).

MAP. Manifold absolute pressure. The absolute pressure that exists within the induction system of a reciprocating engine. It is the MAP that forces air into the cylinders of the engine. MAP is commonly called manifold pressure.

Mass. A measure of the amount of matter in an object. For the purpose of measuring the mass of air flowing through a turbine engine, the weight of the air, in pounds per second, is divided by the acceleration due to gravity (32.3 feet per second).

Matrix (advanced composites). The material that bonds the fibers together in an advanced composite structure. The matrix carries the stresses into the fibers.

Matter. Something that has mass, takes up space, and exists as a solid, liquid, or gas.

Medium-bypass ratio engine. A turbofan engine whose bypass ratio is between 2:1 and 4:1.

MEK. Methul ethyl ketone. A volatile, water soluble, organic chemical compound that is used as a solvent to remove oily contaminants from ignition system components.

Methanol. Alcohol made from wood.

MFD. Multifunction display. A liquid crystal or CRT display that shows a number of parameters and replaces several analog-type indicators.

Microinches rms. A measure used for cylinder wall surface roughness. Twenty microinches rms means that the highest and lowest deviation from the average surface is 20 millionths of an inch.

Micron. A measurement used to identify the size of particles trapped by filters. One micron is a micro meter, or one millionth of a meter. It is 0.000039 inch.

Microprocessor. A single silicon chip that contains the arithmetic and logic functions of a computer.

Milliammeter. An instrument that measures electrical current in units of thousandths of an ampere.

Millibar. A unit of pressure in the metric system. One bar is a pressure of 14.5 psi, or 29.52 in. Hg. One millibar is one thousandth of a bar, or 0.01469 psi, or 0.02952 in. Hg.

Minor alteration. Any alteration that does not fit the definition of a major repair. See major repair.

Module (modular engine construction). The method of construction for mast modern gas turbine engine. The engine is made of several modules, or units, that can be removed and replaced or serviced independent of the rest of the engine.

Momentum. A force caused by the inertia of a moving body as it tries to keep the object moving in the same direction, at the same speed.

Motor. (verb) The act of rotating a turbine engine using the starter, with the ignition system deactivated. An engine is motored to force air through it to purge fuel fumes.

Multiple-can combustor. A combustor used in a gas turbine engine that consists of a series of individual burner cans, each made of an inner liner and an outer case. The individual cans are arranged around the periphery of a centrifugal compressor. Hot gases flow directly from the cans into the turbine.

N1. A symbol representing the rotational speed of the low-pressure compressor in a dual-spool gas turbine engine.

N2. A symbol representing the rotational speed of the high-pressure compressor in a dual-spool gas turbine engine.

NACA. National Advisory Committee for Aeronautics. This organization, dedicated to the technical development of aviation, has been superseded by NASA.

NACA cowling. A long-chord cowling used over a radial engine. The forward portion of this cowling has an aerodynamic shape that produces a forward pull, and the rear portion extends back to fair in with the fuselage. There is a narrow peripheral gap between the rear of the cowling and the fuselage for the cooling air to escape. Some NACA cowlings have controllable flaps over this opening to control the amount of cooling air that flows through the engine.

Nacelle. An enclosed compartment, normally in the leading edge of the wing, in which an aircraft engine is mounted.

Naphtha. A volatile, flammable liquid distilled from petroleum. It is used as a cleaning agent and solvent, and is present in some blended turbine-engine fuels.

NASA. National Aeronautics and Space Administration.

Naturally aspirated engine. A reciprocating engine that depends upon atmospheric pressure to force the fuel-air mixture into the cylinders. Naturally aspirated engines are neither supercharged nor turbocharged.

Net thrust. The thrust produced by a turbojet or turbofan engine in which the acceleration factor is the difference between the velocity of the incoming air and the velocity of the exhaust gases leaving the engine.

Neutral position. The position of the magnet in a magneto when its poles are between the pole shoes and no lines of flux are flowing through the magnetic circuit.

Newton. The unit of force needed to accelerate a mass of one kilogram one meter per second per second. One newton is equal to 1000,000 dynes, or 2.248×10^{-1} pound.

Nichrome. The registered trade name for an alloy of nickel and chromium. Nichrome wire is used for making electrical heater elements and precision wire-wound resistors. Nichrome's resistance is approximately 65 times that of copper.

Nitriding. A method of case hardening steel. Steel is placed in a retort (a sealed, high-temperature furnace), and heated to a specified temperature while surrounded by ammonia gas (NH_3). The ammonia breaks down into nitrogen and hydrogen, and the nitrogen unites with some of the alloying elements in the steel to form an extremely hard surface. Nitriding hardens crankshaft bearing surfaces and cylinder walls in reciprocating engines. It takes place at a lower temperature than other forms of case hardening, and does not cause warping.

Normal category airplane. An aircraft that is certificated under 14 CFR part 23 that is not certificated under the acrobatic, utility, or commuter category.

Normal shock wave. A type of pressure wave that forms at right angles to a surface when air moves at the speed of sound.

Notch sensitivity. A measure of the loss of strength of a material caused by the presence of a notch, or a V-shaped cut.

Nozzle guide vanes. See turbine inlet guide vanes.

Oblique shock wave. A pressure wave that forms on a sharp-pointed object when air flows past it at a supersonic speed.

Octane rating. A system used to rate the antidetonation characteristics of a reciprocating engine fuel. Fuel with an octane rating of 80 performs in a laboratory test engine the same as the fuel made of a mixture of 80% iso-octane and 20% heptanes.

Odometer. The portion of an automobile speedometer that indicates the distance traveled.

Offset throw (crankshaft design). Crank arms on a reciprocating engine crankshaft. The arms, or throws, to which the connecting rods and pistons are attached are offset from the center of the crankshaft to move the pistons in and out of the cylinder. The amount of the offset determines the stroke of the engine.

Oil analysis. A method of measuring the contents in parts per million of various chemical elements in oil. A sample of the oil is burned in an electric arc, and the resulting light is analyzed with a spectroscope which identifies the chemical elements in the oil and gives an indication of the amount of each element. This type of oil analysis is called a spectrometric oil analysis program, or SOAP.

Oil dilution. A method of temporarily decreasing the viscosity of the lubricating oil to make it possible to start a reciprocating engine when the temperature is very low. Before shutting the engine down, enough gasoline from the fuel system is mixed with the lubricating oil in the engine to dilute it so the starter can turn the engine over when the oil is cold and viscous. When the engine starts and the oil warms up, the gasoline evaporates.

Oil-damped bearing. A type of roller bearing installation in a gas turbine engine in which the outer race is installed in an oil damper compartment whose inside diameter is a few thousandths of an inch larger than the outside diameter of the outer race. Oil under pressure fills the oil damper compartment and allows the bearing to compensate for sight misalignment and to absorb vibrations of the shaft.

On-condition maintenance. A maintenance program that closely monitors the operating condition of an engine and allows major repairs or replacements to be made when engine performance deteriorates to a specific level.

On-speed condition. The speed condition in which the engine is turning at the rpm for which the propeller governor is set.

One-hundred-hour inspection. An inspection required by 14 CFR part 91, section 91.409 for FAA-certificated aircraft operated for hire or used for flight instruction for hire. A 100-hour inspection is identical in content to an annual inspection, but can be conducted by an aviation maintenance technician who holds an Airframe and Powerplant rating, but does not have an Inspection Authorization. See 14 CFR part 43, Appendix D for list of the items that must be included in an annual or 100-hour inspection.

Operating cycle. One complete series of events in the operation of a turbine engine that consists of starting the engine, taking off, landing, and shutting the engine down.

Optoelectronic device. An electronic device that produces, modulates, or senses electromagnetic radiation in the ultraviolet, visible light, or infrared portions of the energy spectrum.

Otto cycle. The constant-volume cycle of energy transformation used by reciprocating engines. A mixture of fuel and air is drawn into the cylinder as the piston moves to the bottom of its stroke. The mixture is compressed as the piston moves upward in the cylinder, and when the piston is near the top of its stroke, the mixture is electrically ignited and burns. The burning mixture heats and expands the air inside the cylinder and forces the piston down, performing useful work. The piston then moves back up, forcing the burned gases out of the cylinder.

Overboost. A condition of excessive manifold pressure in a reciprocating engine. Overboosting occurs when the supercharger is operated at too high a speed.

Overrunning clutch. A type of clutch that couples an input shaft with an output shaft. When the input shaft is driven, the output shaft rotates with it. When the output shaft is driven, the output shaft rotates with it. But when the output shaft is driven, the input shaft does not turn.

Overspeed condition. A speed condition in which the engine is turning at an rpm higher than that for which the propeller governor is set.

P-lead. Primary lead. The wire that connects the primary winding of a magneto to the ignition switch. The magneto is turned off by grounding its P-lead.

Pascal. The unit of pressure produced when one newton of force acts uniformly over an area of one square meter. One pascal is equal to $14.503 \cdot 10^{-5}$ (0.00014503) psi. The kilopascal (kPa) is easier to manipulate. 1 kPa = 1,000 Pa = 0.14503 psi.

PCB. Plenum chamber burning. A method of thrust augmentation used on engines with vectored nozzles. Fuel injected into the fan-discharge air is burned to increase thrust.

Peak voltage. The voltage of AC electricity that is measured from zero voltage to the peak of either alternation.

Penetrant dwell time. The length of time a part is left in the penetrant when preparing it for inspection by the fluorescent or dye penetrant method. The hotter the part and the longer the penetrant dwell time, the smaller the fault that will be detected.

Performance number. The rating of antidetonation characteristics of a reciprocating engine fuel that is better than the high rating reference fuel, iso-octane. Performance numbers are greater than 100.

Permanent magnet. A piece of hardened steel that has been exposed to a strong magnetizing force which has aligned the spin axes of the electrons surrounding its atoms. The high retentivity of the material causes the electrons to retain their magnetic orientation.

Permanent-mold casting. A casting made in a reusable metal mold. The walls of permanent-mold castings can be made thinner than similar walls made by sand casting.

Permeability. A measure of the ease with which lines of magnetic flux can pass through a material.

Phase sequence, or phase rotation. The sequence with which the output phases of a three-phase generator are connected to the load. Reversing the phase sequence of a generator from A-B-C to A-C-B prevents the generator from being synchronized with the others on the bus.

Pi (π) filter. An electronic filter used to prevent radio frequency energy produced in the ignition exciter from feeding back into the aircraft electrical system. The filter is made of an inductor with a capacitor on its input and output. The name is derived from the resemblance of the three components on a schematic diagram to the Greek letter pi (π).

Pinion. A small gear that meshes with and drives a larger gear.

Piston (reciprocating engine component). The movable plug inside the cylinder of a reciprocating engine. The piston moves in and out to compress the fuel-air mixture and to transmit the force from the expanding gas in the cylinder to the crankshaft.

Piston pin. See wrist pin.

Pitch angle. The angle between the chord line of a propeller blade and the plane of rotation. See blade angle.

Pitch distribution. The gradual change in pitch angle of a propeller blade from the root to the tip.

Plane of rotation. The plane in which a propeller blade rotates. The plane of rotation is perpendicular to the propeller shaft.

Planetary gears. A type of large-ratio reduction gearing. A series of small planetary gears are mounted on a spider attached to the output shaft. The planetary gears rotate between a fixed sun gear and a driven ring gear.

Plenum chamber. An enclosed chamber in which air can be held at a pressure slightly higher than that of the surrounding air. Plenum chambers are used to stabilize the pressure of the air before it enters a double entry centrifugal compressor.

POH. Pilot's Operating Handbook. A document published by the airframe manufacturer and approved by the FAA that lists the operating conditions for a particular model of aircraft. Engine operating parameters are included in the POH.

Pole shoe. Inward extensions from the field frame of a generator around which the field coils are wound.

Poppet valve. A T-shaped valve with a circular head. Poppet valves are used to cover the intake and exhaust openings in the cylinder head of a reciprocating engine. The valves are held closed by one or more coil springs and are opened by a cam lobe or a rocker arm pushing on the end of the valve stem.

Porcelain. A hard, white, translucent ceramic material that was used as the insulator in some of the early aircraft spark plugs.

Positive-displacement pump. A fluid pump that moves a specific volume of fluid each time it rotates. Spur-gear pumps, gerotor pumps, and vane pumps are all positive-displacement pumps.

Power. The time rate of doing work. Power is found by dividing the amount of work done, measured in floor-pounds, by the time in seconds or minutes used to do the work. Power may be expressed in foot-pounds of work per minute or in horsepower. One horsepower is 33,000 foot-pounds of work done in one minute, or 550 foot pounds of work done in one second.

Power-assurance check. A test run made of a gas turbine engine to determine how its performance compares with its precious performance as new or freshly overhauled.

Powerplant. The complete installation of an aircraft engine, propeller, and all accessories needed for its proper function.

Preignition. Ignition of the fuel-air mixture inside the cylinder of an engine before the time for normal ignition. Preignition is often caused by incandescent objects inside the cylinder.

Prepreg. Preimpregnated fabric. A type of composite material in which the reinforcing fibers are encapsulated in an uncured resin. Prepreg materials are cut to size and shape and laid up with the correct ply orientation, and the entire component is cured with heat and pressure.

Pressure. A measure of force applied uniformly over a given unit of surface area.

Pressure altitude. The altitude in standard atmosphere at which the pressure is the same as the existing pressure.

Pressure carburetor. A carburetor installed on some aircraft reciprocating engines that uses the pressure difference between air inside the venture and ram air entering the carburetor to produce a fuel-metering force. Pressure carburetors have generally been replaced with continuous-flow fuel injection systems.

Pressure cooling. A method of air cooling a reciprocating engine in which the cylinders are enclosed in tight-fitting shrouds. The cowling is divided into two compartments by baffles and seals, with half of each cylinder in each compartment. Ram air is directed into one compartment, and the pressure in the other is decreased by air flowing over a flared exit or adjustable cowl flaps. The pressure difference across the cylinders causes cooling air to be drawn through the fins to remove the unwanted heat.

Pressure-injection carburetor. A multibarrel pressure carburetor used on large radial and V-engines. Fuel is metered on the basis of air mass flowing into the engine and is sprayed under pressure into the eye, or center, of the internal supercharger impeller.

Precailing torque. The torque required to turn a threaded fastener before it contacts the surface it is intended to hold.

Primary winding. The winding in a magneto or ignition coil that is between the source of voltage and the breaker points. The primary winding is normally made of comparatively large diameter wire, and has a small number of turns, typically about 200.

Profile tip (compressor blade tip). The tip of an axial-flow compressor bladed whose thickness is reduced to give it a higher resonant frequency so it will not be subject to the vibrations that would affect a blade with a squared tip. The profile tip also provides a more aerodynamically efficient shape for the high velocity air that is moved by the blade. Profile tips often touch the housing and make a squealing noise as the engine is shut down. For this reason profile tips are often called squealer tips.

Profilometer. A precision measuring instrument used to measure the depth of the hone marks in the surface of a cylinder wall.

Prony brake. An instrument used to measure the amount of horsepower an engine is delivering to its output shaft. The engine is operated at a specific rpm, and a brake is applied to its output shaft. The amount of torque applied to the brake is measured, and this, with the rpm, is converted into brake horsepower.

Propeller end. The end of a reciprocating engine to which the propeller is attached.

PropFan engine. The registered trade name by Hamilton Standard of an ultra-high-bypass turbine engine. See UHB engine.

Propulsive efficiency. A measure of the effectiveness with which an aircraft engine converts the fuel it burns into useful thrust. It is the ratio of the thrust horsepower produced by a propeller to the torque horsepower of the shaft turning the propeller. The nearer the speed of the aircraft is to the speed of the exhaust jet or propeller wake, the less kinetic energy is lost in the jet or wake, and the higher the propulsive efficiency.

PRT. Power recovery turbine. A turbine driven by exhaust gases from several cylinders of a reciprocating engine. Energy extracted from exhaust gases by the turbine is coupled, through a fluid clutch, to the engine crankshaft.

Pulsating DC. Direct current whose voltage periodically changes, but whose electrons flow in the same direction all of the time.

Pulse-jet engine. A type of air-breathing reaction engine used during World War II to power jet-propelled missiles. Fuel is sprayed into the combustion chamber and ignited. As the heated air expands, it closes the one-way shutter valve in the front of the engine and exits the engine through the nozzle at the rear. As soon as the pressure inside the combustion chamber decreases, air enters through the shutter valve and more fuel is ignited. The thrust is produced in a series of pulses.

Push fit. A fit between pieces in a mechanical assembly that is close enough to require the parts to be pushed together. A push fit is looser than a press fit, but closer than a free fit.

Pusher engine. An engine installed with the propeller facing the rear of the aircraft. Thrust produced by the propeller mounted on a pusher engine pushes rather than pulls the aircraft.

Pusher propeller. A propeller installed on an aircraft engine so that it faces the rear of the aircraft. Thrust from the propeller pushes rather than pulls the aircraft.

PV diagram. A diagram showing the relationship between the volume of a cylinder and the pressure during a cycle of engine operation.

Quill shaft. A type of shaft used to couple parts of an engine that are subject to torsional loads. A quill shaft is a long, hardened steel shaft with splines on each end. One end splines into the drive shaft and the other end splines into the device being driven. Torsional vibrations are absorbed by the quill shaft twisting.

Radial bearing load. The load on a bearing perpendicular to the shaft on which the bearing is mounted. Centrifugal loads are radial loads.

Radial engine (static radial). A form of reciprocating engine in which the cylinders radiate out from a small central crankcase. The pistons in the cylinders drive a central crankshaft which in turn drives the propeller.

Radial-inflow turbine. A turbine, similar in appearance to a centrifugal compressor rotor. Radial-inflow turbines are used to drive the compressor in reciprocating engine turbochargers and some of the smaller APU turbine engines. Hot gases flow into the turbine from its outside rim, then radially inward through the vanes and out of the turbine at its center.

Radiation. See electromagnetic radiation.

Ram air. Air whose pressure has been increased by the forward motion of the aircraft. Ram air pressure is the same as pitot pressure.

Ram drag. The loss of thrust produced by a turbojet or turbofan engine caused by the increase of velocity of air entering the engine. Ram drag is the difference between gross thrust and net thrust.

Ram pressure. Pressure produced when a moving fluid is stopped.

Ram-recovery speed. The speed of an aircraft at which the ram effect caused by the forward movement increases the air pressure at the compressor inlet so that it is the same as that of the ambient air.

Ramjet engine. The simplest type of air-breathing reaction engine. Air entering the front of the engine at a high velocity has fuel sprayed into it and ignited. A barrier formed by the incoming air forces the expanding gases to leave through the nozzle at the rear. The energy added by the burning fuel accelerates the air and produces a forward thrust. Ramjet engines are used in some military unmanned aircraft that are initially boosted to a speed high enough for the engine to function.

Ratiometer indicator. An analog temperature measuring instrument in which the pointer deflection is proportional to the ratio between the current flowing in an internal reference circuit and that flowing through the temperature-sensing probe.

Reach (spark plug specification). The length of the threads on the shell of a spark plug.

Reaction engine. A form of heat engine that produces thrust by heating a mass of air inside the engine and discharging it at a high velocity through a specially shaped nozzle. The amount of thrust is determined by the mass of the air and the amount it is accelerated.

Reactive power. Wattless power in an AC circuit. It is the power consumed in the inductive and capacitive reactances. Reactive power is expressed in volt-amps reactive (var) or in kilovolt-amps reactive (kvar).

Reamed fir. The fit of a shaft in a hole in which the hole is drilled undersize and cut with a reamer to the correct diameter. Reamed holes have smooth walls and a consistent diameter.

Rebuilt engine. A used engine that has been completely disassembled, inspected, repaired as necessary, and reassembled, tested, and approved in the same manner and to the same tolerances and limits as a new engine, using either new or used parts. However, all parts used must conform to all production drawings, tolerances, and limits for new parts, or be of approved oversize or undersize dimensions for a new engine. According to 14 CFR part 91, section 91.421, a rebuilt engine is considered to have no precious operating history and may be issued a zero-time logbook. Only the engine manufacturer can rebuild an engine and issue a zero-time record.

Reciprocating engine. A type of heat engine that changes the reciprocating (back-and-forth) motion of pistons inside the cylinders into rotary motion of a crank-shaft.

Rectifier. A device that allows electrons to flow in one direction while preventing their flow in the opposite direction. Rectifiers are used to change AC into DC.

Reheat system. The British name for an afterburner. See afterburner.

Reid vapor pressure. The amount of pressure that must be exerted on a liquid to keep it from vaporizing. Reid vapor pressure is measured at 100 °F.

Reliability. The ability of an aircraft engine to perform its designed functions under widely varying operating conditions.

Residual magnetic particle inspection. A form of magnetic particle inspection for small steel parts that have a high degree of retentivity. The part is magnetized, removed, and inspected away from the magnetizing machine.

Residual magnetism. The magnetism that remains in the field frame of a generator when no current is flowing in the field coils.

Residual voltage. The voltage produced in a generator armature when the armature is rotated in the residual magnetism.

Resistor spark plug. A shielded spark plug with a resistor between the ignition lead terminal and the center electrode. The resistor stops the flow of secondary current when its voltage drops to a specified value. The resistor prevents capacitive afterfiring.

Retarded sparks. The timing of the firing of the spark plugs used to start a reciprocating engine. The sparks for starting occur later in terms of crankshaft rotation than those used for normal operation. Retarding the sparks prevent the engine from kicking back when it is being started.

Retentivity. The ability of a magnetizable material to retain the alignment of the magnetic domains after the magnetizing force has been removed. Hard steel normally has a high retentivity, while soft iron and electrical steel both have very low retentivity.

Reverse-flow combustor. A type of combustor in which the air from the compressor enters the combustor outer case and reverses its direction as it flows into the inner liner. It again reverses its direction as it flows into the inner liner. It again reverses its direction before it flows through the turbine. Reverse-flow combustors are used where engine length is critical.

RF energy. Electromagnetic energy with a frequency high enough to radiate from any conductor through which it is flowing.

Rich blowout. A condition in which the fire in a gas turbine engine goes out because the fuel-air mixture ratio is too rich to sustain combustion.

Rich mixture. A fuel-air mixture that contains less than 15 parts of air to 1 part of fuel, by weight.

Riffle file. A hand file with its teeth formed on a curved surface that resembles a spoon.

Rms. Root mean square. A dimension that is the square root of the average of an infinite number of varying values. An rms dimension is used to indicate the allowable surface roughness of a reciprocating engine cylinder wall.

Rocker arm. A pivoted arm on the cylinder head of a reciprocating engine. The pushrod forces one end of the rocker arm up, and as the other end moves down, it forces the poppet valve off of its seat.

Rocker box. The enclosed part of a reciprocating engine cylinder that houses the rocker arm and valve mechanism.

Rocket engine. A form of reaction engine whose fuel and oxidizer contain all of the oxygen needed for the release of heat energy. The released heat expands the gases which are ejected at a high velocity from a nozzle at the rear of the rocket. Because rocket engines carry their own oxygen, they can operate in outer space where there is no atmosphere.

Rotary radial engine. A form of reciprocating engine used in some early aircraft. The crankshaft is rigidly attached to the airframe, and the propeller, crankcase, and cylinders all revolve as a unit.

Rotating combustion (RC) engine. A form of internal combustion engine in which a rounded, triangular-shaped rotor with sliding seals at the apexes forms the combustion space inside an hourglass-shaped chamber. Expanding gases from the burning fuel-air mixture push the rotor around and turn a geared drive shaft in its center. The RC engine was conceived in Germany by Felix Wankel in 1955.

RPM. Revolutions per minute. A measure of rotational speed. One rpm is one revolution made in one minute.

Run in. A time of controlled operation of a new or freshly overhauled engine that allows the moving parts to wear together.

Run up. A procedure in which an aircraft engine is operated on the ground to determine its condition and performance.

Runout. A measure of the amount a shaft, flange, or disk is bent or fails to run true. Runout is normally measured with a dial indicator.

SAE. Society of Automotive Engineers. A professional organization that has formulated standards for the automotive and aviation industries.

Safety gap. A location in a magneto that allows a spark to jump to ground from the secondary circuit before the voltage rises high enough to damage the secondary insulation.

Sand casting. A method of molding metal parts in a mold made of sand. A pattern that duplicates the part to be molded is made of wood and is covered with a special casting sand that contains a resin to bind it. The mold is separated along a special parting line, and the pattern is removed. The mold is put back together, and molten metal is poured into the cavity. When the metal cools, the sand is broken away from the molded part. Sand casting is less expensive than permanent-mold casting.

Saybolt Seconds Universal (SSU) viscosity. A measurement of viscosity (resistance to flow) of a lubricating oil. The number of seconds needed for 60 milliliters of oil at a specified temperature to flow through a calibrated orifice. The viscosity number used for commercial aviation engine lubricating oil relates closely to the SSU viscosity of the oil at 210 °F.

Scavenge subsystem. The subsystem in the lubrication system of a gas turbine engine that collects oil after it has lubricated the bearings and gears and returns it to the oil tank.

Scimitar shape. The shape of the blades of the propellers mounted on UHB engines. The name is derived from the shape of a curved Asian sword that has its edge on the convex side. See UHB engine.

Scramjet. Supersonic combustion ramjet. A special type of ramjet engine whose fuel can be ignited while the vehicle is mobbing at a supersonic speed.

Scuffing. Severe damage to moving parts caused when one metal part moves across another without sufficient lubricant between them. Enough heat is generated by friction to cause the high points of the surfaces to weld together; continued movement tears, or scuffs, the metal.

Sea-level boosted engine. A reciprocating engine that has had its sea-level rated horsepower increased by supercharging. This is the same as a ground-boosted engine.

Secondary winding. The winding in a magneto or ignition coil that connects to the distributor rotor. The secondary winding is normally made of very small diameter wire and has a large number of turns, typically about 20,000.

Self-accelerating speed. The speed attained by a gas turbine engine during start-up that allows it to accelerate to its normal idling speed without assistance from the starter.

Semiconductor transducer. A piezoelectric crystal that converts input energy of one form, such as pressure, into output energy of another, such as an electrical signal.

Series-wound motor. An electric motor with field coils connected in series with the armature.

Serviceable limits. Limits included in a reciprocating engine overhaul manual. If a part measures outside of the new-parts limits, but within the serviceable limits, it will not likely wear to the point of causing engine failure within the next TBO interval.

Servo system. A type of automatic control system in which part of the output is fed back into the input.

Shaft horsepower. The horsepower actually available at a rotating shaft.

Shielding. The electrically conductive covering placed around an electrical component to intercept and conduct to ground any electromagnetic energy radiated from the device.

Short circuit. A low-resistance connection between two points in an electric circuit.

Shower of Sparks ignition system. A patented ignition system for reciprocating engines. An induction civrator sends pulsating DC into a set of retard breaker points on one of the magnetos. This provides a hot and retarded spark for starting the engine.

Single-shaft turbine engine. A turboprop engine in which the propeller reduction gears are driven by the same shaft that drives the compressor for the gas generator.

Single-spool gas-turbine engine. A type of axial-flow-compressor gas turbine engine that has only one rotating element.

Skin radiator. A type of radiator used on some early liquid-cooled racing airplanes. The radiator was made of two thin sheets of brass, slightly separated so the heated coolant could flow between them. Skin radiators were mounted on the surface of the wing, on the sides of the fuselage, or on the floats of seaplanes. Air flowing over the smooth surface of the radiator removed heat from the coolant.

Slip (propeller specification). The difference between the geometric and effective pitch of a propeller.

Slip ring. A smooth, continuous ring of brass or copper mounted on the rotor shaft of an electrical generator or alternator. Brushes riding on the smooth surface of the slip ring carry current into and out of the rotor coil.

Slow-blow ruse. A special type of electrical circuit protection device that allows a momentary flow of excess current, but opens the circuit if the excessive flow is sustained.

Sludge. A heavy contaminant that forms in an aircraft engine lubricating oil because of oxidation and chemical decomposition of the oil.

Sludge plugs. Spool-shaped sheet metal plugs installed in the hollow throws of some engine crankshafts.

Slug. The unit of mass equal to that which experiences an acceleration of one foot per second, per second when a force of one pound acts on it. It is equal to 32.174 pounds, or 14.5939 kilograms, of mass. Also called a G-pound.

SOAP. Spectrometric oil analysis program. An oil analysis program in which a sample of oil is burned in an electric arc and an analysis is made of the wavelength composition of the resulting light. Each chemical element in the oil, when burned, produces light containing a unique band of frequencies. A computer analyzes the amount of each band of frequencies and prints out the number of parts of the element per million parts of the entire sample. SOAP can predict engine problems by warning the engine operator of an uncharacteristic increase of any elements in the oil.

Sound suppressor. The airframe component that replaces the turbine engine tail pipe. It reduces the distance the sounds made by the exhaust gases propagate by converting low-frequency vibrations.

Specific gravity. The ratio of the density of a material to the density of pure water.

Specific weight. The ratio of the weight of an aircraft engine to the brake horsepower it develops.

Spline. Parallel slots cut in the periphery of a shaft, parallel to its length. Matching slots, cut into the hub or wheel that fits on the shaft, lock the shaft into the device to transmit torque.

Sprag clutch. A freewheeling, nonreversible clutch that allows torque to be applied to a driven unit in one direction only.

Springback. A condition in the rigging of an aircraft engine control in which the stop at the engine is reached before the stop in the flightdeck. The flightdeck control moves slightly after the stop in the engine is reached, and when it is released, it springs back slightly.

Spur-gear pump. A form of constant-displacement fluid pump that uses two meshing spur-gears mounted in a close fitting housing. Fluid is taken into the housing where it fills the space between the teeth of the gears and is carried around the housing as the gears rotate. On the discharge side of the pump, the teeth of the two gears mesh, and the fluid is forced out of the pump.

Squat switch. An electrical switch actuated by the landing gear scissors on the oleo strut. When no weight is on the landing gear, the oleo piston is extended and the switch is in one position; but when weight is on the gear, the oleo strut compresses and the switch changes its position.

Squealer tip (compressor blade tip). See profile tip.

Squeeze film bearings. Another name for oil-damped bearings. See oil-damped bearings.

Stage length. The distance between landing points in airline operation.

Stage of a compressor. One disk of rotor blades and the following set of stator vanes in an axial-flow compressor.

Staggered timing. Ignition timing that causes the spark plug nearest the exhaust valve to fire a few degrees of crankshaft rotation before the spark plug nearest the intake valve.

Standard day conditions. Conditions that have been decided upon by the ICAO for comparing all aircraft and engine performance. The most basic standard day conditions are: temperature, 15 °C or 52 °F; altitude, mean sea level; pressure, 29.92 inches of mercury.

Standard J-1. A World War I training airplane powered by a Curtiss OX-5 engine.

Standpipe. A pipe which protrudes upward from the base of an oil tank and through which oil used for normal engine lubrication is drawn. In the event of a catastrophic leak when all oil available to the engine-driven pump is lost overboard, enough oil is available from an outlet below the standpipe to feather the propeller.

Starter-generator. A single-component starter and generator used on many smaller gas-turbine engines. It is used to start the engine, and when the engine is running, its circuitry is shifted so that it acts as a generator.

Static pressure. The pressure of an unmoving fluid.

Static rpm. The number of revolutions per minute an aircraft engine can produce when the aircraft is not moving.

Steam cooling. A method of liquid cooling in which the coolant, normally water, is allowed to absorb enough heat that it boils. The steam gives up its heat when it condenses back into a liquid.

Satellite. A nonferrous alloy of cobalt, chromium, and tungsten. Stellite is hard, water resistant, and corrosion resistant, and it does not soften until its temperature is extremely high. Stellite is welded to the faces of many reciprocating engine exhaust valves that operate at very high temperatures.

Stepping motor. A precision electric motor whose output shaft position is changed in steps by pulses from the control device. Stepping motors can make high-torque changes in small angular increments to their output shaft.

Stoichiometric mixture. The fuel-air mixture ratio that, when burned, leaves no uncombined oxygen nor any free carbon. It releases the maximum amount of heat, and therefore produces the highest exhaust gas temperature. A stoichiometric mixture of gasoline and air contains 15 pounds of air for 1 pound of gasoline.

Straight-through combustor. A combustor in a gas turbine engine through which the air from the compressor to the turbine flows in an essentially straight line.

Stratosphere. The upper part of the Earth's atmosphere. The stratosphere extends upward from the tropopause, which is approximately 36,000 feet above the surface of the Earth, to approximately 85,000 feet. The temperature of the air in the stratosphere remains constant at -56.5 °C (-69.7 °F).

Stress. A force within an object that tries to prevent an outside force from changing its shape.

Stroboscopic tachometer. A tachometer used to measure the speed of any rotating device without physical contact. A highly accurate variable-frequency oscillator triggers a high-intensity strobe light. When the lamp is flashing at the same frequency the device is rotating, the device appears to stand still.

Stroke. The distance the piston moves inside the cylinder.

Sump (aircraft engine component). A low point in an aircraft engine in which lubricating oil collects and is stored or transferred to an external oil tank. A removable sump attached to the bottom of the crankcase of a reciprocating engine is often called an oil pan.

Sump (fuel tank component). A low point in an aircraft fuel tank in which water and other contaminants collect and are held until they can be drained out.

Supercharged engine. A reciprocating engine that uses a mechanically driven compressor to increase the air pressure before it enters the engine cylinders.

Supercharger. An air compressor used to increase the pressure of the air being taken into the cylinders of a reciprocating engine.

Surface roughness. The condition of the surface of a reciprocating engine cylinder wall that has been honed to make it hold lubricating oil. Surface roughness is measured in micro-inches rms.

Surge. A condition of unstable airflow, through the compressor of a gas turbine engine, in which the compressor blades have an excessive angle of attack. Surge usually affects an entire stage of compression.

Synthetic oil. Oil made by chemical synthesis of a mineral, animal, or vegetable base. Synthetic oils have appropriate additives that give them such characteristics as low volatility, low pour point, high viscosity index, good lubricating qualities, low coke and lacquer formation, and low foaming.

Tachometer. An instrument that measures the rotational speed of an object.

TAI. Thermal anti-ice. A system used to prevent the formation of ice on an aircraft by flowing heated air inside the structure.

Tail pipe. The portion of the exhaust system of a gas turbine engine through which the gases leave. The tail pipe is often called the exhaust duct, or exhaust pipe.

TBO. Time between overhauls. A time period specified by the manufacturer of an aircraft engine as the maximum length of time an engine should be operated between overhauls without normal wear causing parts of the engine to be worn beyond safe limits. TBO depends upon proper operation and maintenance in accordance with the engine manufacturer's recommendations. The overhaul of an engine when it reaches its TBO hours is not mandatory, except for certain commercial operators that have the requirement written into their operations manual.

TDC. Top dead center. The position of a piston in a reciprocating engine when the piston is at the top of its stroke and the wrist pin, crankpin, and center of the crankshaft are all in line.

TEL. Tetraethyl lead.

Test club. A wide-blade, short-diameter propeller used on a reciprocating engine when it is run in a test cell. A test club applies a specific load to the engine and forces the maximum amount of air through the engine cooling fins.

Thermal efficiency. The ratio of the amount of useful work produced by a heat engine, to the amount of work that could be done by all of the heat energy available in the fuel burned.

Thermal expansion coefficient. A number that relates to the change in the physical dimensions of a material as the temperature of the material changes. The thermal expansion coefficient of aluminum is approximately twice that of steel.

Thermal shock. The sudden change in engine operating temperature that occurs when engine power is suddenly reduced at the same time the airspeed, thus the cooling, is increased. Thermal shock occurs when an aircraft is required to rapidly descend to a lower altitude.

Thermistor. A semiconductor material whose electrical resistance varies with its temperature.

Thermocouple. A device used to generate an electrical current. A thermocouple is made of two dissimilar metal wires whose ends are welded together to form a loop. A voltage exists in the loop proportional to the difference in temperature of the junctions at which the wires are joined. The amount of current flowing in the loop is determined by the types of metals used for the wires, the temperature difference between the junctions, and the resistance of the wires.

Thermosetting resin. A plastic resin that, once it has been hardened by heat, cannot be softened by heating again.

Thermostatic valve. A temperature-sensitive valve that controls the temperature of oil in an aircraft engine. When the oil is cold, the valve shifts and directs the oil through the oil cooler.

Thermoswitch. An electrical switch that closes a circuit when it is exposed to a specified high temperature.

Three-dimensional cam. A drum-shaped cam in a hydromechanical fuel control whose outer surface is ground so that followers riding on the surface, as the cam is moved up and down and rotated, can move mechanical linkages to control the fuel according to a preprogrammed schedule.

Throttle. The control in an aircraft that regulates the power or thrust the pilot wants the engine to produce.

Throw (crankshaft design). See offset throw.

Thrust horsepower. The horsepower equivalent of the thrust produced by a turbojet engine. Thrust horsepower is found by multiplying the net thrust of the engine, measured in pounds, by the speed of the aircraft, measured in miles per hour, and then dividing this by 375.

Thrust. The aerodynamic force produced by a propeller or turbojet engine as it forces a mass of air to the rear, behind the aircraft. A propeller produces its thrust by accelerating a large mass of air by a relatively small amount. A turbojet engine produces its thrust by accelerating a smaller mass of air by a much larger amount.

Time-Rite indicator. A patented piston-position indicator used to find the position of the piston in the cylinder of a reciprocating engine. The body of the Time-Rite indicator screws into a spark plug hole, and as the piston moves outward in the cylinder, it contacts the arm of the indicator. A pointer contacted by the arm moves across a calibrated scale to show the location of the piston in degrees of crankshaft rotation before top center.

Timing light. An indicator light used when timing magnetos to an engine to indicate when the breaker points open. Some timing lights incorporate an oscillator or buzzer that changes its pitch when the points open.

TIT. Turbine inlet temperature. The temperature of the gases from the combustion section of a gas turbine engine as they enter the turbine inlet guide vanes or the first stage of the turbine.

Toggle. A T-shaped handle fitted onto the end of a cable used to engage a simple starter with an overrunning clutch.

Top overhaul. An overhaul of the cylinders of an aircraft engine. The valves, pistons, and cylinders are overhauled, but the crankcase is not opened.

Torque. A force that produces or tries to produce rotation.

Total pressure. The pressure a column of moving fluid would have if it were stopped from its motion. Total pressure is the sum of dynamic pressure and static pressure.

Total temperature. The temperature of moving fluid that has been stopped from its motion. Total temperature is the sum of static temperature and the temperature rise caused by the ram effect as the fluid was stopped.

Townend ring. A type of ring cowling used over a single-row radial engine. The cross section of the ring is in the form of an airfoil that produces enough forward thrust to compensate for the cooling drag of the engine. In the United States, townend rings are often called speed rings.

Track. The path followed by a blade segment of a propeller or helicopter rotor in one rotation.

Tractor engine. An engine installed with the propeller facing the front of the aircraft. Thrust produced by the propeller mounted on a tractor engine pulls the aircraft through the air. tractor propeller. A propeller mounted on an airplane in such a way that its thrust pulls the aircraft.

Trailing edge. The thin edge at the rear of a propeller blade.

Transducer. A device that changes energy from one form to another. Commonly used transducers change mechanical movement or pressures into electrical signals.

Transformer. An electrical component used to change the voltage and current in an AC circuit.

Transonic range. Flight at Mach numbers between 0.8 and 1.2. In this range, some air passing over the aircraft is subsonic, and some is supersonic.

Trend monitoring. A system for comparing engine performance parameters with a baseline of these same parameters established when the engine was new or newly overhauled. Parameters such as EGT, rpm, fuel flow, and oil consumption are monitored on every flight, and the baseline is plotted. Any deviation from a normal increase or decrease warns the technician of an impending problem.

Tricresyl phosphate (TCP). A colorless, combustible compound, $(CH_3C_6H_4O)_3PO$, that is used as a plasticizer in aircraft dope and an additive in gasoline and lubricating oil. TCP aids in scavenging lead deposits left in the cylinders when leaded fuel is burned.

TSFC. Thrust specific fuel consumption. A measure of efficiency of a turbojet or turbofan engine. It is a measure of the number of pounds of fuel burned per hour for each pound of thrust produced.

Turbine. A wheel fitted with vanes, or buckets, radiating outward from its circumference. The reactive or aerodynamic force caused by the fluid flowing through the vanes is converted into mechanical power that spins the shaft on which the wheel is mounted.

Turbine engine. See gas turbine engine.

Turbine inlet guide vanes. A series of stator vanes immediately ahead of the first-stage turbine. The function of the inlet guide vanes is to divert the hot gases in the proper direction to enter the turbine, and to provide a series of convergent ducts which increase the velocity of the gases.

Turbine nozzle. Another name for turbine inlet guide vanes.

Turbocharger. An exhaust-driven air compressor used to increase the power of a reciprocating engine. A turbocharger uses a small radial inflow turbine in the exhaust system to drive a centrifugal-type air compressor on the turbine shaft. The compressed air is directed into the engine cylinders to increase power.

Turbo-compound engine. A reciprocating engine that has power recovery turbines in its exhaust system. The power extracted from the exhaust by these turbines is directed into the engine crankshaft through a fluid coupling.

Turbofan engine. A type of gas turbine engine that has a set of lengthened blades on the low-pressure compressor or low-pressure turbine. Air moved by these special blades bypasses the core engine and produces between 30% and 75% of the total thrust.

Turbojet engine. A gas turbine engine that produces thrust by accelerating the air flowing through it. A minimum of energy is extracted by the turbine, with the majority used to produce an exhaust velocity much greater than the inlet velocity. The amount of thrust produced by the engine is determined by the amount the air is accelerated as it flows through the engine.

Turboprop engine. A turbine engine in which several stages of turbines are used to extract as much energy as possible. The turbines drive reduction gears which in turn drive a propeller.

Turboshaft engine. A turbine engine in which several stages of turbines are used to extract as much energy as possible. The turbines drive shafts which are used to drive helicopter rotors, generators, or pumps.

Turbosupercharger. A centrifugal air compressor driven by exhaust gases flowing through a turbine. The compressed air is used to increase the power produced by a reciprocating engine at altitude.

Two-spool engine. See dual-spool gas turbine engine.

Two-stroke cycle. A constant-volume cycle of energy transformation that completes its operating cycle in two strikes of the piston, one up and one down. When the piston moves up, fuel is pulled into the crankcase, and at the same time the fuel-air mixture inside the cylinder is compressed. When the piston is near the top of its stroke, a spark plug ignites the compressed fuel-air mixture, and the burning and expanding gases force the piston down. Near the bottom of the stroke, the piston uncovers an exhaust port and the burned gases leave the cylinder. When the piston moves further down, it uncovers the intake port, and a fresh charge of fuel and air are forced from the crankcase into the cylinder.

UDF engine. Un-ducted Fan™. The trade name registered by General Electric for a type of ultra-high-bypass turbofan engine that drives one or more wide-blade propellers that have between eight and twelve blades. These blades, which are not enclosed in a duct or shroud, are very thin, have wide chords, and are highly swept back in a scimitar shape that enables them to power airplanes flying in the speed range near Mach 0.8.

UHB (ultra-high-bypass) engine. A turbine that drives a pair of ducted or un-ducted contrarotating propellers which have eight to 12 variable-pitch blades. These blades are very thin, have wide chords, and are swept back with a scimitar shape that allows them to power airplanes flying in the speed range of Mach 0.8. The blades are made of advanced composites for high strength and light weight. USH engines may be of either the tractor or pusher type, and have a bypass ratio in excess of 30:1.

Underspeed condition. A speed condition in which the engine is turning at an RPM lower than that for which the propeller governor is set.

Unidirectional fibers. Fibers in a piece of composite material arranged so that they sustain loads in only one direction.

Updraft carburetor. A carburetor that mounts on the bottom of a reciprocating engine. Air entering the engine flows upward through the carburetor.

Upper-deck pressure. The absolute pressure of air at the inlet to the fuel metering system of a turbocharged engine. Upper-deck pressure is the same as the turbocharger discharge pressure.

V-blocks. A fixture that allows a shaft to be centered and rotated to measure any out-of-round condition.

V-engine. A form of reciprocating engine in which the cylinders are arranged in two banks. The banks are separated by an angle of between 45° and 90°. Pistons in two cylinders, one in each bank, are connected to each throw of the crankshaft.

Valence electrons. Electrons in the outer shell, or ring, around the nucleus of an atom. It is the valence electrons that give an atom its electrical characteristics and are the electrons that may be pulled loose from an atom to cause electrical current.

Valve overlap. The portion of the operating cycle of a four-stroke-cycle reciprocating engine during which both the intake and exhaust valves are off of their seats at the same time.

Vapor lock. A condition of fuel starvation that can occur in a reciprocating engine fuel system. If the fuel in the line between the tank and carburetor is heated enough for the fuel to vaporize, a bubble will form in the line. If the vapor pressure of the bubble is high enough, it will block the fuel and keep it from flowing to the engine.

Vapor pressure. The amount of pressure needed above a liquid to prevent it from evaporating.

Vaporize. The changing of a liquid into a vapor.

Vectored-thrust engine. A turbojet or turbofan engine with the fan and/or exhaust nozzles mounted in such a way that they may be rotated in flight to produce forward, vertically upward, or rearward thrust.

Velocity. A vector quantity that expresses both the speed an object is moving and the direction in which it is moving.

Velocity turbine. A turbine driven by forces produced by the velocity, rather than the pressure, of gases flowing through the vanes.

Venture. A specially shaped restrictor in a tube designed to speed up the flow of fluid passing through it. According to Bernoulli's principal, any time the flow of fluid speeds up without losing or gaining any energy from the outside, the pressure of the fluid decreases.

Vernier coupling. A timing coupling used with base-mounted magnetos. The vernier coupling allows the timing to be adjusted in increments of considerably less than one degree.

Vertical tape instrument. A tall rectangular instrument that displays the quantity of the parameter being measured by a movable strip of colored tape. The presentation resembles a vertical bar graph.

Vibration loop. A loop in a rigid fluid line used to prevent vibration from concentrating stresses that could cause the line to break.

VIFF. Vectoring in forward flight. A method of enhancing the maneuverability of an airplane by vectoring the exhaust gases and/or fan-discharge air to produce thrust components not parallel to the longitudinal axis of the aircraft.

Viscosimeter. An instrument used to measure the viscosity of a liquid. The time required for a given volume of liquid at a specified temperature to flow through a calibrated orifice is used to indicate the viscosity of the liquid.

Viscosity. The resistance of a fluid to flow. Viscosity is the stiffness of the fluid, or its internal friction.

Viscosity index (VI). A measure of change in viscosity of an oil as it changes temperature. The higher the viscosity index, the less the viscosity changes.

Viscosity index improver. An additive used to produce a multi-viscosity lubricating oil. The polymer additive expands as temperature increases and contracts as temperature decreases. VI improvers cause viscosity to increase as oil heats and decrease as it cools.

Volatile memory. Computer memory that is lost when the power to the computer is turned off.

Volatility. The characteristic of a liquid that relates to its ability to vaporize or change into a gas.

Volumetric efficiency. The ratio of the volume of the charge of the fuel and air inside the cylinder of a reciprocating engine to the total physical volume of the cylinder.

Von Ohain, Dr. Hans Pabst. The designer and developer of the first turbojet engine to power an airplane. His HeS3b engine was built in Germany by the Heinkel Company and it flew in a Heinkel He178 airplane on August 27, 1939.

Vortex. A whirling mass of air that sucks everything near it toward its center.

Vortex dissipater. A high-velocity stream of compressor bleed air blown from a nozzle into an area where vortices are likely to form. Vortex dissipaters destroy the vortices that would otherwise suck debris from the ground into engines mounted in pods that are low to the ground.

Wake. The high-velocity stream of turbulent air behind an operating aircraft engine.

Wankel engine. See rotating combustion (RC) engine.

Waste gate. A controllable butterfly valve in the exhaust pipe of a reciprocating engine equipped with an exhaust-driven turbocharger. When the waste gate is open, exhaust gases leave the engine through the exhaust pipe, and when it is closed, they leave through the turbine.

Watt. The basic unit of power in the metric system. One watt is the amount of power needed to do one joule (0.7376 foot-pound of work) in one second. One watt is $\frac{1}{746}$ horsepower.

Wet-sump engine. An engine that carries its lubricating oil supply in a reservoir that is part of the engine itself.

Wet-sump lubrication system. A lubrication system in which the oil supply is carried within the engine itself. Return oil drains into the oil reservoir by gravity.

Whittle, Sir Frank. The British Royal Air Force flying officer who in 1929 filed a patent application for a turbojet engine. Whittle's engine first flew in a Gloster E.28 on May 15, 1941. The first jet flight in America was made on October 2, 1942, in a Bell XP-59A that was powered by two Whittle-type General Electric I-A engines.

Windmilling propeller. A propeller that is rotated by air flowing over the blades rather than powered by the engine.
work. The product of a force times the distance the force is moved.

Worm gear. A helical gear mounted on a shaft. The worm meshes with a spur gear whose teeth are cut at an angle to its face. A worm gear is an irreversible mechanism. The rotation of the shaft, on which the worm gear locks the spur gear so its shaft cannot be rotated.

Wrist pin. The hardened steel pin that attaches a piston to the small end of a connecting rod.

Yaw. Rotation of an aircraft about its vertical axis.

Zero-lash valve lifter. A hydraulic valve lifter that maintains zero clearance in the valve actuating mechanism.

Index

A

Abrasion 10-3
Accessory zone cooling 6-40
Aerodynamic factors 7-5
Aerodynamic twisting force 7-9
Aeromax aviation 100 (IFB) aircraft engine 11-12
Afterfiring 10-32
Airflow controls 6-11
Air oil coolers 6-28
Air pressure against the propeller piston 7-9
Aluminium propeller inspection 7-21
Ambient conditions 10-59
Analyzer safety precautions 10-62
Anti-icing systems 7-18
APU fire detection and extinguishing system 9-18
    APU fire warning 9-18
    Fire bottle discharge 9-18
Augmentors 6-34
Authorized personnel that meet FAA regulations 11-4
Autofeathering system 7-20

B

Backfiring 10-31
Baffles 6-33
Balancing procedure 7-26
Basic engine operating principles 10-30
Blade angle 7-3, 7-5
Blade tracking 7-22
Boeing 777 aircraft fire detection and extinguishing system 9-14
    Boeing 777 fire extinguisher system 9-15
        Fire extinguisher containers 9-15
    Continuous fault monitoring 9-14
    Engine fire operation 9-18
    Engine fire switches 9-15
    Fire detection 9-14
    Nacelle temperature 9-14
    Overheat detection 9-14
    Single/dual loop operation 9-14
    Squib 9-15
    System test 9-14

Breather pressurizing system 6-30
Breather subsystems 6-31
Brinelling 10-3
Burning 10-3
Burnishing 10-3
Burr 10-3

C

Carburetor adjustment and checks 11-25
Carburetor air temperature (CAT) indicator 10-22
Carburetor synchronization 11-17
Centrifugal force 7-4
Centrifugal twisting force 7-4, 7-9
Centrifugal twisting moment 7-9
Chafing 10-3
Changing oil 6-17
    Assembly of and installation of oil filters 6-19
    Draining oil 6-17
    Oil and filter change and screen cleaning 6-18
    Oil filter removal canister type housing 6-18
    Oil filter/screen content inspection 6-18
    Troubleshooting oil systems 6-19
Charging the propeller air dome 7-27
Checking alignment 10-11
Checking and adjusting propeller blade angles 7-23
Checking takeoff thrust 10-58
Checking the carburetor actuation 11-20
Checking the friction torque in free rotation 11-22
Checking the propeller gearbox 11-22
Checks and adjustments after engine runup and operation 8-14
Chipping 10-3
Cleaning 10-6
Cleaning propeller blades 7-27
Cleaning the oil tank 11-21
Clearances 10-55
Cloud point 6-3
Cold cylinder check 10-44
Combination splash and pressure lubrication 6-5
Combustion process 10-30
Combustion section inspection 10-49

Components 9-2
Composite propeller inspection 7-21
Compression 10-32
Connecting rods 10-5
Constant-speed feathering propeller 7-15
Constant-speed propellers 7-14
Constant speed unit (CSU) 7-32
Containers 9-9
Continuity check of aircraft EGT circuit 10-64
Continuous-loop detector systems 9-5
    Automatic self-interrogation 9-7
    Combination fire and overheat warning ... 9-6
    Dual-loop systems 9-7
    Fault indication 9-7
    Fenwall continuous-loop system 9-5
    Fire detection control unit (fire detection card) ... 9-7
    Kidde continuous-loop system 9-5
    Sensing element 9-5
    Support tube-mounted sensing elements .. 9-7
    System test 9-6
    Temperature trend indication 9-6
Cooling system 11-7
    Rotax 447 UL SCDI 11-5
    Rotax 582 UL DCDI 11-5
Corrosion 10-3
Cowl flaps 6-34
Cowling 6-33
Crack 10-3
Crankshaft 10-5, 10-11
Cut 10-3
Cylindar removal 10-42
Cylinder assembly reconditioning 10-12
Cylinder baffle and deflector system inspection ... 6-38
Cylinder barrel 10-8
Cylinder bases 6-35
Cylinder compression tests 10-40
Cylinder grinding and honing 10-18
Cylinder head 10-5
    Temperature indicator 10-24
Cylinder installation 10-43
Cylinder replacement 10-42
Cylinder temperature indicating systems ... 6-38

D

Daily maintenance checks 11-22
Decarbonizing 10-6
    Solution 10-7
Degreasing 10-6
Deicing systems 7-18
    Brush block 7-19
    Timer or cycling unit 7-19

Cycling timers 7-20
    Deice boot 7-19
Dent 10-4
Deoiler 6-28
Depreservation of an engine 8-5
Detonation 10-30
Differential pressure tester 10-40
Dimensional inspection 10-8
Direct drive VW engines 11-13
Disassembly 10-2
Discharge indicators 9-9
Discharge valves 9-9
Disconnection of engine controls 8-8
Disconnection of lines 8-9
Dome assembly 7-36
Draining the engine 8-7
Dry sump lubrication system operation 6-12
Dry sump oil systems 6-5
Dual capacitor discharge ignition (DCDI) ... 11-4
Dye penetrant inspection 10-7
Dynamic balancing 7-25

E

Eddy current inspection 10-7
EGT circuit error 10-66
Electrical disconnects 8-7
Electric system 11-6, 11-8
Engine and engine compartment inspection ... 11-24
Engine checks 10-58
Engine cooling systems 6-33
Engine cowling 6-36
Engine cylinder cooling fin inspection 6-37
Engine fire detection systems 9-2
Engine fire extinguishing system 9-8
Engine general requirements 11-1
Engine inspection charts 11-26
Engine installation 8-15
Engine instruments 10-21, 10-25
Engine lubrication 6-1
Engine mounts 8-23
    Mounts for reciprocating engines 8-23
    Mounts for turbofan engines 8-24
    Turbine vibration isolation engine mounts ... 8-24
Engine oil pressure indicator 10-58
Engine oil temperature indicator 10-58
Engine operational problems 8-3
Engine or component lifespan exceeded .. 8-2
Engine preservation 11-24
Engine preservation and return to service ... 8-25
Engine pressure ratio indicator 10-56
Engine ratings 10-55

Engine shipping containers 8-27
Engine shutdown..10-59
Engine speed varies with flight attitude
(airspeed)..7-30
Engine starting 10-26
Engine stopping 10-29
Engine testing of reciprocating engines 10-20
Engine thermocouples out of calibration 10-66
Engine troubleshooting 10-36
Engine warm-up..10-26
Erosion 10-4
Exhaust gas temperature indicating systems................6-39
Exhaust gas temperature indicator (EGT)..................10-56
Exhaust section 10-55
Exhaust system...11-25

F

Factors affecting engine operation...............................10-32
Failure to feather or feathers slowly 7-30
Feathering 7-16
    Operation 7-37
Fire detection system maintenance 9-10
Fire detection system troubleshooting 9-12
Fire extinguisher system maintenance practices..........9-13
Fire extinguishing agents 9-8
Fire switch..9-10
Fire zones 9-7
Fixed-pitch wooden propellers 7-12
Flaking 10-4
Flash point and fire point 6-3
Fretting..10-4
Friction 6-2
    Rolling friction 6-2
    Wiping friction 6-2
Fuel control unit (FCU) 7-33
Fuel-flow indicator...10-57
Fuel flow meter 10-23
Fuel metering 10-32
Fuel nozzle and support assemblies..............................10-51
Fuel oil coolers..6-28
Fuel/oil mixing procedure..11-6
Fuel pressure and oil pressure check 10-28
Fuel pressure indicator...10-22
Fuel system 11-6,11-7
Functional check of aircraft EGT circuit 10-64
Functions of engine oil...6-2

G

Galling..10-4
General maintenance practices for the light-sport
Jabiru engines..11-24

General maintenance practices on light-sport
Rotax engines...11-16
General overhaul procedures 10-2
General procedures for engine removal and
installation...8-3
Gouging..10-4
Governor mechanism 7-10
Governor system operation..7-12
Great plains aircraft volkswagen (VW)
conversions 11-15
Grooving 10-4
Ground check 10-27
Ground operation engine fire 10-58

H

Hamilton standard hydromatic propellers...................7-34
Hartzell constant-speed...7-14
Head bolts 11-25
HKS 700T engine 11-10
Hoisting and mounting the engine for installation........8-10
    Connections and adjustments 8-11
Hoisting the engine 8-10
Hub..7-29
    Assembly 7-36
Hunting and surging..7-30
Hydraulic lock...10-26
Hydromatic propeller..7-35
    Feathering installation 7-37

I

Ice control systems...7-18
Idle mixture 10-34
Idle speed adjustment..11-20
Idle speed and idle mixture checks 10-29
Inclusion..10-4
Induction manifold..10-34
Inspecting the magnetic plug 11-21
Inspection and depreservation of accessories 8-5
Inspection and repair of combustion chambers 10-51
Inspection and replacement of powerplant
external units and systems 8-6
Inspection of stored engines..8-28
Inspection process...10-3
Installation of turbofan engines 8-19
    Completing the installation 8-19
    Installation with cable hoist.......................................8-19
    Installation with dolly..8-19

J

Jabiru 2200 aircraft engine..11-12
Jabiru light-sport engines...11-10

L

Large springs..7-9
Leak testing...10-18
Light-sport aircraft engines..........................11-4
Lock-pitch solenoid valve...........................7-33
Lubrication system.............11-6, 11-7, 11-20, 11-25
    Breather systems (vents) 6-26
    Check valve 6-27
    Instrumentation...6-26
    Maintenance practices 6-14
    Requirements..6-5
    Thermostatic bypass valves......................6-27
Lycoming 0-233 series light-sport aircraft
engine..11-16

M

Magnetic chip detectors 6-28
Magnetic particle inspection 10-8
Maintenance schedule procedures and
maintenance checklist..................................11-17
Manifold pressure indicator 10-23
Marking materials for combustion section parts........10-50
Mechanical failures...9-2
Metal fixed-pitch propellers.........................7-14
Metal particles in the oil 8-3
Metal propeller inspection 7-21
    Tachometer inspection 7-21

N

Nick...10-4
Nonfeathering 7-14

O

Oil change 11-21
Oil cooler 6-10, 6-16
Oil cooler flow control valve 6-10
Oil filters 6-8
    Bypass valve...6-7
    Canister housing filter 6-8
    Check valve 6-7
    Cuno oil filter 6-8
    Spin-on filters 6-8
Oil injection lubrication of Rotax 503 UL DCDE,
582 UL DCDI, and 582 UL DCDI.................11-6
Oil jets 6-26
Oil level check 11-20
Oil pressure gauge..6-9
    Dual-type oil pressure gauge.....................6-9
Oil pressure indicator..................................10-23
Oil pressure regulating valve 6-8, 6-25
Oil pressure relief valve........................6-17, 6-25
Oil pump 6-7, 6-23
    Gear-type oil pump..................................6-23
    Gerotor pump 6-24
Oil tank..6-22
Oil tanks 6-5, 6-14
Oil temperature bulbs...................................6-16
Oil temperature indicator 6-10, 10-23
One or more inoperative thermocouples in engine
parallel harness..10-66
On-speed condition 7-10
Operational effect of valve clearance 10-34
Opposed light-sport, experimental, and certified
engines 11-7
Optical fire detection systems 9-4
    Principle of operation 9-4
Optimizing engine running 11-20
Other disconnections.....................................8-9
Overspeed condition 7-10

P

Peening...10-4
Personnel authorized to perform inspection and
maintenance on light-sport engines 11-2
Pistons 10-5, 10-13
    Piston pins 10-5, 10-13
    Piston repairs 10-18
Pitting...10-4
Pneumatic synchronization 11-18
Pneumatic thermal fire detection 9-5
Pour point..6-3
Power check...10-28
Powerplant vibration....................................7-22
Pratt and Whittney PT6 Hartzell Propeller System......7-32
Pre-flight checks..11-23
Pre-ignition 10-31
Pre-oiling..10-26
Preparation of engine for ground and flight
testing..8-13
    Fuel system bleeding................................8-13
    Pre-oiling..8-13
Preparation of engines for installation 8-3
Preparing the engine for removal..................8-7
Preservation and depreservation of gas turbine
engines 8-28
Preservation and storage of engines............8-24
    Corrosion-preventive compounds 8-25
        Heavy compound 8-25
        Light mixture 8-25
    Corrosion-preventive materials 8-24
    Dehydrating 8-25

Silica gel 8-25
Pressure and scavenge oil screens....................................6-16
Pressure indication 9-9
Pressure subsystem 6-30
Pressure system...6-29
Propeller aerodynamic process 7-2
Propeller auxiliary systems 7-18
Propeller balancing 7-24
Propeller blade 7-3
    Flyweights 7-9
Propeller check..8-14
Propeller controls and instruments.....................................7-6
    System 7-31
Propeller governor 7-9
    Oil on the propeller piston side 7-9
Propeller inspection and maintenance 7-20
Propeller location 7-6
    Pusher propellers 7-6
    Tractor propeller...7-6
Propeller overhaul 7-28
Propeller pitch...7-3
    Check...10-28
Propellers 7-1,7-2,7-6
    Constant-speed propellers 7-8
    Controllable-pitch propeller 7-7
    Feathering propellers 7-8
    Fixed-pitch propeller 7-6
    Ground-adjustable propeller 7-7
    Lubrication 7-28
    Principles 7-2
    Removal and installation 7-26
    Reverse-pitch propellers 7-9
    Test club propeller..7-7
    Troubleshooting 7-30
    Vibration..7-22
Propellers used on general aviation aircraft...................7-12
Propeller synchronization and synchrophasing 7-20
Prop reassembly..7-29

Q

QECA buildup method for changing of engines............8-4

R

Reassembly 10-20
Receiving inspection..10-2
Reciprocating engine cooling systems...........................6-33
    Maintenance 6-35
Reciprocating engine lubrication systems 6-5
Reciprocating engine operation 10-25
Reciprocating engine overhaul 10-1
    Major overhaul and major repairs 10-2

Top overhaul...10-2
Reciprocating helicopter engine and QECA..................8-23
    Installation, rigging, and adjustment of
    helicopter QECA...8-23
    Removal of helicopter QECA 8-23
    Testing the engine installation...................................8-23
Reduction gear assembly 7-31
Refacing valve seats...10-13
Removal and installation of an opposed-type
engine..8-14
    Engine removal..8-14
Removal of reciprocating engines 8-2
Removing hard carbon...10-6
Removing the engine 8-9
Repair and replacement...10-12
Requirements and characteristics of reciprocating
engine lubricants 6-2
Resistance and insulation check...................................10-65
Resistance of circuit out of tolerance...........................10-66
Revmaster R-2300 engine..11-13
Rigging, inspections, and adjustments..........................8-20
    Adjusting the fuel control...8-21
    Rigging power controls 8-20
Rotax 447 UL SCDI...11-4
Rotax 503 UL DCDI 11-4
Rotax 503 UL DCDI 11-5
Rotax 582 UL DCDI 11-5
Rotax 912/914..11-7

S

Scavenger subsystem 6-31
Scavenge system 6-29
Scoring 10-4
Scratches 10-4
Sender 11-25
Servicing propellers 7-27
Setting the propeller governor 7-40
Shorts to ground/shorts between leads.......................10-66
Single capacitor discharge ignition (SCDI) 11-4
Spark plugs...11-25
Specific gravity 6-4
Spectrometric oil analysis engine inspection
program 8-3
Spectrometric oil analysis program 6-21
    Parts per million (PPM)..6-21
Stain 10-4
Static balancing..7-24
Structural inspection 10-7
Sudden reduction in speed 8-2
Sudden stoppage 8-2
Surge protection valves...6-10

Swivel outlet fitting..6-22
Synchrophasing system..7-31

T

Tachometer 10-56,11-25
    Check...10-65
    Indicator..10-24
Teledyne Continental 0-200 engine 11-16
Test cell requirements 10-21
Thermal discharge indicator (red disk) 9-10
Thermal switch system 9-2
Thermocouple 9-3
    Systems..9-3
Torquemeter...10-25
    Turboprop engines..10-56
Troubleshooting aircraft tachometer system.............10-66
Troubleshooting and abnormal operation 11-23
    Exceeding of maximum admissible cylinder
    head temperature 11-24
    Exceeding of maximum admissible exhaust
    gas temperature..11-24
    Exceeding the maximum admissible engine
    speed...11-24
        Engine keeps running with ignition OFF............11-24
        Knocking under load..11-24
Troubleshooting EGT system 10-66
Troubleshooting turbine engines................................10-60
Turbine blade inspection 10-51
Turbine blade replacement procedure........................10-52
Turbine disk inspection..10-51
Turbine engine analyzer uses.....................................10-62
Turbine engine calibration and testing.......................10-60
Turbine engine condition monitoring programs 8-3
Turbine engine cooling 6-39
Turbine engine ground fire protection 9-9
Turbine engine instruments..10-56
Turbine engine insulation blankets 6-41
Turbine engine lubricants 6-19
    Bulk stability 6-20
    Cleanliness 6-19
    Compatibility...6-20
    Load-carrying ability...6-19
    Seal wear 6-20
    Vapor phase deposits...6-19
Turbine engine lubrication systems 6-21
Turbine engine maintenance 10-46
    Blending and replacement....................................10-49
    Causes of blade damage 10-46
    Compressor section 10-46
    Inspection and cleaning.......................................10-46
Turbine engine oil system maintenance.......................6-32

Turbine engine operation 10-58
Turbine engine powerplant removal and
installation..8-16
    Install apu powerplant 8-16
    Removal and replacement of an auxiliary power
    unit (APU) 8-16
Turbine engine wet-sump lubrication system.............6-31
    Reservoir 6-32
        Magnetic drain plug...6-32
        Provision 6-32
        Sight gauge 6-32
        Vent or breather 6-32
Turbine lubrication system components 6-22
Turbine nozzle inlet guide vane inspection 10-54
Turbine oil filters...6-24
Turbine oil health and safety precautions 6-20
Turbocharger and control system..............................11-10
Turbofan powerplant QECA removal.........................8-18
    Removal of QECA accessories 8-19
Turbo-propeller assembly 7-31
Turboprop engines and propeller control systems 7-30
Turboprop operation 10-60
    Troubleshooting procedures for turboprop
    engines..10-60
Turboprop powerplant removal and installation..........8-22
Two-cycle engine..11-4
Two cylinder rotax engine 11-4
Two-stroke engines...11-5
Two-way check valve 9-9
Typical dry-sump pressure regulated turbine
lubrication system 6-28
Typical dry-sump variable pressure lubrication
system 6-30

U

Ultrasonic Inspection 10-8
    Pulse-Echo..10-8
    Resonance...10-8
    Through Transmission..10-8
Underspeed Condition 7-10
Unfeathering 7-17
    Operation...7-39
Universal Propeller Protractor 7-23
Upsetting 10-4

V

Valves 10-10,10-13
    Blow-by..10-40
    Lapping...10-18
    Reconditioning 10-16
    Springs.. 10-10,10-13

Train 10-5
Viscosity 6-3
    Index 6-3
Visual inspection 10-3

W

Warning systems 9-10, 10-25
Wear metals and additives 6-21
    Aluminum 6-21
    Chromium 6-21
    Copper 6-21
    Iron 6-21
    Lead 6-21
    Molybdenum 6-21
    Nickel 6-21
    Phosphorous 6-21
    Silver 6-21
    Tin 6-21
    Titanium 6-21
Wet-sump lubrication system operation 6-14
Wood propeller inspection 7-21

X

X-ray 10-8

Y

Yellow disk discharge indicator 9-10

www.ingramcontent.com/pod-product-compliance
Ingram Content Group UK Ltd.
Pitfield, Milton Keynes, MK11 3LW, UK
UKHW051351180426
11947UKWH00014B/874